Power
and
Political Theory

# Power
# and
# Political Theory

## Some European Perspectives

*Edited by*

**Brian Barry**
*University of British Columbia,*
*Vancouver, British Columbia, Canada*

## JOHN WILEY
London · New York · Sydney · Toronto

Copyright © 1976, by John Wiley & Sons, Ltd.

*Library of Congress Cataloging in Publication Data:*

Main entry under title:

Power and political theory.

   Includes rev. versions of papers delivered at a workshop sponsored by
the European Consortium for Political Research and held at the
University of Strasbourg in Apr. 1974.
   Bibliography: p.
   Includes index.
   1. Power (Social sciences)—Congresses. I. Barry, Brian M. II. European
Consortium for Political Research.
JC330.P69     301.15'5     75-25556
ISBN 0 471 05424 0


Printed by The Pitman Press Ltd., Bath

# Preface

The European Consortium for Political Research (ECPR) was created so as to provide an opportunity for scholars in different countries in Europe to meet and work together. This book could not have come into existence without the ECPR and without the vision and drive of its Director, Jean Blondel. It is a great pleasure and a great privilege to have the opportunity of paying tribute to him here.

I was asked to do what I could to further the ECPR's ends in the field of political theory by organising a 'workshop' at which papers contributed by the participants would be discussed. This task was peculiarly daunting because of the lack of any basis (such as existed, for example, in the study of political socialization or electoral behaviour) in any clearly established common definition of the scope or method of the subject and the lack of paradigmatic works to which all those defining themselves as belonging to the field were oriented. In the light of this, I proposed that I should be permitted to begin by calling a planning meeting in order to see if enough common ground existed to make it appear profitable to proceed further.

The ECPR executive committee generously accepted this proposal and I convened a meeting of a dozen people which took place during the joint sessions of workshops at the University of Mannheim in April 1973. That we were starting from scratch is vividly illustrated by the fact that nobody (including myself) had ever met more than two participants from outside his own country before (counting Scandinavia as one country for the purpose of this computation).

As well as being great fun, the meeting was a revelation to us all as we discovered the extent to which we had been working on similar problems and thinking along similar lines. After a rather wary first day spent largely in sizing one another up, the meeting took off on the second day as alternative themes and topics followed one another on the blackboard in dizzying succession. By the end of the third day (under the pressure, I must admit, of some fairly ruthless chairmanship in the final stages) we were not only in a position to report that the basis existed for a workshop in political theory but we also had an elaborate programme with topics and names.

The programme was nothing if not ambitious for a first venture in international collaboration. It was divided into three sections. The first was concerned with evaluation, ideology (understood as the notion of a total theory of society) and the possibility of rational planning. The second was concerned with a contrast between the 'economic' and 'systems' approaches to the study of politics, as exemplified in the treatment of power. The third was concerned with problems about the nature and method of the study of politics.

Within each section there were to be a number of papers, with a very early deadline for delivery. These papers were then to be read by commentators, who in turn were to circulate their own papers in time for *further* comments to be written and circulated before the meeting. In order to ensure as far as possible that the discussion at the workshop took up general issues rather than becoming a disjointed affair with an hour spent on each paper, we arranged that writers of discussion papers would be invited to deal with groups of papers.

Naturally, this did not all go precisely as planned, but the reality approximated the plan far more closely than, I now confess, I had ever dared to hope. A few (though only a very few) of those approached to give papers declined the invitation. Others were brought in by various means: some were suggested as alternatives by the original planning group, some offered their services when they read or heard about the workshop and a few were added more accidentally. Jon Elster, whose *tour de force* concludes this volume, was introduced to me at Oslo Airport. According to Dr Johnson, 'if a man were to go by chance with Burke under a shed, to shun a shower, he would say "this is an extraordinary man" '. The equivalent in this case was a hurried coffee while we waited for our planes and it was enough to impart to me a powerful conviction that here was a man, if any, who could take on the whole range of our topics and bring them into intellectual order.

A few of those who had agreed to participate fell by the wayside and more were late with their papers, but the structure of original papers, discussion papers and a paper commenting on everything else stood up well to the test. A lot of the credit for this must go to my secretary at Nuffield, Mrs Audrey Skeats, who kept it under control from the outset and took complete charge during the last three months, while I was in the United States.

After all the preparation, the workshop itself, held during the joint sessions of workshops in April 1974 at the University of Strasbourg, was perhaps a little of an anticlimax. Since our officially allocated meeting place was a raked lecture theatre with fixed seats, it is something that the participants managed to overcome the obstacles to multilateral exchange as well as they did, and in any case there was plenty of excellent discussion in the more congenial surroundings of the restaurants of Strasbourg.

It will be appreciated that, with twenty-eight papers of various kinds circulated among the participants, the sheer bulk of paper generated by the workshop was quite formidable. Indeed, participants in the theory workshop could be distinguished by their lopside gait as they staggered towards the meeting place each morning. It was therefore unavoidable that over half of the original material would have to be left out of this volume. I am grateful to the participants for encouraging me to go ahead and for giving me *carte blanche* to make the selection.

With much reluctance to lose some really excellent papers, I decided that the most important thing was to retain coherence by cutting whole areas, rather than present a sample from the whole workshop. I have therefore dropped all the papers from the first section (evaluation, ideology and planning) and the 'systems' papers from the second section. Almost all the papers have been revised for this volume. Three (Barry, de Vree, Midgaard) have been extensively changed and expanded, while two more

(Lehner and Schütte, van Gunsteren) are completely rewritten. Finally, Professor Felix Oppenheim, who attended the workshop while spending the year at the Netherlands Institute for Advanced Study in the Humanities and Social Sciences at Wassenaar, agreed to write a paper specially for this volume.

The book begins with two papers on the exchange theory of power which provide an interesting contrast. Although both focus on the inadequacy of an exchange theory for explaining the distribution of power in a society, Lively's criticism accepts the validity of the kind of exercise represented by exchange theory whereas Birnbaum treats the defects as inherent in the whole individualistic approach of which exchange theory is one manifestation.

The next three papers, by Mokken and Stokman, Chazel and myself, are concerned with other issues in the conceptualization and analysis of power and each of them tries to deal with problems that have persisted from the earliest speculations until the present: what, for example, is the relation (empirical or analytic) between power and such things as authority, the ability to manipulate rewards and punishments, the actual application of force, the restriction of the range of actions and getting what one wants? Oppenheim's paper, which follows, refers to these discussions while developing its own line of analysis.

The papers of Midgaard, Lehner and Schütte and de Vree, which come next, follow up a theme that is explicit in the first two papers and my own: the limitations of an 'economic' approach to the analysis of social and political phenomena. What is interesting is that each of the three is motivated by a desire to enrich the 'economic' style of analysis while accepting that it at present provides the only well worked out paradigm of rigorous social analysis. Midgaard proposed to set the underlying game—theoretical analysis of bargaining situations in the context of a more subtle analysis of the actual process of negotiation and in particular the varieties of communication involved. The papers by Lehner and Schütte and by de Vree are concerned with an attempt to modify the postulate of contentless 'maximizing' that is made in orthodox economic theorizing, and to allow for more complex psychological processes that may not be 'rational'.

Next come three papers concerned with problems of political analysis. Van Gunsteren discusses the way in which theorists of planning are (apparently without always being aware of it) constructing their own variants of classical themes in political theory and putting forward, in the guise of 'theories of planning', conceptions of the way political institutions should be restructured that have enormous—and sometimes sinister—implications. Vedung discusses the way in which writers on 'comparative government' have conceived of the purpose, method and subject-matter of comparison and proposes his own solution. The paper by Lane is a logically refined examination of the way in which 'politics' has been defined in the work of Weber, Easton and Lasswell and Kaplan.

The book concludes with the general discussion paper by Elster. Having already described it as a *tour de force*, I do not intend to be so rash as to attempt to summarize it. I hope that the reader will find these essays interesting both in themselves and as indications of the kind of questions at least one group of European political theorists are asking themselves and the kind of work they are doing.

Most of the pieces that appear in this book have been written in English by people who are neither native English speakers nor immigrants of long standing in an English-speaking country. Without exception, their ability to express themselves in

English is extraordinarily high, but it is almost impossible when writing in such an anarchic language to avoid an occasional order or combination of words that falls outside the standard range of variation. In editing the manuscripts I have tried to ensure that everything reads completely idiomatically, while at the same time taking care not to impose any uniform style of my own within the limits of normal usage. My ideal is that each chapter should come over as having been written by an author with his own distinctive style while containing nothing that feels unnatural or uncomfortable to a native user of English. If I have fallen short of this ideal, as I am sure I have, I hope that I have erred on the side of *laissez faire* rather than that of unnecessary intervention. In all cases where my revisions amount to more than changing an occasional preposition and a few points of punctuation, the revised manuscript has been seen and approved by the author. I am very grateful to contributors for the trouble that they have taken in checking over such revisions.

The paper by Lehner and Schütte was translated from the German original by Kark-Peter Markl. The last half of the article was than rewritten in English by Franz Lehner, who has approved the final version of the whole piece, as edited by me, in the form in which it now appears. The Chazel paper was translated from the French original by Karl-Peter Markl and the Birnbaum paper by Ulla Kasten. Both have been edited by me and discussed in detail with the authors during visits to England. I hope that the considerable labours of all those concerned have paid off by producing readable and accurate texts.

The appearance of this book would have been seriously delayed if my wife Joanna had not kindly taken on the onerous and time-consuming job of creating and checking the consolidated bibliography. I am very grateful to her and I must also thank those authors who provided the additional information we needed where this could not be obtained locally.

Brian Barry
Nuffield College, Oxford
1 June 1975

# About the Contributors

BRIAN BARRY (b. 1936, London) is an MA and DPhil (Oxon) and has held positions in Britain at the Universities of Birmingham, Keele, Southampton, Oxford and Essex, where he was Professor of Government. In the United States he was a Rockefeller Fellow in Legal and Political Philosophy and Honorary Fellow of Harvard College in 1961–62, Visiting Professor at Pittsburgh University in Autumn 1967 and Hinkley Visiting Professor at Johns Hopkins University in Spring 1974. During the preparation of this book he was an Official Fellow in Politics at Nuffield College, Oxford. He is now Professor of Political Science at the University of British Columbia, Vancouver, Canada. His books are: *Political Argument* (Routledge and Kegan Paul, London, 1965), *Sociologists, Economists and Democracy* (Collier-Macmillan, London, 1970) and *The Liberal Theory of Justice: a Critical Examination of the Principal Doctrines in A Theory of Justice by John Rawls* (Clarendon Press, Oxford, 1973). He was founding editor of *The British Journal of Political Science*.

PIERRE BIRNBAUM is a Docteur ès lettres (1974, Sorbonne). He is a Professor at the University of Paris I and at l'Institut d'Etudes Politiques de Paris. He has published the following books: *Sociologie de Tocqueville* (1969), *La Structure du pouvoir aux Etats-Unis* (1971) and, with F. Chazel, (eds.), *Sociologie politique* (1971) and *Théorie sociologique* (1975). He has also published *La Fin du politique* (1975), a critical work on the principal contemporary models of political theory (Parsons, Easton, Deutsch, Dahl, etc.). In this he aims to show how these writers have departed from the classical models of democracy. He is now working on a study of power in contemporary France.

FRANCOIS CHAZEL (b. 1937) studied at the Sorbonne and at l'Ecole Normale Supérieure and in addition spent a year at Harvard University. He is a Docteur ès Lettres and has been at the University of Bordeaux, where he is now Professor of Sociology, since 1966. He has published a book *La Théorie analytique de la société dans l'oeuvre de Talcott Parsons* (Mouton, Paris, 1974) and articles on, among other topics, Durkheim, Parsons, power and political mobilization. With Pierre Birnbaum he has edited books on *Sociologie politique* (A. Colin, Paris, 1971) and *Théorie sociologique* (PUF, Paris, 1975), and with Paul Lazarsfeld and Raymond Boudon one on *L'Analyse des processus sociaux* (Mouton, Paris, 1970). In addition to his substantive interests, he is concerned with the logic of inquiry in the social sciences.

JON ELSTER (b. 1940) is Associate Professor of History at the University of Oslo and Associate Professor of Sociology at the University of Paris VIII. He has been Visiting Professor at the University of California at Berkeley, at the University of Aarhus (Denmark) and at Stanford University. Main publications include his *Thèse pour le Doctorat d'Etat, Production et reproduction* (Mouton, Paris, forthcoming) and *Leibniz et la Formation de l'ésprit capitaliste* (Aubier, Paris, forthcoming).

HERMAN VAN GUNSTEREN is a political theorist and a musician. He studied law at Leiden University, where he is now a Reader in Political Theory. The title of his inaugural address, which was given in October 1974, is 'Thinking about Political Responsibility'. His present research interests are the theory of contemporary citizenship, the concept of legislation and the practical implications of rational methods of policy-making. He spent a year at Berkeley, California, where he wrote a book, *The Quest for Control: a Critique of the Rational-Central-Rule Planning Approach in Public Affairs* (Wiley, London, 1976).

JAN-ERIK LANE (b. 1946) studied at the University of Umeå in Sweden, where he is now Associate Professor in the Department of Political Science. He has worked in the fields of history, political science and philosophy of science and has been affiliated as a lecturer to the corresponding departments in Umeå. He has contributed articles to Swedish and English—American journals and books, including among the latter: 'Two kinds of means-end sentences: on the use of the means-end terminology in Weber, Parsons and Simon' in *Scandinavian Political Studies,* No. 9, 1974.

FRANZ LEHNER is an *assistent* at the Department of Social Science of the University of Mannheim. In 1974–5 he was a German Kennedy Fellow of Harvard University. He has published a book, *Politisches Verhalten als sozialer Tausch* (*Political Behaviour as Social Exchange*) and several articles on the psychology of perception and on modern political theory. He is currently engaged in research on the new political economy.

JACK LIVELY read History at St John's College, Cambridge. After research in Cambridge, he moved to a Research Fellowship at St Antony's College, Oxford. Since then he has taught politics at the University of Wales, the University of Sussex and St Peter's College, Oxford. He is now Professor of Politics at the University of Warwick. Publications include *The Social and Political Thought of Alexis de Tocqueville* (1962), *The Works of Joseph de Maistre* (1965), *The Enlightenment* (1966) and *Democracy* (1975).

KNUT OLAV MIDGAARD (b. 1931, Oslo) passed his *magistergrad* in the History of Ideas in 1959 at the University of Oslo and was then for several years a Research Fellow, mainly at the Institute of Philosophy at the University of Oslo, combining philosophical work with the study of conflict and co-operation. A year's stay at Harvard University was the background of the publication in 1965 of a book in Norwegian on game theory and its application in the study of international politics (*Strategisk Tenkning: Noen Spillteoretiske Emmer med Saerlig Tanke på Internasjonal Politikk*) and various articles on game theory and strategy. The problem of the rules of the game in various types of political interaction and an interest in political communication led to a mimeographed work, 'Communication and Strategy' (English edition 1970), which focused on the constitutive elements of 'interlocutions' with a view to a systematic understanding of strategic and non-strategic verbal behaviour. Since 1968 he has been associated with the Institute of Political Science at the University of Oslo where he is now a Professor. He teaches political theory and has for some years directed research in the fields of negotiations, political debates and voting.

ROBERT J. MOKKEN (b. 1929, Djakarta) graduated in 1952 from the Dutch Royal Naval Academy at Den Helder and subsequently studied political science and mathematical statistics at the University of Amsterdam, receiving his PhD in political science in 1970. He worked from 1961 to 1966 on the staff of the Department of Mathematical Statistics of the Mathematical Centre, Amsterdam, and the Institute of Mass Communications of the University of Amsterdam. After that period he was appointed to the Institute for Political Science of the University of Amsterdam, since 1971 in his present position of Professor of Political Science and Methodology. In 1974–5 he was Visiting Professor at the University of Michigan. He has published numerous books and articles in Dutch and English covering varied subjects in such areas as mass communications, electoral and participatory analysis and mathematical methods of research.

FELIX E. OPPENHEIM, who holds a law degree from the University of Brussels and a PhD in political science from Princeton University, is a Professor of Political Science and Philosophy at the University of Massachusetts (Amherst). He was the recipient of a Guggenheim Fellowship (1956), a Fulbright Lecturer at the University of Florence (1968), a Visiting Fellow at Wolfson College, Oxford (1970), and a Resident Fellow at the Netherlands Institute for Advanced Study (1973/4). He was Visiting Professor at Columbia and Yale, and lectured at various English and Italian universities. He is the author of *Dimensions of Freedom* (New York, 1961) and *Moral Principles in Political Philosophy* (New York, 1968). He contributed to the *International Encyclopedia of the Social Sciences*, the *Handbook of Political Science, Nomos* and the *Dizionario di Politica*. His articles have appeared in various political science and philosophy journals.

HANS GERD SCHÜTTE is an *assistent* in the Department of Sociology of the University of Mannheim. He has done research on regional mobility, town-planning, industrial relations and occupational problems, and has published articles on the methodology of systems analysis and organization theory and a book, *Der empirische Gehalt des Funktionalismus (The Empirical Content of Functionalism)*. A book on problems of sociology and political economy, *Rationalität, Konsens und Konflikt (Rationality, Consensus and Conflict)*, is in press.


FRANS N. STOKMAN (b. 1941) is Assistant Professor in Political Science and Research Methodology at the Institute for Political Science of the University of Amsterdam. His fields of specialization include research methodology; influence and power structures among political and economic élites and the analysis of legislative behaviour, in particular in the United Nations. Publications: (with R. J. Mokken) 'A theory and method of roll call analysis', paper delivered at IPSA congress, Munich, 1970; with H. M. Helmers, R. J. Mokken, R. C. Plijter in collaboration with Jac. M. Anthonisse, *Graven naar Macht. Op Zoek naar de Kern van de Nederlandse Economie (Traces of Power)* (Van Gennep, Amsterdam, 1975); *Shifts in leadership among the developing nations in the United Nations*, forthcoming; articles in *Acta Politica*.


EVERT VEDUNG is Associate Professor in the Department of Political Science at the University of Uppsala, Sweden. His dissertation, *Unionsdebatten 1905* (1971), is a comparative study of Swedish and Norwegian foreign policy during the dissolution of the union between the two countries in 1905. In an article entitled 'Content-oriented and function-oriented analysis of political ideas' (*Scandinavian Political Studies*, 10, 1975) he has conducted an inquiry into some methodological problems of the study of political ideologies and controversies. In co-operation with Professor Sverker Gustavsson he is currently working on a study of 'Focus and Method of Comparative Government'. His research interests also include the application of game and decision theory to political action.


JOHAN K. DE VREE is Professor of International Relations at the State University at Utrecht. He received his PhD from the University of Amsterdam. He has taught at the University of Amsterdam and written about philosophy of science as well as empirical political theory. He is working on an axiomatic general theory of politics, applicable both to domestic and to international affairs, formulated in a mathematical language, and to be described in a book that is provisionally called 'Foundations of Politics'. He has written the following: *Political Integration: the Formation of Theory and Its Problems* (Mouton, Den Haag, 1972), 'Behaviour, Learning and Conversion: Elements of a General Theory of Politics' (Amsterdam, 1972, *mimeo*), *Syllabus Inleiding Internationale Betrekkingen* (Utrecht, 1973), *Syllabus Capita uit de Leer der Internationale Betrekkingen* (Utrecht, 1973/74) and a number of articles.

# Contents

# 1

# The Limits of Exchange Theory

JACK LIVELY

## 1 THE THEMES OF CATALLACTICS

The eighteenth century saw the emergence of a number of radically different types of social theory which had one feature in common, an emphasis on spontaneous forms of social organization and a corresponding stress on the autonomy of the social sphere from political direction. Within this broad assumption, three distinct modes of theorizing developed. The first, embodied largely in contract, utilitarian and classical economic theories, sought to explain society in terms of individual intentions and saw social coherence as emerging from the willingness of individuals to serve the needs of others in order to satisfy their own. The second, taking shape in what might be called cultural sociology, derived social coherence from the shared values of a society, varying from community to community but in all constituting severe limits to political action. The third, expressed in various historicist philosophies, asserted the patterning of social development over time and the possibility of predicting as well as retrodicting this patterning, thus again setting bounds to political possibilities. The political uses of these varieties of social analysis have been complex, but again, broadly, the first has been identified with classical *laissez faire* liberalism, the second has been developed by and supported conservative thought of one kind of another, while the third has been peculiarly although not exclusively associated with Marxist socialism. Whatever their political applications, these theories have in common served the purpose of underlining the limited efficacy or even the positive disutility of political intervention in social arrangements, the marginal use of politics.

I am concerned here with the first of these modes of theorizing, exchange theory. The central assumptions of exchange theory, necessarily postulates about individual psychology or motivation, have been egoism, the self-interest axiom and rationality—the capacity and inclination of men to choose appropriate means for the ends they have in mind. The central assertion of the theory has been that social cohesion may be achieved through (if men are egoistic and can be taught to be rational) or is based on (if men are both egoistic and rational) the adaptation of individual actions to the needs of others and to general social ends in the course of their pursuit of their own interests, and without any appeal to cohesive values other than those involved in the acceptance of common media of exchange. The central intellectual construct of the theory has been the notion of the market (or, as Hayek has called it, in order to free the term of its narrowly economic implications, a catallaxy), the notion of a spontaneous and self-adjusting order which emerges from the mutual exchange of benefits between self-interested individuals.

The political requirements seen as necessary to sustain such a catallaxy were minimal. One arose from the need to enforce agreements. Rational egoists in a world of rational egoists had to have some insurance against the excesses of egoism and some assurance therefore that promises and bargains would be enforced. The other problem demanding a political solution was the need to prevent monopoly and perhaps to stimulate competition, so as to maintain sufficient alternatives for the individual, either as supplier or demander, meaningfully to measure opportunity costs. Another political problem that might seem to present itself—that different individuals carry different resources into the market—was ignored, or rather, it was ignored as a moral problem requiring perhaps a political solution, while it was explained as a social fact in exchange terms through the division of labour, inequality of capacities, demand differentials and thus exchange inequalities. The moral problem of inequality was avoided by insisting on the moral neutrality of the market and also on the claim that inequalities in the distribution of resources derived from exchange inequalities.

There have thus been two analytical thrusts in catallactics or exchange theory: firstly and primarily to explain and predict the behaviour of individuals or groups engaged in exchange within a given distribution of resources; secondly and secondarily to describe how differential distributions emerge, are maintained and may change, primarily through division of labour explanations. Used ideologically, as a justification for a particular type of political system or programme, the theory has claimed some moral superiority for the spontaneous order of a catallaxy over an order decided on politically and maintained by political power. One basis for such a claim has been utilitarian in form, but most of the weight of justification has rested on the supposed voluntary character of entry into and agreement within exchange relationships in contrast for example with the coercive character of power relationships. Bargains are freely arrived at, political obedience is essentially unfree; and thus the *prima facie* preferability of the first is obvious.

## 2 AN EXCHANGE THEORY OF POWER

At least in classical *laissez faire* thinking, then, exchange relations and power relations have been viewed as polar opposites. A necessary condition of interpersonal and intergroup exchange is the reciprocal and voluntary provision of benefits, and this condition cannot be met within a power relationship in which—one may say as a crude starting-point—one person is forced to do something by or to provide something for another. The purpose of this paper is to examine a recent attempt to dissolve this distinction by casting power relations in exchange terms, the attempt made by Peter M. Blau in his book, *Exchange and Power in Social Life* (Blau, 1964). It will be my contention that Blau is largely occupied with what I have defined as the second and secondary concern of exchange theory, the explanation of the emergence of differential distributions, and that he is unsuccessful in providing such an explanation in exchange terms.

However, Blau's failure to do this does not imply that lack of success must necessarily attend exchange theory in its first concern, that is to explain or predict behaviour within a given distribution of power or within a given changing distribution of power. More specifically, my arguments will be that Blau's genetic account of power distributions is faulty; that nevertheless power relations are amenable to exchange analysis; that the scope of exchange analysis is both wider and narrower than Blau claims, wider in that physical coercion (which he seems to wish to exclude) can easily be accommodated within it, narrower in that authority relations (which he wishes to include), cannot; that, precisely because power relations *can* be discussed in exchange terms, the identification of exchange relations as free relations and of exchange agreements as voluntary agreements is doubtful. Blau may be right in trying to remove the *laissez faire* opposition of exchange and power, but he is right for the wrong reasons. It is not (as the general tenor of Blau's argument suggests) that power relations are like all exchange relations, voluntary, but that power relations like many other exchange relations cannot plausibly be discussed in voluntaristic terms.

Blau, as I have said, is primarily concerned with the genesis of power relations and his basic etiology of power can be briefly stated. His general intention is, he tells us, to explain 'how social life becomes organized into increasingly complex structures of associations among men' (Blau, 1964, p.2.); and he believes such an explanation can be found in the concept of social exchange which can be analysed most succinctly in microcosmic face-to-face groups but which has equal explanatory force in large and complex social structures. A major part of interpersonal relations are based on exchange processes, that is to say processes in which benefits are given to others in the expectation that some equivalent will be returned by them. The root characteristics of exchange are thus reciprocity and voluntariness. Social exchange 'refers to the voluntary actions of individuals that are motivated by the returns they are expected to bring and typically do in fact bring from others' (Blau, 1964, p.91). These returns or benefits can be either extrinsic or intrinsic—extrinsic if the nature of the association or the participants in it are irrelevant to the services mutually provided (the salesman and his customer), intrinsic if the rewards derive from the relationship itself and are peculiar to a particular relationship (the salesman and his wife). There is a tendency towards imbalance in interpersonal exchange, since men are apparently reluctant debtors but willing lenders. The desire to stay out of debt in the mutual provision of benefits results in the strain towards reciprocity. However, men also wish to achieve the superior status that a credit balance will bring and so, when particular benefits are in short supply and great demand, imbalances can occur. This disequilibrium in service provision is balanced by an imbalance of power. A person who supplies services to others obliges them to provide some return. If those who accept his services cannot provide any acceptable return, they must, in order both to fulfil obligations and to ensure continuance of supplies, comply with his wishes, in other words submit to his power. The unilateral provision of services in this way gives rise to a differentiation of power that brings the exchange back into equilibrium. This is the basis of interpersonal power and, with qualifications that are largely derived from the distinction between direct and indirect exchanges, large and complex power structures.

## 3 POWER AND IMBALANCE OF EXCHANGE

There are no doubt many different ways in which this theory could be approached and evaluated. What I wish to do here is to examine the internal coherence of Blau's argument. I hope, by doing so, to establish some limits on the capacity of catallactics in general as both an explanatory and a justificatory theory. In this section I will look at Blau's derivation of power from an imbalance of exchange and at his movement from microsociological to macrosociological explanations. In the following two sections I will examine his treatment of the notions of power and authority.

The first difficulty presented by Blau's argument has to do with his claim that power originates in an imbalance of exchange, when it would seem less tortuous to talk of power relations in terms simply of exchange. A Person who needs services from some Other has a number of alternatives open to him, argues Blau. He can offer reciprocal services to Other which Other needs and will accept, in which case a straightforward exchange takes place. If he has nothing acceptable to offer, Person can choose between a number of alternative strategies. He can tighten his belt, ascetically limit his needs so as to require less from Other; he can shop around and look for another supplier who has a lower asking price or needs what Person can provide; he can force Other to provide the wanted service; or he can subordinate himself to Other, comply with his wishes, give Other power over himself. Clearly, on Blau's argument, the first two strategems do not account for the rise of power relations. Equally clearly, they are not strategems available in the political market, even supposing they are ready to hand in the economic market. We cannot make power-holders go away by ignoring them or refusing their services; and it has become less plausible since Locke's day to argue that we can, by emigration, choose our political supplier. The third alternative, forcing Other to provide the wanted service, is odd in the context since it seems to offer an alternative etiology of power to that which Blau puts forward. It is not odd as an etiology; indeed, if we are to speculate on the origins of power structures, the paradigm of conquest seems intuitively at least as reasonable as that of the free market. It is however the last strategem that, according to Blau, gives rise to power differentation. Yet it is rather difficult, I suspect, to differentiate this fourth case from the third.

Blau's argument implies a particular hypothesized chronology of events: (*a*) Other provides Person with services, (*b*) Person is unable to provide reciprocal services, (*c*) in order to repay Other (or to secure his future services), Person has to comply with Other's wishes. The division between stage (*b*) and stage (*c*) depends on a distinction between the provision of reciprocal services and compliance with wishes to which it is impossible to hold. For presumably, in complying with Other's wishes, Person is providing (reciprocally) goods or services that Other desires. So perhaps the stages can be cut to two: (*a*) Other provides Person with services; (*b*) to repay Other (or to secure his future services), Person complies with Other's wishes. This is a move towards a simple exchange rather than the imbalance of exchange of which Blau talks.

At the same time, the chronology is still insecure for it depends upon whether Person complies to repay Other or to secure future services. In his derivation of power from an imbalance of exchange, it is the first that Blau stresses. In getting services from Other that he does not return, Person incurs a debt of obligation which he has to repay by subordination. Now this depiction of the origins of interpersonal power is both odd in itself and difficult to reconcile with egoistic assumptions. On the second count, it is difficult to see why a rational egoist should repay debts, fulfil obligations, unless the non-payment will affect his future position. The egoist is constitutionally forward-looking, a man of appetites, not of gratitude. This is why the account is odd in itself. Even if Person subordinates himself to Other because Other (and perhaps no Other) provides wanted services, it would be more natural to derive Other's power from his capacity to threaten the future non-provision of services rather than from his past provision of services. Other has power not because other Persons are obligated to him but because he possesses resources that other Persons want or need continuously and which he can utilize, through threats, to secure compliance. The chronology then suggested is: (*a*) Other possesses resources that enable him to harm Person; (*b*) Person complies with his wishes to escape harm. Or, Other can force Person to supply him with services. One only has to turn strategem four round to find strategem three.

In fact, Blau tacitly recognizes this by defining power itself in terms of threats and sanctions. But he does this without realizing how far it weakens his depiction of the genesis of power in the imbalance of voluntary exchange transactions. A second difficulty in Blau's genetic account of power relations arises from his move from the examination of micro-structures to his examination of macro-structures. He assumes a fairly close correspondence between power relations (as he describes them) in small face-to-face groups and those within large collectivities. It is, however, problematic whether or not this genetic account, derived from the supposed processes governing interpersonal relations, can be applied to complex political structures. The major obstacle to such a translation is that the benefits that might be said to be exchanged in complex structures may be products of that system itself and of the distributions or power within it.

The main difference between exchange relations in small groups and those in large collectivities lies, according to Blau, in the role of shared values in the latter. While the general thrust of exchange theory is to diminish the force of shared values as an explanation of social behaviour, some appeal to them has to be made by exchange theory in general in order to explain the acceptance of common media of exchange, and Blau in particular has to appeal to them to explain authority relations. More specifically the differences between the micro- and the macro-levels consist in the substitution of groups for individuals as the actors within exchange transactions and in the substitution of indirect for direct exchanges. Both processes depend on shared values. A sub-group within a wider collectivity can become an exchange transactor because its members share particularistic values distinguishing them from other groups. Universalistic values on social achievement or proper behaviour are necessary to replace the individual assessment of relative values possible within interpersonal exchanges by a common media of exchange. Given the existence of such universalistic values, Blau argues, indirect rather than direct exchange can take place.

I do not find Blau's discussion of indirect exchange either very clear or very consistent, but there are at least two usages of the concept that can be isolated. Firstly, given the existence of universalistic standards of achievement and behaviour, those who achieve highly on these standards will be rewarded by status and, Blau implies, power. Secondly, given universalistic standards, there will be social pressures on all both to conform to these norms and to obey those who achieve highly on them. I will return to this second usage when I discuss authority and exchange; for the moment I will concentrate on the first. The difficulties here seem to be threefold. In the first place, even in political systems in which it can be said that those holding power do so because they satisfy demands from below, the role of indirect exchange might be slight. In the second place, power (or even status) in complex and ongoing structures does not derive from the personal capacities of those with great power or high status but from their position within a particular distribution. Thirdly, the existence of a stable power structure changes the nature of the benefits that can be said to be exchanged by those with and those without power. Binding together these three criticisms is the general objection that the approval of those who obey is not necessarily an element of power relations.

To illustrate the first point, let us take a democratic system in which more than in other systems, it might be supposed, governors have to seek the approval of the governed. It is by no means clear that here men with power achieve it because they score heavily on some universalistic scales of personal worth. In choosing governors, voters might reasonably prefer rat-like cunning to nobility of character. Of course they would probably do so if they thought the cunning men would be more likely to secure what they wanted from their governors than the noble man. The point is, however, that this motivational pattern suggests a direct rather than an indirect exchange. The voter is not rewarding someone attractive on universal standards or seeking the social approval of his peers; he is trading off his vote in return for an expected performance in office.

The second objection, that social power derives from position within a structure of distribution rather than from personal capacities, is more fundamental. What are the benefits sought in Blau's quasi-state of nature, the small group? He talks mainly in terms of advice, friendship and love on the one side, approval, status and, finally, power on the other. Those with the personal capacity to give good advice or to inspire affection gain in return approval or, if that approval is valueless, power (compliance with wishes). The language of approval, and the rooting of approval in the appreciation of personal capacities, is carried over by Blau from his discussion of direct to his discussion of indirect exchange, and thus from his examination of small groups to his examination of large collectivities. It is easy, I think, to see how strained this language is. Already we have seen that, even using this language, power is most plausibly defined in terms of the capacity to hurt. And clearly, in complex power structures, the capacity to hurt is related rather to position within that structure than to personal characteristics. Even with status, this may be true. (The English, it is said, all love a Lord; but they do not necessarily make those they love Lords.) It is more clearly the case with power. In an unstructured situation, the capacity to inspire love, or friendship or respect (which may well be supposed to be innate) may give a personal influence over others. But, given situations in which the capacities that confer on men a strong bargaining position depend on their position within a particular distribution of resources, it is impossible to derive that distribution from differences in capacity. This is not to say that individual qualities may not be needed to achieve favourable positions. A silver tongue may be necessary for the successful democratic politician, phlegm in the face of risk-taking to the successful capitalist. But even if a particular ability is needed to reach a particular power position (or a favourable position within any other distribution), the possession of power depends on control over particular resources and not on the possession of the capacity.

Moreover, what counts as a benefit is different within a stable power structure and in an unstructured face-to-face situation; and the difference lies precisely in the degree to which the existing distribution of resources determines the rate and the nature of exchanges. In an unstructured situation what A requires by way of services from B is decided by A himself; in a stable and structured situation it may well be decided by B. Let us suppose a structured situation in which A has stable power over (the capacity to direct through the threat of some harm) B, C and D. Now B may be benefited by A's power. It may prevent C and D from harming him; it may co-ordinate his activities with C and D in a mutually beneficial way; it may protect him with C and D against E and F. It may be even that B is willing to obey A precisely because A does provide these general benefits (although it is hard to see why as a rational egoist he should). However, A's power over B does not depend upon this willingness, or necessarily upon A's securing of these benefits for B. It consists in the capacity to harm B. Yet the very existence of a unilateral capacity to harm does allow us to talk of an exchange between A and B, the exchange of B's obedience for A's not harming him. The exact terms of the exchange will depend on how great A's power is (how extensive his capacity to harm) and what the distribution of power resources is in this community of four. What is clear, however, is that the benefits conferred by power-holders need not be extrinsic to the power itself; that the exchanges taking place are direct rather than indirect in Blau's first sense; and that a voluntaristic element is no more necessary a feature of direct exchanges in complex structure than it is of direct exchanges in interpersonal relations.

The difficulties involved in Blau's move from small groups to large collectivities are revealed most clearly in his explanation of the continuity of power relations, perhaps the outstanding characteristic of complex structures. He explains the continuity of power in terms of mechanisms through which shared values are perpetuated. The major mechanisms are processes of socialization and support by dominant groups of those existing values that legitimize their dominance. Now this seems to run directly counter to the account of the derivation of power differentials given in his discussion of interpersonal associations. There he derived power differences from free exchange transactions. However, if a dominant power group has the ability to perpetuate itself, through its ability to control socialization processes or in other more obvious ways, the explanation of power differentials in terms of free exchange transactions becomes irrelevant to actual distributions of social power, or at the most relevant to that hypothetical moment in time when power differentials first emerged. The point cannot be better put than by Blau himself:

Sufficient power enables individuals to monopolize resources and to make others increasingly dependent on themselves. While the perpetuation of their power is contingent on their continuing to provide *some* benefits to others, if only by refraining from punishing them, it is evident that the very power that makes others dependent for these 'benefits' cannot be considered in any sense to constitute a deserved reward for supplying services or an incentive necessary to produce them. In short, once superior power has been attained by furnishing services, it can be sustained without furnishing these same services. [Blau, 1964, p.197]

What Blau does not realize is that, if this is so, exchange theory fails to provide an explanation of power distributions in complex structures (as distinct from an explanation of behaviour within given distributions). At most it could perhaps explain how power differentials ever arose in the first instance. If so, it seems a flight into a historical anthropology as much beyond empirical verification as Locke's state of nature—to which Blau's small group bears a close resemblance.

## 4 POWER, COERCION AND FREE EXCHANGES

Early in his thesis, Blau argues that exchange processes cover only part of the whole field of power relations. He excludes two cases from their ambit, physical coercion and disinterested action, on the grounds that the requirement of voluntariness is absent from the first and that of reciprocity in the second. Surrender of money to the gunman cannot be regarded as an exchange because it is not voluntary. And giving conscience money to the poor cannot of itself be viewed as an exchange because no reciprocal benefit is provided. Now it might seem that any schema claiming to depict political relationships that excludes force on the one hand and duty or obligation on the other must of necessity be extremely partial and thus highly unrealistic. Blau preserves some realism by a restricted and confused definition of physical coercion and by explaining, in his discussion of authority, obligation in terms of indirect exchanges. I shall argue that he is mistaken both in his wish to exclude physical coercion from the compass of exchange analysis and in his wish to include authority relations in it; and I shall suggest that the wish in both cases stems from a desire to characterize exchange transactions as voluntary.

The clearest definition Blau gives of the term 'power' is at the same time the most linguistically plausible. Here he defines power in terms of the capacity to affect intentionally the acts of others through the use of threats, and notices that threats can have a very wide range including the threat to deprive someone of habitual rewards. Power is, he says, 'the ability of persons or groups to impose their will on others despite resistance through deterrence either in the forms of withholding regularly supplied rewards or in the form of punishment, inasmuch as the former as well as the latter constitute, in effect, a negative sanction' (Blau, 1964, p.117). This definition may be limited and certainly does not cover all the ways in which one person can affect the actions of others in desired and intended ways. However, it does cover most of the obvious instances in which we would want to talk of an exercise of power.

The difficulties that arise are not over the definition itself, but over the inconsistencies between it and the general tenor of Blau's argument. One, already touched on, is the incompatibility of this definition with his depiction of the emergence of power as the result of an imbalance of exchange. Another difficulty emerges if one asks why (on this definition) any power relations, including those arising from physical coercion, should be excluded from exchange analysis. Obviously, a distinction has to be made between the exercise of physical force and the threat of physical harm (killing, maiming or incarceration, say). The actual exercise of physical force can have only limited use as a means of power. Having led the horse to the water, I might just be able to make him drink by pushing his head under, but this and analogous cases illustrate rather cumbersome and unusual methods of exercising power. I might also make someone do nothing by physical force—tying him up, imprisoning him, destroying his physical capacity to act in certain ways—and nothing might be precisely what I want him to do. But such methods of enforcing one's will must be of limited applicability. Normally, when we talk of physical coercion as a basis for power (certainly when we are talking of regularly exercised social power), we are referring to the threat of physical harm as a means of imposing one's will. Not imprisonment, but the *threat* of imprisonment, is the usual instrument of social power. Clearly, physical coercion in this sense is both a regular element in political power and quite susceptible to exchange analysis. Blau's appreciation of this, but his desire also to maintain the voluntarism of exchange relations, is shown in a passage following closely on the definition of power quoted: 'the punishment threatened for resistance, provided it is severe, makes power a compelling force, yet there is an element of voluntarism in power—the punishment could be chosen in preference to compliance, and it sometimes is—which distinguishes it from the limiting case of direct physical coercion'. (Blau, 1964, p.117.) Physical coercion is now drastically narrowed (it would not now cover the gunman example) and the implication is that all deliberate actions are voluntary actions. In terms of my relations with others, my only non-voluntary actions would be those in which I am physically manhandled or perhaps when I am under hypnosis. The argument is reminiscent of that of Hobbes in his discussion of what he genteelly calls sovereignty by acquisition. Submission to a conqueror constitutes a contract as binding on men as their mutual agreement to obey a sovereign in a covenant. In both cases, the motive for contracting is fear, and in both cases a free choice is made. What is nonsensical in this argument (and there is a parallel with Blau here) is the depiction of the bargain as one made of free choice which consequently entails a moral obligation to obey. What is not nonsensical in either Hobbes or Blau is to picture the decision in exchange terms. Those who submit to a conqueror can compare the costs of submission with the costs of resistance, and act rationally on the comparison. Power consists precisely in the ability to vary the costs for others of different courses of action, usually by making all but one more costly, sometimes by making one more rewarding. There seems no reason at all for excluding fear of physical harm from the range of fears (of economic loss or prestige, eternal damnation and so on) that can form the basis of threats.

All that is required for bargaining and exchange to take place is the presence of alternatives enabling the participants to measure opportunity costs. Bargaining decisions may be 'voluntary' only in the sense that Hobbes's man agrees voluntarily to submit (the alternative being to be killed). Acts of exchange take place within a context that itself determines the bargaining power that different participants can wield, which distributes differentially the 'services' they can offer, which indeed defines what is to count as a benefit. I may agree on an exchange as the best I can get in the circumstances, but to talk of my decision as thereby 'voluntary' is to drain the notion of free choice of all that normally we think characterizes it.

This criticism of Blau—that exchange transactions in power terms cannot be identified as 'voluntary'—has perhaps a wider implication. This is that it is only in special circumstances that any exchange can be cast in voluntaristic terms. When we talk of bargaining and agreement, we commonly speak as though the bargain agreed on, the exchange made, must be one that provides benefits for all parties to the agreement. Agreement implies co-operation, and co-operative activity (given the assumption of rational egoism) implies mutual advantages. In one sense, this is true. It may however be misleadingly true for, while the fact that an agreement is reached implies that there is one position that parties prefer in common, the ranges of choices open to them may not necessarily (will not commonly) be ones that they would themselves, if outside the situation, have most preferred.

The point can be illustrated by looking at the distinction made between zero-sum conflicts and non-zero-sum conflicts, which I shall take roughly to be the distinction between on the one side conflicts in which protagonists have exactly contrary preferences and a gain for one yields a corresponding loss to the other, and on the other side a conflict in which there is at least one outcome for which the preferences of protagonists are not strictly opposed, one mutually advantageous outcome. In one sense all settlements of conflicts must be based on a non-zero-sum solution. Even if we fight to my death, it could be said that I preferred death to other alternatives (dishonour, submission) and you preferred my death to other alternatives. The distinction between the two types of conflict does in fact hold only if the preferences of protagonists are abstracted from the conflict or bargaining situation itself. I want your money, you do not wish to give it; one racial or religious group wants equality of civil rights, another wishes to maintain discrimination; one state wants a stretch of territory, the other does not wish to cede it. The objectives here are incompatible and, if one protagonist achieves his, the other must necessarily fail in his. However, once the bargaining or conflict situation has been entered (and conflict here can be regarded in Clausewitzian terms as nothing more than the continuance of bargaining by other means), the range of alternatives and the costs of different alternatives are normally altered within the process itself. I want your money, you do not wish to give it; but if your refusal would lead to public disclosure of some private shame, or to physical harm, or to exclusion from a job, and if I can plausibly threaten such consequences, you might well choose to be blackmailed or robbed, or to offer a bribe. We have, in the situation, reached a mutually advantageous outcome, a non-zero-sum solution. The zero-sum conflict can be defined only in terms of the *status quo ante bellum.* This is not surprising, for the process of bargaining or conflict is one of trying to modify the objectives of an opponent by adding to the preferability to him of an outcome preferable to oneself. And, since it is difficult to think of conflicts that are literally endless, presumably this process of modification of goals (which may or may not be mutual) is normally achieved, perhaps at very considerable and damaging costs to one or other of the combatants. The example of competitive games, which is commonly brought forward to illustrate the zero-sum situation, is of little relevance to social conflict, for the absolute win-or-lose outcome is dependent on the game having a finite term—the referee blows the whistle and has authority to end the play. (Even in games, it is possible in football, usual in cricket, for teams to 'settle' for a draw.)

A zero-sum conflict therefore is one in which not only is there incompatibility of objectives but also the combatants are mutually incapable of modifying their opponent's objectives by any means (persuasion, inducements, threats). Since the utilization (and perhaps the buildup) of such means is a normal part of the process of bargaining of conflict, a zero-sum conflict is usually unstable. It will persist only so long as the resources available to the combatants are, or are thought to be, in some sense equal and so long as the recognition of equality does not itself lead to a modification of goals (settling for a draw). On the other side, any agreement reached (even if as the result of coercion, the threat of harm or further harm) can be defined as a non-zero-sum settlement. But little can be implied about the 'voluntary' character of the agreement from the fact that agreement has been reached and that there are advantages for all in it. How far a settlement is willingly agreed on in any real sense will depend upon the distribution of those resources that can be employed in bargaining. It is likely that the voluntariness of the simple barter model will be present only to the degree that there is some rough equality in such distributions.

## 5 AUTHORITY AND EXCHANGE

As has been seen, Blau initially excludes disinterested action from the scope of exchange analysis. This seems at once to be plausible and to limit the explanatory capacity of this kind of analysis. To do something because it is right, to obey someone because his commands are rightful, to accept a decision because it has emerged from a rightful procedure, is not to be engaged in exchange, unless (at the cost of the intellectual coherence of exchange theory) it is claimed that the self-satisfaction that the righteous are supposed to feel is to count as the reciprocal benefit. Perhaps *dulce et decorum est pro patria mori;* and perhaps men die thinking so. If they do, they do not seem to die in the marketplace. Nor is this a lonely example in a sparsely populated class. If I give blood as a donor, if I take the trouble to vote in a secret ballot, if I help a pupil over and beyond official requirements of the norms of my colleagues, if I accept the result of a democratic decision-making procedure even when I dislike the decision and could do otherwise, if in other words I act on a sense of obligation, I seem to step beyond the purview of exchange analysis. The fact that the values from which this sense of obligation derives and which determine its direction may be socially induced does not affect the issue, so long as I am not incurring costs in the expectation of returns from others. If love and friendship, the promptings of conscience, feelings of duty or obligation, notions of proper behaviour and legitimate claims cannot be encompassed by catallactics, its relevance to the real world must be diminished, for it would need not a hard heart, but a resolute lack of realism to discount these entirely as factors in interpersonal and social relations.

Despite his initial exclusion, Blau does nevertheless try (unsuccessfully in my opinion) to bring such factors within the scope of his analysis. In interpersonal terms, on friendship and love, he contests Blake's view that 'Love seeketh not itself to please, Nor for itself hath any care'. In an excursus on love, he pictures love as the exchange of (largely) intrinsic benefits, my love for your love. The partiality of his success here is of a piece with the partiality of the success of his general theory. What he tries to explain but does not succeed in explaining is why anyone should love at all and what behaviour would follow from being in love; what he may perhaps illuminate are the strategems of courtship or seduction, particularly in the case where resources are unequal (not-loving counting as a resource).

When he turns to the notions of authority, legitimacy and rightful command, which he recognizes as important elements in social obedience, his argument is not altogether clear. He suggests a number of stages through which an authority relation (involving the recognition that a command is rightfully given or a leader rightfully obeyed) emerges. For power to be stable, the collective approval of the community is necessary. For that collective approval to arise, the leadership must conform to generally held norms and/or (which is not clear) must contribute to the common welfare. Thus far, nothing has been said that brings authority relations within the ambit of exchange analysis. Suppose a subordinate to be one of those sharing the social norms to which leadership conforms and who believes that leadership of the sort that exists contributes to the general welfare. No exchange has taken place if he obeys for these reasons, unless he has assumed either that virtue is its own reward or that incurring costs for the general welfare must be in the net interest of each individual—in which cases he has ceased to act respectively as an egoist and as a rational egoist. Blau does not in fact utilize either of these assumptions, but argues that the benefits an individual receives from compliance to authority are indirect, in the second sense isolated earlier. The cost of accepting authority is for the individual covered by the social approval of his peers. Social constraints imposed by subordinates on each other in defence of common values create the possibility of reciprocity in obedience to rightful authorities.

There are a number of difficulties about this argument as an explanation either of the emergence of authority systems or of their maintenance. The first point to be made is that this derivation of authority from indirect exchanges might be culture-bound, or at the least that the social-psychological mechanism on which it relies might vary in efficacy in different social environments. Certainly it would seem to operate best in an environment in which man's moral sense is little more than a barometer sensitive to social pressures. If, say, Tocqueville and Riesman are right in setting 'the tyranny of the majority' and the 'outer-directed' man in an American context, this mechanism might be particularly or even peculiarly operative in American society.

Even if we assume this to be a constant in all complex social structures, there are still limitations in the indirect exchange explanations of authority relations. Clearly it does not explain the origination of particular authority systems, since the generally held norms have to be present before the constraints on which indirect exchange is based can be operative; and the theory does not attempt to explain the emergence of this collective approval. Nor patently can it explain changes in ideas of legitimacy. It seems to have more leverage as an account of how authority systems are maintained, but even here it is in some respects clumsy and uneconomic. If there is general approval in a community for a particular leader or a particular procedure for selecting leaders or deciding on social rules, it seems less wasteful to attribute general obedience to the persons or rules so authorized to that approval rather than to mutual constraints. For those who approve, social constraints can at most be a reinforcement of their own commitments. For those who do not approve and are consequently potentially disobedient (and these, if the constraints are to be of any force, must presumably be either few or uninfluential), social constraints might be one among a number of disincentives to disobedience. A particular actor facing a particular command which he is inclined to disobey might take social disapproval into account as one cost (and not necessarily the highest cost) of insubordination. But this does not help us to explain the behaviour of those in any case inclined to obey. Even rebels, as Blau himself observes, will often be fortified in their rebellion by sub-cultural norms reinforcing the rejection of authority. In this case, indirect exchange operates to weaken rather than stiffen existing authority structures.

It seems then that Blau's first thoughts might be better than his second. There seems to be little theoretical mileage to be gained by trying to draw disinterested action (as exemplified by obedience to authority) into the ambit of exchange theory.

## 6 CONCLUSIONS

To sum up the conclusions of this examination of Blau's theory of power and exchange:

(1) Exchanges depend on reciprocity; and reciprocity can be seen as a characteristic of power relations, even if they involve physical coercion. Given this, they are susceptible to economic or catallactic analysis.

(2) But exchanges are distorted if they are seen as necessarily voluntary. Men may have to make choices they do not want to make. The decisions they do make as between alternatives may be (and exchange theory must suppose will be) based on a rational choice of the best available.

(3) What choices anyone has will depend upon the distribution of these resources which can affect the bargaining power of individuals or groups.

(4) Exchange theory cannot explain how actual distributions of power emerge.

Blau's attempt to base such an explanation on some initial 'free' exchange transactions fails.

(5) Nor can exchange theory explain adequately 'voluntary' obedience, that is obedience to rightful authority springing from the commitments of subordinates.

(6) A catallaxy or market cannot be justified on grounds of voluntariness or free choice. Or, to qualify this, the degree to which it can be so justified depends upon the actual distribution of resources within which exchanges take place. The degree of 'freedom' in choice is related directly to the degree of equality in the distribution of those resources.

# 2

# Power Divorced from its Sources: a Critique of the Exchange Theory of Power

Pierre Birnbaum

### 1 UTILITARIANISM AND INDIVIDUALISM

The outstanding example of exchange theory is to be found in the work of Peter Blau. In his book *Exchange and Power in Social Life* the author maintains that one particular kind of exchange may be located as the major source of power. In his conception, social exchange 'is limited to actions that are contingent on rewarding reactions from others and that cease when these expected reactions are not forthcoming' (Blau, 1964, p.6). In linking power with the profit obtained from inter-individual exchange Blau is, of course, inspired by George Homans's works on elementary individual behaviour. But to understand both the interest in and the flagrant shortcomings of the writings of Homans and Blau, it seems necessary to draw out their links with the theory of utilitarianism from which they spring. We must also, before tackling our main subject, recall the historic origins of the individualistic movement from which the work of both Blau and Homans springs.

At the end of the eighteenth century and the beginning of the nineteenth, Jeremy Bentham founded the utilitarian school which, in accordance with the views of Hume, maintained that man seeks before all else personal profit in his relations with others. According to Bentham: 'By the principle of utility is meant that principle which approves or disapproves of every action whatsoever, according to the tendency which it appears to augment or diminish the happiness of the party whose interest is in question' (Bentham, 1960, Ch. 1, para. 2). In his view, then, 'Nature has placed man under the empire of pleasure and of pain. We owe to them all our ideas; we refer to them all our judgements and all the determinations of our life' (Bentham, 1960, p.125). The science of pleasure will thus replace any pure morality allegedly founded on reason: it determines the behaviour of the individual who must strive, through social exchange, to accumulate the maximum personal advantage. Bentham holds the principles of natural law to be 'fictions': politics as well as morals are nothing but 'the regularization of egoism'. Morality becomes a 'matter of arithmetic', and Bentham disallows any notion of disinterested behaviour: 'Show me', he says, 'the man who deprives himself of a greater amount of some good that he has revealed to nobody, and I shall show you a man who ignores even the first element of moral arithmetic.' (Quoted by Guyau, 1904.) To publicize this behaviour, so deeply anchored in human nature, Bentham created a mathematics of pleasure that was to be valid for all ages and all men. To this end he tried to measure the hedonistic characteristics of human acts by calculating the intensity, the duration, the certainty and the proximity of the pleasures they produce.

John Rawls has shown how, in the utilitarian theory, 'the good is defined independently from the right and the right is defined as that which maximizes the good' (Rawls, 1971, p.24). This teleological reasoning radically distinguishes utilitarianism from an ethics based on reason of the kind embraced by the social contract theorists. Placing himself in the tradition of Rousseau and Locke, Rawls opposes Bentham's utilitarianism which reappears in the work of Homans. He proposes to replace utilitarian ethics by what he calls 'justice as fairness'. These ' . . . principles of justice are agreed to in an initial situation that is fair' (Rawls, 1971, p.12). The concept of justice now precedes the notion of profit and implies, at least in the title of the theory, a situation prior to the exchange situation which is itself 'fair'. In abandoning the ideal of moral and rational exchange prior to experience in favour of a hedonistic search for pleasures, Bentham, and with him Homans and Blau, are bound to find it impossible to take account of the situation prior to exchange based on utilitarian calculation, from either an empirical or a moral point of view. As one examines it, this difficulty largely explains the ambiguities in the ideas of Homans and Blau.

Furthermore, the principle of utility rests on an individualistic and nominalistic concept of society: according to Bentham, 'the community is a fictitious *body,* composed of . . . individual persons' (Bentham, 1960, p.126). Utilitarian exchange consequently seems to be universal and purely individualistic, the State's sole mission being to co-ordinate everybody's search for individual profit. Bentham eliminates politics, since the State is transformed into a simple administration that increases the happiness of all by a rigid division of labour, impersonal rules and the increased competence of the bureaucrats. According to Bentham these principles of government can be applied to all countries with slight variations (Bentham, 1960, p.25). Consequently he puts aside the 'labyrinth of history', made up of inexact facts, and prefers to concentrate on the 'human heart', which one finds at the origin of the individual search for happiness (quoted by Manning, 1968, p.28).[1] This individualistic, atomistic and a-historical vision reappears later in Homans, and in a more ambiguous form in Blau. One must note, however, that it has been opposed by Durkheim as well as by Marx. In *The Division of Labor in Society* Durkheim criticizes utilitarianism and shows the absence of any link between the division of labour and the search for individual happiness. For him, 'social science must resolutely renounce this utilitarian comparison in which it has too often been involved' (Durkheim, 1964, p.250). It is, 'therefore, outside the individual, in the surrounding environment, that the determinant causes of social evolution are to be found' (Durkheim, 1964, p.251).[2] Durkheim opposes the psychological aspects of utilitarian theories as well as their individualistic conceptions: sociology must mark out a separation between individual psychology and social facts, and dissociate itself from individual action.

Referring to Bentham's psychological utilitarianism which was to be valid for all societies, Marx says that 'With the driest naïvete he [Bentham] takes the *petit bourgeois,* especially the English shopkeeper, as the normal man. Whatever is useful to this queer man, and to his world, is absolutely useful. This yard-measure then, he applies to past, present and future.' (Marx, 1967, I, p.609, n.2.) It is in this unjustified fashion that Bentham extends his utilitarian philosophy to everybody, whatever their social situation, and to all societies regardless of economic structure. Furthermore, the criticisms offered by Durkheim and Marx may also be applied to the works of Homans and Blau.

However, Homans and Blau are equally inspired by the atomistic and interactionist perspective set out by Simmel and Weber. Unlike Bentham, Simmel tries to describe the forms of inter-individual exchange. Although he was possibly inspired by the utilitarian philosophy, Simmel recognizes that: 'if the concept "society" is taken in its most general sense, it refers to the psychological interaction among individual human beings' (Simmel, 1950, p.9). The goal of Simmel's 'pure' sociology is to describe the forms taken by exchanges among those individuals whom he considers as 'real' entities. By means of this atomistic and psychologistic sociology he wishes to identify within the social system those exchanges that are specifically social. These processes of 'sociation' seem even more devoid of structural facts than they were in the work of Bentham: according to Simmel, 'Wealth, social position . . . may not play any part in sociability. At most they may perform the role of mere nuances.' (Simmel, 1950, p.46.) Thus, the sociologist will study pure exchange among people without worrying about influences that might arise from what Homans will later call the 'external system'. It seems that Simmel's project is predicated on this separation, which raises big problems, between a process of pure exchange and the global system within which it develops. Cut off from the external system, 'the forms [of the exchange] develop from the contact of individuals independently of the material causes (specific, unique) of this contact, and their sum constitutes this concrete whole which, by abstraction, is called society' (Simmel, 1894, p.498).[3] It is not surprising that Emile Durkheim also objects to this atomistic and voluntaristic sociology. (See for example Durkheim and Fauconnet, 1903.) As well as rejecting Tarde's individualistic and mechanical imitation (Durkheim, 1962), he also condemns this pure sociology which—even more so than utilitarianism—refuses to distinguish facts that are properly social from facts that are strictly individual.

The oppositions Bentham—Durkheim and Simmel—Durkheim seem essential in understanding the work of George Homans: indeed it is not accidental that the latter says, 'I necessarily reject Durkheim's view that sociology is *not* a corollary of psychology' (Homans, 1961, p.12, n.10). That is, by opposing Durkheim (and in a certain way Marx), Homans adopts an individualistic sociology which also can be found in the works of Bentham, Tarde, Simmel or Weber, despite other differences that exist between these authors. If Homans rejects Durkheim's theses, his definition of social action must repeat the same individualistic character as the one put forward by Weber. More explicitly, Blau appeals not only to Homans, but also to Simmel and Weber when he introduces the foundations of his model (Blau, 1964, pp.2,5).

This last opposition, between Weber and Durkheim, helps to account for the grave difficulties in the theories of exchange and power. Weber states, for example, 'if I have become a sociologist . . . it is mainly in order to exorcize the spectre of collective conceptions which still lingers among us. In other words, sociology itself can only proceed from the actions of one or more separate individuals and must therefore adopt strictly individualistic methods.' (Quoted in Mommsen, 1965, p.25.) This methodological individualism (see Lukes, 1973, Ch. 13) that Homans accepts is fundamentally alien to Durkheim's thought. Even if the Weberian method is not psychologistic (though Homans falls into this trap), they both regard it as essential to examine 'face-to-face' relations. Weber defines social activity in the following way: 'Action is social in so far as, by virtue of the subjective meaning attached to it by the acting individual (or individuals), it takes account of the behaviour of others and is thereby oriented in its course.' (Weber, 1964b, p.88.) Unlike Weber, and under the influence of Skinner, Homans maintains that people react more or less mechanically like pigeons (Homans, 1961, pp.18ff). He thus refuses to take an interest in subjective reality, in the intentional aspect of human action. Homans is content, like all behaviourists, to observe 'from the outside' the course of human activities in which negotiation and exchange occurs (Homans, 1961, p.34). From this point of view there is a great difference between Weber's perspective and that of Homans. We must again emphasize, however, that both are supporters of an atomistic and nominalistic sociology, who wish to clarify the nature of interpersonal exchange.

It has often been pointed out that, according to Weber, an activity is not social if it is devoid of intentionality; traditional or emotional behaviour 'stands on the borderline' of social activity (Weber, 1964b, p.116). Weber, and with him Homans and Blau, cannot account on this definition for the social quality of many items of more or less collective behaviour, since the behaviour occurs under the influence of social control. These authors find it impossible to analyse exchange as a structural, collective and non-intentional process. Moreover, for Weber, activity oriented toward a structure is not a social activity, since 'the economic ability of an individual is only social if, and then only in so far as, it takes account of the behaviour of someone else' (Weber, 1964b, pp.112-13). This means that Homans and Blau cannot, any more than Weber, study the relationship that is established between an actor (or a group of actors) and a structure, or that of a trade union facing a company rather than facing the director of this company. Desiring at all costs to avoid the holistic conceptions that attribute an existence to the whole, independent of the component parts (Weber, 1964b, pp.115-16), Weber does not succeed in reconstructing the social system, as Talcott Parsons has pointed out (Parsons in Weber, 1964b, p.20). And the same goes for Homans and Blau.

Durkheim, on the other hand, defined social facts as 'ways of acting, thinking and feeling, external to the individual, and endowed with a power of coercion, by reason of which they control him' (Durkheim, 1962, p.3). Since he also maintained that 'a whole is not identical with the sum of its parts,' and that 'the group thinks, feels and acts quite differently from the way in which its members would were they isolated' (Durkheim, 1962, pp.101,104), he has often been considered a holistic theorist who reifies reality and in that respect is opposed to Max Weber's individualistic perspective.[4] This difference really does exist, but there is a more direct contrast between Weber and an author who claims that as far as he is concerned 'there are in societies only individual consciousnesses', and who insists that 'because individuals form a society, new phenomena emerge caused by this association' (Durkheim, 1962, p.98). This allows him to conclude that collective life does not grow out of individual life but that on the contrary it is the second that grows out of the first (Durkheim, 1964, p.279). Consequently, Durkheim takes a different line from Weber without proposing a theory that involves the reification of society. In contrast to the theorist of social action, he is able to show, by distinguishing between social facts and individual facts, how a society forms a specific whole which functions according to its own laws. As a result of their taking the other side and adopting an atomistic perspective close to that of Simmel and Weber, Homans and Blau find themselves up against the impossibility of analysing in other than individualistic terms the phenomena that lead to the formation of a structure of power.

## 2  GEORGE HOMANS: POWER AND EXCHANGE IN THE INTERNAL SYSTEM

Homans's work is deliberately presented as an extension of the individualistic, anti-Durkheim line: for example, he rejects the definition of social facts proposed by Durkheim, since he does not accept the idea that social facts can function as external constraints on the individual. Robert Blain has shown how this opposition to Durkheim's conception of sociology has profoundly marked all of Homans's work. Thus, since his early writings he has wanted to assert that society is not distinct from individuals, and that it has to come back to inter-individual exchanges if it is to be able to tie people together (Blain, 1971, pp.4-6). According to Homans, 'the institutions, organizations and societies that sociologists study can always be analyzed, without residue, into the behavior of individual men. They must therefore be explained by propositions about the behavior of individual man.' (Homans, 1964b, p.231.) This self-conscious methodological individualism in Homans's work is accompanied by psychological reductionism, and these two views do not necessarily lend support to each other. As Murray Webster has pointed out, 'psychological reductionism does entail methodological individualism, but the implication does not work the other way' (Webster, 1973, p.261). Homans adopts the psychological perspective when he observes, in 'Bringing Men Back In', 'I now suspect that there are no general sociological propositions, propositions that hold good of all societies or social groups as such, and that the only general propositions are in fact psychological.' (Homans, 1964a, p.817. See also Homans, 1968, p.6.)

While Durkheim would replace individual psychology by the sociological study of social facts, fully recognizing the fecundity of social psychology (Durkheim, 1962, pp.51-2 of Preface), Homans tries to reduce sociology entirely to individual psychology. This rejection of Durkheim's positions, which we have already mentioned, must lead Homans to attack the French sociological school and particularly Claude Lévi-Strauss. Just as Peter Blau makes use of Marcel Mauss's *The Gift* by giving it a psychological interpretation and by eliminating its highly determinate structural aspect, so Homans proposes a psychological reinterpretation of *The Elementary Structures of Kinship*. In both cases, Homans and Blau criticize a study of primitive societies carried out according to the Durkheim principles that prescribe a structural conception of society. According to George Homans and David Schneider (1955), the structures of kinship in primitive societies result from individual sentiments, from the attraction that one person feels towards another. Lévi-Strauss showed that 'exchange—and consequently the rule of exogamy which expresses it—has in itself a social value. It provides the means of binding men together, and of superimposing upon the natural links of kinship the henceforth artificial links—artificial in the sense that they are removed from chance encounters or the promiscuity of family life—of alliance governed by rule.' (Lévi-Strauss, 1969, p.480.) Homans and Schneider, on the other hand, abandon the structural aspect of kinship and (as pointed out in Needham, 1962, pp.125-6) replace the prescriptions and the rules by the psychological preferences of the actors. Their 'psychological preoccupation' forces these authors to dissolve the structure in order to concentrate on the individual emotional involvements.

The opposition to Durkheim's school is evident in Homans's examination of the notion of social control. For Homans, social control does not imply domination or power exercised in the name of the entire society, but it simply 'emerges' from reciprocal exchanges among individual actors. (Homans, 1950, pp.288,310,319; cf. Webster, 1973, p.269.) From within an atomistic conception, Homans thus presents social control as a process issuing naturally from simple 'elementary' social relations, at the same time abandoning any relationship of domination that might augment the structure of power. This renunciation, indicative of Homans's orientation, results from his intention of studying only the 'elementary' direct relations that place individuals 'face-to-face' in a setting where exchange is beneficial to all. Like Bentham and Simmel, Homans considers that such face-to-face relations are characteristic of human nature and consequently always and everywhere identical (Homans, 1961, p.7). Besides its universalistic aspect, this vision is also profoundly reductionist: from fear of falling into an essentialist theory, Homans proposes to study only elementary behaviour in order to proceed in an inductive, not a deductive way (Homans in Faris, 1964, pp.968-9. See on this Buckley, 1967, p.109). Following Skinner's work on pigeons, he maintains that people react mechanically in order to procure profits; that is to say, they react to the extent to which the cost of their action is lower than the reward that the action will bring them. In the tradition of Bentham's hedonistic and utilitarian philosophy, he tries to construct a mathematics of pleasure that rests on the cost and quantity of the values exchanged among the actors. For Homans, the actor is always taken to have calculated correctly (Homans, 1961, p.80), his behaviour thus being accounted rational regardless of the end pursued. Thus, 'the open secret of human exchange is to give the other man behavior that is more valuable to him than it is costly to you, and to get from him behavior that is more valuable to you than it is costly to him' (Homans, 1961, p.62). On the basis of such an individualistic and behaviourist definition, exchange seems fairly well balanced to begin with: in order to 'pierce' the secret of this exchange in quasi-equilibrium, we must ask questions about the origin of the resources thus put into circulation. As we shall see, Homans, like Bentham, does not take into account the production of these resources, and this omission allows him to present exchange as a quasi-equilibrium (Homans, 1961, p.113).

Since authority arises out of respect, which is created in the course of interaction and exchange, and since, according to Homans, the move from influence to authority is a simple quantitative, non-qualitative change (Homans, 1961, pp.286-7), it becomes necessary to measure the influence an individual can acquire during the course of an inter-individual exchange. No more than could the hedonistic theorists does Homans succeed in creating a rigorous method for evaluating the influence of each actor. (See Abrahamsson, 1970, pp.281-2; Buckley, 1967, p.112.)

It is interesting to note that Homans uses Moreno's sociometric method to determine the respective power of the actors during the process of their interaction. In *The Human Group,* for example, he readily adopts this sociometric method, placing it in the atomistic and individualistic perspective of Tarde and Simmel. There too, he finds no place for society as such and we see that he views exchange purely as an interpersonal psychological process (see Gurvitch, 1963, I, p.261.) In Moreno's book *Who Shall Survive?* we may find as well a definition of social structure similar to the one that will later be put forward by Homans in *Social Behaviour:* for Moreno, indeed, a social structure is reduced to 'the form of inter-individual actions' (Moreno, 1954, p.254). It is thus from Moreno that Homans takes the anti-Durkheimian arguments that strengthen his individualistic and psychological conception of social relations; for him, as for Weber, Simmel or Moreno, the whole is reducible to its component parts.

Consequently Homans allies himself with Bentham and emphatically rejects the criticisms that could be addressed to him by Marx or Durkheim. He could instead adopt this remark of Moreno: 'We have opposed to the macro-sociologies of Comte, Marx and W. G. Sumner . . . microsociology, of which sociometry is one of the most devoted apostles.' (Moreno, 1947, p.89.) Beyond August Comte, it is clearly Durkheim and Marx with whom Homans wishes to engage calling to his aid sociometry and the study of the elementary forms of social relations. As Pitirim Sorokin forcefully notes, this 'wonderland' gives us 'a picture of a mainly imaginary, hypothetical, wishful web of social relatedness' (Sorokin, 1956, p.220). Thus, the 'internal system', which is always identified by Homans with the sole site of interaction, will always find itself cut off from the 'external system'; hence the power relations that may be established within it are totally 'imaginary'.

Before we return to the distinction between internal system and external system, we must note that Homans makes much use of the research of Elton Mayo and his team (Western Electric Inquiry: Bank Wiring Group) in order to prove, in the manner of Moreno, that power is born out of the respect accorded to the leaders as the process of interaction develops (Homans, 1950, p.133). In addition to criticism of a methodological nature (see Carey, 1967), one can raise the same kind of objections to this research as those already directed at Moreno. George Friedman, for example, emphasizes that 'the main weakness in the psycho-sociology basic to the Hawthorne survey is the obstinate view of the corporation as a rounded, closed social structure, an entity which evolves independently of all other social groups.' (Friedman, 1946, p.326.) The internal system is again arbitrarily isolated from the external system. Furthermore, as with Bentham or Simmel, it seems that the forms of power thus established must remain static: in a commentary on the Western Electric study, Mayo wrote as follows: 'Since this seems to be as characteristic of Russia as of the United States, it is probable that the human problems involved are fundamental and contain no "political" element . . . The question is not who is to control, but, rather, what researches are essential to the development of intelligence in control.' (Mayo, 1960, p.174.) Power relations will thus always remain the same within the corporation because these relations result from specific processes of social interaction and are totally independent of the external systems (the corporation as institution or, *a fortiori*, as its own environment).

Thus, from the works of Moreno, of Elton Mayo or again of Festinger, Schachter and Back (Festinger *et al*, 1950), Homans constantly makes use of psycho-sociological researches directed roughly along the lines of the sociometric method: the deviants, like those who hold power, owe their strength to purely psychological interaction or to its absence, this interaction unfolding within a system cut off from the outside and entirely closed in upon itself. This distinction between the internal and external system seems to occupy a central place in Homans's writings. He simply takes the geographical conditions or economic structures as 'givens', that is to say as external systems without any effect upon the actions that go on within the internal system. He says, 'Since our interest is in elementary social behavior, we shall be more concerned with persons who acquire authority by their own action than with persons who have it handed by appointment or inheritance.' (Homans, 1961, p.283.) Homans also admits that 'this book will not undertake to explain the nature of the rules themselves and instead will simply take them as given.' (Homans, 1961, p.4.) He furthermore refuses to attach the least importance to the behavior of an individual (*a fortiori* of a union) facing a corporation, since on his theory 'it is not two individuals that are dealing with one another here, but an individual and a corporation' (Homans, 1961 p.4). Thus, extending the Weberian definition of social action, Homans will take into consideration only actions directed by one individual towards another individual. Obviously this perspective does not permit one to take into account the power held by a large industrial corporation because it would not be able to take part in the psychological interactions that link individuals. Like Mayo, Homans sees in the corporation a structural system external to the system of internal interaction, which alone occupies his attention.

Even if in *The Human Group* Homans recognizes that the separation between the two systems is arbitrary, as they both are not independent but mutually dependent (Homans, 1950, p.152),[5] he also asserts that this dependency is unilateral since the internal system, which alone interests him, must 'adapt' itself to the external system, without challenging it further (Homans, 1950, p.155). Thus, in the Bank Wiring System the system of internal interaction preserves its specificity and adapts itself to the external system without calling into question the structure of the corporation or the system of salaries. According to Homans, these external problems do not interfere with the life of the internal system. He adds that 'as students of elementary social behavior . . . we do not undertake to explain . . . why there are classes at all . . . we use these givens.' (Homans, 1950, p.221.) It is quite clear that if one takes no account of 'exterior' resources held by individuals, if one refuses to see that they belong to wider social groups from which they draw values and norms, one necessarily ends up with a psychological conception of power, attributed to certain actors through the process of interaction that unfolds within the closed internal system.

To conclude, this refusal to consider the role of the external structures is based on a complete rejection of functionalism inasmuch as it is a purely deductive method. For Homans, the sociologist must proceed inductively from an examination of behaviour. Weber rejected functionalism when he said: 'We are in a position to go beyond merely demonstrating functional relationships and uniformities. We can accomplish something which is never attainable in the natural sciences, namely the subjective understanding of the action of the component individuals.' (Weber, 1964b p.103.) Homans sets out his own concerns as follows: 'We are not talking here about the leader's functions; we are talking about the results of his acting or failing to act.' (Homans, 1961, p.196.)[6] By prejudicially separating the internal system from the external system, Homans reduces his object of study to inter-individual actions. Thus he finds himself faced with the impossibility of knowing if these actions are determined simultaneously both by the external system and by the functions that the actors perform within the internal system. Setting out from such premises as he does, he can draw conclusions only as to the psychological basis of exchange underlying authority and power.

## 3  BLAU ON POWER (1): THE INDIVIDUALIST ORIGIN OF POWER

Peter Blau's book *Exchange and Power in Social Life* is openly indebted to Homans's work, but whereas Homans declares that 'there is no functional prerequisite for the survival of the society except that the society provide sufficient rewards for its individual members to keep them contributing to its maintenance' (Homans, 1961, p.384), Blau hopes to steer between 'the Scylla of abstract conceptions too remote from observable empirical reality and the Charybdis of reductionism that ignores emergent social and structural properties' (Blau, 1964, p.3). In contrast to Homans, Blau claims to make use equally of a functional analysis and an inductive examination of the behaviour of individuals. Such an approach would be more fruitful, since it would allow an analysis of power both in the functioning of the internal system and in the external system in which the actors occupy positions and from which they derive resources. We propose to show, however, that Blau has not carried out the double task that he sets himself and that he too seems to favour the reductionist approach.

Right from the opening pages of his book, Blau emphasizes that the examination of global social structures must be 'derived' from elementary social processes (Blau, 1964, pp.2-4). For him, 'the concept of social exchange directs attention to the emergent properties in interpersonal relations and social interaction' (Blau, 1964, p.4). The concept of exchange applies only to actions that are contingent on rewarding actions from others and that cease when these expected reactions are not forthcoming' (Blau, 1964, p.6). If Blau, in contrast to Homans, thus refuses all mechanical and strictly behavioural explanations, he none the less builds his model out of the activities of individuals engaged in a process of exchange. In so doing, he refers especially to those types of action that are most rational, according to the Weberian definition itself (*zweckrational, wertrational*). In an effort to avoid an essentialist perspective, Blau presents an atomistic and voluntaristic conception of social reality, based on exchange between individuals. For him, as for Weber or Homans, an activity directed towards a structure does not establish a social exchange. By this move, he too becomes involved in a serious distortion of reality.

As against Homans, Blau does recognize that social exchange can create an institutionalization of social relations that makes some kind of sense of the progression from the elementary level to the global level of society. He thereby avoids at once both reductionism and essentialism by recognizing the distinctiveness of social facts in relation to individual facts. (See Blau, 1964, pp.273-81.)[7] In spite of this concession, we must still press our criticism of reductionism further and show that exchange can unfold only in the context of an existing 'total social phenomenon' (Marcel Mauss) which antedates it. Blau himself deduces from inter-individual exchange the existence of specific social structures. But one can, on the contrary, with the help of the passages from Mauss that are cited by Blau, demonstrate that exchange obeys the rules imposed by the system.

Blau in fact relies on *The Gift* to provide evidence for his interactionist conception of exchange, just as Homans had recourse to the work of Moreno and Mayo. Blau's assimilation of Mauss's work should not however be accepted because, for Marcel Mauss, exchange is a structural fact. These are not individuals who create exchanges *à la* Moreno; they content themselves with sticking to the rules. In Mauss, the system is antecedent to interaction which does not have any individualistic character (Blau, 1964, pp.88-9). What Blau does not retain from Mauss's analysis is the idea that the obligations to give, receive and return are imposed by the social system; studying these gifts, Mauss emphasizes that 'the form usually taken is that of the gift generously offered; but the accompanying behaviour is formal pretence and social deception, while the transaction itself is based on obligation and economic self-interest.' (Mauss, 1954, p.1.) These total social phenomena cannot be reduced to simple inter-individual exchanges.

Let us consider as a further example the love relations on which Blau dwells at such length. For him this exchange, like all other exchanges, is based on 'attraction'. Analysing with a good deal of sensitiveness the development of a love relationship between a man and a woman, Blau describes, for example, how a woman has an interest in bargaining about the dates she accepts or the kisses she gives in order to obtain additional 'rewards' (Blau, 1964, pp.76-85). This exchange must, however, be studied in the context of the global social system, because the choice of spouse, as has been shown by Alain Girard (1964), depends strictly on social class membership or type of occupation. Once again, exchange cannot be reduced to a clear inter-individual trade since its nature is heavily determined by the social system within which it takes place.

Approximating to Simmel's position, Blau appears to attach great weight to processes of 'sociation'. According to him, 'social exchange refers to voluntary actions of individuals that are motivated by the returns they are expected to bring and typically do in fact bring from others. Action compelled by physical coercion is not voluntary ... conformity with internalized standards does not fall under the definition of exchange presented.' (Blau, 1964, pp.90-2.) Like Bachrach and Baratz (1963), Blau excludes the use of force from counting as an exercise of power. Thus, 'power refers to all kinds of influence between persons or groups including those exercised in exchange transactions, where one induces others to accede to his wishes, by rewarding them for doing so.' (Blau, 1964, p.115.) So power grows out of an asymmetric exchange which occurs when one person with superior resources can 'reward' other persons and by doing so obtain from them what he wants. As with a number of authors who reason in individualistic terms (Homans, Dahl, etc.), power here comes to be identified with a form of exchange: they are distinguished only quantitatively.

According to Blau, when force is exercised or when certain values impose some behaviour that is specific and independent of the actor's own wishes, power is no longer present. Nothing can justify such an exclusion. This does, however, explain the example of the hundred dollars put forward by Blau (Blau, 1964, p.116). He holds that it is a case of coercion when a man obliges another to act in a particular way by threatening to take a hundred dollars from him if he refuses to comply, whereas it is influence that is at work when one person gives a hundred dollars to another in order to get him to do what he wants. In the second case an exchange takes place that gives influence (or power according to the preceding definition) to one person over another. In the first case, coercion is definitely distinct from influence (or power thus conceived).

This example seems very ambiguous since Blau does not succeed in explaining how the one person comes to possess a hundred dollars—and yet this resource is the one instrument of his power. Blau seems to find it normal for one person to 'influence' another by means of 'reward': this exchange probably even appears to him balanced. Power (in the sense of coercion) no longer has to be exercised, because one person can more easily attain his goal by using his own resources. We might suggest, however, that the individual who agrees to act in a certain way in order to receive the hundred dollars very probably experiences his action as submission to a power that can buy him, rather than as the result of a process of balanced influence. Like Homans, then, Blau does not pay attention to the non-egalitarian origin of resources which facilitates the subsequent balanced exchange: thus, he too separates the internal system from the external system.

## 4 BLAU ON POWER (2): POWER, STRUCTURE AND SOCIAL CONTROL

On the basis of these premises, Blau employs the model put forward by Emerson (1962) to indicate the strategies by which one person can successfully escape from the power of another person: he can resort to a third person, decide to abandon a project that will entail his subordination, etc. (Blau, 1964, pp.188ff.). He also gives great weight to applications of marginal analysis in economics with respect to relations of exchange between two actors, from which may develop one person's power over another (Blau, 1964, Ch. 7). In this connection Anthony Heath has shown, from the standpoint of internal logical coherence, the difficulties encountered by such an application. By analysing indifference curves as well as by the process of exchange in a bilateral monopoly, he stresses the atomistic and individualistic presuppositions of Blau's model, which ignores the structure of the group, and simply adds the individual curves (Heath, 1968).

The main example that Blau analyses in this context is that of a number of employees in a work group, some of whom are more skilful at the task than others (Blau, 1964, pp.168-98). Exchange processes develop in which advice is given in return for deference. Without going into the detail of this analysis, we should note that Blau again treats the process as one in which both parties, the one who gives the advice and the one who seeks it, stand to gain. Once more, as in the example of the hundred dollars, it is assumed that the exchange is 'voluntary' in spite of the fact that it may seem rather more like a forced exchange: just as we have seen that one person needed a hundred dollars, so, in exactly the same way here, an inexperienced worker needs the advice of a more expert worker. Blau's atomistic conception prevents him from throwing light on the social preconditions that help to determine the nature of the exchange. Paradoxically, he does himself acknowledge at the end of the analysis the importance of these social determinants, but he does not amend his model as a result (see Blau, 1964, p.197). Yet the action in question is surely scarcely voluntary: the actor who abases himself socially in order to obtain advice lacks precisely those resources that give the expert the opportunity of increasing his own social standing within the group.

Instead of lingering further on the uses of marginal analysis in the field of social exchange, I would rather return to the ineluctable consequences of Blau's definition of power. It is because he is interested in the asymmetric exchange which, according to him, gives rise to power, without at the same time asking questions about the resources the actors possess *before* entering this relationship exchange, that Blau attributes little importance to zero-sum power (Blau, 1964, p.15). Without going back to the debate between Parsons and Wright Mills, one can simply point out that, in Blau's work, power is never exercised unilaterally, because the author presupposes a non-cumulative distribution of resources. Since all the actors are supposed to possess resources (whatever may be their nature), the power that is exercised through exchange can be called influence. The example of the hundred dollars is relevant in this connection: in Blau's view, the actor is not subservient to pure unilateral power in the case where he receives the hundred dollars. This reward, however, does not modify the sense in which power is applied, and this seems to preserve its constraining character in spite of the promised reward. At the same time, it is important to understand the origin of the hundred dollars held by one person and the structural reasons why the other finds himself in a state of deprivation, and to ponder the fact that he is obliged to act on the basis of an imperative need.

As the power resulting from the exchange does not constitute a zero-sum relation, the setting in which it is exercised may more easily qualify as 'fair'. On the basis of the law of supply and demand, Blau judges that an equilibrium will establish itself which could be considered 'fair'. In order to define this notion, he first recalls the way in which Homans puts forward the notion of 'distributive justice'. According to the author of *Social Behaviour*, 'A man in an exchange relation with another will expect that the rewards of each man be proportional to his costs—the greater the rewards, the greater the costs—and that the net rewards, or profits, of each man be proportional to his investments—the greater the investments the greater the profit.' (Homans, 1961, p.75.) Blau adds, in contradiction to Homans, that fair exchange depends on social norms, indispensable in measuring the cost of the investment.

This statement seems fruitful, but unfortunately Blau does not pursue it further. He could, for example, have looked into the nature of these social norms defining a fair exchange: as Peter Berger and Thomas Luckman stress, 'power in society includes the power to produce reality' (Berger and Luckman, 1967, p.119). Who possesses this kind of efficacy before there is power in Blau's sense, and who controls the means? By not pressing further into an analysis of the role played by these social norms in the definition of 'fairness', Blau seeks to avoid getting himself into a self-contradiction. His own definition of exchange actually prevents him from considering such social norms since, as we have already seen, he takes the line that social exchange 'refers to voluntary actions of individuals ... Action compelled by physical coercion is not voluntary ... [C]onformity with internalized standards does not fall under the definition of exchange presented ...' (Blau, 1964, pp.91-2.) Suddenly, the criticism directed against Homans is cut short.

Instead of following the road that would lead him towards a rediscovery of the role played by social control in determining the nature of exchange, Blau assures us that an 'unfair' exchange, which provides an excessive advantage to one of the parties to it, inevitably entails strong 'social disapproval', which would make the cost to the beneficiary too high (Blau, 1964, p.157). Blau does not, then, try to establish further connections between the internal system and the external system (the origin of resources, the nature of social control, etc.) but instead returns to examining the behaviour of actors within a closed system. In this interpersonal system, the desire for strong social approval seems, for Blau, to prevent all unfair power, or even all zero-sum power, both at the level of elementary social relations and at the level of the global system. In the very improbable event that power should be exercised in an 'unfair' way, those who were exploited would feel angry and, carried away by an 'emotional' desire to retaliate, they might well come to take the desire for revenge as an end in itself (Blau, 1964, pp.228-9). But Blau considers this possibility of revolt purely academic, since the collective norms curb fraud and the use of violence (Blau, 1964, p.225).

Not only are the norms that govern interpersonal exchange fair, but they are reinforced by the conception of 'fair exchange' implicit in the collective norms of the social system. The criticism of Homans's definition of distributive justice is without danger, because it now turns out that the norms of the internal system reproduce the same idea of 'fairness' as the norms of the external system. Unfairness thus has little chance to occur, since the external system is itself governed by norms of fairness: the historical development of societies simply restores easily avoidable emotions.

The exchange may be all the more 'fair', according to Blau, to the extent that individuals nowadays find themselves tied by the bonds of professional reputation. It is very interesting to observe how the professionalization described by Parsons is brought in here to reinforce the idea of fair exchange, from which develops legitimate power, that is to say authority. According to Talcott Parsons, 'The professional complex has already not only come into prominence but has even begun to dominate the contemporary scene in such a way as to render obsolescent the primacy of the old issues of political authoritarianism and capitalistic exploitation.' (Parsons, 1968, p.546.) In corporations, for example, authority is more legitimate inasmuch as it is now (according to Burnham, Galbraith, Parsons, etc.) separated from the ownership of the means of production. The professionalization of authority in turn reinforces the separation between the internal system and the external system. Universal, non-particularistic values, neutrality, absence of immediate benefits, etc., in proportion as they are features that must check 'exploitation', must operate to reinforce the legitimacy of authority and to assure the integration of the collectivity (Blau, 1964, pp.261-7). In this pacified society, where fair exchange rests on professionalization and everybody's increasing expertise, where power is legitimate by virtue of the collective norms, we still—in spite of all this—continue to find quasi-structural and non-emotional opposition, which Blau cannot omit to mention but which he totally fails to explain.

## 5 BLAU ON POWER (3): BLAU'S PARADOXES

At the level of the entire social system, as well as at the level of exchange between the actors themselves, Blau begins by tracing sentiments of antagonism similar from a psychological viewpoint to the sentiments of attraction upon which exchange is founded. Both at the elementary level and the level of the global system, he therefore analyses the beginnings of opposition in the same way (see Mulkay, 1971, p.211). The author of *Exchange and Power in Social Life* records the existence of structural facts at all levels that form conflicting elements. The essential paradox in Blau's work lies in the fact that he persists in his 'pure' analysis even though he shows himself at numerous points to be aware of the structural aspect of certain facts that are bound to make 'fair exchange' impossible and which can perhaps by themselves more adequately explain the creation of opposition among those treated 'unfairly'.

Blau indicates, for example, that fairness is not something immediate, as it is with Homans, and that it is now to be conceived of as being mediated by the collective norms of the social system. This observation surely ought to lead him to turn his attention to the social structure that generates such presumably 'fair' collective norms—the social structure that ordinarily regulates inter-individual exchanges to the satisfaction of all. Yet Blau does not follow up this line of thought (see MacIntyre, 1967, and Martin, 1971). Such a move would have enabled him to put an end to the separation between the internal system and the external system, especially since he himself recognizes that the dominant groups in the social system have the power to make their ideas prevail even if these cut across the collective norms. (Blau, 1964, p.276; and see Mulkay, 1971, pp.204-5.) How can norms developed by the group be fair for all? The power structure of the internal system (in terms of asymmetric influence) as well as the use of force and manipulation (which Blau excludes from his concept of power) can become explicit only when they are 're-immersed' in a social system that itself recognizes the phenomena of structural power.

Blau does not always put qualifications on his conception of power as individualistic, just and voluntaristic, though he does emphasize that the high status derived from great wealth can explain by reference to the social structure why 'the rich in power tend to get richer in power' (Blau, 1964, p.136). Blau does not ask where these unequally distributed resources come from: he accepts them as a 'given', to borrow Homans's expression. The exchanges on which power is founded are themselves taken to derive from a previous exchange which had worked 'fairly'. Social exchange takes place when the distribution of resources has already occurred: Blau does not ask what happened in the earlier stages of the society.

Even so, in contradistinction to Homans, he always remains aware of the fact that an unequal distribution of resources, reinforced by norms favourable to dominant groups, makes it difficult to maintain 'fair' exchange. He rightly sees a further obstacle in the weakness of social mobility and the 'crystallization' of classes (Blau, 1964, p.194) which almost leads to a confrontation between the owners and the workers (Blau, 1964, pp.164-7). Following this, Blau admits that 'large differences in power occur without corresponding differences in services' (Blau, 1964, p.197). In Blau's picture, opposition little by little loses its emotional aspect: it ceases to be the consequence of a desire for revenge; on the contrary, it derives from kinds of structural differentiation that make all 'fair' exchange impossible.

As a final example of Peter Blau's paradoxical attitude, one may cite his appraisal of the crosscutting cleavages which all the time become a more important feature of Western industrialized democracies. Following Lipset, he emphasizes the way in which multiple affiliations of the various groups permit a diminution in the intensity of conflicts. However, he further stresses that 'crosscutting conflicts fortify democratic institutions at the expense of the most oppressed strata, whose political influence they diminish.' (Blau, 1964, p.309.) Here again, the structural opposition to the global system is founded on the structural arrangement of the social forces in the system itself and not on the psychology of the actors or on their more or less fair inter-individual exchanges.

Blau, then, seems quite conscious of the existence of structural causes that can by themselves provoke conflicts between groups and that make very unlikely the occurrence of 'fair' exchanges between actors considered as individuals. The paradox is that he keeps sweeping this difficulty under the carpet. In order to illustrate this contradiction once again, we may draw attention to the way in which Blau believes that he can use Gouldner's analysis to support his main thesis. So, while Blau is able to throw light on the structural causes of the development of an opposition, he takes over Gouldner's (1959) framework, which limits the opposition's room for manoeuvre to the amount of autonomy that the global system will confer on it in order to keep down a source of conflict and preserve its own stability (Blau, 1964, pp.302-4).

Blau skilfully utilizes Gouldner's very flexible model, which confers great autonomy on sub-systems and even allows for the possibility of new structural 'dedifferentiation'. The principle of reciprocity, which equally underlies exchange in the theories of Homans, Blau and Gouldner, is here intensified by the high degree of autonomy bestowed on elements within the system. But here again, as in Homans's work, the opposition in achieving the status of a sub-system adapts to the degree of freedom of action that is cleverly granted to it by the global system in order to assure its own survival. A lack of reciprocity in the exchange, which, by virtue of its unfair character, could provoke serious conflicts and call into question the survival of the system itself, thus does not lead to decisive breakdowns. Gouldner's model justifies the separation between the internal system and the external system and limits the long-run consequences of an 'unfair' external system.

While Blau incorporates those of Gouldner's observations that enable him to put the emphasis on the autonomy of the parts, he also hastens to adopt Erving Goffman's analyses demonstrating the great freedom that all actors enjoy in relation to the roles they occupy in social institutions. From his opening page, Blau acknowledges the influence of Goffman as well as of Simmel (Blau, 1964, p.2). It is only on the microsociological level that these authors have taken on the task of describing the vast freedom that one has in the choice of behaviour *vis-à-vis* others, an effort that might appear to resemble in its viewpoint that pursued by Gouldner on a macrosociological level. For Gouldner, an element may depart a certain distance from the function it must assume in the system. For Goffman too, the actor may establish a 'role-distance' in relation to his role. To the extent that individuals can choose the 'presentation' that they offer to others, they can to the same degree maintain a certain distance with respect to the expectations of others and thus succeed in disengaging themselves from the roles that others call on them to assume (Goffman, 1959).

For Goffman, 'the individual limits the degree to which he embraces a situated role, or is required to embrace it, because of society's understanding of him as a multiple-role performer rather than a person with a particular role' (Goffman, 1961, p.142). In a rather curious way Blau extends this freedom that actors enjoy in their inter-individual relations to more structural and collective phenomena. He thus gives a psychologistic interpretation of the Kula, similar to the kind of characterization he has already offered of *The Gift*: in both cases, the actor is free to enter into the process of exchange from which he can gain power (Blau, 1964, p.111).

Such a perspective tends to underestimate the weight of social structures from which depend the allocation of resources and roles (Burns, 1973). The actors certainly possess some latitude of action which enables them to 'present' themselves to others, but its extent depends on the roles that are already occupied and is in any case never very great. The power that individuals acquire by 'presenting' others with their gifts, and the distance they can maintain, presuppose that they must have some prior resources. In the Kula process, which is reserved especially for chiefs, power in the end depends less on the impression made on another by a gift than on the resources that make such a gift possible. In wishing always to play up the subject's freedom in the exchange that determines the structure of power, Blau does not grant the external system the importance it deserves.

## 6  BLAU ON POWER (4): CONCLUSION

Blau admits that the structural distribution of resources can often give rise to opposition directed against the beneficiaries of a social organization when their power does not result from a previous exchange relationship. But he does not investigate the origin of this unequal distribution of resources, which sets in train non-peaceful and even violent exchanges between individuals (see Lenski, 1966, p.40). Instead, he returns to psychology as an explanation for the 'desire for revenge' experienced when the actors are confronted with an 'exceptional' situation that does not conform to the norms that are supposed to commend fairness. The effect of this line of analysis is to deny the opposition its structural characteristics: opposition is transformed into a matter of simple psychological demands that find a certain form of rationalization in some ideology or other.

Following Simmel, Blau presents a purely instrumental conception of ideology: on his account, desire for revenge and rage at unfair exchange (not at an unacceptable structural distribution) gives rise to 'revolutionary ideology which converts these base tendencies into noble ideas pursued not for selfish reasons . . . but for bettering the conditions of humanity at large' (Blau, 1964, p.232). Ideology thus has no rational basis. World-visions, messianic fervour or moral attitudes are reduced to the defence of particular egoistic interests. One may also note that Blau almost always describes ideology as 'revolutionary', 'radical' or 'extremist': as with Bell or Lipset, ideology is always identified with a homogeneous and enclosed system, that is with the traditional 'isms'. It does not encompass more hidden forms of social control. One can therefore understand why, according to Blau, it does not develop except under 'exceptional' conditions—as a consequence of 'severe oppression' which has little chance of developing to the extent that the collective norms favour fair exchange (Blau, 1964, p.252).

In putting forward this purely psychological interpretation of ideology, Blau can only reduplicate the reductionism and methodological individualism of Homans. For him the various structural causes of social change (social organization, ideology, etc.) do not deserve to be mentioned, and the internal system (within which the fair exchange between individual actors takes place) is separated, as we have seen, from the external system. This, despite the unequal distribution of resources linked with a particular power structure, is the source of fair collective norms.

In conclusion, one can reproach Homans and Blau in the same terms that Marx and Durkheim have applied to Bentham. Marx wrote:

This sphere that we are deserting, within whose boundaries the sale and purchase of labour-power goes on, is in fact a very Eden of the innate rights of man. There alone rule Freedom, Equality, Property and Bentham. Freedom, because both buyer and seller of a commodity, say of labour-power, are constrained only by their own free will . . . Equality, because each enters into relation with the other, as with a simple owner of commodities, and they exchange equivalent for equivalent. Property, because each disposes only of what is his own. And Bentham, because each looks only to himself. [Marx, 1967, I, p.176] [8]

Homans and Blau also depend on this 'sphere', or the circulation of merchandise where individuals exchange their resources fairly in accordance with the law of supply and demand. Neither of them (in spite of some hints from Blau) shows what is the relation between this sphere of circulation (internal system) and the sphere of production (external system, the 'given'). Power therefore results from face-to-face interactions, and not from the structures that precede them.

Durkheim showed that social facts by their very nature tend towards an independent existence outside the individual consciousness which they dominate (Durkheim, 1962, p.30). Consequently, he demands of the sociologist that he apply the following rule: 'The determining cause of a social fact should be sought among the social facts preceding it and not among the states of the individual consciousness.' (Durkheim, 1962, p.110.) He also rejected the absolute individualism of Bentham, oriented entirely towards personal advantage, and providing no support for the rules that he wished the global system to impose. 'For Bentham,' Durkheim points out, 'morality like legislation constitutes a sort of pathology.' (Durkheim, 1961, p.36.) The collective morality arises from the social facts prior to the inter-individual exchange. Like them, it is part of the 'external system'. In the light of the comments that we quoted from Marx and Durkheim, we may emphasize that the internal system (the exchange between individual actors) constitutes a product of the external system, even if it is capable of acquiring considerable specificity.

The 'pure' sociology of exchange offers a rather artificial interpretation of the constitution of power in global societies. It rests entirely on a conception of justice that neither Homans nor Blau has really succeeded in explicating.[9] Exchange, however, has not always put on the aspect of individual calculation, conceived in egoistic terms of particular advantage. In no sense is it a universal and timeless phenomenon, determined by an unchangeable human nature. To conclude, one can distinguish with Rawls real justice from utilitarian justice, according to which 'the satisfaction of desire has its value irrespective of the moral relations between persons' (Rawls, 1962, p.150). For Rawls, on the contrary, 'where the conception of justice as fairness applies, slavery is always unjust' (Rawls, 1962, p.152). The utilitarians were unable to make a similar distinction.

# 3

# Power and Influence as Political Phenomena

R. J. MOKKEN AND F. N. STOKMAN

## 1 INTRODUCTION

For an analysis of the network of interrelations between the boards of major business concerns among themselves and with departments, institutions and committees of the central government in the Netherlands we shall need an appropriate theoretical perspective. We think that in particular the structure and distribution of social power and influence may provide an appropriate background for such an analysis. In order to achieve this, however, we shall need a conceptualization of 'power' and 'influence' of of sufficient precision and coherence to serve at least two important conditions. In the first place, power and influence and associated concepts should be related as much as possible to observable phenomena in order to make problems of power and influence in principle amenable to empirical analysis and research. Moreover, theory will then point the way to methods and data necessary for such investigations. Secondly, the concepts of power and influence, in as far as they are not defined directly in terms of observables, should provide a theoretical framework in terms of which observable facts and research data can be explained and understood in a meaningful way. We did not find in the vast and richly varied literature a ready-made theory that we could use as such. This led us to an endeavour to provide a theoretical perspective more appropriate for our purposes.

In fact, 'power' and 'influence' seem to suffer from the same defects as the concept of 'illness': we all know what we mean when we use the word, and yet it seems to be impossible to define it in a satisfactory way (Rothschild, 1971, p.15). Numerous definitions and thorough theoretical analyses have been suggested in a discussion that has been going on to this day. Yet it cannot be said that the many, often paradoxical, aspects and 'faces' of power and influence have been caught in one encompassing theory. One can therefore feel some sympathy with the somewhat negative attitude of Riker. Having demonstrated that much thinking on power and influence seems to suffer from the same conceptual confusions that pervade discussions of the concept of causality, he wonders whether we should not abolish both concepts altogether (Riker, 1964, p.348).

We should not want (any more than Riker) to proceed that far. Power and influence are associated with such important phenomena in social life that we simply cannot afford to drop them from consideration in social analysis. The least we can do is to try to glean from the many paradoxes, contrasts and restrictions those elements that might promote our insight and understanding. That is what we shall try to do in the following sections, yet without any ambition or pretence of producing a fully developed and closed theory.

## 2 POWER AND PURPOSE

In a number of definitions, power and influence are introduced as the capacity to determine the actions of others in accordance with the will or the purposes of the holder of power or influence. An example is the well-known definition of Max Weber: 'Macht bedeutet jede Chance, innerhalb einer sozialen Beziehung den eigenen Willen auch gegen widerstreben durchzusetzen, gleichviel worauf diese Chance beruht.' (Weber, 1964a, I, p.38.) Power is, therefore, according to Weber, the capacity to carry through one's will in a social relation against resistance, irrespective of the sources of that capacity. This definition contains already a number of possibilities and difficulties, which, as we shall see, arise also in later definitions. For our purposes here the important element is the restriction to will and purpose. This voluntarism implies a stress on purposefully held positions of power and the conscious exercise of power.

Van Doorn disputed this voluntaristic emphasis with the argument that through it psychological contents, such as 'will', 'motivation' or 'consciousness', were introduced as defining elements. Desiring a purely sociological definition, he therefore circumscribed power as the possibility to restrict, in accordance with the purposes of a person or group, the action alternatives of other persons or groups (van Doorn, 1957, p.82; 1966, p.10). The problem, however, amounts to more than just the elimination of psychological connotations. The main point is that such definitions of power are restricted to the *purposeful* exercise of power. And that is the case with van Doorn's definition too. This association of power with the capacity to manipulate in correspondence with the purposes and ends of persons or groups in positions of power tends to emphasize the possibilities of *rational* applications of power. For a suitable definition of power and influence, this rationality *motif* seems to be no more revealing than the elements of psychological volition that van Doorn tries to avoid.

Obviously, motivated and purposeful applications of power and influence are among the most important phenomena in any society. We would overstep our mark, however, if we were to restrict power and influence to this area just 'by definition', because then we would define away other important phenomena of power. Seemingly or evidently irrational applications of power are equally a part of the social reality to which we want to relate our concepts. Many of these applications relate to the impact of positions of power of which the wielders of that power are unaware, either because they do not sufficiently know the range of their power, or, perhaps, because they are not able to master it fully. That can be the case with respect to the *values* whose allocation they dominate: industrialization may lead to environmental pollution. It can also apply to the *subjects* to which their power in fact extends: closing down certain works may effect the level of employment and welfare of the population of a whole region. The 'side effects' of standard economic theory cover many such power phenomena. For these reasons we shall not need such voluntaristic or purposive elements for an appropriate definition of power or influence.

### 3  POWER AND FORCE

Power is often associated with force and sanctions. An overemphasis in this respect tends to ignore the fact that in a society many, if not most, phenomena of power occur in a way not involving a clear application of force or coercion or even a remote threat of those. Less extreme conceptualizations do not imply actual force, but proceed from the availability of compulsion (e.g. Weber) or, more specifically, of sanctions. This last approach characterizes the well-known definition of Lasswell and Kaplan, in which power is given as participation in decisions. Defining decisions so that 'a *decision* is a policy involving severe sanctions (deprivations)', they then introduce power as follows: 'Power is participation in the making of decisions: G has power over H with respect to the values K if G participates in the making of decisions affecting the K-policies of H.' (Lasswell and Kaplan, 1950, pp.74-5.)

Against these or similar approaches, in which power is more or less defined in terms of force or coercion, or the somewhat milder form of sanctions, we can raise two objections. Our first objection again concerns the restrictions imposed by these approaches. Compulsion based on the threat of force or sanctions is certainly characteristic of many positions of power. Indeed force, coercion and sanctions are *sufficient* characteristics of power. Our point is, however, that they are not *necessary* ones. Many phenomena of power occur where force or sanctions cannot be said (in a way that preserves the meaning of these terms) to be present. Van Doorn, whose definition we referred to before, for these reasons considers the capacity to *restrict* action alternatives as primarily characteristic of the concept of power. This line of argument has been followed by others in the Netherlands. Van Doorn and Lammers (1959, p.66) used it in their introduction to modern sociology and Droogleever Fortuijn (1968, p.7) applied it in the field of community power structures. Valkenburgh (1968, p.32) also seemed to take this position when he defined power as a relation creating the possibility of restricting action alternatives of others (persons or groups).

Our second objection concerns the biased meaning of these definitions: they tend not to be ethically neutral. Their focus on the forceful or coercive nature of power seems to imply a predominantly negative concept of power. An analytically efficient concept should, however, allow for all possibilities of power evaluation (positive as well as negative) in its application to social reality. This objection can also be levelled against the broader definition of van Doorn. Various authors (e.g. Droogleever Fortuijn, 1968, p.8; Hoogerwerf, 1972, p.85) have mentioned the bias implicit in concepts that envisage power as the capacity only to *restrict* alternatives. Situations where action alternatives are *expanded* for actors (persons or groups) would escape this perspective of power. Examples of such situations can be found in the emancipation of groups of people through policies of redistribution or by the liberation of areas under foreign domination. Such a negative power concept certainly reflects the negative connotations that seem to pervade popular discussions of power through an association of power with social struggle and conflict. Hoogerwerf (1972, p.85) rightly states that these definitions are based implicitly on a conflict model. He makes a plea for a concept that will also cover positive power relations in co-operative contexts, so that it can explain, for instance, the mechanics of coalition formation. Hoogerwerf's own definition goes far towards achieving this goal but it leads to other problems, as we shall see in later sections.

For these reasons we shall prefer to delineate power as the capacity to determine action alternatives. Power has a dynamic as well as a static aspect. The dynamic aspect consists in the possiblity of change, the restriction or expansion of action alternatives. The static aspect consists in the possibility of fixing or conserving the existing sets of alternatives. These two strongly differing types of power, the conservative and changing forms, may be closely associated but they do not imply each other. An actor (person, group or institution) may possess the power to maintain an existing situation but not the capacity to change it. The expression 'balance of power' suggests such a situation for the parties concerned in such an equilibrium. Both sides, dynamic and static, can be included in the word 'determine' but are insufficiently expressed by that term. We prefer therefore to relate power to the possibility of fixing or to changing the action alternatives or choice alternatives of others.

## 4 POWER AND INFLUENCE

Hoogerwerf defines *power* as the possibility to influence the behaviour of others in accordance with the actor's own purposes (Hoogerwerf, 1972, p.84). According to Hoogerwerf, *influence* occurs wherever behaviour leads to change in behaviour. In his view, power is therefore potential influence in accordance with the ends of an actor. Hoogerwerf states emphatically that power and influence are different concepts, which is not clear in many authors. Kuypers (1973, pp.85ff.) also follows this line of argument and introduces power as the capacity to exercise influence. We have reached here a thorny point in popular debate and academic discussion on power and influence, in which both concepts often are used indiscriminately or conceived in very different ways. If we rely on our intuition and common parlance, we seem to be confronted with two closely related yet distinct concepts. But what is that relation and how is the distinction to be conceived? Is power the general concept and influence a special case? Or should rather the reverse be considered to be true, and power be a special case of influence? Or is it not expedient to relate power and influence to each other in such a simple inclusive way?

An example of this confusion of ideas can be found in the work by Dahl. In a much cited article (Dahl, 1957) he introduces power as follows: 'A has power over B to the extent that he can get B to do something that B would not otherwise do.' A and B are designated as 'actors'. They can be persons, but also groups, roles, institutions, governments, etc. Power is elaborated by Dahl as a relationship between a pair of actors. His further contribution consists of a more or less formal, semi-mathematical analysis of that relation, which we shall not need to consider here. In a study that appeared later, however, Dahl defined 'influence' in nearly the same wording as we cited above for his earlier definition of power (Dahl, 1963, p.40). Power is defined here as influence based on the applicability of severe sanctions (Dahl, 1963, p.50). Thus, in this case Dahl considers influence as the general concept and power as a special case. In still another study, the well-known controversial study of the structure of power in New Haven (Dahl, 1961), the concepts of power and influence are used indiscriminately and more or less synonymously.

Lasswell and Kaplan also use a general concept of influence, which includes power as a special case distinguished by the involvement of severe sanctions. 'It is the threat of sanctions which differentiates power from influence in general.' (Lasswell and Kaplan, 1950, p.76.) Their conceptual approach was widely accepted among

American political scientists, including Dahl. In the Netherlands, van Doorn (1966, p.5) also considers power as a special form of influence. (See also Banfield, 1961, pp.312, 348.) Others, for instance Hunter (1953, p.164), tend to consider power as the more general phenomenon and influence as a sub-category. We saw that both Hoogerwerf and Kuypers distinguished power and influence in a different way. Power is potential influence and influence is behaviour that changes the behaviour of others. In the next section we shall raise a number of objections to this approach.

How can we gain some clarity in this conceptual confusion? We suggest that the characteristic feature of *power* is given by the possibility to restrict or expand freedom of action, or the capacity to preserve that freedom to a given degree. This can be achieved by the application of force, coercion and sanctions, but also in a positive sense through the allocation of necessary resources. (Freedom of action is determined by the set of action and choice alternatives which the actor has at his disposal.) On the other hand *influence* can be characterized as the possibility to determine the outcomes of the behaviour of others, without the restriction or expansion of their freedom of action. (Compare Bierstedt, 1950, p.731.) These outcomes are therefore determined within and take as given the set of alternatives that are available to others. The exercise of influence takes place mainly by means of persuasion, information and advice. The most important, if not the only, source of influence is in particular associated with strategic locations in the communication and information networks that other actors use for the determination of their behaviour.

Summarizing, we may therefore define power and influence as follows. *Power* is the capacity of actors (persons, groups or institutions) to fix or to change (completely or partly) a set of action alternatives or choice alternatives for other actors. *Influence* is the capacity of actors to determine (partly) the actions or choices of other actors within the set of action or choice alternatives available to those actors.

We have in this way introduced power and influence as essentially different phenomena—however intricately interwoven they may be in social reality. In principle, we can therefore conceive power to exist without influence. In this sense, man has power over wild animals, because he can restrict their territory, without having any influence on their freedom of movement within that territory. The power position of the white American settler in relation to the original Indian population showed elements of this.

Every form of social organization implies some restrictions and expansions of freedom for individuals, groups and institutions, as well as the possibility of exercising influence through the communication structures that give shape to that social organization. Any social organization, whether at the micro-level (the family, a peer-group, a workshop) or at the macro-level (a community, nation or political system), consists also of a structure of interconnected positions of power and influence. A close relation exists between power and such concepts as freedom, sovereignty and anarchy. The freedom of an actor can be defined as his capacity to determine his *own* sets of action or choice alternatives. In a social organization, the freedom of an actor can then imply power over others in so far as their alternatives are restricted by his freedom. Freedom for *Ego* implies lack of freedom for *Alter*. The struggle for freedom and the struggle for power are for that reason two sides of the same coin.

In our Western economic system, entrepreneurs have the power to fix or change the composition of the bundle of commodities and services available for consumption.

The consumer has the freedom to determine his choice of articles and brands given that composition. Advertising through the mass media is one of the channels through which the entrepreneur exercises influence on that choice. A government, and through that government and parliament the political parties, have the power to determine the number and identity of political parties in the parliament. The voter is free to express his preference for any of those given parties in elections. The mass media again serve those parties as a channel to exercise influence on the voter's choice. In some models of an organization in which line and staff structures may be distinguished, the staff organization formally reflects an influence structure whereas the more hierarchical composition of the line organization formally designates it more as a structure of power.

The analysis of power and influence structures in social reality is certainly not as simple as these examples may suggest. There are roughly two reasons why it is hard to distinguish power and influence in practical situations. First, power can be a source of influence and influence a source of power. And second, processes occur whereby positions of influence are transformed into positions of power or, conversely, positions of power into positions of influence.

*Power itself can be a source of influence.* This is so when actors, in their choice from the action alternatives open to them, let themselves be guided by information from other actors who have a position of power with respect to them. The well-known 'law of anticipated reactions' of Friedrich (1963, pp.199-215) seems to be based mainly on this mechanism. The same is true for the reputation of power, which, as we shall see in section 9, forms the basis of the reputational method of power observation.

*Influence can also be a source of power.* This is the case where an actor has a particular influence relation with an actor who holds a position of power with respect to other actors. An obvious example is the type of the *éminence grise,* the councillor behind the scenes on whose advice or expertise holders of power particularly rely. This position is one of influence with respect to the holder of power, but it is also a source of power over the subjects of that actor's power. More generally, such a situation is likely to prevail whenever, in relation to holders of power, certain actors have a relative advantage of information or advantage of access (see section 8).

The cases where *influence is transformed into power* are seemingly related to the former examples. Yet they should be distinguished. They occur whenever the influence of an actor with respect to others develops into power, because his influence has expanded so that it also determines the set of alternatives open to the other actors. In a city like Amsterdam the board of mayor and aldermen and the city council have the formal power to determine municipal policies in such basic areas as urban development, public transport and housing. In these policy areas the tasks of the local department of public works are, formally again, restricted to the planning and execution of decisions. This department provides the plans and blueprints for the highest decision-making centres of the city, who, in theory that is, can decide their choice from the multitude of policy alternatives. At a first glance one might assess their position with respect to mayor and aldermen and the city council as one of influence. In actual practice, however, developments have led to a situation in which the department of public works in fact apparently determines the set of policy alternatives from which a decisive choice is to be made. In many cases, only one alternative is at issue. The original position of influence that this city department may have held in the past has been transformed into a position of power.

In a former example we saw that entrepreneurs have a position of influence through the availability of advertising through the mass media. If access to those media on a scale necessary for effective advertising can be acquired only with high costs such as can be afforded only by large enterprises, then this one-sided possibility to influence consumer behaviour results in a position of power for these enterprises as a group. From our perspective, basic statutory rights involving fundamental civic freedoms such as freedom of the press (or, more generally, freedom of opinion) serve the function of guaranteeing to all relevant actors the capacity for exerting influence and of forestalling a process of transformation whereby certain actors acquire positions of power.

The reverse process can also be observed. *A relation of power between actors can develop into a relation of influence.* The 'promotion' to a staff position of officials from the line organization in the reorganization of a business can for that reason sometimes be interpreted as such a transformation. The efforts of modern urban civic action groups in the Netherlands to make an effective contribution of their own in the planning and execution of local decisions in borough or township can thus be seen as an effort to convert the actual position of power of certain government services to one of influence.

Power and influence are the warp and woof in the dynamics of social organization. For these reasons it can often be observed that evident holders of power are not conscious of their power in certain areas and even tend to deny it on the basis of formal influence relations.

## 5 POTENTIAL OR BEHAVIOUR?

In the definitions referred to thus far, another aspect can be brought out clearly, which has been treated in very different ways. Is power (or influence) a *potential* or *capacity*, or is manifest *behaviour* (i.e. the actual application of power or exercise of influence) the more important element? In other words, should we conceptualize power and influence as *latent* or as *manifest* concepts? (van Doorn, 1957, p.80.)

The definitions of Weber, van Doorn and Hoogerwerf made power a capacity, whereas Lasswell and Kaplan (and in their trail many other American scholars, who emphasized participation in decisions) tended to define power in terms of behaviour. We saw that Hoogerwerf and Kuypers followed a different approach, defining power as a capacity, and influence as actual behaviour. (See also Riker, 1964, p.347.) Lasswell and Kaplan seem to proceed precisely the other way around. Influence is for them a potential and power a particular form of behaviour: influence exercised (Lasswell and Kaplan, 1950, pp.60, 71, 75).

We do not favour a line of reasoning in which power and influence are conceived of as latent and manifest concepts in different ways. This we have argued already in section 4. If power is a capacity, for what reasons should we preclude influence from being one also? Yet choice of definition cannot be made an arbitrary one. Simon has raised a number of objections against a latent power concept (Simon, 1953, pp.501-2). They are partly methodological in nature, involving the argument that power as an observable and verifiable phenomenon should be defined directly in terms of observables. A strictly operationalistic requirement, this seems to us unnecessarily rigid and narrow. Another argument by Simon seems more to the point. He states that, when conceived as a potential, power will be equated by definition with the sources of power, the power base. Propositions such as 'the wealthy are powerful' will then be true by definition and no longer amenable to empirical verification. We should certainly guard against such a conceptual confusion. In the next section we shall see that that is possible.

Here we want to emphasize the dangers underlying an approach in which power and influence are identified with their observable applications: manifest power behaviour or influence behaviour. One then tends to lose sight of the fact that the *non*-exercise of power can often be considered also as the exercise of power: non-behaviour is behaviour, and 'non-decisions' can be 'decisions' too (see Bachrach and Baratz, 1962, p.949). We shall run the risks of strongly biased insights if we neglect this perspective. If a government systematically refrains from action in certain policy areas, or on behalf of certain segments of the population, one might well be led to the sometimes spurious conclusion that it lacks the necessary power in these fields. The army of a nation has the manifest function to defend it against aggression from abroad. Modern armed forces can also, however, be *within* that nation an internal power factor of importance. Countless *coups d'état* and juntas in contemporary history have made that evident. Whether such an internal power does exist is determined by the organization of the armed forces in relation to the political and social structure of the nation concerned. That can be different according to time and space. Such power is *not* determined by its *applications*. By those it is made manifest only afterwards (and sometimes too late).

Conversely, an exclusive concentration on evident power behaviour or influence behaviour can easily result in an overestimation of the actual power and influence of certain actors. This may, for instance, be the case where relatively powerless groups resort to intensive and extreme forms of application of power, such as the occupation of factories, wildcat strikes and the like. Where solidly established positions of power are concerned, it can more readily be said that clearly recognizable and manifest forms of the exercise of power are unnecessary and will therefore seldom be observed as such. Positions of power that are asserted in that way are threatened and therefore unstable. Force and action are usually more the resources of the powerless than direct indicators of power. Methods of observing power and influence that emphasize manifest behaviour and the success or otherwise of power initiatives are therefore particularly vulnerable to such a bias. This is, for instance, the case with the 'decision method' in the forms in which it is usually applied (see Section 9). We shall see that much of the criticism of the 'pluralist' studies of Dahl *et al.* can be traced to this point.

Concluding our argument, we propose that for these reasons power and influence should both be defined primarily in terms of potentials or capacities. The application and exercise of power and influence, the actual power behaviour or influence behaviour, important in its own right, should be distinguished. Power behaviour and influence behaviour may be important as indicators, but they can derive their significance only in connection with potentials or capacities. It will not be easy to measure these capacities, or rather to make them amenable to empirical investigation. In principle, this should be done in terms of observable elements, which should also however include items other than observable behaviour.

## 6 ATTRIBUTE OR RELATION?

Power and influence are often seen as more or less personal attributes or properties of a substantial nature. We talk about the *possession* and *accumulation* of power, about the *distribution* of power and the *equality* or *inequality* of power of persons, groups or institutions. Power and influence thus stand as attributes that can be measured and qualified (see for example Simon, 1953). On the other hand a different approach may be mentioned, in which the relational aspects of power and influence are central. Power and influence in this view find their origin in specific social relations between actors. For that reason they should be investigated primarily by examining the form of those social relations. This contrast between power as attribute and as relation reaches far back in the history of political ideas. Friedrich (1950, pp.17-19) states that originally the concept of power as an attribute prevailed in political thinking. It is found with Hobbes, the philosophers of natural right, the utilitarians and Hegelian thinkers up to modern thinkers of totalitarian inclination. The relational aspect of power was brought to the fore by Locke, and is predominant among social scientists.

Both aspects, the substantial as well as the relational, can be found in Parsons (1963b; 1969) and Deutsch (1966). Parsons, however, seems to lend such an emphasis to the former aspect that his theory of power seems to be predominantly a substantial one. It is based on the stream of processes of exchange and transactions between and within the major functional sub-systems of a society. He considers these processes as general forms of exchange, such as may be observed in a particular form in the economic sub-system. These general transaction processes are conducted and facilitated with the help of a social mechanism or medium, serving the role of a generally accepted 'currency'. In the economic sub-system money in its varying forms serves that purpose. Consequently, in that sub-system two complementary and reversed streams of transactions can be distinguished: a flow of commodities and services, and a flow of money. In the political sub-system of a society a similar process appears to hold, according to Parsons. There he considers power to be the major currency, the coin which enable such transactions to take place. Again two complementary streams can be distinguished: a stream of value allocations on the one hand and a stream of power transfers on the other. Power is therefore divisible to a refined degree. It can be transferred and deposited 'on term', in a similar way to money. (He presents a similar theory of influence as a 'generalized medium of persuasion'—see Parsons, 1963a.)

Deutsch refers in this respect of a number of other interesting analogies relating money and means of power such as sanctions (force). Prestige is for power what reliability and solvency are for money. Banks can invest and lend out money to an amount that is a multiple of what they receive in the form of deposits because a reliable bank can be sure that its clients will not claim their deposits all at the same time. A similar observation can be made with respect to a government with prestige and authority. 'In much the same way, governments can promise to back with sanctions many more of their binding decisions, rules and laws, and to do so against many more people, than any government could possibly do if all people started disobeying it at one and the same time.' (Deutsch, 1966, p.121). The economic and political sub-systems are interconnected closely in their transaction flows for Deutsch also. Economic transactions such as credit policies and investment policies in business ought to be considered as (political) inputs in the economy for that reason, as demonstrated by the close co-ordination of government policies and those of the central banks in these areas. This can lead to *political* power located in the economic sub-system, the main theme of the project at the Institute for Political Science of the University of Amsterdam, of which this paper forms a part. (See also Mokken and Stokman, 1974.) Deutsch points this out with some emphasis: 'To the extent that such central banking functions are carried out by wholly private and unsupervised banks, or other financial organisations—or to the extent that such organizations share in these policies—it might be surmised that banks and their executives have acquired a substantial amount of political power.' (Deutsch, 1966, pp.119-20.)

The imaginative metaphors of Parsons, referred to above, are certainly appealing. However, they satisfy us only partly. The conception of power and influence as divisible and transferable substances, media of exchange, does tell something about the instrumental use that can be made of power and influence, but it does not provide us with an explanation of the emergence and occurrence of power in social systems. The separation of the medium of circulation (substantial aspect) from the nature of the social structure (relational aspect) in which it operates seems to us to rule this out. The two faces can be distinguished. Power and influence in a community or society emerge and develop, however, primarily in a *relational* framework—a specific complex of particular social relations between actors, by means of which certain actors, or groups of actors, acquire the capacity to fix or to change the action alternatives of other actors (power) or to determine the behaviour of those actors in relation to the alternatives available to them (influence). This complex of social relations forms a part of the institutional framework of that community, the network of channels of interaction, transaction and communication that shapes its social organization over time.

The power or influence of actors as a capacity is inherent in the particular position or configuration that they occupy in that relational complex. We shall designate that place or configuration as a *power position* or *influence position*. The position of power refers to the relational aspect of power. The instrumental or substantial aspects of power (or influence) bear a close connection to the resources by means of which power (or influence) as a capacity can be put into effect. That capacity is also determined by these resources, but even then only in a particular relational context. The mere possession of possible power resources alone does not necessarily produce power. Wealth, military skills and social background can be sources of power. Nevertheless well-to-do generals of upper-class descent are not likely to possess much power in a foreign country where they are residing in exile or retirement. They will have power, for instance, in a society in which the highest social positions, including those in the army, are occupied mainly by people representing a small upper class—a situation, for instance, that seems to be characteristic of the larger part of Latin America. The same can be said concerning influence. We have stated that expertise is one important source of it. The mere possession of expertise does not necessarily lead to influence. An eminent lawyer who regularly plays golf with a chief executive of a big concern need not have any relation of influence with him in which this expertise plays a role. The position is different where his office has a close connection with that concern.

The various means of power, as resources of power, are therefore tied to the position of power in which they can be put into effect. The specific combination of resources of power that are available to and can be commanded by actors in a particular position of power we call the *power base* of those actors or that position. The position as well as the basis determines the capacity or potential that defines power or influence. The power position or influence position refers to the relational aspect, the power base or influence base to the substantial aspects of that capacity. The substantial aspect is determined by the relational one. This distinction also has its consequences for the instrumental aspects of power and influence: the manner in which that power or influence is wielded and applied, in short the actual power behaviour or influence behaviour, as exercised by actors. These also have a relational side, when we pay attention to the utilization of positions of power and the relations to other actors. These can be observed, for instance, when power is redistributed, transferred or delegated in the course of rearrangements or changes of an existing social organization that create new positions of power and/or abolish old ones. The substantial aspects stand out when we focus on the application of resources, the power base. It is this aspect in particular to which Harsanyi refers when he introduces as 'opportunity costs' the costs entailed in the application of power resources (Harsanyi, 1962b; Banfield, 1961, p.312). Simon (1953) also treats this aspect when he points out that power and influence can be 'invested' to enlarge the power base, as well as 'consumed' in such a way that the base is not increased and may even shrink.

Many concepts in frequent use such as the *structure and distribution of power* of a community can likewise be reduced to these aspects. The structure of power then relates particularly to the relational aspects, the pattern of social relations of that community and the positions of power that can be observed in it. We shall argue that the structure is associated with the form and construction of major processes of value allocation and decision-making in that community. The distribution of power refers mainly to the substantial aspects. For a given structure of power we are then concerned with the distribution over actors (persons, groups or institutions) of the capacities to determine the alternatives that enter those processes as well as their outcomes. It comprises also the distribution of actual resources of power and influence and the possibility of occupying positions of power or influence in their application.

## 7 MICRO-LEVEL AND MACRO-LEVEL

In many theories and studies of power and influence, it is often not clear whether the authors apply their observations to relations between individuals or to those between groups or institutions. Our insight may then be hampered because power and influence at the macro- and micro-level cannot simply be treated in the same way. Often theories are formulated and elaborated mainly at the micro-level and subsequently applied to the macro-level, leaving open the question what the units (actors) represent. Dahl's approach exemplifies this point, as does the work of March (1955, 1957), Shapley and Shubik (1954), Harsanyi (1926b, 1962c) and Karlsson (1962). It is essentially a micro-level theory that cannot be generalized directly to the macro-level. If it is so generalized, an *atomistic* bias may be introduced because individuals were the starting point, and a *relational* bias may result because limited relations are considered.

The *atomistic* error may threaten because right from the beginning power and influence are thought of in personalistic terms. Even though the term 'actor' is meant to cover individuals as well as collective entities such as groups or institutions, in actual discourse its personalistic meaning tends to prevail. Expressions such as 'A influences B' or *'Alter* has power over *Ego'* abound. Concepts as 'power holder' and 'power subject' (van Doorn, 1957, p.83) also induce this mode of thinking. Consequently, power and influence tend to be thought of as personal attributes assigned on the basis of relations between persons. This has manifested itself in most of the power studies in communities and other sites. It applies, for instance, to Hunter's (1953) study as well as that of Dahl (1961). These analyses are mainly in terms of individuals. The groups and institutions from which persons derive their power do not seem to enter the perspective. As far as groups are distinguished, they serve to characterize persons or they are represented as aggregates of personal characteristics. Specific institutional attributes, such as the degree of organization of a group, do not come into the picture. In Dahl's study of participation in local decisions, for instance, an economic élite is distinguished, but the mutual connections and interrelations of the institutions that they represent remain obscure.

The *relational* bias may be introduced when only relations of pairs of actors are considered instead of relational networks. 'A influences B', *'Alter* has power over *Ego'* and the concepts of power holder and power subject all suggest this mode of thinking. Moreover, power and influence are also often perceived as asymmetric relations: A has power over B, but not *vice versa.* The possibility of a balance of power suggests, however, that we should also take account of symmetric relations and mutual influence. We can also construct examples where the (binary) power relations between two actors A and B contain no account of their relations of power with 'third parties' C, D, . . . Z. These relations, however, can determine the relation between A and B strongly. A power relation of A over B can be cancelled by an influence relation of B with respect to C, when C has power over B. Moreover, the relation of a power holder A to each of the subjects of power B– Z is shaped by the nature of the relations that exist between those subjects of power. A coalition among them (i.e. an organizational and communication structure) can sometimes reduce A's position of power with respect to the set of actors B– Z considerably. Suppressing the formation of trade unions (as occurred in most European countries in the nineteenth century) reinforced the position of the employers in their dealings with individual workers, since these relations then became mainly bilateral (binary). Through the organization of trade unions as actors, the power position of employers was reduced. Again, the bargaining position of the employer's organizations is stronger whenever they have to meet the unions separately and weaker when they have to confront them in coalition.

From the macro-perspective we need therefore to supplement atomistic viewpoints with collectivistic, and personalistic viewpoints with institutionalistic. These considerations are of special importance for the macro-problems that arise in the study of the structure and distribution of power in a community. And it is just there that the focus of sociological and political science research studies on power and influence is to be found. Here, therefore, the origin of the great controversies and heated debates that have taken place in this field should especially be found. This long-winded series of polemics, focused around the studies by Hunter (1953) and Dahl

(1961), known as the élitist—pluralist debate, proved to be of considerable importance for the development of thinking on power and influence.[1] It will be sufficient for our purposes to characterize its outcome with the statement that Hunter's reputational approach had its built-in biases and that Dahl's focus on the study of actual decision processes, instead of reputational élites, led the way to more promising studies.

Yet Dahl's type of decision analysis, with its exclusive focus on actual participation in on-going decisions, does not take into account the possibility '. . . that an individual or group in a community participates more vigorously in supporting the *non-decision-making* process than in participating in actual decisions within the process' (Bachrach and Baratz, 1962, p.949). This is in fact the second face of power, designated by Bachrach and Baratz 'non-decision'. It is mainly concerned with the determination and composition of what Crenson (1971) has called the *political agenda* of a community: the set of issues and policies that are allowed to enter the established decision-making bodies and procedures of that community. It may apply, however, to later stages of decision-making also, as when the effective execution or implementation of decisions is impeded or obstructed. Both aspects of the structure of power in a community should therefore be taken into account: participation in decisions as well as in non-decisions.

Apart from the limitations owing to the *local* context of these studies, we should stress their essentially *personalistic* nature. Dahl shared this with Hunter. Power and leadership were from the start considered as personal attributes apart from any institutional framework. Dahl, for instance, did not venture beyond recording successful influence initiatives of individuals. He did not investigate the degree to which these influential persons were interconnected in terms of a community of interests through the organizations and institutions that they represented. This suggests the (in itself rather naïve) proposition that representatives of a ruling élite should be active and hence observable in all conceivable issue areas. More plausible, however, would seem to be the assumption that a properly cohesive ruling élite would operate mainly on the basis of a reasonably efficient social organization and a division of labour derived from it. Dahl's study for these reasons gave no conclusive evidence concerning the existence of either a pluralist or an élitist system in New Haven. People realize and develop themselves in institutions and are moulded by institutions. Therefore, we should not ask, with Hunter, 'Who are the most important persons in this community?' but 'What are the most important institutions in this place?' Nor should we wonder, with Dahl, 'Which individuals participate in local decisions?' but 'What institutions play their part in local decisions?'

Finally, the whole debate is an example of how misleading and confusing such research can be when it is not guided by and interpreted in terms of a clear and adequate theoretical delimitation of the closely related concepts of power and influence. None of the participants in the debate provides such a perspective. If we use the concepts as introduced by us above, we can view the élitist—pluralist controversy in a different light. Dahl then did not so much investigate the structure of *power* in New Haven (the determination of the set of most important policy alternatives available to that community) as the degree of *influence* that certain members (or groups of members) of that community had in the choice to be made from given alternatives. The criticism of neo-élitist authors like Bachrach and Baratz or Crenson,

46

with its emphasis on non-decisions, was concerned mainly with the determination of the political agenda, that is the set of policy alternatives open to the community. That is power in our conception. Their critique can therefore straightforwardly be summarized with the statement that studies of influence are not necessarily studies of power. And the whole crux of the élitist—pluralist debate may well be summarized in the proposition that in a society pluralist influence structures can exist within élitist structures of power: gardens where under the regime of one gardener a hundred flowers blossom. About such questions these studies gave no satisfactory evidence at all.

## 8 POLITICAL POWER AND INFLUENCE

We may now collect and summarize the major points of our argument. Power and influence were introduced in section 4 as follows:

> *Power* is the capacity of actors (persons, groups or institutions) to fix or to change (completely or partly) a set of action or choice alternatives for other actors.
> *Influence* is the capacity of actors to determine partly the actions or choices of other actors within the set of action or choice alternatives available to those actors.

Our focus is therefore the sets of action or choice alternatives that actors have in a social system. *Power* in particular refers to the possibility of determining such sets to a certain extent in either a dynamic or a static sense. The dynamic aspect, 'progressive' or for that matter 'reactionary', is shown in the capacity to change sets of alternatives. The static (or 'conservative') aspect we find in the capacity to fix alternatives. *Influence* concerns the behaviour of actors within the given set of alternatives available to them. It is the capacity to determine that behaviour to a certain extent. Power and influence are thus introduced as closely related, yet essentially different, concepts. Power is associated with the restriction or expansion of freedom; influence on the other hand does not interfere with the degrees of freedom of actors. The availability of positive or negative sanctions is a characteristic, but not a necessary source, of power. The ability to persuade or to supply information and expertise are characteristic sources of influence. Power and influence we view as *capacities* to be distinguished from their *application:* the actual power or influence behaviour. They should also be distinguished from the *resources* of power and influence.

Power and influence in a community find their origin primarily in a relational context, a structure of social relations, whereby certain actors acquire these capacities to determine in certain respects the action alternatives of other actors. That structure is part of the institutional framework of that community, the network of interactions, transactions and communications between relevant actors which determines its social organization. The power or influence of an actor or group of actors with respect to other actors is determined by the location or configuration in that network from which they derive that capacity. It is called their *position of power or influence*. Obviously, such positions, as well as the actors occupying them, can themselves be subject to power relations or influence relations in a wider social setting.

The power position refers to the relational aspects of power. Power and influence also have substantial aspects, where we consider the means and resources of power. These also are determined by the relational context, the power position. The specific combination of resources of power than can be applied in a specific power position is called the *power base*. Position as well as base determine the capacities we call power or influence. The instrumental aspects of power and influence concern the behaviour of actors, the application of power or influence. These also have relational as well as substantial sides. Where the focus is relational, we mainly pay attention to the ways in which positions of power are employed in their relation to those of other actors. Where the focus is substantial, on application of resources, the power base assumes prominence.

Similar observations apply to such concepts as *power structure* and *distribution of power*. The power structure concerns the relational side of power in a community: the structures of actors and their social relations in which positions of power can be discerned. We shall look for that structure in the organization and construction of those processes of decision-making or value allocation that are important to that community. The distribution of power concerns especially the substantial aspects, the question being how, for a given structure of power, the capacity to determine the outcomes of those processes is dispersed over relevant actors in that community. It includes the distribution of means and resources of power. Power can be a source of influence ('law of anticipated reactions') and influence a source of power (*éminence grise*). Positions of influence can be transformed into positions of power and positions of power can be converted into positions of influence. The dynamics of social organization are pervaded by such processes.

With these definitions and related concepts we face power and influence as highly general sociological concepts, which can be applied to any social context and at any level. But how should we derive from these our definitions of *political* power and influence? Roughly, there are two ways in which political power is circumscribed in the literature. The first approach introduces political power as a special case of a more general definition of power. It is prevalent among sociological theorists, where political power usually is seen as a particular form of social power. That, for instance, is true of Weber, who considered the political context as linked to a well demarcated geographic territory and the availability of the means of physical force (Weber, 1964a, I, p.39). Nowadays, it is more usual to restrict political power to government and the state (see for example Neumann, 1950; and van Doorn, 1957, pp. 98-9; 1966, pp. 23-5).

The second approach is prevalent among those political scientists who have tended to conceive political science mainly as the study of power phenomena. The power concept thus becomes the more or less central and defining object of their discipline. This approach therefore leads to a very broad delimitation of the discipline and simultaneously to a too-narrow definition of power. Obviously, for them a concept like 'political power' did not stand out clearly, because power as such was a political phenomenon anyway. We refer to the well-known 'Chicago power school' of political science, which, since the thirties, inspired by the thoughts of Charles E. Merriam and Harold Lasswell, has had and still indeed has much influence on American political science.

For our definition of political power we prefer the first approach. Political power and influence will be defined as particular forms of the general concepts we described before. A restriction to the domain of state and government, however important they may be in themselves, seems too narrow for our purpose. Many important social events of immediate political relevance occur outside the sphere of government and state. Wage negotiations, investment decisions, occupations of factories, business mergers and closures and so on have an impact that clearly designates them as political matters even before governments come into our view. We therefore prefer a perspective, such as that provided by Easton (1965b), according to which political phenomena can be said to occur in those social processes by means of which values are authoritatively allocated for a community. The allocation of values (e.g. education, medical care, production of goods and services) takes place in a chain or network of interconnected institutions and organizations, and these networks form certain allocation structures (e.g. educational system, system of medical care, production system). In those systems, according to Easton, certain institutions play a decisive role: the authorities. Easton (1965b, p. 212) unnecessarily restricts his concept of authorities to agents and agencies in the governmental sphere. Our interpretation of this concept is a wider one. These authorities may be considered to effect the binding and final allocation of values in a specific area. If necessary, we can see these allocation processes also in another light, namely as processes of social decision-making or chains of such processes, through which these value allocations are effected. In those decision-making processes where the governmental authorities are involved, we can, for instance, distinguish on the input side the institutions of the bureaucracy, the political parties and the numerous pressure groups, lobbies and organizations that act in an on-going effort to determine the outcomes of those processes. On the output side we can discern among others (as authorities) the government, the parliament, and again the bureaucracy and judicial bodies, which are involved in the conversion, realization and effective execution of policies.

In allocation processes of economic values we can also regard such a communication and information network as a decision-making structure with input and output aspects. On the input side we have the mobilizing and channelling of savings through financial institutions in capital and money markets, of labour in the labour market, raw materials in commodity markets and consumer behaviour in consumer markets. These inputs are converted in enterprises by entrepreneurial institutions (as authorities) in investment and production decisions, which entail an allocation of economic values (commodities, services, primary income and so on).

We can distinguish in such social decision processes two aspects that are relevant for our definitions of power and influence. The first one concerns the composition of the set of admissible choice alternatives, the available value alternatives that are taken as the starting point for the choice of alternative policies or value allocations in a community or group. In every political system this spectrum of possible value allocations is in various ways restricted from the start. The ways in which this happens and the identities of actors who play a determining role at this level tell us something about politically relevant relations of power. The capacity to fix or to change sets of admissible alternative value allocations for a political community is political power. As such we may consider it to be a special case of power as defined before.

For example, the requirement of profitable production for given production relations indicates a mechanism behind which important relations of power are concealed. Those actors who determine profitability possess economic as well as political power. This aspect can also be distinguished at the micro-level. For a business enterprise, the admissible value allocations are determined by its goals, opportunities and resources. These are determined partly by circumstances and actors outside that enterprise, i.e. external power factors. Within the enterprise, the basic alternatives are determined by those actors (persons or organizational parts) who exercise the entrepreneurial function: the top managerial level, in our study of the boards of chief executives and directors.

The second aspect concerns the choice that is ultimately made from the given set of alternatives. This is the conversion process proper, which results in a policy: the effectuation of a specific value allocation. The possibility that an actor has to determine these outcomes indicates his (political) influence. Here again we are facing a particular form of the more general concept of influence, defined before.

We therefore define political power and influence in a social system as follows:

> *Political power* in a social system is the capacity to fix or to change (partly) a set of alternative value allocations for the members of that system or for parts of it.
> *Political influence* is the capacity to determine (partly) within a given set of available alternative value allocations the outcomes of the allocation process.

The availability of sanctions (positive or negative value allocations) that determine the alternatives open to actors (members of the system) is often characteristic of political power. Political power, however, is especially associated with the concept of non-decision: the capacity to predetermine basic alternatives and to prevent changes in them. This non-decision aspect can be distinguished in all phases of processes of value allocation and decision-making (Bachrach and Baratz, 1970, pp. 52-63; Van der Eijk and Kok, 1974). On the input side the non-decision manifests itself in the form of *non-initiation.* Here the construction of a community's political agenda is at issue, the determination of basic alternatives for the allocation of values. On the output side, the non-decision takes the form of *non-implementation.* Here, for instance, we are concerned with the non-execution of formally completed decisions or with the perverted use that can be made of the outcomes of decision processes and the value allocations determined by them. Examples of such 'output perversion' can occasionally be found in development aid, when development funds are locally used for purposes other than the social and economic development of a community and its population.

Again, political influence is strongly associated with the effective aggregation and organization of information, intelligence and expertise and the availability of good opportunities for access to levels of decision-making. When the political influence of an actor or group achieves a one-sided character in comparison with that of other actors, that influence can be a source of power or it can be converted into power (see section 4). We have mentioned two ways in which this may occur. The first one arises by means of an *advantage of information,* based on superior, efficient or timely knowledge, arguments and know-how. The possession of such information is not in itself sufficient to constitute influence or power in the social decision processes. There has to be a thorough aggregation and organization of the intelligence, information and skills concerned. Only then can we speak of an advantage of information and, occasionally, of an information monopoly. This is the case, for instance, when specialized agencies possess more or less uniquely the knowledge that is necessary for the determination of certain policies.

Second, the possession of superior means of access to decision-making levels or centres, authorities and policy-makers may be not only a source of influence but indeed a source of power. We may designate this situation as one of *advantage of access*. Well-aggregated and well-organized information can lead to influence only if the actors concerned have the capacity to introduce (or derive) their information in (or from) decision-making at the right times and in the right agencies. An advantage of access therefore has two aspects: that of *timing* and that of *representation*.

Effective information should be channelled at the right time through the openings for access, i.e. at those moments and in those phases of decision-making when such information will be operative in the selection of alternatives. Examples abound of decision procedures in which certain actors are allocated access in phases and at levels where their information will come too late to have appreciable effects.

Representation involves the question: which actors are to be allowed to have access to decision-making? One example is that of the 'recognized' organizations, which are accepted by the authorities as their exclusive discussion or 'influence' partners in their decision-making procedures. Any legislative or administrative process is teeming with these cases. Collective wage negotiations, land re-allottment procedures and urban redevelopment are just a few areas in which there are many positions that are apparently influence positions but that through an advantage of access are more like power positions.

In such cases, therefore, we can speak of an advantage or even a monopoly of access. Schattschneider's statement (1960, p.171) that 'organization is the mobilization of bias' is illustrated here with the organization of information and the organization of access.

In our discourse, we have repeatedly underlined the importance that information positions have as a source of influence and, where they exist in a one-sided form, of power. We have therefore emphasized that positions of power and especially of influence can be traced in the form of critical positions in interaction and communication networks. We needed this emphasis because a reference to these aspects is virtually lacking in the literature of power in political science. Lasswell and Kaplan (1950, pp. 83–97), for instance, give a more than elaborate enumeration of sources of power, as did Bachrach and Baratz (1970, pp. 52–63) twenty years later in their elaboration of a decision model. Yet information is hardly mentioned as a source. Only Deutsch develops his concepts of power and influence in the context of communication theory, referring explicitly to power positions as critical positions in communication networks. For example, he points to the strategic middle level between the top of a system and the mass. In military organizations, this level coincides with positions that are usually associated with the rank of colonel. Hence the important role colonels frequently are observed to play in juntas (Deutsch, 1966, pp.145–62).

A different situation can be observed in small group research in social psychology. In numerous studies it has been demonstrated convincingly that positions of power and influence (leadership) are to a large extent determined by the appropriate communication structure (e.g. Bavelas, 1960; Glanzer and Glaser, 1959; 1961).

Collins and Raven (1969, pp.166-80) for that reason distinguish various forms of
power based on information or expertise.

All the other concepts that we defined before, such as power position and power
base, can be adapted without many problems to our definitions of political power and
influence. We may however need an additional pair of concepts, *value scope* and
*system range* in relation to power and influence. We shall develop these for power
only, as the reader can well adapt them to influence. By *value scope* we shall
understand that set of values the allocation of which is (partly) controlled from a given
power position. In relation to the objects of our study, the big concerns, or 'big
business', there are first the values that are directly associated with the firm's position
in economic production: the commodities and services that are produced and
distributed, the employment that is generated and the (primary) incomes that are
created and distributed. But also less obvious values can be involved: environment and
ecology as a result of industrial construction and forms of distribution and marketing,
education in as far as it is inspired by or geared to industrial problems, the arts and
sports in as far as they are sponsored by industry or whenever they are subjected to
such norms as that of good (industrial) management and marketing. A modern central
government has in principle a still larger value scope, encompassing virtually any
conceivable value sector in social life.

As *system range* we shall denote the set of actors (or members of the social system)
for which value alternatives can be determined. It is the collection of actors to which a
power position extends. For the big concern it may include the workers and
employees and their organizations in the labour market, suppliers, retailers and
consumers and their organizations. But it can also include authorities such as local
governments in the fields of housing and schools, for example, and the mass media as
far as the latter depend on business through advertising. Scope and range can be larger
than the occupants of power positions realize. The system range of a banking system
can be larger than formally stated when, for instance, the withdrawal of credit for
certain unprofitable firms proves to result in the dislocation of employment in a
region or town. The value scope of energy works is unintentionally larger when the
production of energy is accompanied by (negative) values in the area of living
conditions and environment. (Again, the side effects that merit marginal attention in
standard economic theory hide many of such transgressions of formal scopes or
ranges.)

## 9 TRACING POWER AND INFLUENCE METHODS

Power and influence are elusive matters. They can not often be observed clearly
because they are rarely manifested in the form of clearly recognizable 'power' or
'influence' behaviour. In the case of solidly established power positions, it can more
readily be stated that clearly identifiable, manifest forms of exercised power are
superfluous. Power positions that are asserted in that way are being threatened and are
unsteady. Moreover, really important power and influence are usually characterized
by an atmosphere of discretion and secrecy. The disguise of power is often an
important means for the maintenance of power. For that reason solid positions of
power are often presented in pluralist and fragmented forms, which constitute the
appearances of that power.

In Western society, for instance, we often meet such appearances when the concealment of economic power is at issue. Minority holdings in concerns, joint ventures and a proliferation of subsidiaries and numerous other legally differentiated forms of undertaking can serve to lend a pluralist look to concentrated power. A similar pluralist camouflaging principle of organization can be observed in totalitarian groupings such as Communist parties. The formation of cells and undercover organizations may also disguise their character in a society that is proclaiming pluralist democracy rather than democratic centralism.

Finally, relations and positions of power are not often recognized as such, because they often develop without a conscious striving for power. We argued before that power and influence are the result of social organization developed to achieve certain goals. In the resulting social organizations, those goals are primarily being served and relations of power and influence form the sediment of the ways in which these are striven for.

For all these reasons it has proved to be a rather forbidding task to develop methods of tracing and analysing power and influence satisfying our requirement of observability in empirical situations. Currently four methodological approaches may be roughly distinguished. Two of them have been mentioned before: the *reputational method* and the *decision method.* The two others may be referred to as the *positional method* and the *method of policy analysis.* In the literature these methods are usually compared in a rather unsystematic way. Most frequently they are treated as competing alternatives and then certified (or stigmatized) in terms of some well-known particular application. In this way the reputational method has been associated with Hunter's study and the decision method with that of Dahl's group. In the longer run we do not see much sense in a classification of methods according to their similarity to specific applications. The result is often that methods that are fundamentally alike are not characterized as such but presented as different ones. In the Netherlands a case in point is the interesting study by Braam which according to its strategy should be counted under the decision approach, although Braam disputes the correspondence and claims to present a new method (Braam, 1973, pp.3,41-4,311). It seems better to classify methods in terms of the basic research strategy that they seek to implement. We have argued in our introduction that one of the functions of an efficient conceptualization of power and influence should be to point the way to the development of methods, as well as to provide a framework within which these methods can be interpreted. Our conceptualization gives us the opportunity to do so.

We have described power and influence as a capacity originating in a relational context. The power position emphasizes this relational aspect and indicates the location in the network where this capacity is situated. The power base is the combination of power resources that can be applied in that position. The base, which also determines the capacity, is more an indicator of the substantial aspects of power or influence. Power as a capacity should be distinguished from its application, power behaviour as exercised. These three basic aspects should all be studied for a more or less exhaustive analysis of power and influence relations in decision-making or allocation structures. Moreover, it will be necessary to decide whether alternatives can be fixed or changed (power) or whether mainly behaviour can be guided or determined with respect to available alternatives (influence).

None of the methods reflects all these aspects equally; each tends to emphasize certain aspects more than others. Two methods emphasize the capacity in particular: the reputational method and the positional approach. In the two other methods, the decision method and the policy analysis, the applications (observed behaviour) assume prominence.

The *reputational method* is essentially based on the perception and strength of the overtly established power position and, in connection with it, Friedrich's 'law of anticipated reactions'. It relies on the validity of the reputation for power and influence generally attributed by the knowledgeable members of a community. Therefore, it seems to be oriented more to the power base and its elements than to the position, so it may well accentuate the substantial rather than the relational aspects of power. The method seems to be useful in clearly laid-out situations, such as in small, local communities where face-to-face relations and communications may cover the whole area. The method has the tendency in particular to produce types of well-publicized general leadership and not to be sensitive to more specialized but no less important types of leadership (Wildavsky, 1964a, pp.303-19). In large, urbanized communities, where reputations, stereotyped by the mass-media, serve as a substitute for direct experience, the method is less useful.

The *positional method* is focused primarily on the relational aspects of the power or influence position. This approach is aimed at detecting critical or central points or key positions in structures of decision-making or allocation. Its basic principle is that an analysis of the relevant interaction and communication structures underlying those processes may reveal positions that can be considered as centres of power or influence. Although informal structures also can be analysed by this method, most of its applications in the literature involve models of formal organization.

The other two methods are aimed primarily at actual behaviour that can be interpreted as an exercise of power and influence. The capacities stay more or less in the background.

In the *decision method*, the basic assumption is that power holders and influentials will reveal themselves through their actions as participants in concrete decisions. The term 'decision method' refers to the study of concrete decisions and not to the study of the whole process and context of decision-making or value allocation. In the latter sense any study of political power is also decision-making (or value allocation) research. The decision method was designed to detect those actors who play an active role in the realization of certain decisions. In this method one should try to take account of relational aspects such as coalitions of actors (persons as well as institutions) that by coalition and division of labour can block undesirable value alternatives (non-decision) as well as regulating controversial but admissible allocations.

Finally, the *method of policy analysis* has recently been advocated with respect to another aspect of the actual exercise of power, the outcomes of allocation processes: policies as they are actually effected. The strategy has been proposed among others by Bachrach and Baratz, and is based on the assumption that an analysis of policy outputs can reveal which actors profit in particular from these policies and which ones suffer relative deprivation. This approach seems to be based in particular on the notion, not unrealistic in itself, that power is exercised mainly for one's own benefit. As a matter of theory, one might raise the objection that, when confronted with the case of an altruistic exercise of power on behalf of powerless actors, one might come to wrong conclusions about the actual power relations. An altruistic dictator may be no less powerful than his egocentric successor. The method of policy analysis no more leads to direct observations of power than do the other methods.

Each of the four methods that we sketched summarily above concerns different aspects of power and influence. It will be clear from the perspectives of this paper that all methodological possibilities will not be exhausted by these four approaches. Moreover, it is to be expected that studies that are based exclusively on methods applying to one aspect in particular will lead to results that are characteristic for those methods. Walton (1966a, 1966b) demonstrated this rather convincingly in an analysis of over thirty studies of more than fifty local communities. He noted that the resulting power structures were closely related to the methods used to uncover them. The reputational method led to élitist, pyramidal power structures, whereas the decision method suggested more disconnected pluralist structures. (See also Ellemers, 1968, pp. 15-17.)

The point is, of course, that in the empirical analysis of power structures, different methods should be used so as to cover all the most important aspects of power relations. Indeed, in more recent studies of local power structures, combinations of methods have been used with some profit in a comparative analysis across communities. Researchers such as Agger *et al.* (1964) and Gamson (1966) used particular combinations of the reputational and decision methods. Crenson's study of the issue of air pollution also led to a certain redress of the reputational method (Crenson, 1971).

Our analysis of interlocking directorates between large concerns, some results of which are presented in another paper (Mokken and Stokman, 1974), can be considered as a version of the positional approach, focusing on one basic aspect of power: the relational structure. Such a study necessitates application of efficient and penetrating methods appropriate for the analysis of sometimes highly complicated networks. Of such analyses relatively few satisfactory applications are known thus far. Brams (1968; see also Russett, 1968) gave for formal organizations a first, though not very convincing illustration of the analytical and conceptual possibilities of the mathematical theory of graphs. As far as we know, we are the first to adapt and apply elements of this theory to the analysis of the networks of interlocking directorates between large corporations and of networks involving government institutions.

# 4

# Power, Cause and Force

F. CHAZEL

## 1 POWER AND CAUSE

Over ten years ago Herbert Danzger pointed out that the studies of community power suffered most from the abuse of the concept of power (Danzger, 1964, p.712). This observation still holds true. And it is not only true of community power but much more generally, so it is still relevant to ask what are the dimensions of the concept of power. Students of the subject have fallen into serious ambiguities in the area of power, and my main concern here will be to tackle these.

Undue reliance has been placed on certain analogies and this has tended to make us lose sight of what may be said to characterize power and to neglect the specific type of social relation that constitutes power. Despite the fact that a systematic survey of such analogies and their variations might be interesting I shall limit myself in this paper to examining only one case, namely the relation between power and cause.

Herbert Simon, for instance, suggests in *Models of Man* that the proposition 'C *has power over* R' be replaced by the proposition 'the behavior of C *causes* the behavior of R' (Simon, 1957, p.5), while William Riker in a more recent article (Riker, 1964) essentially views power as capacity and equates it with a potential cause. To avoid any misunderstanding, the object of my criticism is not to underrate the value of Simon's approach from a formal point of view. It consists in an attempt to translate a concept—power—that is confused and unclear into a methodological language that is appropriate for causal analysis. Even though this particular application of causal analysis seems to me mistaken, I have no wish to question causal analysis in principle. It has marked a stage of social science even if it is now perhaps time for us to become conscious of its epistemological and methodological limits. I do not deny that it could be useful to locate the concept of power in relation to the concept of cause, as McFarland (1969) has tried to do. I object only to the reduction of the former to the latter. This would unhappily deprive the concept of power of any fruitfulness, as we shall see. The investigator finds his attention turned away from the most significant aspect of power relations, i.e. the mechanisms that it comprises.

First of all, there are some fairly obvious differences between the notions of power and cause even before they are conceptually refined. As far as Simon's formula is concerned, it accounts only for the most elementary distinction according to which power refers to a causal relation between human beings. Power would correspond to the form causality takes in social interaction, and the association of power and cause would remain legitimate. Yet if we want to characterize C's power it seems to me problematic to ignore C's intentions and not to relate them to the change brought about in R's behaviour. More precisely, we can speak of power only if the change in R's behaviour goes in the direction intended by C and corresponds to the strategy for carrying out his intentions that he has worked out (McFarland, 1969, p.13). To pursue the matter further, power can be identified not only by the results it brings about but also by the mode of action that constitutes it, namely the recourse to sanctions or rather the possibility of having recourse to sanctions. The precise nature of the process will have to be elaborated, but in a power relationship sanctions certainly constitute the lever which C uses in order to obtain from R those changes that he wants.

From this we see that as we apply minor corrections of the most obvious kind to Simon's formulation we move away from the perspective that tends to reduce power to pure social causation. Certainly it is true that none of the features of power we have mentioned prevent us from seeing it as a type of causality. But, at the least, it is a kind of causality *sui generis*, applicable to the interrelation of social actors; more precisely, it implies an adjustment of R's behaviour in accordance with the wishes of C as a result of whatever sactions the latter is in a position to inflict. David Easton said much the same thing when he wrote: 'Power, therefore, is present to the extent to which one person controls by sanction the decisions and actions of another.' (Easton, 1953, p.144.) This is so whether C makes his move as a pre-emptive threat in order to discourage resistance of whether he actually applies a sanction in order to prevail.

This leads to an opposite position to that proposed by William Riker in his article, 'Some Ambiguities in the Notion of Power' (Riker, 1964). I take his argument to be as specious as it is subtle. Riker's main idea is the distinction between two concepts of power. The first is *ego-oriented* and based on the capacity to influence the result (of a decision-making process). The second is *other-oriented* and rests on the ability to control the action of other social agents (Riker, 1964, p.344). Each of these two concepts implies a different meaning of the concept of cause (Riker, 1964, pp.346-7). The causality that corresponds to the other-oriented kind of power is the naïve idea of what Riker calls 'recipe causality'. This involves an exclusive preoccupation with the means that an actor can put to work to obtain a given effect. The ego-oriented version of power on the other hand presupposes a more sophisticated handling of causality understood as what Riker calls 'necessary-and-sufficient condition causality'.

This may well be an elegant argument, and yet I find Riker's play on the opposition of the two concepts unacceptable. It is rather surprising to see an author as versed in questions of method as Riker satisfied with a definition of causality that is obviously inadequate for empirical social research, even if the expression 'necessary and sufficient condition' is the exact equivalent of the concept of mutual implication: if A then B and if B then A.

It was long ago demonstrated, notably by Lazarsfeld, that it is practical and convenient, in accounting for the connections between social phenomena, to substitute probability statements for statements embodying a pattern of necessary relations (see Lazarsfeld, 1970, p.121). Terms like 'necessarily' or 'always' are to be replaced by less absolute words like 'generally' or 'most frequently'. Hubert M. Blalock argued along similar lines when he wrote that 'in real-life situations we seldom encounter instances where B is present if and only if A is also present' and concluded emphatically that 'the use of "necessary and sufficient" terminology may work well for the logician but not the social scientist' (Blalock, 1964, p.30). We actually meet only cases of weak implication (Boudon, 1971a, p.27). The logic of mutual implication with which Riker works without making it explicit takes the attenuated form in a social-political reality; if A, then in most cases B; and if B, then in most cases A. Similarly, when this weak mutual implication is translated into the language of sets, there are no longer totally excluded combinations but only *rare* combinations.

Riker is seduced by the paradigm of the minimum winning coalition, each of whose members is *necessary* to produce the outcome but the last person to join—the eleventh-hour recruit—is alone identifiable as *sufficient*. Apart from the fact that it is not always easy in an election to determine who (or which group) gave the last and decisive push (McFarland, 1969, p.11), it is to be noted that this imagery relates to coalition formation and not to the actual result, that is the decision flowing from the vote of the participants. The stress here is on the methods of controlling the result of the vote (i.e. the formation of a majority) rather than on the outcome itself. Unintentionally, we arrive back at the degenerate type of 'recipe causality' that Riker set out to avoid at all costs.

Riker's position in this matter thus appears both strained and imprudent. It is strained to the extent to which it leads straight to the complexities of mutual implication and bypasses the case of simple implication (if A then B) which in our field of study usually takes the weaker form of: if A then in most cases B. And it is imprudent if it is true that there are no necessary causes to be found in the kind of analysis typical of the social sciences. Hayward Alker reminds us of this when he prefers to speak of 'potential sufficient cause' in relation to the concept of power or more precisely in relation to the generic and classical concept of power to which he adheres (Alker, Deutsch and Stoetzel, 1973, p.311, n.3).

Riker is also at fault, I believe, in incautiously setting his whole analysis of power over others in the framework of an impoverished concept of causality, seen as limited to simple maxims for action. His evaluation also strikes me as unfair with regard to the 'formal definitions' of Dahl (1957), Cartwright (1959) and Karlsson (1962) which he especially criticizes, because the criticism reveals a basically reductionist attitude. It demands that the study of the *inherent* aspects of the exercise of power, which has proved useful and even indispensable, be converted to a pure study of *pragmatic action rules*. Power in real life exists in a context of interaction. Trying to discover how power is sustained and exercised is therefore a scientifically legitimate task for sociologists and political scientists.

It definitely does not seem very fruitful to contrast a rigorous type of causality based on mutual implication with a pragmatic concept of causality seen from the perspective of the exigencies of action and no longer from the perspective of precise empirical knowledge. First, the type of situation analysed by social scientists is such that it has to be interpreted in terms of weak implication and they are led to work in terms of probability, though this manifestly fails to satisfy the criterion of causality conceived as a necessary and sufficient condition. And second, studying the exercise of power over others is not a camouflaged return to the level of 'recipe causality' but an integral part of the study of the phenomenon.

Thus the first type of causality is too ambitious for the social sciences while the second would correspond to a misrepresentation for polemical ends of the underlying methodological orientation of a view he does not share. Neither of these types of causality is to be found in actual analyses of power, so it is not acceptable to make play with it in the way that Riker does, and still less to use this opposition as the focus of his critical examination.

This conclusion should not, however, be rashly extrapolated to reject the distinction established by Riker between two essential conceptions of power, a distinction whose relevance I shall seek to test. We may remember here that each conception is formed out of two elements. One of them concerns the assumed object of power and the other the actor taken as a point of reference. In the theoretical perspective that Riker prefers and which is illustrated by the Shapley-Shubik index (1954) or to a lesser extent by J. G. March's (1957) formalization, the accent is on the results and power is attributed to Ego. The other tradition of thought represented by Karlsson and less markedly by Cartwright and Dahl focuses on power exercised over others and puts it in the centre of the stage. Riker's distinction implies that the first choice (action for results *or* action over others) predetermines the second (reference to Ego *or* reference to Alter). Our priority must therefore be to examine this fundamental dichotomy.

In the abstract this distinction between the capacity to determine the final decision and the ability to control the behaviour of others is perfectly acceptable to the extent that it isolates two *analytically* independent dimensions. But its great disadvantage is its empirical inadequacy in the context of power. Dissociating these two dimensions, however useful it may be at the level of conceptual clarification, effectively hides the fact that I consider essential, namely that they are always both present wherever power is. They are therefore united in a certain way which we shall have to specify. Riker sticks to the separation of elements, although Alker *et al.* (1973, p.311) have suggested that we ought to concentrate upon the form in which they are synthesized within the context of power. March was certainly on the right track when he proposed to use as a criterion for influence (in the broad sense) the capacity to restrict the range of possible outcomes. Thus, role $R_1$ will be considered to be more influential than role $R_2$ in relation to a given behaviour $B_1$ if, when $R_1$ adopts the behaviour $B_1$, the range of outcomes is narrowed more than it is when $R_2$ adopts $B_1$. Similarly the behaviour $B_1$ would be said to be more influential than the behaviour $B_2$ in respect to some role $R_1$ if, within this role, the behaviour $B_1$ narrows the range of outcomes more than does the behaviour $B_2$. It is the reduction of the set of possible outcomes that marks out influence. Unfortunately, March's notion of influence remains a generic one, since he does not study the specific modes of this determination or the types of interaction to which they correspond; he stops in mid-course.

Although this criterion concentrates on the right phenomenon, it does not suffice on its own to characterize power. It does not in my view obtain its full significance unless it is used together with another indicator, and it would be still better to speak of a combination of these two indicators in a single criterion so as to emphasize the intimate connection between them in the workings of power itself. The reduction to which March wants to direct our attention concerns essentially the outcomes that Alter is liable to obtain. We could therefore say provisionally that power is constituted by a limitation of the range of outcomes that Alter is liable to obtain, or rather *by the restriction of the range of courses of action open to Alter.*

Such a perspective leads us to reject outright Riker's second opposition, between other-directed power and self-directed power, the second of which totally fails to account for the relational character of power. It must not be confused with the simple ownership of a resource, as Dahl as shown. No sort of power whatever can be attributed to an actor A without paying attention to his ability to control more or less the actions of B (or of C or of B and C). We have here an essentially rhetorical dichotomy. If we take up again Riker's imperfect terminology, we must say that power is inevitably directed towards others in virtue of the simple fact that it is always exercised *over* other social actors and at their expense.

Since Riker founded his whole argument on the radical dissociation of two elements (determination of results *v.* action over others) that in reality are fused within power and its exercise, this artificial contrast cannot but lead to an impasse. This is why the attribution of a special kind of causality to each of Riker's two major conceptions of power is illusory, however ingenious it may be. It is illusory not only because these types of causality do not match actual research done in the social sciences, but also because of the artificial character of the oppositions and asymmetries applied throughout the analysis of power itself.

The shortcomings of Riker's analysis show how rash was his claim to have established a relation of equivalence between well-defined types of causality and theoretical approaches that deal specifically with power. Such a quest for a correspondence relation of one term to another impoverishes or, indeed, sterilizes the concept of power. This is the conclusion I wish to draw from this examination, but Riker's article might also give us an opportunity to emphasize the distance between a simple analogy of the sort with which he is satisfied and a real analogical paradigm. (According to Raymond Boudon (1971b, p.162), the latter is characterized by the fact that explicanda are not deduced from a theory but drawn by analogy from a body of knowledge in another field.) Riker suggests in the final paragraph of his article that the concept of power ought no longer to be used. 'Ought we to redefine it in a clear way or ought we to banish it altogether? My initial emotion, I confess, is that we ought to banish it. But this suggestion will, I am sure, find little sympathy among my colleagues.' (Riker, 1964, p.348.) Is this not admitting the unsatisfactory character and lack of empirical applicability of a generic notion of power understood in terms of causality? Riker is not the only one to express his disenchantment with power. Although his article does not perhaps entail such a sceptical conclusion, March also, although he proposes a rigorous reordering, finds the concept of power deceptive and its explicative value relatively small (J. G. March, 1966, p.70).

The reader may feel a little alienated by some of my objections, inspired above all by realism, to nominal definitions of power that, being deliberately chosen, must first and foremost satisfy the criterion of usefulness (see Bierstedt, 1959). The problem lies not in this or that particular formulation but in the underlying notions. Hence, all these formulations have been scientifically disappointing and our reservations are justified *a posteriori* by the mediocrity—honestly admitted by the proponents—of the results obtained by this system of explanation. Those who have insisted on the classical and constricting forms of the causal model at all costs have lost sight of some of the most significant dimensions of power at the same time.

There remains only one apparent paradox that needs to be at once stressed and clarified. On the one hand, the notion of power is conceived in such a fashion as to be *operational* in the framework of a causal analysis in the guise of an intervening variable. On the other hand, it is not really *fruitful* in this respect. It is not of course a matter of questioning the general requirement—evoked by the term 'operational'—of adapting our concepts to the exigencies of research. But as our example illustrates (in contrast to the tenets of methodology) a concept can be at once operational and of little relevance. That is to say, it may be usable in research without being useful in virtue of its position in explicatory schemata. The fact that someone disposes of a whole battery of operational concepts does not therefore constitute an element of success and is far from always being a guarantee of it. This elementary truth appears to me to be sometimes forgotten in the particular case of power. More than one author has moved on to the specific *measures* of power, especially in the shape of indexes, without previously isolating by conceptual clarification the *dimensions* themselves to which the measure is to be applied. (See, for an example, Riker and Ordeshook, 1973, especially pp.154–75.) In fact, as J.G.March (1966, pp.68-9) has stressed, the move to measurement should not always be made, because it raises a problem that is prior to the construction of any index. This step must not be taken until the measurement can be based on a firm conceptual foundation that clearly relates to theoretical choices. It is precisely the fragility of this conceptual base that, together with the doubtful analogy between power and cause, constitutes the biggest weakness of the conception of power presupposed in Riker's article and revealed in all his writings. Measurement is not a process that could ever be totally independent of theory, as Bell (1969, p.26) has pointed out. It is the inadequacy of work at this theoretical level, on which the choice of a measure should be founded, that chiefly explains the disappointment of some representative contributors to research in this area.

The concept of power—and with it the vernacular language whose ambiguities it reflects—should not be allowed to become the scapegoat. As March observed, we must instead emphasize the limitations of the work so far done on the conceptualization and the measure of power without at the same time denying their contribution. Perhaps a second generation of research projects can rehabilitate the concept of power if they are conducted from different perspectives. This at least is what I hope to suggest in the next section.

## 2 POWER AND FORCE

If the preceding considerations were in the main critical they have still led me to distinguish two central characteristics of power. One is the reduction of the range of action open to others, the other the possibility of using sanctions. But I have not yet outlined precisely the nature of these sanctions; nor, more generally, have I specified with the necessary clarity the means and mechanisms by which power is exercised. It is by the (adverse) effects on Alter that we recognize power, and we have at the best only an imprecise intuition of the real connection between the application of sanctions by Ego and the consequences observed in Alter. In order to get a picture of the phenomena of power that may be at the same time more complete and more clear it remains to analyse more closely the typical mode of operation. To do this we must elucidate the relation between power and force.

It is to Robert Bierstedt's credit that he did not evade this difficulty in his effort to achieve terminological precision by comparing the concept of power with some cognate notions (Bierstedt, 1950, 1957). But he still did not succeed in overcoming the difficulty because he defined each of the two concepts in terms of the other, 'power' as 'latent force' and 'force' as 'manifest power' (Bierstedt, 1950, p.733). Because of the circularity of the definition it does not really tell us anything about the relation between power and force. Besides it seems difficult to speak of power as manifest on the basis of a single, one-shot, employment of force—an isolated act of physical coercion. The power relation is not limited to any single occasion and to any single instant but inheres in a certain kind of situation, and implies some minimum of temporal continuity. Power thus has a certain degree of generality, as Parsons (1963b) has rightly emphasized, even if he was wrong to see this as an indication of its symbolic character. Perhaps we could also reproach Bierstedt with failing to make a distinction between the most typical case of power, where the threat of sanctions for non-compliance precedes their actual employment, and the limiting case constituted by the 'direct' use of force without warning. Finally, we may well be unhappy that, on Bierstedt's formulation, pure power (as distinct from manifest power) invokes force in only a latent form.

We are even more inclined to deplore the fact that, when Bierstedt employs this notion of latency for further analysis, it gives rise to an ill-founded distinction between power and force such that power is reduced to the sheer *capacity* to apply sanctions while force is envisaged as their actual *application* (Bierstedt, 1950, p.734). Such a dichotomy between a capacity and its actual employment seems to me unacceptable. It is as arbitrary as would be a separation between the dexterity of a workman and the actual manual work in which he exercised his dexterity. This will be the main line of my criticism, which I can develop by reference to a different distinction between power and force, this time the one drawn from Bachrach and Baratz (1963).

Perhaps it sounds odd to relate them to Bierstedt in view of the theses put forward by him to which they have explicitly refused to subscribe; but in the course of my analysis I shall show that, despite their rejecting certain theses out of hand, there are some similarities between their conception and that of Bierstedt. According to Bachrach and Baratz, four dimensions of power and force can be distinguished.

(1)    The power relation is expressed by the submission of B to A. A comes out the winner in a confrontation, while the use of force is a response to disobedience or recalcitrance on the part of the other.

(2)    Consequently, whereas, in the case of a relation based on force, A alone decides the action to be adopted, in the case of a power relation B retains the possibility to choose (between obedience and non-compliance).

(3)    On the basis of this, one can oppose the 'rationality' of power to force, since force does not possess this property.

(4)    Finally, it may happen that force, unlike power, may be non-relational, for example where B is killed by being shot in the back by a thief he does not see (Bachrach and Baratz, 1963, p.103 in Bell, 1969).

In this perspective, power has only one weapon, simple threat of the use of sanctions, and success (which it gains, by definition) is based on nothing but it, or rather on nothing but its credibility. Conversely, the actual use of sanctions would mean implicitly admitting defeat in that the threat had not sufficed to produce the intended effect. It would thus be, in as far as it indicated a setback, fundamentally foreign to power.

This is obviously a web of sophistry. It would seem convenient to specify in advance the criteria by which (and especially the period over which) victories and defeats are to be judged. Bachrach and Baratz themselves restrict the scope of their own argument quite a lot by admitting that 'if the resort to force against one party effectively deters noncompliance on the part of others, now or in the future, the employment of sanctions becomes a *fresh declaration of the existence of power*'. (Bell, 1969, p.104.)

Let us now modify the last words of this conditional proposition and suppose that the application of sanctions does not deter—or not only deter—the 'witnesses' C, D, etc., but deters actor B himself from any impulse to disobey from that moment on. Clearly A's first objective, the submission of B, is thus attained, and, even if its success was not obtained at the very beginning, his power cannot be doubted. Certain B has not given in *immediately* to the mere threat and this 'deferred obedience' can sometimes be a nuisance to A, especially if the delay threatens the achievement of some ultimate objective by throwing out the timetable of his overall strategy in which B's compliance is only one step. Thus we are led to distinguish variable degrees of power as a function of the speed with which B has 'adjusted' his behaviour to the designs of A and the consequences liable to result from this greater or less speed. But this differentiation in terms of more or less—amounting to a measurement—must not be confused (as by Bachrach and Baratz) with a difference in nature, a distinction between two independent phenomena.

Let us go one step further and suppose now that the sanctions applied (such as imprisonment) radically preclude any insubordination of the part of B. A succeeds by this measure in preventing any interference by B with his own projects. Even if his success is only in a sense negative it is none the less the outcome of a power relation. Doubtless this situation is not as desirable to A as would be compliance based on pure threat, especially if with B's 'collaboration' he might have obtained his objectives with greater ease or certainty. But one does not abandon a field of power simply because one recognizes that it can present itself under two fundamentally different aspects according to whether A does or does not obtain by coercion the active 'complicity' of B. And it is legitimate to measure the degree of power by the extent of this complicity.

I do not wish to retain this dichotomy between power understood as dissuasion (by the use of threats alone) and force understood as punishment (by the actual use of sanctions). Dissuasion is not always a result of threats alone but, as we have seen, may also result from the actual application of sanctions. It can become manifest in the behaviour of both the 'witnesses' and the 'victim'. This is enough already to throw some doubt on the fruitfulness of such an opposition, which, furthermore, can also help to conceal the basis upon which the threats rest in so far as they are not 'in the air', and which guarantees their credibility.

Bachrach and Baratz totally fail to see the privileged connection between the threat addressed to B and the capacity to resort to force which alone gives it any weight. If the announced sanctions are effectively at the disposal of A, B does not normally ignore this. Also there is a tendency for the holder of power to play on two registers and change from one to the other according to the situation: that is, from a simple 'prohibition' to the punishment of the disobedient party. Certainly we ought to recognize, as Bachrach and Baratz to their credit do, the role played in complex societies by threats and their widespread efficiency. But we must not reduce power to that by cutting it away from its indispensable support, the control of force.

My refusal to dissociate power and force absolutely must lead me to reject the fundamental proposition put forward by Bachrach and Baratz and the corollaries of that proposition. It is artificial, because it is too extreme, to insist on a sharp contrast in terms of freedom between a power relation and one of force, and to say that when A exercises power B retains freedom of action, whereas when A uses force all possibility of choice on the part of B is taken away. It is also indicative of a certain naivete—or, to be more polemical, or an ideological bias—to draw such a contrast, if I am right in saying that Ego's power always manifests itself in a restriction of the courses of action open to Alter. A continuum could therefore be formed according to the size of this reduction, extending from the limiting case in which all alternatives are excluded (say, certain death) to more minor but still detrimental limitations. Precisely because it does not always use the same weapons, power should be seen as covering a whole area, at the core of which the use of force occupies a relatively important place—not one end of a continuum as Bachrach and Baratz erroneously believe.

Their insistence on the 'rationality' of power calls for a deeper analysis; but, while proposing to take up this problem in a different context, I shall rest content here with expressing some reservations about the use without preliminary clarification of a notion whose significance has been obscured by careless usage. In this way I wish to show an ambiguity in the use made of the concept by Bachrach and Baratz, for whom rationality is related now to B's choice and now simply to his perception of the demands formulated by A (first dimension in Bell, 1969, p.103; second dimension in the table on p.107).

Finally, we may be surprised to see Bachrach and Baratz giving special status to situations where force does not really occur within a social relationship, situations where a social relationship is either only implicit or is totally absent. These are cases, however genuine they may be, that are extreme and are far from being the most significant. As Talcott Parsons reminds us, it is essentially as an 'aspect of social interaction' that force gains its true significance and deserves the attention of the social scientist (Parsons, 1967, p.265). Parsons's reflections on this theme show a greater interest in clarifying the notion of force than do those of either Bierstedt or Bachrach and Baratz. This concern for terminological rigour, which is characteristic of the best parts of Parsons's work, first of all leads him to stress that force is a 'way' of acting before being an instrument or a 'means'. He then throws light on the intimate relation between force and physical constraint. And finally he distinguishes three functions of force: from the point of view of Ego (or A) they are respectively dissuasion, punishment and symbolic demonstration of the control of a situation (Parsons, 1967, p.266). Despite these presuppositions (and the first point particularly, from which perhaps fails to draw all the consequences), Parsons still does not in my view succeed in illuminating the relation between power and force. This is basically the result of his allegiance to one analogy that is too limited and, one may add, too mechanistic. That is the analogy between power and money. This analogy has often been discussed and I have myself questioned its fruitfulness elsewhere (Chazel, 1964). Certainly it is true to say that the application of negative sanctions would not always and necessarily lead us to call it 'force', since that word may be reserved for the more serious penalties. But perhaps it is less legitimate to deduce directly and, so to speak, automatically its degree of importance from its relative frequency. On the basis of such a deduction, Parsons is quick to affirm that the use of force is not important in complex societies (see especially Parsons, 1967, p.296).

The visible occurrence of force is not the only relevant criterion of its role, which is not restricted to the critical situations where it is in the limelight. It also occupies an important place as a *guarantee* or *caution* for other negative sanctions while it remains in some way off stage. It appears rather difficult under these conditions to turn it simply into a 'reserve' weapon comparable to a 'reserve' currency, since in reality it is always present whatever the sanctions actually used. Thus, Parsons stretches the slender links which in my view unite power and force so as to arrive at a metaphorical linkage—based essentially on the image of a reserve—between force and gold (see especially Parsons, 1967, pp.277-8). He increasingly loses sight of the central fact that power is a *function* of the control of force, even if it is not a matter, as he rightly says, of an elementary link of a linear kind (Parsons, 1967, p.272), and if other intervening variables will have to be introduced into the construction of necessarily complex models. He also progressively reduces force to a pure means of enforcement of the law, in contrast to his initial intuition: 'Force in power systems is, we suggest, a particular means of enforcement.' (Parsons, 1967, p.277.)

At the very least this way of looking at it allows us to avoid the difficulty that arises from postulating a hermetic seal between coercion on the one hand and legitimacy on the other. Robert Dahl himself failed to escape this. For the sake of the *analytical* independence of these two dimensions he denies their possible *empirical* interdependence, even though this characterizes so many situations (Dahl, 1963, p.19). This supposed empirical opposition—between on the one hand illegitimate coercion (implying an eventual use of force or in any case based upon such a use) and on the other hand legitimate authority—indicates a dangerous Manichaeism, even if it comforts out tendencies towards conformist acquiescence. It consists in 'idealizing' legitimate power, in misunderstanding its bases and its weapons. It ignores Weber's insight that is no less domination for having the trappings of legitimacy. This is what Weber formulated in the context of his general presentation of types of domination when he concluded that all kinds of domination seek to arouse or to maintain the belief in their 'legitimacy' (Weber, 1964b, p.325).

Parsons's article has other merits. Adhering to a long tradition (e.g. Laswell and Kaplan, 1950), he associates power with negative sanctions, the more severe deprivations being associated with 'force'. And he adds that these sanctions affect others by a more or less profound change in their situation. More precisely, for Parsons it is 'coercion' that corresponds to this action or change of another's situation by means of negative sanctions, but this is intimately connected with power (Parsons, 1967, pp.269-70,310,364). The question formulated at the beginning of this section about the nature of the sanctions connected with power has thus found an answer adequate enough for us to adhere to.

I am not pretending to have totally and rigorously answered the other more ambitious question that concerned the means and mechanisms of action inherent to power. As it is, I believe we can say that power has two registers at its disposal and sometimes plays on threats, whereas at other times it proceeds actually to apply sanctions. In both types of relation—this is what I have tried at least to shows—force plays an essential role apart from its direct application. It either *sustains* the credibility of threats or it *guarantees* the use of other and less brutal forms of sanction.

### 3 BY WAY OF CONCLUSION

Let me draw together the main threads that have guided these reflections in which I have tried to clarify the concept of power. These can be summarized in four propositions.

(1) It is not helpful to conceive of power as no more than a simple intervening variable between a stimulus and a response, available for general use in examining modifications in behaviour or (more ambitiously) analysing the mechanisms of social choice.

(2) Therefore, it is advisable to go beyond the generic and common notion of power, in virtue of which power would describe only the capacity to achieve ends. Rather we ought to try, through the analysis of its mode (or modes) of action, to discern the effects of Ego's action on Alter. From this perspective I think I can assert that power consists in a reduction of the range of possible courses of action open to others.

(3) This limitation is imposed on B (Alter) by A (Ego) either through threats of sanctions to be applied or through actually employing them. So power does not reduce itself to threats, even though threats belong to it just as much as does punishment. And of course power cannot be reduced to punishment either. Power is defined by the combined—which does not mean simultaneous—use of threats and punishments. Thus A moves from the one or the other according to what the situation seems to demand. Let me finally point out that, even when it is not overt (directly employed), force is equally present, forming the basis of threats and the guarantee for other sanctions.

(4) Sanctions that are tied to the exercise of power affect B's situation negatively. We may therefore call them negative situational sanctions.

It occurred to me as useful in finishing off this chapter to propose a definition of power in which the principal elements of the concept I have tried to outline are brought together. My formulation is as follows:

> *Power consists of the probability that a social unit A will obtain from a social unit B (or from social units B and C) compliance with its strategy by reducing the range of courses of action open (or permitted) to B. This is achieved through negative situational sanctions which may be simply invoked as threats or actually applied.*

This definition is constructed around three essential criteria:
 (1) the probability of compliance,
 (2) the reduction of possibilities for action offered to B, and
 (3) the threat or the carrying out of negative situational sanctions, which allow a ready means for the measurement of the importance of deprivations risked or really suffered.

Equally, the extent of power can be determined by the number of persons belonging to the social unit B. And it is also possible to refine this indicator by taking into account not only the members of B but also the value objects held by this social unit. From the point of view here adopted, nothing after all prevents us from inquiring into the speed with which B is subjugated or even the degree of reorientation in his behaviour arising from the result of the threat or as a result of sanctions actually used.

This shows that our definition does not depart from any of the seven dimensions elaborated by Dahl in his analysis of the so-called 'Newtonian' criteria (Dahl, 1968, p.414) even though it is obviously biased in favour of some of them and could lead to a reformulation of others. Perhaps, however, it needs to be clarified by a more general analysis, in which 'choice models' and 'coercive models' would be compared. Immense difficulties even more than lack of time have so far prevented me from accomplishing this task.

# 5

# Power: an Economic Analysis

BRIAN BARRY

## 1 INTRODUCTION

Although controversy continues to rage about the proper definition and analysis of power, we find no great difficulty in understanding in a general way what is meant by ascriptions of power. The Norwegian government, for example, in a brochure for visitors entitled *Glimpses of Norway*, tells us: 'Today, Norway is a constitutional monarchy, with political power centered in the 150 member parliament (Storting).' (Royal Ministry of Foreign Affairs, n.d. p.3.) Obviously, political scientists might not be entirely happy with this. Stein Rokkan, in his contribution to *Political Oppositions in Western Democracies* (Dahl, 1966, pp.70–115) speaks of 'numerical democracy and corporate pluralism', suggesting that much of the power of the Storting has been delegated to corporate groups so that in practice the Storting often merely ratifies their deals. But even so the statement that political power is centred in the Storting serves to distinguish Norway from, for example, contemporary Chile, where it would not be true to say that the National Assembly has any political power at all, since it has been dissolved by the military junta. And we know roughly what is meant by saying that in Chile the President and the Assembly both *had* power until a group of generals *seized* power. One crude but practical criterion of power would be to ask: suppose you were an officer of the CIA or some multinational corporation with large funds available for buying favours in terms of public policy, what kind of person would it be rational to spend the money on? And it does seem reasonable to say that you could do worse than buy some members of the Storting (if any were for sale) but would be wasting your money in Chile on anything except a member of the government or perhaps the armed forces.

Robert Dahl's (1957) 'intuitive idea of power', in his essay on 'The Concept of Power', was that 'A has power over B to the extent that he can get B to do something that B would not otherwise do' (Bell, 1969, p.80). Power is thus the ability to cause things to happen when the object is actions by other people. Bertrand Russell, in his book *Power* (Russell, 1938), goes further and in effect identifies power with the ability to cause things to happen. He equates the use of power with the production of intended effects. The ability to cause actions of other people (social power) is then a sub-class of power in general. The word 'power' is indeed employed in this general sense, as when we say that a man is 'powerfully built': we mean that he has strong muscles and is thus able to produce more intended effects by his own exertions than most people can. But there is no sense in looking for a general theory of power in this sense. We should simply be asking for a general theory of the ability to cause things to happen. Nor is it much more sensible to look for a general theory of social as against natural power. We should then be asking for a general theory of the ability to get people to do things.

What we have to do is divide up the phenomenon of getting other people to do things so that each method of getting people to do things can be analysed in the terms appropriate to it. And I think that as a first shot at this Talcott Parsons's division of the methods into four categories has much to commend it. He calls these methods 'activation of commitments', 'persuasion', 'inducement' and 'coercion' (Bell, 1969, p.258). I propose to put inducement and coercion together but then add a further category, physical constraint, which has often been included—for example by Hobbes. I now want to explain these four categories and show that each calls for different techniques of analysis.

## 2 FOUR VARIETIES OF POWER

Getting somebody to do something by 'activating a commitment' is a matter of cashing in on some norm that he already has to the effect that he *ought* to act in accord with a demand from a certain source. If B accepts a norm giving authority to A, A has the ability to 'activate commitments' for B. To take a central political example, let us say that someone has a general belief that he ought to obey the law of the country in which he lives. A new law is passed by whatever procedure constitutes the 'rule of recognition' for a valid law in the country, and the person obeys it. Obviously, this process raises questions about the circumstances under which people acquire and retain such norms. The relevant studies are in the sociology of law and more generally of legitimate authority.

The second way of getting somebody to do something is to bring about a change of mind so that he does now want to do it. In principle we can distinguish between on one hand supplying him with new information (whether true or false, sincerely or insincerely believed by the giver) which leads him to conclude that a different action will be a more effective means of reaching his goals, and on the other hand working on his goals by some method or another so that they become different. But in practice the distinction is often not clear because many goals are valued only (or partially) as means to something further. In any case, it is apparent that the kind of analytic tools necessary to discuss this phenomenon (Parsons's 'persuasion') are those relevant to the psychology and sociology of attitude change, the sociology of knowledge, propaganda analysis and so on.

The third process involving power that I want to mention is one that Parsons does not. (It is, of course, characteristic that, compared with most discussions, he should include a normative conception that is not usually mentioned and leave out a conception involving the direct use of physical force.) Sir George Cornewall Lewis, in his *Remarks on the Use and Abuse of Some Political Terms*, said that the word power 'appears to signify the possession of the means of influencing the will of another, either by persuasion or threats; or of constraining his person by means of physical force' (Lewis, 1898, p.92). This process is embodied in the usage of 'overpowering' someone and also (less explicitly) in that of 'having someone in one's power'. Notice that Lewis carefully sets off this kind of power from others in that it does not act on the will but directly reduces the range of actions open to the person over whom power is being exercised. By holding fast to this distinction we can see that power in this sense need not be embodied in anything as dramatic as chains or prison walls. If someone wants to do something that involves his travelling by car and I immobilize the only car available to him then I have prevented him from doing what he wanted more surely than if I had, say, threatened to burn down his house if he went.

An important case of physical constraint in this extended sense is that of reducing the capability of another to resist the imposition of sanctions, increasing his need to accept offered advantages, reducing his capacity for doing similar things to oneself or reducing his capacity to impose sanctions on oneself. Thus, in a war one side may improve its relative bargaining position by destroying the other side's anti-missile system so that its cities are more vulnerable, by destroying its stores of food so that the offer of food in return for compliance is more attractive, or (covering the last two categories) by destroying the other side's offensive capabilities. Thus, physical constraint may be used as an instrument for increasing power in the fourth sense, which I now discuss.

The fourth and final method by which one person (A) can get another (B) to do something is for A to change the incentives facing B. A can do this by attaching the promise of something B desires to gain to some action that he would not otherwise propose to do (Parsons's 'inducement'). Or A can do it by attaching the threat of something B desires to avoid to some action which he would otherwise propose to do (Parsons's 'coercion'). It is possible to combine a promise and a threat in respect of the same action.

This method of getting someone to do something he would not otherwise do is different from the 'activation of commitments' in that it appeals purely to self-interest. In effect, A says to B: 'I will make it worth your while to do X'. It differs from the second method–Parsons's 'persuasion'—because it does not alter the attractiveness of the action in question in the eyes of B. In itself, the action demanded by A remains unattractive. What happens is that, if B's behaviour is successfully modified by A, this comes about because B has been convinced that A will provide rewards or sanctions, or refrain from providing them, according to the way B acts; and that the balance struck when he takes account of the direct effect of his own actions or inactions and the consequential actions or inactions of A is such as to make it more advantageous to do what A demands than not to do it. Finally, this fourth process of inducement and coercion differs from the third one in that, although force may be used, it is used in order to affect the will rather than to affect the capabilities. The distinction, which is central to Clausewitz's analysis, is between changing someone's choice among his options from what it would otherwise have been and actually removing some options from him.

For many purposes—ethical, legal and (as we shall notice later) practical—threats have to be treated as different from promises. But for analytical purposes we can assimilate threats and promises into one theory. This is important because it means we can handle the case where A combines the two and says: 'If you don't comply with my demand I'll do something you don't like but if you do comply then I'll do something you do like.' As Alexander George has observed (George *et al.* 1971), foreign policy-makers tend to neglect the combined use of sticks and carrots—though one gathers from *The Godfather* that the Mafia have encapsulated the theory in the immortal Brando remark, 'I'll make him an offer he can't refuse'.

This fourth variety of power lends itself naturally to theoretical development from within an 'economic' or 'rational choice' framework. It falls within the province of ordinary economic theory, since an exchange in a market is in effect a case in which A promises B that he will do something B likes (give him money or some commodity) provided that B does something he would not otherwise do that A wants him to do (give him some commodity or some money). And obviously the whole subject is centrally related to bargaining theory and to the theory of games.

## 3 POWER AND POLITICAL EXPLANATION

Since power is the *ability* to get people to do things, we can obviously construct a characterization of power corresponding to each of the four methods of getting people to do things that we have just outlined. Thus, power in the first sense is the ability to activate commitments: the capacity at one's own discretion to get people to do what they would not otherwise do by invoking some standing commitment to obey some source of instructions. Power in relation to the second process is the capacity at one's own discretion to change people's perceptions or goals by some means or other so that they want to do something they would not otherwise do. Power in relation to the third process is the capacity physically to restrain or constrain the actions of others. And, finally, power in the fourth sense is the possession by one actor (A) of the means of modifying the conduct of another actor (B) by means of an expectation in B that one or more of the alternative actions available to him will (with some probability) result in reward or punishment brought about by A. The exercise of power on a given occasion is the threat or promise by A of employing his means of modifying the conduct of B contingently upon B's doing some action (or one of a set of actions) out of the alternatives open to him.

There are two points about this fourth variety of power which are worth clearing up at once. First, if A has the means of modifying the behaviour of B by making B better off or worse off contingently upon what B does, it must follow that A also has the ability to make B better off or worse off unconditionally. Thus, if A has power he has the means of making B better off or worse off than he would be if A did not exert himself. But if A in fact chooses to make B better off or worse off unconditionally this is not an exercise of power. The converse relationship usually but not invariably holds: if A can make B better off or worse off unconditionally he can normally also create an expectation in B that he will make him better or worse off depending on B's actions. Thus possession of the means of making someone better off or worse off normally constitutes power, that is to say possession of the means of modifying behaviour. But a prerequisite of there being a connection between the two is the possibility of (i) some kind of communication from A to B and (ii) some kind of system whereby A can find out whether B has in fact complied or not. Thus, as Schelling has suggested, if the families of kidnapped persons were locked up and kept incommunicado, it would make it impossible for kidnappers to get their demands through to their victims (Schelling, 1960, p.39, n.11), and, while the integrity of the secret ballot is believed in, nobody can exercise power over an elector in respect of the way he votes.

Second, following on from this, it should be noted that the communication of threats and promises need not be explicit—all that is needed is that A should be able with some reliability to create an expectation in B that certain acts will have certain consequences brought about by A. This may be done explicitly or implicitly in speech, in writing or even in gesture; or it may be done (where the situation is of an appropriate kind) purely by a sequence of reactions to moves by B. In other words, if every time B does something of one sort something nasty happens to him, or if every time he does something of another sort something nice happens, he is liable or later to get the message, especially if A is visibly behind the nice or nasty things that happen each time.

Power, to repeat, is not an event but a possession. The event that is associated with this possession is the *exercise* of power. A man *has* power over a period of time and during that time he has the means of modifying the behaviour of more or fewer people to a greater or less extent. He *exercises* power at a particular time within that period, in relation to a particular person or persons and in respect of a particular modification of action. The exercise of power may of course be either successful in achieving its object or unsuccessful. Dahl remarks in 'The Concept of Power' (Dahl, 1957) that 'unfortunately, in the English language power is an awkward word, for unlike "influence" and "control" it has no convenient verb form . . .' (Bell *et al.*, 1969, p.80). But this is a mere grammatical deficiency in English (as, for example, the fact that there is no infinitive or past tense of 'must') or does it (like most linguistic phenomena) reflect something about the nature of the concept itself? In the present case, the answer is surely the latter. Since 'power', like 'wealth', refers to something possessed, there is no more sense in regretting the absence of a verb form than there is for regretting that there is no expression 'he wealths'. In both cases everything that can be said logically, given the meaning of the word, can be said with auxiliary verbs: he has power (or he has wealth); he exercised his power (or he spent his wealth).

If politics is, as Harold Lasswell said, the study of 'who gets what, when, how' (Lasswell, 1958) it is easy to see why we should feel that a knowledge of the distribution of power is so basic to the explanation of political events. But a knowledge of the distribution of power is not enough to enable us to predict with complete confidence who will get what. Someone may try to exercise his power but, through lack of skill, fail to alter behaviour in the way he wants. This possibility of slippage is not a defect but is in fact what saves the whole idea from triviality: it means that we have a framework for causal explanation. Weber and Dahl close the logical gap by equating power with the *probability* of one actor's being able to change the behaviour of someone in the direction desired. To say that A got B to do something that B would not otherwise have done because A had power over B becomes as vacuous as saying that someone became angry on a given occasion because he had an irascible temperament, or that opium makes people sleepy because it has the *virtus dormitiva*.

In any case, a complete explanation of 'who gets what' must take account of the fact that there are ways of getting things other than by the exercise of social power. First, you might get what you want by your own unaided efforts (the exercise of natural power). Second, there is the possibility of getting something without exercising power at all: people may simply give you what you want. (We all started our life this way—if we hadn't done we wouldn't be here now.) And, third, if (as I shall suggest later in my analysis of the fourth variety of power) we want to reserve the word 'power' for a relationship in which there is an asymmetry between the costs and benefits of the parties, we shall need a separate category (exchange) for getting what you want by offering equal value—trading on equal terms—though it can be handled as well as the asymmetrical case from within the model to be developed.

But although these three ways of getting things are obviously of great significance in determining the exact form that the 'what' takes, they have rather little importance in determining the relative success of different people or social groups in getting *whatever* it is that they want. As Hobbes pointed out, the distribution of natural power is fairly equal—certainly such inequalities as there are in its distribution are dwarfed by the inequalities that exist in social power. Getting things by being given them is of course important in small groups but again has little effect in producing large inequalities. And exchange, by the definition given which distinguished it from power, has the characteristic of leaving the parties in roughly the same relative positions as they were before. If by 'what' we mean 'how much' in the question 'who gets what, when, how', then is remains true that the distribution of social power is by far the most important determinant.

## 4 THE MEASUREMENT OF COMPLIANCE

Power, we have said, is the possession by A of the means of modifying the conduct of B. To begin with, then, we need some way of talking about how much the conduct of B is modified. In 'The Concept of Power', Dahl throws up his hands over this: there can be nothing except an unsorted list of things that B can be got to do. 'Suppose that I could induce my son to bathe every evening and to brush his teeth before going to bed and that my neighbour could induce his son to serve him breakfast in bed every morning. Are the two responses I can control to be counted as greater than the one response my neighbour can control?' (Bell *et al.* 1969, p.84.) But there is not necessarily any difficulty about this. Surely, if both sons agree that providing breakfast is a bigger chore than bathing and brushing teeth, the neighbour is incontrovertibly obtaining more compliance than is Dahl, if the neighbour is obtaining compliance with the first demand and Dahl with the second demand.

This example is, of course, complicated by the fact that we are asked to compare responses of different people. Even here, as I have suggested, it can be done quite simply in some cases, but Dahl does not even suggest a technique for the easy case of comparing the responses of a single actor. Surely, there is an obvious criterion: A can be said to secure more compliant behaviour from B the more B doesn't like complying with A's demand. Thus, in any area where A and B have some conflict of goals, i.e. where the preference orderings of A and B for outcomes are not identical, we need to begin by constructing a compliance schedule for B. In its most modest form this can consist simply of a listing of all the possible demands that A might make, with at the top the item that B would least mind conceding, and then the other demands in order of increasing reluctance on B's part to accede to them. When a negotiation is being undertaken by agents, the principle will normally brief them in precisely these terms (see Iklé, 1964).

For the purpose of geometrical representation, let us put B's degree of possible compliance on a horizontal axis, with zero compliance on the left and increasing compliance as we move right. In Figure 5.1, 0 represents zero compliance—the

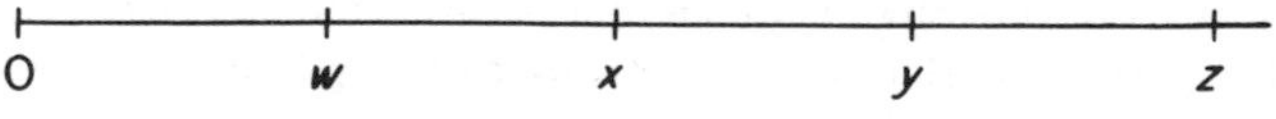

Figure 5.1

baseline against which the degree of compliance is to be measured. It is what B would choose to do if his behaviour were entirely unmodified by A. Moving right from 0, we get to $w$, which is the possible demand of A that B would least mind conceding. Compliance with successive demands as we move right would be increasingly objectionable to B. Let us call this horizontal axis B's compliance line, since it is constructed from B's compliance schedule. It is important to notice that compliance is measured entirely in terms of B's reluctance and takes no account of A's satisfaction. Zero compliance by B may in fact be quite satisfactory to A if what B most wants to do suits A well. And there is no suggestion that greater compliance by B is necessarily preferred by A.

For some purposes an ordinal scale is all that is needed. For other purposes, it is very useful to have a cardinal scale, and the obvious one is to have monetary units. Sometimes, money is actually the subect of A's demand—as in blackmail, kidnapping, protection rackets and all other forms of demanding money with menaces. In many others, money is not itself the subject of the demand, but it would make sense to ask B how much money he would have to be given to just compensate him for complying with each demand. Thus, we can now space out the four demands on a cardinal scale, as in Figure 5.2.

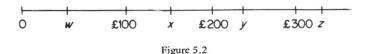

Figure 5.2

It is important to notice that 'getting someone to do what he does not want to do' must be understood to include 'inhibiting someone from doing what he does want to do'. Both are equally an exercise of power. What this means in terms of the compliance line is that the zero point—no compliance by A with B's demands—may be a point at which B is doing something that A doesn't like. The point at which B is *not* doing anything that has any interest for A may, by contrast, be a long way along the compliance line.

Figure 5.3 provides an illustration. Suppose that B owns the land at the bottom of A's garden and has planning permission to erect four houses on it. A would most like the *status quo*, that is to say open space, but if there is to be any building he would

Figure 5.3

prefer one house to two, two to three, and three to four. B's preferences are the inverse, as shown in Figure 5.3: he would most like to build four houses and would like least the continuation of the *status quo*. Suppose now that A somehow has the means to make it worth B's while to desist from building more than three houses. The outcome is that B builds three houses, but he is complying with A's demand to the extent that he does not build the fourth house that he would otherwise have built.

That non-action can constitute compliance as well as can action has an obvious bearing on the 'community power' debate. Inaction where we might have expected action requires just as much explanation as action where we might have expected inaction. In both cases the answer may (though it may not) lie in discovering that the agent is complying with the wishes of someone else. Moreover, it is no refutation of the existence of a 'power élite' to show that some things happen contrary to the wishes of the putative 'power élite'. There may nevertheless be many things that this 'power élite' would intensely dislike that it is able to prevent from happening.

For example, a Labour government in Britain undoubtedly does things that the Confederation of British Industries dislikes. But are there other things that the CBI would dislike much more that the government would like to do and is inhibited from doing because of the sanctions that the members of the CBI could deploy? It seems as if the CBI believes so, since its spokesmen have developed over the years an elaborate Aesopian terminology for threatening Labour governments that unless 'business confidence' is created businessmen will not invest and may contract their operations.

The standard 'behaviouralist' objection to counting inaction as compliance is that we can see compliant action but we can't see compliant inaction. This is an absurd piece of (to use a word of which the behaviouralists are fond) metaphysics. Action and inaction themselves are equally observable. On the other hand, *compliance* is never observable: to say that a piece of behaviour is compliant is always a theoretical statement entailing a counterfactual conditional. But this, again, is the same whether compliance is ascribed to action or to inaction. In one case we say that an actor is doing something that he would otherwise not do. In the other case we say that an actor is refraining from doing something he would otherwise do.

Obviously, this analysis of compliance fits most naturally into the analysis of our fourth variety of power, the ability to modify behaviour by the manipulation of rewards and costs. And it is on this that the rest of this chapter will concentrate. But consider also our first variety of power: your ability to get someone to do what he would not otherwise do by appealing to a norm that says he *ought* to obey you. Surely we wish to be able to say whether his accepting your authority and obeying your order changes his behaviour a lot or a little. And I do not see any alternative way of answering that question except by asking how much he has to give up by obeying, in other words what it costs him, taking what he would have preferred to do in the absence of the order as the baseline.

Our other two varieties of power require rather different treatment. Although both are instances of 'getting someone to do what he wouldn't otherwise have done', neither is a case of 'securing compliance'. In the second case you persuade someone to change his preferences so that his 'zero compliance' position is nearer your own. You do not move him along his compliance line. And in the third case you reduce the number of alternatives open to him (in extreme cases to one) so that what he would originally have chosen to do (his original zero compliance position) is no longer available. In a different way, this is also therefore a matter of changing the compliance line rather than moving someone along it.

The analysis of the second and third varieties of power in terms of changing the compliance line is especially useful where one of these methods of changing behaviour is combined with one of the others. It enables us to think of the methods in relation to one another. Thus, for example, you might (starting from an initial position of sharply opposed goals) modify someone's behaviour in the desired direction partly by changing his mind so that his zero compliance position is no longer as distasteful to you as it was and partly by operating on his new compliance schedule by (say) offering rewards or threatening sanctions. Or, again, you might physically limit the alternatives open to someone (by putting a wall around him, for example) but then, within this restricted range of choices, attempt to elicit a choice he would not otherwise make by the exercise of authority or by offering a reward for certain behaviour.

## 5  GAINS AND LOSSES FROM COMPLIANCE

It is tempting to pursue further the possibility of fitting into a broad framework the special analyses appropriate to each of our four varieties of power. But the space limitations of a chapter (even a long one like this) demand that if I am to reach some definite conclusions I must follow up only one line of analysis. In the rest of this chapter, therefore, I shall concentrate on the analysis of the fourth, 'economic' variety of power.

Obviously, such an analysis must rest on the relations of gains and losses for the actors. We therefore introduce these on the dimension lying at right angles to the compliance line.

The vertical axis then, measures various gains and losses for A and B associated with any given level of compliance on the part of B. The curve that can be drawn in most directly is the curve representing B's loss from each level of compliance with A's demands. Where the same units are used on both axes, the curve becomes quite trivial, since it is just a straight line running at 45° to the horizontal downwards to the right

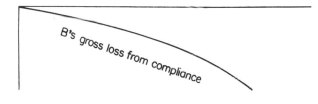

Figure 5.4

from the origin. But the units on the two axes do not, of course, have to be the same. Thus, if compliance is measured in money and loss in cardinal utility, we might suppose the curve to have the shape shown in Figure 5.4. The curve is marked 'B's gross loss from compliance' (the significance of 'gross' will be explained below). The weakest interpretation of the vertical axis is that it measures ordinal utility, in other words that a greater distance from the origin measures a greater loss than a smaller distance (and the same for gains) but that any part of the vertical axis could be arbitrarily stretched or contracted without changing the information given. All we can say here, of course, is that the curve for B's gross loss from compliance will slope down strictly monotonically from the origin. (In other words, it will go down all the way.) But any assertion about its shape would be meaningless. As I shall show, quite a lot can be got out of curves constructed on this very undemanding basis.

Let us now turn to A's gross gain from B's compliance. (The significance of 'gross' will, again, be explained below.) Everything that has been said about the units for measuring B's loss applies here, but the question of the shape is much more interesting.

We could say definitely that the curve for B's gross loss from compliance must slope strictly monotonically down to the right, because this was guaranteed by the rules for constructing the horizontal axis; i.e., the further right, the more distasteful the thing in question. There is no such inevitability about the shape of A's gross gain curve. It is, of course, quite possible for it to slope up to the right strictly monotonically, as in

Figure 5.5

Figure 5.5. This would be a situation in which (within the amount at stake in the issue) there was maximum conflict of interest: the more B dislikes doing something, the more A would like him to do it. Situations which are straight transfer of money or of something else that is valued by both sides (e.g. territory for states) inevitably have this form. So are situations in which B's suffering is itself the source of A's satisfaction.

Many other situations, however, are not of this kind—the fact that B dislikes doing $y$ more than he dislikes doing $x$ does not entail that A would prefer his doing $y$ to his doing $x$. There are then, as it were, pockets of relative congruence of interest within a general context of conflict of interest. For example, T. R. Marmor and D. Thomas have pointed out that in negotiations between doctors and those responsible for running national health schemes, doctors are deeply interested in both more money and in getting a method of payment that they like (in fact, normally what they have been used to). Governments, however, are interested almost entirely in keeping down the cost of the settlement, with the result that the deal always includes virtual adoption of the doctors' preferred position of methods of payment (Marmor and Thomas, 1972).

Graphically, the doctor—government position might look something like Figure

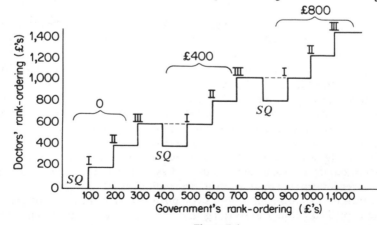

Figure 5.6

5.6. The horizontal axis here represents compliance by the government with the doctors' demands and the curve represents the utility (which need be measured only ordinally) that the doctors get from each level of compliance. If each point on the compliance line represents some combination of total cost and method of payment, the far right end is obviously a very large total cost plus the government's least relished payment method. Assuming that there is a conflict of goals over payment methods as well as total costs, but that the government cares less about payment methods

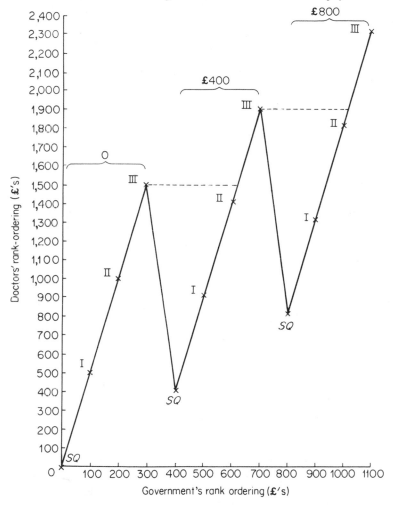

Figure 5.7

relatively to costs that do the doctors, we get the first trough (from the left) where the government, having begun by conceding on methods of payment, starts giving away more money; the second trough represents the same thing at a higher cost. On the figure it is imagined that there are three possible concessions on methods (I, II, III) and two on pay (£400, £800). If the concessions on methods are thought by the

78

government to trade off against £100, £200 and £300 respectively, we get a compliance line as shown; and if the concessions on methods are worth £200, £400 and £600 respectively to the doctors, we get a curve for the doctors like that shown. This is, of course, fairly mild coincidence of interest. If there is greater disparity in valuation between the parties, we get bigger dips in the curve. Thus, if the doctors value the three payment methods at £500, £1,000 and £1,500, we get Figure 5.7. Of course, in both these cases the thing most disliked by the government is still the thing most wanted by the doctors, but this is by no means inevitable. A blackmailer, for example, may be able to drive his victim to suicide but he would sooner stop short of exercising that degree of power at the point where his victim is paying as much as possible. We may thus often get a turning point on the curve which does not again change direction or which at any rate has no higher peak to the right of it (see Figures 5.8 and 5.9).

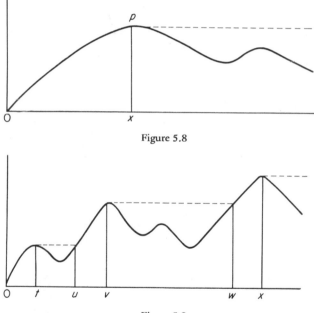

Figure 5.8

Figure 5.9

   The dotted horizontal lines in Figures 5.6–5.9 are there to assist the exposition of a simple theorem: that no point to the right of and below any other point on the gain-from-compliance curve can be an equilibrium position for a settlement. In other words, the sections of curve under a dotted line can be ignored as feasible outcomes. Thus, in Figure 5.8, there is no advantage to A in securing more compliance than $Ox$, since he can gain no more than $px$ and beyond $x$ stands to gain less. And in Figure 5.9, if the most compliance A can get is a little less than $u$, he cannot do better than get $t$ compliance—as he moves to the right from $t$ he actually makes himself worse off. He is also, of course, making B worse off, but we can see from the shape of the curve that that in itself is not what he wants. (If A simply wants B to comply because it makes B suffer, A's curve must inevitably rise strictly monotonically; i.e., it can't have any dips or even flat sections in it.) In the same way, A can get no advantage from enforcing compliance between $v$ and $w$ or beyond $x$.

Naturally, other things being equal, the greater congruence of interest, the smaller the length of the compliance curve that forms a possible location for an equilibrium. Thus, in Figure 5.6, with only a relatively small congruence of interest between the doctors and the government, we can see that of the twelve possible outcomes (including that of no compliance with the doctors' demands by the government) only two are ruled out—£400 and £800 plus no change in payment methods. In Figure 5.7, however, where there is a bigger difference between the preference rankings of the two sides, six of the twelve possibilities are ruled out. In the combinations with £400 and £800, only payment method III stays in the set of equilibrium outcomes. (Incidentally, especially where the things at issue are finely divisible, there may be more than one outcome associated with a given degree of compliance by B. In such a case we need only take notice of A's highest-rated outcome at that point, since he would obviously not press for something equally hard to obtain but which he liked less.)

## 6 OBTAINING COMPLIANCE BY 'ECONOMIC' MEANS

Having now introduced the basic idea, I shall explain how the analysis of a given situation can be carried out, and then go on to discuss the implications for the study of power.

How does A actually get B to comply with his demands? The process we are analysing is one where A makes it worth B's while to comply. A must in other words make B believe that on balance he will be better off if he complies than if he does not. Thus, if A operates by means of threats he must threaten B that if B does not comply with the demand A will see to it that he suffers a loss greater than the cost to B of complying. The incentives facing B are therefore rigged so he will be better off if he complies than if he does not comply. Or if A operates by means of promises he must promise B that if he does comply he will receive a reward that will more than compensate for the loss represented by complying. Thus, taking the loss and the reward together, and comparing them with the no compliance/no reward alternative, B must find that he will be better off by complying than by not complying. Or,

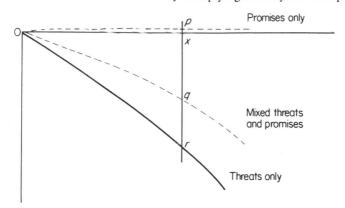

Figure 5.10

thirdly, A must offer a mixture of rewards and threats which between them make the choice of compliance-with-reward-without-sanction preferable to non-compliance-without-reward-with-sanction.

In all three cases, of course, B must believe with some degree of confidence that A will carry out his promises and threats. He must also believe that A will not carry them out otherwise. A's threat must be 'sanction if *and only if* compliance'. There is nothing to motivate B to comply in a belief that A will apply the same sanction even if he does comply. Conversely, the prospect of a reward following compliance will be effective only if B does not believe the reward would be forthcoming anyway.

We can see how all this works out diagrammatically by looking at Figure 5.10. Let us suppose that A wants to obtain an amount of compliance $Ox$ from B. (We shall ask what determines the level of A's demand later.) This means that A is trying to get B to incur a loss of $rx$. This is B's gross loss from compliance, and $r$ is simply the point on B's gross-loss-from-compliance curve perpendicular to the point $x$ on the compliance line. Somehow, A has to overcome the degree of reluctance on the part of B expressed in the length of the line $rx$. How can he do it? As we have seen, he can use threats or promises, or he can use a combination of the two.

Let us suppose that A uses threats exclusively. He then has to make B believe that a sanction bigger than $rx$ will be applied if he does not comply. If B believes this and consults his own short-term advantage, we expect him to comply. The outcome therefore is that B complies (with a loss of $rx$) and A subsequently does nothing. If we define B's *net* loss from compliance as the loss he suffers from compliance adjusted to take account of A's actions in response, the net and gross losses are in this case the same, because there is no action by A in response to B's.

Now suppose that A operates entirely by promises. He then has to convince B that his net loss will be negative, in other words that the reward will more than outweigh the loss. Thus, in Figure 5.10 he is shown as offering a reward of $pr$ to B in return for compliance. B therefore stands to make a net gain of $(pr-rx=px)$. B's gross loss is $rx$ but his net loss is $-px$.

Finally, suppose that A employs a combination of threats and promises. Obviously there is an infinite variety of possible combinations which would be adequate to make it pay B to comply. We have illustrated one in Figure 5.10. Here, A threatens B with a sanction of more than $qx$ if he does not comply. Obviously this by itself would make it preferable for B to refuse to comply (and accept the sanction) rather than comply and incur a loss of $rx$. But to make up the difference A also offers a reward of $qr$ if B does comply. B's net loss from compliance is therefore $(rx-qr=qx)$.

I have, for ease of exposition, considered a single point on the compliance line $x$. But the same analysis can be applied to every point along the compliance line. The result of joining up the points so obtained is the two curves for B's net loss under conditions of promises only and mixed promises and threats. The net and gross loss curves under conditions of threat only always, of course, coincide.

Let us now turn to the other side of the relationship and focus on A, the actor making the demands on B. What, within our model, determines the demand that he makes—or indeed whether he makes any demand at all? To begin with, let us make the simplifying assumption that A has at his disposal means of rewarding and/or punishing B of infinite size and that it costs A nothing to deploy these resources if he so chooses. We can in this case read off the demand that A will make from a knowledge of A's gross gain curve. A will demand whatever degree of compliance maximizes his own gross gain. Thus, in Figure 5.11, we simply look for the point at which the gross gain curve

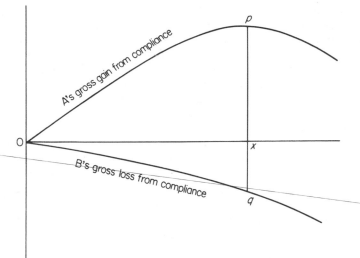

Figure 5.11

reaches its greatest height ($p$) and drop a perpendicular to the compliance line. The point of intersection ($x$) gives the level of compliance A will demand.

Figure 5.11 also shows B's gross loss curve. From our previous discussion we know that if A's demand for the degree of compliance $Ox$ is to be successful, he must lead B to believe that he has a high probability of carrying out threats and/or promises, contingently on B's behaviour, that make it preferable to comply (with the associated loss $qx$) than not to comply. In the present case, we are assuming that A disposes of infinite rewards and/or sanctions at zero cost. If B knows this then any threat or promise made by A will seem extremely plausible, since he knows that it will cost A nothing to carry it out. A simply has to make a threat and/or promise big enough to counterbalance the inherent loss $qx$ involved in doing the thing demanded, and he wins. His gain from the operation is, of course, $px$.

However, the assumption that A has threats and promises of infinite size available for use at zero cost is not realistic. Normally, it costs something, in time, money, effort, personal risk, etc., to carry out a promise or a threat. And, though there are no doubt exceptions, it is reasonable to suppose that in general there larger the threat or promise to be delivered on, the greater the cost of doing so. How should we work this fact into the model?

## 7 COSTS OF CARRYING OUT PROMISES

The situation is most straightforward in the case where A operates by making promises, so we shall take this one first. Let us assume that A does in fact intend to carry out the promise he makes to B, if only to maintain credibility with B—and whoever else knows about it—on future occasions. The anticipated cost to A of carrying out his promise may then be deducted from the anticipated gain from B's compliance. The gross gain minus the cost of carrying out the promise gives us A's anticipated profit from B's compliance with any given demand.

Leaving aside for the moment the question what now determines the level of demand made by A, let us take as given that A makes a particular demand upon B. What determines the cost to B of carrying out the promise appropriate to that demand? Pretty clearly, there are two factors involved. First, there is the size of the reward (measured in terms of B's values) that B requires to compensate him for doing the thing demanded. The more distasteful the object of A's demand the larger the reward B will require for compliance. The other factor is how much it costs A to generate any given level of reward for B. This is, if you like, the transformation function for A's costs into B's rewards.

Thus, the cost to A of producing the reward appropriate to elicit a given degree of compliance from B is given by the size of reward multiplied by the cost to A of producing a reward of that size. Given a certain transformation function, the cost to A of carrying out the appropriate promise will be lower the less onerous to B is the demand. Conversely, given the onerousness of the demand, the cost to A of carrying out the appropriate promise will be lower the less it costs A to provide any given amount of reward for B, measured in B's terms.

It obviously follows from what has been said that we can in principle associate with each point along the compliance line a cost to A of carrying out the appropriate promise for securing that degree of compliance from B. If we draw A's gross gain curve and at each point deduct from the gross gain the cost associated with obtaining it, we get a second curve under the first, giving A's profit or net gain. The net gain curve will coincide with the gross gain curve at the origin, since zero compliance requires zero promises at zero cost. Thereafter, it will fall increasingly far below the gross gain curve if we accept that bigger promises cost more to carry out. Figure 5.12 illustrates the relation hypothesized between gross and net gain curves.

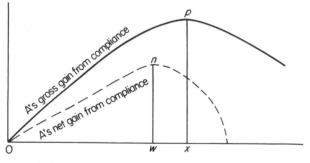

Figure 5.12

We are now in a position to return to the question of what determines A's demands when it costs something to carry out promises. The answer is that the optimum demand for A is the one that maximizes his net gain. In Figure 5.12, A's net gain curve reaches its highest point at *n,* which is perpendicular to *w* on the compliance line. A therefore demands O*w* degree of compliance from B. We can in fact now say looking back that our example with costless promises was a special case where the gross and net gain curves happen to coincide. It too therefore falls under the general rule that A's demand is the one that maximizes his net gain.

There are three implications for A's optimal demand that are worth noticing. First, there will be many cases where A's gross gain from B's compliance would at every point cancelled out by the cost of securing that compliance. Graphically, these are cases where, although the gross gain curve is (at least at some point along the compliance line) higher than the origin, the net gain curve is at no point higher than the origin. The maximum height of the net gain curve then occurs at the origin, in other words at the zero compliance point. The optimum demand by A would therefore, of course, be nothing (see Figure 5.13).

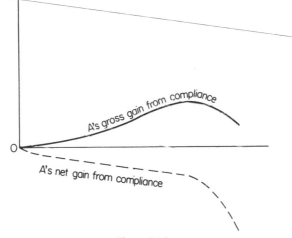

Figure 5.13

Situations of this kind are so ubiquitous that we do not usually even think about them. Almost any human being could find some way of benefiting from the compliance of almost any other human being. But the vast majority of these possibilities are never realized, or even contemplated, because the cost of securing any level of compliance would outweigh the gain. In a market economy there is no limit to the goods and services one can obtain from other people if one is willing and able to pay. But out of the vast gross gains obtainable from the shops we in fact, of course, pursue only that tiny fraction that we expect to yield a net gain. In political analysis, too, we do not bother to think about gains, however large, that would obviously cost more than their value to obtain.

The second point is also illustrated by Figure 5.12. It is this: wherever the highest point on the gross gain curve occurs, the highest point on the net gain curve must fall to the left of it if there are costs of securing compliance and these costs increase strictly monotonically with the degree of compliance secured. What this means is that the existence of costs will always make the optimum demand less than it would be in the absence of costs. And we can add that, for any given gross gain curve, the higher the costs of securing compliance (and the greater the gap between gross and net gain curves) the smaller will be the optimum demand. Our first point, that the optimum

84

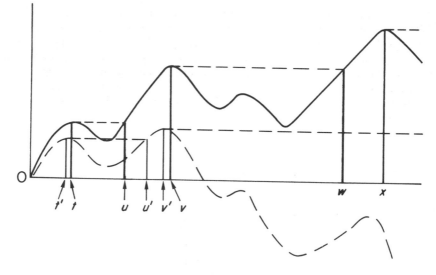

Figure 5.14

demand may be zero, is simply a special case of this general implication of the existence of costs.

The third point is illustrated by Figure 5.14. This is like Figure 5.9 in that horizontal lines have been drawn from the top of each peak to indicate segments of the compliance line that it would not pay A to move B on to. But this time the same exercise has been carried out on both the gross gain curve and the net gain curve. It will be seen that the segments of the compliance line (*tu*, *vw* and beyond *x*) that were unavailable even with zero cost of carrying out any promise are still unavailable when we allow for a gap between gross and net gain. But the segments that are unavailable when carrying out a promise has costs are greater: $t'u'$ and everything beyond $v'$ are now ruled out. This is necessary consequence of the assumption that the gap between gross and net gain increases the greater the degree of compliance demanded. We can say generally, then, that the unavailable segments where there are costs must include the segments that would be unavailable if there were no costs and will extend from these at both ends.

We might wish to relax the assumption that it always costs more to carry out a bigger promise. Rewards may be 'lumpy' rather than finely graded, so that the cheapest way for A to offer a reward over some size is to offer a reward that (in B's eyes) is much bigger. All the intermediate degrees of compliance will then cost the same. In other words, costs of securing compliance will go up in steps instead of smoothly. If we have 'lumpy' rewards like this, the truth of the first of our three implications of costs of promising remains intact. The other two, however, have to be withdrawn. It *may* still be that the optimal demand will be to the left of the maximum height of the gross gain curve, but all we can assert categorically is that it will never be to the right. And, similarly, although the available segments of the compliance line cannot exceed those available in a zero-cost situation, they will not necessarily be smaller.

## 8 COSTS OF CARRYING OUT THREATS

It is my intention to analyse the use of threats using the same apparatus of gross and net gain as for promises. As before, it will be maintained that A's optimum demand upon B for compliance is given by the point at which A's net gain curve reaches its maximum height. But, because of the basic difference between the way in which promises operate and the way in which threats operate, the interpretation of A's 'net gain' must inevitably be different for threats and, unfortunately, rather more complicated.

If A makes a promise to B and B does what is demanded, A has to provide the promised reward to maintain credibility. It is therefore reasonable to deduct the costs to A of providing the reward from the gain he would make from B's compliance, and say that the result is A's net gain from B's compliance. For this simply reflects the nature of the process. But if A threatens B and B does what is demanded, A is committed to *not* doing anything. His total gain therefore is the whole of the gross gain that he derives from B's compliance. It is only if B does not comply that A is committed to acting, and in that event A's final position will be worse than it was before he made the threat, since he gains nothing from B but incurs the cost of carrying out the threat.

How, then, are we to interpret the notion of A's net gain from B's compliance? The answer is that we must understand it as the *expected value* of A's gain from threatening B. 'Expected value' has its usual meaning here: the expected value of an action is the value of each of the possible outcomes discounted by the probability of its occurring. Just as we assumed that A will in fact carry out his promise if B complies, so let us simplify things by assuming here that A will in fact carry out his threat if B does not comply. We do not therefore allow in calculating A's expected value of threatening for A to bluff. But we must allow for A to think that there is some probability that B will believe that A is bluffing. For suppose that A does not think that B will ever suspect him of bluffing, or more precisely suppose that A does not think that B will ever believe that A will fail to carry out his threat (whatever his intentions may have been at the time of making it) if B does not comply with A's demand. On this supposition, it will always pay B to comply so long as A's threatened penalty for non-compliance is greater than the costs to B of compliance. However great the cost to A of carrying out the threat would be, therefore, he will still expect with certainty that B will comply, even if (to borrow Schelling's example) A's threat is that he will blow his brains out over B's new suit unless B gives him the last slice of toast (Schelling, 1960, p.127). (We assume that A is sure that having to get the suit cleaned is worse for B than forgoing the toast.)

If we assume, then, that A will always in fact carry out his threat, but does not know whether or not B will comply, his expected value (or net gain) from threatening B is made up of two items. The first is the gross gain ($G$) from compliance discounted by the probability ($p$) of obtaining compliance. The second is the cost of carrying out the threat ($C$) discounted by the probability of having to carry it out. This probability is simply the probability that B will not comply, so that if the probability of B's complying is 0.9, the probability of having to carry out the threat is 0.1. The expected value (or net gain) is the expected gain minus the expected cost: symbolically, we can write it as follows: $pG-(1-p)C$.

Let us consider in more detail the precise mechanism by which threats work. We know already that to have any hope of succeeding, the sanction threatened must be greater than the cost of compliance. Otherwise it would obviously always pay to accept the sanction—even if one were certain it would be applied—rather than comply. But this sets only the minimum level below which a threat will not be at all effective. If B has any doubt about A's willingness (or ability) to apply the threatened sanction for non-compliance, he may not comply even if the sanction is a little greater than the cost of compliance. For any given expectation by B that A will carry out his threat (and let us suppose for now that this expectation is independent of the level of the threat), we can say that the probability of compliance is greater the more the sanction exceeds the cost of compliance.

Now turn the situation round and look at it from the point of view of A. For any given demand (represented by a point on the compliance line) he knows that there is a minimum threat below which B certainly will not comply. But beyond that minimum, the more he threatens the better the chance of B's complying. Thus, as the level of threat goes up $pG$ increases. At the same time, however, $(1-p)C$ may or may not go up. $C$ will definitely go up, if we assume that a greater sanction costs more to carry out. But $(1-p)$ will obviously go down, since $p$ has gone up. In effect, there is a trade-off between the advantage that B is more likely to comply and the disadvantage that if he nevertheless does not comply the cost of carrying out the threat will be greater.

The optimum threat corresponding to any given demand will depend on the precise interaction between the size of sanction (to A) and the probability of compliance. For our present purpose we need only say that our 'net gain' curve will reflect the optimum choice corresponding to each point along the compliance line. We may note here that if A can carry out costlessly a threat of infinite size, he will threaten an infinite sanction whatever the degree of compliance he demands. The earlier statement that the gross and net gain curves are identical for costless threats and promises can now be seen to require a slight qualification. The formula for net gain, as we know, is $pG-(1-p)C$. The second item $(1-p)C$ must be 0 because $C$ is 0. But $pG = G$ only if $p = 1$. We should therefore say that gross and net gain are identical only if an infinitely large threat is certain to secure compliance. Provided that the cost of compliance is finite (as it was at the maximum point on the gross gain curve in Figure

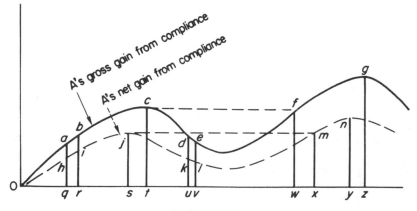

Figure 5.15

5.11), this seems reasonable. But if the cost of compliance is also infinite the outcome is indeterminate: even the most appalling tortures do not always succeed in obtaining compliance.

Now that we have seen how A's choice of threat is determined, we can raise the question of the relation between the gross and net gain curves. In Figure 5.15 we have taken two pair of points, $q$ and $r$ and $u$ and $v$ fairly close together on the compliance line. How does the gap between gross and net gains change as A moves from $q$ to $r$ and from $u$ to $v$, making the optimal threat at each point? In terms of Figure 5.15, this means that we have to compare the lines $ab$ with $bi$ and $dk$ with $el$. It can be shown that, provided a bigger threat costs more to carry out, the gap necessarily widens as we move along the compliance curve under a gross gain curve that is rising to the right, and that no point at which it is falling is a possible point for a demand by A. Let us suppose that A has selected the optimum threat for the demand represented by $q$ on the compliance line. He now wants to find the optimum threat for $r$. Let us consider two possibilities: that he maintains the same threat and that he maintains the same probability of compliance.

If A maintains the same threat, the probability that B will comply must go down, because the cost of compliance relative to the sanction is higher. $(1-p)C$ will therefore increase, since the cost of carrying out the threat remains the same but the probability of having to carry it out increases. Whether $pG$ goes up or down or stays the same depends on what happens to $G$ as well as what happens to $p$. $G$ is going up between $q$ and $r$, and the gap between $G$ and $pG$ widens for two reasons. So long as $p<1$, the gap $(G-pG)$ will increase as $G$ increases if $p$ stays the same. But in addition $p$ here declines as $G$ increases, so the difference between $G$ and $pG$ is even greater.

We are looking for the way in which $G-[pG-(1-p)C]$ changes as we move along the compliance line. At points where $G$ is increasing, both of the other expressions change in value to increase the gap: $pG$ at best goes up more slowly than $G$ and $(1-p)C$ increases. Where $G$ is decreasing as we move to the right, $(1-p)C$ will still necessarily continue to increase but the gap between $G$ and $pG$ need not increase, though $pG$ will of course decline. This is because if $p$ were to stay the same, the gap between $G$ and $pG$ would decrease as $G$ declines. Whether or not the gap widens, however, the important fact is that net gain must decrease because $pG$ is decreasing while $(1-p)C$ is increasing. It remains true therefore that points at which the gross curve is declining are not available as possible demands by A. Thus, in Figure 5.15 we have shown the gap narrowing between $u$ and $v$. In other words $dk$ is greater than $el$. But the net gain curve is necessarily falling.

The same conclusions may be derived by supposing that, in moving from $q$ to $r$ or from $u$ to $v$, A is concerned to keep the probability of B's compliance constant. In this case $pG$ must obviously stay the same as a proportion of $G$, while $(1-p)C$ will increase because the only way in which the same probability of compliance can be obtained for a demand further along the compliance line is to threaten a larger sanction, and we are assuming that a larger sanction costs more to carry out. Therefore, as before, the gap between the gross and net gain must increase while the gross gain curve rises, moving right along the compliance line, and when the gross gain curve falls the gap may widen or narrow but the net gain curve must move down.

In any particular case, the optimum move as the demand changes is hardly likely either to constitute keeping the threat exactly the same or to constitute keeping the probability of compliance exactly the same. But, since these two moves have the same general Implications, so would the most likely actual optimum: a bigger threat but not enough bigger to prevent the probability of compliance from falling.

What are the general implications? The answer is that all the general findings for promises carry over to threats. First, the net gain curve will always start turning down before the gross gain curve (provided the curve is smooth, that is differentiable) because the gap between the two widens all the time the gross gain curve rises. The optimum demand by A will therefore always be less than it would be with costless threats or rewards ($y$ as against $z$). And second, it remains true that all the segments of the compliance line that are ruled out because the gross gain curve is below a peak to its left ($tw$) are also ruled out because the net gain curve has a peak to its left. And, thirdly, more of the compliance line is ruled out on the basis of the net gain curve than the gross gain curve ($sx$ as against $tw$).

## 9 CREDIBILITY AND COST OF THREAT

The analysis set out in the previous section may be strengthened by suggesting a further reason why the net gain curve will tend to fall relatively to the gross gain curve as one moves along the compliance line. Until now, we have assumed that the probability of B's complying with A's demand is a function of the difference between the cost to B of complying and the cost to B represented by the sanction threatened by A. But it is surely reasonable to postulate that B will also try to form an estimate of the likelihood that A will in fact be willing or able to enforce the sanction in the event that B does not comply with A's demand. Other things being equal, the less likely B believes it to be that A will enforce the threat, the less likely B is to comply with A's demand. And, other things being equal, the less likely B is to comply, the lower is $pG$ and the higher is $(1-p)C$.

What determines B's estimate of the likelihood of A's enforcing his threat? No doubt there are many factors entering into the estimate, most of which cannot be accommodated within our simple model. But I suggest that one factor is the cost to A of carrying out the threat. Other things being equal, the higher the cost to A of carrying out the threat, the less likely B is to believe that it will in fact be carried out if he fails to comply with A's demand.

If this line of argument is acceptable, it means that an increase in $C$ has a direct effect in depressing $p$, therefore lowering $pG$, and in increasing $(1-p)$, therefore raising $(1-p)C$ in two ways at once. Since we have been assuming all along that a bigger threat costs more to carry out, the addition of this new consideration means that it is more likely than we have suggested previously for any attempt by A to step up the level of threat to be self-defeating. So far we have envisaged the possibility that as A moves rightward along the compliance line he may increase the level of threat so as to keep the probability of compliance constant. The drawback so far emphasized has been that because $(1-p)C$ goes up as $C$ goes up and $p$ stays the same, it may not pay A to make a bigger threat, even if the gross gain from success in obtaining more compliance would be greater. Now, however, we have to add that increasing the threat will in itself have an adverse effect on $p$. The increase in threat that would otherwise have been necessary to maintain the level of $p$ has to be augmented yet further to overcome the depressing effects on $p$ of the cost of carrying out that greater threat. So the cost of maintaining the same probability of compliance goes up more than it would otherwise do.

Indeed, the cost may be infinite, as each increase in threat actually makes the goal of compliance recede further. This will be so if each successive dose of possible threat in relation to a given degree of compliance increases the cost to A of carrying it out so much that it more than counteracts in B's mind the greater incentive to compliance contained in the greater excess of the sanction over the cost of compliance.

In other words, there may be no way of maintaining more than some particular probability of compliance at any given of demand for compliance, however great the cost A would in fact be willing to bear it. This observation reflects the line of argument used against the Dulles strategic doctrine of 'massive retaliation' against even a minor Soviet incursion and in favour of so-called 'flexible' or 'controlled' response. The Soviet Union would simply not believe, it was suggested, that the United States would unleash the full devastation of a Third World War—an exchange of nuclear weapons targeted on civilian populations—merely as a response to the seizure of a few square miles of territory. The fact that the adoption of the new strategic doctrine led to the abomination of the Vietnam War does not, it seems to me, show that it was incorrect. Rather, what happened was that the same mistake was made on a smaller scale. The leaders of North Vietnam and the Vietcong were simply not prepared to believe, however often American presidents reiterated it, that the United States would indefinitely bear the costs of fighting in Vietnam when the real bearing of Vietnam on the security of the United States was so minimal—one might even say symbolic only. And in the long run they proved to be correct.

Incidentally, it should be borne in mind that among the costs of carrying out threats is the repugnance that A may feel about it. This clearly played a part in the US withdrawal from Vietnam, and an even clearer example is provided by the way in which the death penalty for sheep stealing and theft of over £2 proved counter-productive in England in the eighteenth century because juries refused to convict even on clear evidence. At a more domestic level, a parent is more likely to obtain compliance by making a threat sufficiently moderate to make it plausible that he or she would be willing to carry it out than by uttering some blood-curdling threat like 'I'll skin you alive'.

So far we have been assuming that a bigger threat costs more to carry out. But as with promises, this need not always be so. Threats, like promises, may be 'lumpy': if you want a sanction bigger than a certain size, there may be nothing efficient between it and a much bigger one. That is to say, intermediate-sized sanctions (if available at all) may be even more expensive to carry out than the much bigger one. The cost of making threats will thus go up in steps.

As with promises, once we allow for 'lumpiness' we have to modify our arguments in some respects. It remains true, of course, that if there are costs at all the net gain curve will be below the gross gain curve at all points; and it will still be true that many cases in which a demand for compliance would be profitable with zero cost will show a net gain curve that is at no point positive once costs are taken into account. Moreover, the conclusions of Section 8 remain valid. Whereas with promises 'lumpiness' made it no longer true that the net gain curve would turn down before the gross gain curve, the effect of the size of the 'excess' sanction on the probability of compliance saves the relationship for threats. We are, *ex hypothesi*, dealing with a case where the size of the threatened sanction (and its cost, of course) stays the same along a stretch of the compliance line. This being so, $p$ must decline and $(1-p)C$ increase as the demands become more unacceptable, so the gap between $G$ and $pG-[(1-p)C]$ will increase while $G$ increases and the net value itself $pG-[(1-p)C]$ will start to decline before $G$ does.

All that is lost is the reinforcement for that conclusion provided by the present section, which does depend on the assumption that at each point there is a slightly bigger sanction available at a slightly higher cost.

## 10  THE 'MYSTERY OF POWER'

I suggested at the beginning of Section 3 that power in the 'economic' sense should be understood as the possession of the means of securing compliance by the manipulation of rewards or punishments; and I have now set out a model of the process by which rewards and punishments may be used to modify behaviour. It is now time to come back to the concept of power, and look at it in the light of this analysis. What are the problems with which we have to deal?

First, 'getting someone to do what he would not otherwise do' (Dahl's 'intuitive idea') is not necessarily the same as 'getting someone to do what you want him to do'. A may be able to secure massive compliance from B without this enabling him to get B to do anything that he (A) wants him to do. For there may be nothing that A wants B to do. This might incline us to follow Goldman and say that 'the extent of a person's power with respect to an issue is (*ceteris paribus*) inversely related to the degree of desire required for him to obtain a preferred outcome' (Goldman, 1972, p.253).

On the other hand, we might regard A as lucky rather than powerful if he can get something he wants a great deal by overcoming only small resistance on the part of B. To push it to an extreme: would we wish to say that A was exercising infinite power if he could get something he wanted very much from B merely by asking for it? If not, should we not concentrate on the amount of resistance A can overcome? We may then be inclined to adopt a definition of power like that of Karlsson (cited in Bell *et al.*, 1969, p.112) according to which A's power over B is a function of the difference between how *well off* A could make B if he tried and how *badly off* A could make B if he tried.

These two approaches would lead us to say widely differing things about power in some situations, for the ability to get what you want and the ability to secure compliance need not be correlated. But both of these conceptions have one feature in common: they deal in terms of A's *gross* gain and B's *gross* loss. This however, itself seems implausible. If we concentrate on what A gains, should we not deduct the expected cost of getting it from the gross gain and say that A has more power the larger his *net* gain from securing compliance?

Alternatively, if we start from B's end and identify power with compliance, do we really want to ignore the distinction between compliance secured by promises and compliance secured by threats? In other words, should we not look at B's *net* loss (if any)? Perhaps we should not call a case where there no net loss to B a case of 'power' at all: we might say that threats are associated with power and promises with exchange, as Blau (1964) does, though, as Jack Lively has shown in his Chapter above, Blau confuses the question.

Here, then, we have four quite different conceptions of A's power over B: as A's gross gain, B's gross loss, A's net gain and B's net loss. More could be added. For example, we might identify A's power with the smallness of the *difference* between his gross gain and his net gain. Nor is this the worst. For I have deliberately skated round the problematic relation between having power and exercising power. Obviously you can't exercise power that you don't have, but you can have power that you don't exercise. When we talk about power are we talking about what A *could* do or what A *does* do? Or should we perhaps be talking about what it would pay A to do?

It is not my intention exactly to *answer* these questions. In the tradition of philosophical analysis developed by Wittgenstein and Austin, I would say rather that my object is to attempt to dissolve the puzzlement that such questions reflect. My method, however, is not the orthodox 'linguistic' one of minute attention to nuances of meaning, but the construction of a model designed to give insight into the processes involved. When we see the way in which the various uses of 'power' reflect a concentration on different aspects of the process, we will be, I hope, relieved of the feeling that it matters to ask what is the meaning of power. What has been called ironically 'the mystery of power' (Kaufman and Jones, 1954) results from the fact that there are a number of aspects of power, and it is easy to move between them without noticing that they are different. De-mystification requires that we get them clear. Whether, after that, we want to go on using the word 'power' and, if so, how we use it, is of secondary importance.

## 11  A PARADIGM OF POWER

I think that the best way of approaching the analysis of power relationships in terms of the model is to construct a case such that nobody would have any doubts in saying that A did have power over B. I shall then offer an example. Finally, I shall take each element in turn and see what happens if we vary it.

I     *A has the opportunity of exercising power over B.*
(1)   A can communicate demands, threats [and offers*] to B.
(2)   A can monitor B's degree of compliance with his demands.
(3)   A can, at low cost to himself, impose severe sanctions on B [and/or provide large rewards to B*].

II    *A has the motive for exercising power over B*
(1)   There is at least one demand on B that A could make, compliance with which by B would be (in gross terms) highly advantageous to A and highly disadvantageous to B.
(2)   There is no alternative demand to that specified above that would be (again in gross terms) at least as advantageous to A while being less disadvantageous to B.

III   *A has an incentive to exercise power over B.*
(1)   There is at least one demand on B that A could make, compliance with which by B would be highly advantageous to A in net terms and highly disadvantageous to B in gross terms.
(2)   There is no alternative demand to that specified above that would be at least as advantageous to A in net terms while being less disadvantageous to B in gross terms.
(3)   The optimal mix of threats and promises for A to make is such that compliance with the demand specified in (1) will be highly disadvantageous to B in net terms.**]

(N.B. If promises are to be included, the sections in brackets marked * should be included and the section in brackets marked ** excluded; if promises are to be excluded, the sections in brackets marked * should be excluded and the section in brackets marked ** should be included.)

Crudely, the logic of this is

I.   Could A probably obtain a lot of compliance cheaply if it paid him to?
II.  Would it pay A to attempt to obtain a lot of compliance if he could probably obtain in cheaply?
III. Putting the two together: will it pay A to attempt to gain a lot of compliance, given the cheapness with which he can probably obtain it?

Thus, to give an example from industrial relations, the *opportunity* of a trade union to improve its members' pay by striking increases (i) the less the cost of a given length of strike (e.g. the more the state pays strikers or their families in lieu of wages) and (ii) the greater the cost to the employer of a given length of strike (e.g. the more capital-intensive the process and the more full the firm's order books). The *motive* of the trade union would be greater the more profitable the firm was, since this would mean that there was more in the kitty to share out.

An example that scores high on all the elements listed above may be drawn from Benjamin Barber's book about history of the Swiss canton of Graubünden. After the Raetian Republic took possession of the fertile Tellina valley (now part of Italy) in 1512, 'the executive and judicial office which comprised the colonial administration were officially put up for sale to the highest bidder' and 'corruption was limited only by the confines of the officeholders' imagination'. 'One judge . . . passed an arbitrary sentence of death on anyone who appeared before him, for whatever reason. It is a tribute to the catalyzing effect of fear on human generosity that this particular official amassed in fifteen months a fortune surpassing that of his most imaginative colleagues.' (Barber, 1974.) Running through the list, it is clear that this provides for communication of threat, monitoring of compliance and a low-cost means of applying a severe sanction. The Tellina valley was fertile and prosperous, so there were resources of high value to be transferred to the judge's pocket, and money has the characteristic that the more A gets the more B loses. The two factors together meant that the judge was in fact in a position to extort large rewards at low cost.

## 12  ARE PROMISES AN EXERCISE OF POWER?

The first point we ought to take up is one that was left open in the paradigm for 'A has power over B'. This is the question whether compliance secured by offering a rewards is an exercise of power. As I have already suggested, it matters less how we answer a question like this than to see what is at stake in giving different answers.

The argument for ignoring the net loss (if any) of B is, I suppose, that compliance is compliance whether it is induced or coerced. A rich man can have servants around him who will do his bidding. Is this not power? And when people (in either a capitalist or a socialist economy) work at the direction of others in return for pay, are they not subject to power?

The argument on the other side is that power should be contrasted with exchange. To be in someone's power is something we would prefer to avoid: people seek to escape from the power of others. But the possibility of exchange is never something we would prefer to avoid, because it enlarges our freedom of choice without the same time ruling out the opportunity of staying as we are if we do not like any of the additional alternatives. Here, too, plausible cases can be cited in support. If I buy a pound of parsnips in the greengrocer's shop, there is an exchange—money for parsnips—but am I exercising power over the shopkeeper by promising him money for complying with my demand for parsnips?

If we are unhappy about either saying that we look only at the degree of compliance (and therefore ignore the question of means) or saying that no case of gaining compliance by promises can ever be a case of exercising power, we must look for some other criterion that will sort out the cases in the way we feel happy with. I think this is the right move, but it is not at all easy to formulate the criterion precisely. There are two false trails that can I think be found in the literature.

One of these misguided suggestions is that we use 'power' only to refer to cases where someone can obtain a large amount of compliance with a high degree of probability, and it is simply a matter of fact that most cases of this sort are cases where the means are coercion rather than inducement. As a matter of usage, I think it is true that if we simply say that someone has power we imply that he has a lot of power. In the same way, though, if we say that someone has money we mean he has a lot of money. This does not entail that we cannot say someone has a little money, and similarly we can say someone has a little power. The other misguided suggestion is that we use 'power' for relationships of which we disapprove, and as a matter of fact we are more likely to disapprove of coercive attempts to produce compliance than attempts employing the prospect of rewards. Again, usage is against this idea. It makes perfectly good sense to say that one approves of someone's power, while there are some attempts to modify behaviour that we may disapprove of without calling them an exercise of power, for example a competitor in a village flower show buying one of the judges a drink just before the judging is due to take place.

I am myself inclined to think that the criterion for a power relation is an asymmetry between the parties. The tendency for power to be disapproved of could then be explained as a reflection of our disapproval of asymmetry in social relations, since there is a close connection, though not a perfect one, between asymmetry and unfairness. By 'asymmetry' I mean simply that one party stands to gain more out of the relationship than the other, because it is in a position to exploit the weakness or necessity or vulnerability of the other. On this criterion, we get the result, which I think in accordance with common usage, that threats are *always* an exercise of power, rewards only sometimes. If A is in a position to make a plausible threat against B, this must mean that he is able to exploit B's vulnerability; and if he succeeds in obtaining compliance by issuing a plausible threat, then the transaction must be one-sided because it is inevitably one in which A gains and B loses. But an exchange may take place between parties with sufficiently equal positions to enable us to say that there is no asymmetry in the relationship. In terms of the model, we can indifferently describe an equal exchange as a case where A offers B a reward in return for compliance or a case where B offers A a reward in return for compliance. There is no reason in general why in an equal exchange both sides should not share the benefit arising from the transaction roughly equally. However, an exchange may be between unequally placed partners. If A is a single buyer or seller, facing an unorganized mass of sellers or buyers, he can set the price so as to get almost the whole surplus from the transaction.

Similarly, as Marx correctly argued, the fact that a labourer in nineteenth-century Britain could survive only a short time without a job gave employers a great advantage in the labour market and enabled them to extract almost the whole surplus from the transaction of employment. Obviously, in terms of our model, to say that A is in a position to get nearly all the total gain out of the transaction is precisely to say that A can obtain a large amount of compliance of high value at low cost, while B has to accept, because of his weak position, compensation for the gross loss inherent in compliance that is only just enough to make compliance better on balance than non-compliance.

One final point. I noted before that if A makes B worse off unconditionally this is not an exercise of power, because it is not associated with any attempt to modify B's behaviour. But suppose that after A has made B worse off he then comes along and, taking advantage of B's distressed situation, is able to obtain compliance in return for an offer that B would have turned down before. Even more, suppose that A's reduction of B's wellbeing was deliberately designed to bring about a state of dependence. I think that in such a case we would be inclined to say that A was exercising power over B through offering rewards for compliance even if we might not say the same if the relative positions of A and B had come about without the intervention of A. This has an obvious bearing on the question whether the countries of the 'third world' are subject to the power of the developed (and especially the ex-colonial) countries. Those who argue that they are not point to the existing pattern of trade relations and say that these relations are mutually beneficial. But if what has just been said is true, the 'dependence' theorists are right to say that we have to ask how these patterns of trade came about in the first place.

## 13  THREE CONCEPTS OF POWER

Having decided to admit the ability to make promises as a form of power under certain circumstances, we can now return to the other questions that were raised in Section 10. As I said there, I do not think that there is anything much to be gained from simply picking a definition and saying 'That's the one everybody ought to use'. But I do think that it is useful to see the implications of alternative definitions and to notice the way in which the choice of a definition is affected by what it is that we want to explain.

If we are interested in predicting how people will behave, then we want to know when it will *pay* A to try to get B to do something. It is no good A's being able to derive enormous potential benefit from some compliant action by B if either A has no way of getting B to do it or if the cost to A of getting B to do it is so great as to cancel out the benefit. At the same time, it is also no good A's being in a position to make sizeable threats or promises to B at low cost to himself if there is nothing that B has that A wants, or, more generally, if no compliant behaviour of B would produce a worthwhile gross gain for A.

In other words, if you are interested in predicting *action*—attempts by one actor to achieve compliance by another actor—you need both motive and opportunity. And that means that you have to insist on a certain amount of both **I** and **II** in the paradigm, such that between them they satisfy **III**. The resulting definition would be on the following lines: A has power over B if and only if A can profitably get B to do something A wants or, more formally, if and only if there is some level of compliance by B such that A's net gain from it would be positive. The *measure* of power would be the maximum net gain obtainable by A at any level of compliance by B.

Notice that this definition concentrates on A's net advantage from B's compliance. Any given net advantage may arise either from $x$ gross gain and $y$ cost to A (e.g. a huge gross gain and high cost) or from $x-a$ gross gain and $y-a$ cost (e.g. a small gain and a minuscule cost). The present measure of power would produce the same result in both cases, and this is reasonable if what we are interested in is predicting action by B. For it is surely plausible, if we accept a general cost-benefit framework of analysis, to predict that the greater the profit to A that can be anticipated from action (in this case making an attempt to obtain compliance from B) the more likely A is to undertake that action.

But prediction of actions is not the only thing we may be interested in. I have already mentioned the Lasswellian conception of the *explananda* of politics as 'who gets what, when, how'. This implies a distributive focus to our inquiries: we are interested in the outcomes of social behaviour, in who gains and who loses. The obvious way of defining power from this point of view is in terms of inequality. A's power over B will consist in A's ability to gain at the expense of B.

In the simplest case this means that A has the ability to make a profit from gaining B's compliance while B makes a net loss, in other words in A's ability profitably to coerce B. But, as I argued in section 12, there can also be an asymmetry in net gains. Suppose that both sides make a net gain from the transaction but that one of the parties (A) is able to appropriate almost all the profit by manoeuvring the other (B) into a position where the choice is between the *status quo* and a small improvement on it. There is then an unequal distribution of the gains from trade between A and B.

The implication of this is that power should be defined in terms of the *difference* between what A gets and what B gets if A pursues the course most profitable to him. It would follow from this that there were two ways in which A could have no power over B. If it would not pay A to attempt to obtain compliance from B, the equilibrium position would obviously be one in which no attempt was made, and there would by definition be no gains and no losses to either party, so no power relation. But even if it would pay A to obtain compliance from B by offering a reward for compliance to B, there may still be no power relation because the outcome may be a fair exchange between A and B in which both make a roughly equal gain over their positions in the *status quo ante*. (Of course, A and B might both lose equally from an attempt by A to coerce B that fails. But it must be recalled that our analysis of net gains and losses is *ex ante* not *ex post*. If *ex ante* the net gain that A anticipates is negative, because the product of the probability of B's non-compliance and the cost of carrying out the threat exceeds the product of B's compliance and the gross gain from B's compliance, then A has no incentive to attempt to obtain compliance. The case is therefore *ex ante* of the first type.)

Formally, then, the definition of power on this conception would be on the following lines: A has power over B if and only if the maximum net gain for A from compliance by B entails *either* a net loss by B *or* a smaller net gain by B than that enjoyed by A. And the measure of A's power would be the size of the difference between A's net gain and B's net loss of between A's net gain and B's net gain, measuring these values at the equilibrium level of compliance demanded by A, that is to say the point that maximizes A's net gain.

Unlike the first definition, this would enable us to predict changes in the pattern of distribution: if A has power over B we predict that A will become better off and B worse off relatively to the *status quo*. But it does not predict behaviour as well as the first definition does. First, all equal exchanges are simply ignored, so we eliminate a great deal of market behaviour. Second, if the probability of action by A is related to prospect of profit by A, the second definition, by contaminating A's profit with B's loss, entails that we can no longer mover from power to motive so confidently. If what pays A most is to try to get B to do something he very much doesn't want to do, that must entail on this definition a great deal of power for A. Yet the net gain to A may be quite tiny, either because the gross gain is small (recall that B's hating to do something does not entail that A loves having him do it) or because the cost of getting B to do it is so hight that it almost outweighs a large gain. This observation of course illustrates the general point that different definitions serve different intellectual (or indeed practical) interests.

Both of the definitions canvassed so far have one thing in common: they both include within them a reference to the prospective gains of A from securing B's compliance with a demand. And clearly to predict either behaviour or distributive outcomes we do need to take A's prospective gains into account. But I think there is a further object we may have in attributing social power to people or groups and that in order to pursue that object we ought to leave A's prospective gains out of the definition of power. I want to argue that, in some sense, we grasp social reality at a deeper level by looking at what A *could get at low cost* rather than what it *actually pays* A to get. In other words, I am suggesting that we might conceptualize power purely in terms of opportunity and not at all in terms of motive. A's power would then consist simply of the ability to obtain low-cost compliance. Even if there were currently nothing B could do that A would wish him to do, A would still, on this conception, have the same amount of power as would be attributed to him if there were something B could do that A very much wanted him to do.

What interest would be served by such a definition? My answer is that an interest in *security* will lead us to such a definition, and that we ought to take an interest in security because of its importance for the dignity of individuals and societies and (related to this) their capacity to plan for the future with confidence. If A has power over B in the sense that A can at low cost to himself obtain compliance from B, then A has B *in his power*. B may not be subject to demands from A at the moment but he cannot count on that happy state of affairs continuing. B's freedom depends on A's not choosing to exercise his power. (In our cost—benefit framework this means that it depends on A's net gain from securing compliance being negative, and if the cost of obtaining compliance is low this can come about only if A's net gain is low.) If at any time B happens to get into a position where he *does* have something that A wants to more than a negligible degree, he knows that A is in a position to get it.

Let me give two examples of this kind of power in practice, the first from interpersonal relations, the second from international relations. The first is a little frivolous but illustrates an important point. It occurred to me, while reading an omnibus edition of the Jeeves short stories by P. G. Wodehouse, how often the plot turns around the dependence of one of Bertie Wooster's fellow Drones on an allowance from some aged relative, and on the need to meet (or appear to meet) the more or less cranky demands of this relative in order to keep the allowance. Even Bertie, in one of his more philosophical moments, remarks that 'It's a curious thing how many of my pals seem to have aunts or uncles who are their main source of supply' (Wodehouse, 1973, p.180).

It may be noted that this constitutes a case where A (the aunt or uncle) operates on B (the Drone) by rewards rather than sanctions. The Drone would prefer a situation in which he has the option of complying with the whims of his aged relative and getting an allowance to a situation in which this option is withdrawn. (Of course, he would like even better to get the money without having to placate the aged relative, but this opportunity is not normally available (if at all) until the decease of the relative.) If we reflect on this, we can see that the relationship may not be one of power in the sense of an unequal exchange. It may be that the relative receives less benefit from the Drone's compliance than the Drone does from the allowance. But the point is that the Drone *is* dependent—his behaviour is open to control by the aunt or uncle—and the truth of this is not affected by the fact that he prefers dependence to independence on the only terms on which independence is available.

At the other extreme, many grave illustrations may be drawn from relations between states. If we define a weak state as one which at least one other state could, if it chose, occupy and control at fairly low cost, it must follow that the independence of a weak state at any time depends on its not having anything that makes it worth the while of a state that could occupy and control it to do so. Woe betide it if in an industrial era valuable raw materials are discovered on its territory or if economic and technical developments mean that its land and perhaps its inhabitants could be used profitably to grow some valuable cash crop like cotton, rubber, tea or coffee. Woe betide it if, because of its location, it suddenly becomes strategically or commercially significant, as a coaling station or the site for a canal, for example. What has protected the independence of mountainous areas like Montenegro, Switzerland or Ethiopia over the centuries? Partly the relative difficulty of conquering such mountainous territories but more, I suggest, the fact that their poverty has made them unattractive acquisitions. The possession of a mass of gold was the undoing of the Incas, and the Transvaal would no doubt have remained an independent state of poor farmers but for the discovery of diamonds in extraordinary quantity on the Rand. (The fact that the ultimate upshot of Britain's victory in the Boer War was to create a single state of South Africa in which Afrikaners had a numerical majority among the white population and thus in the long run dominated its politics is one of the sadder ironies of history.) Again, Egypt lost its independence to Britain and France largely to protect the Suez canal and the state of Panama was carved out by the United States to create a buffer for the Panama Canal. And so on.

The argument in favour of the conception of power as the ability to secure compliance at relatively low cost is that it focuses on the realities of dependence. Even if a state is independent, it is surely a relevant fact about it that its independence is contingent on the apathy of those states with power, and that its independence will be in jeopardy should it ever happen to become interesting to such a state.

## 14  TECHNICAL LIMITATIONS OF THE ANALYSIS

I shall not expand any further on the limited *scope* of the 'economic' approach to the analysis of power. Instead I want to end this chapter by asking what are the limitations on the analysis that I have developed earlier *within* the general area where it applies. I shall consider three kinds of limitation: technical limitations, limitations on applicability (in the sense of operationalizability) and limitations on applicability in the sense of limitations on the usefulness of threats and promises themselves.

The model that has been presented here is extremely simple and primitive. Three technical limitations in it are, I think, especially serious. First, we were always considering cases where A is trying to get B to change his behaviour but never cases where B is also trying to get A to change *his* behaviour. Of course, we can say that B is trying to change A's behaviour if B refuses to comply until A offers a larger reward for compliance. And indeed the 'pure reward' case can often be equally well presented with either party as the active one trying to change the behaviour of the other. (For example, in an ordinary economic exchange we could make either party A or B.) But where each party has threats at its disposal and each is trying to move the other to a position worse than that of non-compliance, we do have to extend the model.

Second, we need to be able to allow for the fact that B may respond to a demand of A backed by a threat not merely by refusing to comply and then leaving A to decide whether it is worth the cost inherent in carrying out the threat: B may in addition attempt to reduce the probability of A's carrying out the threat by making a conditional threat in turn to the effect that if A carries out his threat then B will do something to A that A won't like. (A may, of course, counter with a conditional threat against B to the effect that if B retaliates A will do something else.) The threat of retaliation differs from the case of mutual threats that I mentioned first in that B's move here is defensive in nature: B is content to be left alone by A and simply to deter A from carrying out his threat, but B is not using his threat-capacity to attempt to get A to comply with a demand from B for a change in his behaviour.

Third, there is a rather worrying tendency to slither between subjective and objective values in the model. Ideally, we want one set of curves to represent A's *actual* benefits from any degree of compliance by B and the *actual* costs to A of carrying out any given threat or promise; and another set for A's *estimate* of what a given degree of compliance would cost B and his *estimate* of what a given threat or promise would be worth to B if carried out. And the same *mutatis mutandis* for B.

I shall not discuss these three extensions further since any serious exposition of the model with these extensions incorporated would require a paper several times the already considerable length of this one. I shall simply affirm my belief that technical problems of this kind can be overcome, though the problem is that a small additional input of complexity can be a terrifyingly large additional output of complexity.

## 15 LIMITATIONS ON OPERATIONALIZABILITY

Can the model (in its simple or extended form) be applied in the sense of having measures found for each of the curves and precise hypotheses developed for each case on the basis of such measurements? I have three answers to offer.

(1) I think that a model may be said to be applicable to real life even if it is not possible to operationalize it. It may still illuminate real life to have a worked-out formal model in our minds even if we have to make do with something more scrappy when we get down to the analysis of real-life cases. One way of illustrating this point is, I think, to observe that in many ways my model can be regarded as a formalization of the theoretical exposition of 'coercive diplomacy' and its alternatives in the first chapter of Alexander George *et al.*, (1971), *The Limits of Coercive Diplomacy*, though in fact I came across the book only while drafting the workshop paper, and the basic model was worked out several years ago. It would be an interesting exercise to get someone to read George and then this chapter and to see if he found that it

made clearer the logic of George's implicit model. I believe that it would be found to.

(2) In any case, although that is my fall-back position, I don't despair of the possibility of being able to make reasonable estimates of the variables in some situations. And it might be possible to get the actors in a real-life (but not life-and-death) negotiation to set down their own estimates of the quantities in advance, if necessary in a sealed envelope. One could then deduce from the theory the expected equilibrium outcome and compare it with the actual one. Of course, it is to be explicitly allowed that skill is an intervening factor between the model's predicted outcomes and actual outcomes. But over a number of cases it would become pretty clear whether skill was at all plausible as a gap-filler or whether there was something wrong with the theory's predictions in a more fundamental way.

(3) In any case, in spite of the limited usefulness of tests in artificial conditions because of the hazard of generalizing beyond the special circumstances, it would I think be interesting to test the model in the laboratory situations that social psychologists create. This certainly could be done. Much work already has been done on the use of threats and promises (see most issues of *The Journal of Conflict Resolution*), but this has been mostly vitiated by poor theory: if you don't have a clear idea of the critical variables you muddle things together experimentally and not surprisingly get confused results. So I do not regard the lack of clear guidance from these experiments so far as conclusive but rather as a consequence of poor (or even worse no) model-building.

## 16  LIMITATIONS ON THE USEFULNESS OF THREATS AND PROMISES

(1) Obviously, in any given case, what someone can get is conditioned by the threats or rewards he has at his disposal or is willing to use. George's *Limits of Coercive Diplomacy* treats limits in this rather uninteresting way. (As George Canning wrote in a despatch to the British government, 'In matters of commerce the fault of the Dutch/Is giving too little and asking too much.') Of course, although this phenomenon is uninteresting theoretically it may be of great importance practically. The continuation of the Vietnam War, if George is right, was due to the Americans underestimating the size of the demand they were making on the North in asking them to give up national unification under their leadership.

(2) But this raises a more interesting question. Suppose we say: this account may be true up to the mid-1960s though after that rational calculation based on false premises seems less likely to contain the answer than some explanation in terms of psychopathology or US domestic politics. This, of course, raises a central question about applicability: the requirement of rationality. Where single individuals are concerned, we can say that operating a strategy of threats and promises requires some sort of ability to work things out and to provide at least the appearance (which in the long run means also the capacity) to control the rewards and sanctions; and there is no point in even trying to use threats or promises on someone who is too stupid to understand them or too lacking in self control to act on them. We don't rely on deterrence with young children, for example: we put bars around the fire or across the windows (i.e. what I called physical constraints).

The biggest questions along these lines about applicability, however, arise when the actors are not individuals but collectivities (e.g. states). Obviously, all the difficulties that individuals experience in putting together coherent behaviour (in which information is processed, calculations made and decisions reached and then implemented) are greatly magnified when a number of different people are involved in each stage. For this reason Graham Allison in his book *Essence of Decision* (Allison, 1971) cast doubt on the applicability of what he called a 'rational actor' model to international politics. I think that it is important to recognize limitations on the rationality of organizations, and in the case of relations among the super-powers this ought to entail very great caution in making use of strategies that rely on a quick and precisely calculated reaction by another (see Cornford, 1974, p.233). But even so I think that Allison overstates the case for pensioning off the 'rational actor' model. For his other two models—that involving the examination of the standard operating procedure of an organization and that involving the analysis of in-fighting among top-level decision-makers—can in my view be made sense of only in relation to the 'rational actor' model.

The bureaucratic machine, although it of course develops a life of its own, is after all set up with the object that it should serve the interests of the collectivity (say, the United States) rather than the individual interests of its members; and its 'standard operating procedures' are designed with the object of producing appropriate responses in the organization, 'appropriateness' again being conceived of in terms of serving some overall collective goal. Moreover, if a state (or any other organization) is to survive in a challenging environment, I think we can predict that constant efforts will have to be made to correct tendencies towards the pursuit of personal self interest at the expense of organizational goals and tendencies for 'standard operating procedures' to degenerate into rituals which play no useful role. We can only understand the notion of *correcting* tendencies in relation to some norm, and this norm is provided, I suggest, by the 'rational actor' model.

Similarly, it is no doubt a cliché that in the in-fighting that takes place in a cabinet or committee (such as the Excom in the Cuban Missile Crisis) 'where you stand depends on where you sit', but first, 'multiple advocacy' is often built into the process (e.g. it is expected that the education minister sticks up for education if there are cuts to be made in the overall government budget), and secondly, arguments are still put forward *in terms* of the 'national interest' etc. Anyway Allison's account doesn't suggest that positions had much relevance in determining attitudes on the Excom: Robert Kennedy was hardly acting to build up the office of the attorney general, for example.

(3) A different though related question is that of the relative effectiveness of promises and threats as against alternative ways of getting people to do what you want. It may be possible to combine them so their *relative* efficacy doesn't matter (e.g. in a smoothly running state the demands of the criminal law are backed both by normative acceptance—'mobilization of commitments'—and by sanctions). Here the existence of the sanctions does not detract from the authority of the law because the sanctions themselves are regarded as legitimate. But in other cases it seems likely that the introduction of promises and threats into a situation shifts people on to a self-interested way of looking at the matter, thus undermining the possibility of a normative appeal. This is the argument put forward by Richard Titmuss in his book *The Gift Relationship* (Titmuss, 1970), where he suggests that the introduction of payment for blood has the effect of drying up the supply from voluntary unpaid donation of blood. The two kinds of motive—in this case social responsibility and commercial self-interest—cannot, the argument goes, coexist in the same society in

respect of the same category of transaction. Again, the attempt to mix punishment and rehabilitation in prisons may founder on the inflexibility of prison personnel but it may also be affected by the problem of one method of eliciting desired behaviour cutting across another. I don't know that there is much to be said about this but I simply draw attention to it.

(4) Finally, there is a point mentioned very much in passing by George in *The Limits of Coercive Diplomacy* but which has big implications for the applicability of the 'economic' approach in both senses of 'applicability' I have distinguished. George points out that an almost invariable effect of actually carrying out a threat—i.e. imposing sanctions—is to harden the attitude of the person subjected to the sanction to the original demand. In our terms, a given concession (expressed in descriptive terms) becomes greater in terms of the loss it would be felt to represent. To the extent this is so we can say two things. (i) This means that recurrent demands backed by successively greater threats—even if the demand stays the same—may well actually fall further and further short of being sufficient to overcome resistance. The cost represented by the demand may, in other words, increase faster than the sanction for non-compliance. And (ii) as far as the analysis of bargaining is concerned, as against the practice of it, the implication is that, if we want to analyse a series of threats, we may need to allow for a shift in curves between stages. We can of course carry out the analysis of each stage on the basis of a new set of curves giving us a comparative statics of bargaining with an equilibrium outcome corresponding to each set of curves. But how do we get from one set of curves to the next? That seems to take us outside the 'economic' approach. It requires some propositions in individual psychology (e.g. the frustration—aggression hypothesis) and where groups are concerned some notions about the way group solidarity intensifies as a result of common experience of deprivation.

# 6
# Power and Causation

FELIX E. OPPENHEIM

## 1 INTRODUCTION

This chapter proposes to explicate various concepts of power, to connect them with the notion of causation, and to determine whether causality refers in such contexts to necessary or to sufficient conditions. I shall not consider the concept of degree of power, nor shall I examine the connection between power and exchange—two topics of some of the other chapters in this volume.

I shall deal with the notion of power in only one of its meanings, but it is the meaning in which it occurs most frequently in political science. The expression I shall examine is: 'P has power over R's doing x', where the variables 'P' (symbolizing the power holder) and 'R' (the respondent) range over actors—persons or groups (not only government and citizens, of course)—and where 'x' stands for a possible action of R. Since, at least in the area of politics, P most often wields power over R with respect to R's *not* doing x, I shall consider mainly this negative expression.

Power in this sense is a relational concept. 'But ordinary language suggests that this is not true. "Power" is something which one may "have" or "not have", "exercise" or "not exercise." ' (Pitkin, 1972, p.276.) Here, as so often, ordinary language is an unreliable guide to uncovering the logical structure of concepts. I may 'have' a headache or a television set, but I do not 'have power—period'. I have (perhaps) power over my students with respect to their reading *Leviathan*. This is the type of expression to be analysed if we want power to function as a fruitful concept in political theory.

## 2 EXERCISING POWER AND HAVING POWER (1): EXERCISING POWER

Like most authors I shall distinguish between exercising and having power, but my analysis of the latter concept will differ from theirs. I shall say that *P exercises power over R's not doing x* $=_{df}$ *P influences R not to do x or restrains R from doing x or punishes R for having done x.*

### 2A. Influence

I am defining influence as a sub-category of power (like Barry), not *vice versa* (as does Dahl, 1963, p.50), or synonymously (see Riker, 1964, p.347), or as excluding each other (as do Mokken and Stokman in this book or Benn, 1967, p.424). I shall say that *P influences R not to do x* $=_{df}$ *P performs some action y as a result of which R chooses not to do x*. It follows from this definition that, before P does y, R has not yet chosen to abstain from doing x; he either intends or at least contemplates doing x (e.g. to vote Conservative). As a result of P's intervention, R makes the choice—in the sense of *final* decision—not to do x (e.g. not to vote Conservative, but to vote Labour). If R has already set his mind definitely on not doing x, then P cannot influence R not to do x—'cannot' in the logical sense, given the proposed definition. On the other hand, merely by asking R not to do x, P exercises influence, and power in that respect, if only to a small degree.

P's action y may consist of dissuading R from doing x, and P may do so by rational argument or by playing on R's irrational feelings. Prior to P's dissuasive action y, R may either contemplate doing x or be undecided or even be mildly disinclined to do x. Persuasion therefore does not necessarily involve P and R having opposing interests, unlike the other forms of exercising power to be mentioned. To say that some degree of conflict of goals is a necessary condition of the exercise of power would exclude persuasion, a conclusion drawn by Benn (1967, p.424) for example: 'To offer a man good reasons for doing something is not to exercise power over him, although it may influence his decision.' But if P successfully persuades R to vote Labour, doesn't he exercise power over R in that respect? It seems therefore more fruitful to consider all forms of influence by persuasion as instances of power.

*Deterrence,* the other form of influence, consists of P's communicating to R that he (or someone else) would inflict some harm on him, should he do x. As a result, R judges the negative utility of the threatened penalty sufficiently great, and the probability of its application sufficiently high, to determine him to choose compliance as a lesser evil. Deterrence (and the exercise of influence and of power in general) is thus necessarily successful by definition—that is, by the definition I am proposing, contrary to Barry (section 3 above). If R decided to do x in spite of P's (unsuccessful) effort to influence him (through dissuasion or deterrence) not to do x, then P did not exercise power in this instance. Not does the government exercise deterring power over citizens whose compliance is motivated not by their fear of sanction but by their moral conviction that legitimate authority ought to be generally obeyed. Making it illegal to do x will then be sufficient to dissuade them from doing x. I therefore consider 'activation of commitments' in the sense of 'cashing in on some norms that [somebody] already has' (Barry, p.68 above) as a form of persuasion rather than deterrence but not a separate power process. R's general law-abiding disposition may in turn be the result either of his own autonomous moral conviction or of his having been persuaded by others (for example those in authority) to accept official enactments as morally (as well as legally) binding. Inducement—promising R some benefit if he abstains from doing x—may be considered a special form of deterrence, where P threatens to withhold some benefit from R in case he does x (see Lively, section 3 above, referring to Blau; similarly Held, 1972, p.54).

## 2B. Restraint

*P restrains R from doing x* $=_{df}$ *P performs some action y as a result of which R's attempt at doing x fails*. Restraint or coercion differs from influence in the following respects: (i) before P's intervention, R has not only positively chosen to do x, but has overtly embarked on a course of action which he expects to bring about x; (ii) restraint does involve a conflict of interest between P and R, since R intends to realize x and P wants him not to achieve this goal; (iii) P's action y impinges not on R's mind, but on his body or environment; and (iv) coercion or restraint makes R unable to do x, and unfree to do x as well. On the other hand, influence (whether by discussion or deterrence), while motivating R not to do x, does not restrict either his ability or his freedom to do x (contrary to Chazel who in section 3 above *defines* exercising power as restricting the range of actions open to R). It is this difference between influence and coercion that makes the distinction between these two forms of power so important (see Oppenheim, 1961, p.82).

*Physical coercion* is perhaps the first situation that comes to mind in connection with power. Yet, coercing someone to *do* something or restraining him from *acting* in a certain way covers only such face-to-face interactions as a guard forcing a resisting prisoner into his cell or frustrating his attempt to break out. If R remains passive, P does not exercise power with respect to his *doing* (or not doing) something. 'The actual exercise of physical force can have only limited use as a means of power.' (Lively, p.8 above.) Here it seems practical to follow ordinary language and to extend the meaning of restraint or coercion to cover also *coercive threats*, where the threat is so severe and so credible that R has 'practically no choice' but to give up his attempt at doing x (Lasswell and Kaplan, 1950, p.97; Oppenheim, 1961, p.36). Thus, in the typical situation of 'your money or your life', R—at least in theory—first attempts to keep his money but soon realizes that he 'must' surrender it. Doing so still constitutes an action, and an intentional one, though not a voluntary (in the sense of preferred) one. Analogously, we may assimilate the promise of a reward that R 'cannot refuse' (see Barry, p.69 above) to coercive threats and, hence, to coercion. Surely, promising someone lost in the desert some water 'if he does x' amounts to threatening him with keeping it from him if he doesn't.

Influence through deterrence thus slides over into restraint through coercive threats. There is, however, a widespread tendency to include even mild threats under coercion.[1] It would then follow that my keeping within the speed limits to avoid a fine is an instance of being coerced, rather than deterred (and influenced). From there it is only one step to take the threat of sanction as a defining characteristic, not only of coercion, but of power in general (as does, e.g. Chazel, sections 1 and 2 above, and Blau as paraphrased by Lively, section 4 above; *contra* Mokken and Stokman, section 3 above). But the definitional equation 'power = coercion = deterrence' would leave out three other important power processes: influence through persuasion, physical coercion, and (as we shall see) actual punishment (which Chazel does introduce as a form of power: see Chapter 4, Section 2).

## 2C. Prevention

*P punishes R for having done x* $=_{df}$ *P believes that R did x, as a result of which P performs some action y which deprives R.* The definition does not refer explicitly to any norm. This is not to deny that, as a matter of fact, there is usually some legal or customary rule accepted as binding by members of the given society (including P and R) stipulating that whoever occupies office P is empowered to inflict penalty y on any R he finds guilty of having done x.

While influence is, as we have seen, often disregarded as an instance of exercising power, punishment is hardly ever considered in this connection. It is true that punishment, unlike influence and restraint, does not constitute *control*. On the contrary, P's punishing R for having done x indicates P's failure to exercise control (influence or coercion) over R with respect to his not doing x. It is also true that 'not imprisonment but the threat of imprisonment is the usual instrument of social power' (Lively, p.8 above), since penal legislation is usually enacted to deter people from acting in a certain way and to punish only those who have not been deterred. Nevertheless, imprisoning someone for having broken the law is surely an exercise of power, no less so than deterring him from committing an infraction.

Deterrence and punishment are different power processes: the former by definition implies compliance, the latter non-compliance. But punishment must also be distinguished from yet another power relation. P, by punishing R for having done x, may thereby deter R (and others as well) from performing some other action z, similar to x, in the future. Here one and the same action y of P constitutes two different power processes, referring to two different actions, x and z. Chazel, failing to make that distinction, considers P's punishment of R an exercise of power only to the extent that it succeeds in deterring R from disobeying P 'from that moment on' (p.62 above). No: even if R turns out to be a recidivist, P exercised power over R—punitive power—with respect to his having done x, but not deterring power over his later action z. Finally, P's action y (e.g., imprisoning R) may at the same time be an instance of coercion, depending on whether or not R puts up resistance which P overcomes.

## 3 EXERCISING POWER AND HAVING POWER (2): HAVING POWER

Exercising power usually involves face-to-face relationships among individuals. The social sciences are more interested in relationships of interaction between groups than between individuals and more in potential than in merely actual interaction. The more inclusive concept of having power captures such relationships and is therefore the more fruitful one. P may thus have power over R with respect to his not doing x without R's actually intending or attempting or doing x, and hence without P's exercising power in that respect. And the more power an actor has the less power he needs to exercise. *P has power over R's not doing x* $=_{df}$ *P has influence over R's not doing x or prevents R from doing x or makes it punishable for R to do x.*

### 3A. Influence

*P has influence over R's not doing x* $=_{df}$ *P performs some action z such that, were R to contemplate doing x, R would choose not to do x.* In analogy to exercising influence, we may distinguish between *having dissuading power* and *having deterring power*. By publishing pro-Labour articles, P may have persuading power even over voters who have already decided to vote Labour but who, were they to contemplate switching to Conservative, would stick with Labour as a result of these articles. Through acts of legislation involving threats of sanction, the government may acquire power even over many citizens who comply on their own initiative. Thus, the Ministry of Transport, by enacting and enforcing speed limits, has deterring power over the following group of drivers who stay within the speed limits: (i) those whom it thereby deters from speeding (and over whom it thereby exercises influence and power); and (ii) those who do not care to speed but who, were they to contemplate speeding, would change their mind as a result of the threatened penalty. The Ministry of Transport has no deterring power over: (i) speeders (regardless of whether or not they are apprehended and fined); (ii) non-speeders who, were they to contemplate speeding, would decide to do so regardless of the penalty; and (iii) non-speeders with a general law-abiding disposition who would not even contemplate breaking the law. (Over this group the Ministry has dissuading power, as we have seen.) Similarly, the Catholic Church has influence (either dissuading or deterring power) even over Catholics who do not think of divorcing but who, were they to contemplate divorce, would decide against it; the Church has no power over those who would in that case carry out their original intention.

### 3B. Prevention

*P prevents R from doing x =*$_{df}$ *P performs some action z as a result of which R cannot do x.* That R cannot do x means that R would not do x even if he wanted to, in the sense of 'would like to' (see von Wright, 1971, p.102). Analogously, to say that P makes it necessary for R to do x means that P performs some action z as a result of which R cannot help but do x. Making it—either literally or for all practical purposes—impossible or necessary for a person or group to act in a certain way is perhaps the most widespread form of power; yet it is often not mentioned, or not clearly distinguished from actual coercion (see Barry, section 2 above). Even so, preventing someone from doing something without the latter's attempting to act otherwise occurs more frequently than actually restraining him. If R first attempts to break out and then P locks the door (does y) before R reaches it, P exercises power over R by means of physical coercion. If P locks the door first (does z) so that R cannot get out, P *physically prevents* R from leaving, no matter whether or not R actually attempts or even merely contemplates getting out. Military occupation, blockade, protective tariffs or breaking of diplomatic relations are policies by which a government makes it impossible for another government and its citizens to do certain things and thus has power over the latter. The gunman's making it practically impossible for his victim even to attempt any resistance would be an example of *prevention by coercive threats.* Similarly, in a dictatorship, penalties might be so severe and their enforcement so effective that disobedience becomes practially impossible. But the most effective way by which governments in general acquire power over their citizens without having to exercise it is to make certain actions *legally impossible:* outlawing divorce, cancelling a franchise, witholding a passport or declaring certain type of contract null and void. Or policy-maker A may have power over policy-maker B by preventing him 'from bringing to the fore any issues which might in their resolution be seriously detrimental to A's set of preferences' (Bachrach and Baratz, 1962, pp.947-52). On the other hand, P does not have power over R by making it possible for him to do x (*contra* Mokken and Stokman, section 3 above) unless P makes it thereby practically necessary for R to do what he has enabled him to do.

### 3C. Punishment

*P makes it punishable for R to do x =*$_{df}$ *P performs some action z such that, were R to do something which some agent Q who is under P's authority believes to be an instance of x, this would motivate Q to perform some action y harmful to R.* Penal legislation is of course the prime example. Here P, the legislator, enacts a penal statute and bestows law-enforcing power on certain office-holders Q (policemen, judges, prison guards and so on). P thereby acquires power not only over law-breakers (real and alleged) who are actually being penalized by Q by virtue of the statute, but also over those who would be apprehended and punished if they broke the law. Thus, the Ministry of Transport, while lacking influence over speeders and would-be speeders who would not be deterred by the penalties, nevertheless has power—punishing power—over those who would be fined if they speeded, as well as over those who are actually being fined. It is true that government, by enacting penal legislation, acquires both deterring power (over those who comply to avoid the penalty) and punitive power (over law-breakers who are apprehended). But, analytically, these are two distinct forms of power, as are actual deterrence and actual punishment. 'P has made it punishable for R to do x' in the behavioural sense must also be distinguished from the notion of illegality. While the Ministry of Transport has no punitive power over those who would not be detected and fined if they speeded, speeding is illegal for all drivers. At least in principle, the percentage of drivers over whom the Ministry of Transport has punitive power (that is, the percentage who would be punished if they speeded) could be statistically determined.

## 4 EXERCISING POWER AND HAVING POWER (3): ABILITY TO HAVE POWER

All other authors known to me who use the concept of having power define it as the ability to exercise power.[2] It is true that the word 'power' is often used as a synonym for 'ability': that John has the power to jump six feet means that he can jump six feet, in other words that he will do so provided he wants to. But we are dealing here not with power as a relationship between *one* actor and his *own* potential action but with the narrower concept of one actor having power over *another* actor with respect to a possible action of the *latter*. Even in such contexts, having power often stands for the capacity to exercise it. That parents have power over their children may simply mean that they *can* influence or coerce them to do certain things or punish them if they don't. However, having power over the activities of others is more often used in the narrower sense in which I am taking it and must then be distinguished from the ability to acquire power as well as from its actual exercise. True, whoever *exercises* power also *has* power and also *can* have (and exercise) it. But not necessarily *vice versa*. P may have the resources (for example, wealth) enabling him to acquire influence over a wide group, for example by buying a television station. But P does not *have* such power unless he actually *does* avail himself of that possibility ('performs some action z . . .') by, for example, acquiring a television station; and the audience over which P now has power may be larger than the group over which he exercises influence. Having power, as well as exercising power, must be distinguished from the bases or resources of power (see Lasswell and Kaplan, 1950, p.84).

Here are some other illustrations. That the United States has power over Mexico's foreign policy implies not merely that the former government is capable of, for example, deterring or preventing the latter from joining the Soviet bloc; it means that the United States has acquired and now possesses sufficient military and economic resources so that, in the—very unlikely—event that Mexico attempted or even merely contemplated joining the Soviet bloc, the United States *would* prevent or deter

Mexico from doing so. Most who have the technical skill and the psychological stamina to hijack a plane would never do so; and only someone who actually hijacks a plane gains control over passengers and crew, making certain actions practically impossible or necessary for them. Governments have the legal authority to lower speed limits and hence the capacity to have and to exercise power over drivers in that respect. But the Ministry of Transport does not *have* such power unless such legislation has been enacted. 'To say that the policeman has the power to stop the traffic is to say that *if* some traffic came along and he held up his hand it would stop.' (Gibson, 1971, p.105.) More precisely: to say that policeman P has power with respect to R's stopping when P raises his hand is to say that P has acceded to and now occupies the office of a policeman so that R would stop upon P's raising his hand, even if R had at first contemplated going on.

'It is perfectly possible to have power without doing anything at all.' (Gibson, 1971, p.102.) Without exercising that power, yes; but not without having done something to acquire that power. 'Done something' is to be taken in the broad sense which includes not only such 'basic actions' as raising my hand, but also their immediate and long range effects (see Goldman, 1970, p.20). These include such lasting results as occupying an office (after having acceded to it), playing a role (that one has assumed), owning something (that one has acquired) or possessing a skill (that one has developed). Using 'power' in the two senses I have distinguished, one might say that someone has the power to have power: that he has the ability, say, to make others unable to act in a certain way.

Compared with Barry's definition of power—'the possession of the means of securing compliance by the manipulation of rewards or punishments' (p.90 above)—my proposal is both narrower and broader. It is narrower in that P not only has the ability or means to control R's behaviour, but actually does something that would secure R's compliance under certain conditions; it is broader since it includes not only deterring and inducing power, but also prevention, having influence not involving threats of punishment or promise of reward, and punitive power (which implies P's failure to secure R's compliance).

## 5  POWER AND CAUSE (1): POWER IDENTIFIED WITH CAUSE

Having clarified these various power concepts, we are ready to examine whether any or all of them are conceptually linked to the notion of causality. We begin by noting that the proposed definitions of the three forms of *exercising* power do indeed refer to causation. To bring this out, we can replace in the defining expressions 'as a result of which' by 'which causes'. For example, that P influences R not to do x means that P performs some action y which causes R not to do x. This does not imply, however, that 'for the assertion "A has power over B" we can substitute the assertion "A's behavior causes B's behavior." ' (Simon, 1957, p.5). 'Having power' and 'causing' are not synonyms. Rather, these are overlapping categories. There may be power without causation and causation without power.

We have seen that, unlike exercising power, having power involves no actual causal links, since P may have power over R in some respect without causing him to do (or not to do) anything, or without causing him any harm. The advantage of the concept of having power is precisely that it covers situations in which there is no punitive or restraining or dissuading action y of P and where R neither does nor attempts nor even contemplates doing x. The problem of the logical status of hypothetical and contrary-to-fact conditionals need not concern us here. Suffice it for our purpose to say that such statements—which pervade the social sciences—can in principle be tested by reference to empirical evidence, like affirmations of actual causal connections.

Conversely, P may perform some action y that causally affects R, and yet no power may be involved. P does not have power over R with respect to any *action* of R if he does something *to* R: if for example he causes him to be better off or worse without controlling his future behaviour or punishing him for some past action (see Barry, Sections 3 and 12 above). We have seen that P does not exercise coercive power over R's not doing x unless R makes an unsuccessful attempt at doing x. If the guard pushes the prisoner into his cell and the latter does not put up any resistance, the guard does not exercise power over the prisoner with respect to his not breaking out. Nor is R under the power of any actor if his inability to do x is the causal result not of someone else's intervention but of his own lack of skill or of his upbringing or of some physical obstacle or of general social or economic conditions. If North Africans cannot work in Western Europe because these governments have closed their borders to them, the latter have power over the former in that respect. But no power relations are involved if North Africans living in Europe cannot find work because of large-scale unemployment caused in turn by depression—unless these general economic conditions are in turn considered the causal result of the policies of some Arab sheikhs, a rather far-fetched and simplistic explanation and a rather lengthy causal chain. While this example illustrates the problem of borderline cases, it also shows the fruitfulness of distinguishing between social causation generally and power relations in particular. To consider both coextensive would deprive the concept of power of its proper and distinctive linguistic function and of its usefulness for political science.

## 6 POWER AND CAUSE (2): POWER CONSIDERED AS NOT INVOLVING CAUSATION

There are various arguments for the opposite view, that 'cause' should not occur in the defining expression of any power concept. First, causality, like power itself, has been viewed as an outmoded notion. Suffice it to quote Patrick Suppes's rejoinder that 'the words "causality" and "cause" are commonly and widely used by physicists in their most advanced work' (quoted by von Wright, 1971, p.36, together with other statements to the same effect). And surely such fields as medicine and law could not do without speaking of the causes of various infections or crimes. The same goes for the social sciences studying the causes of wars or revolutions or depressions.

Again, the concept of causality is often mistakenly associated with that of necessity. It is then objected that social and behavioural relations are probabilistic, and therefore not causal. However, these are not contradictory notions. There is strict causality and probabilistic causality. Power relations are of the latter type. That P exercises control over R's action x does not imply that R necessarily does x, but that it is more or less *likely* that he will do so, or that members of group R tend to comply (see Chazel, Section 1 above).

Speaking of causation is often thought to imply the classical mechanistic, billiard ball view of cause and effect. No, using the terms 'cause' and 'effect' in the area of individual or social behaviour does not commit one to crude behaviourism, but is perfectly compatible with the contemporary view that mental states or events like R's beliefs, wants, preferences or choices function as intervening variables between P's and R's overt actions. The proposed definition of influencing—P causes R to *choose* to do x—explicitly refers to such unobservable mental factors.

This particular definition raises the recently much debated question whether an actor's reasons for acting in some specific way may be considered the cause of his action. While von Wright denies that such motivational mechanisms are causal (1971, p.69), Goldman holds that 'reasons—explanations *are* a species of causal explanations' (1970, p.69), and hence (p.91) that 'acts are caused by mental events'. We need not take sides on this issue here since we are concerned with R's motives and choices not in relation to his own subsequent action x but in relation to P's antecedent action y. There cannot be any doubt that the connection between one actor's action and another actor's choice is a causal one. 'We most naturally speak of causes where some agent does something which results in an interference with the natural operations or conditions of some other agent or substance.' (Alston, 1967, p.408.)

We come now to the most serious objection against the use of the notion of causality in connection with the study of human interaction such as power. It is claimed that causality is linked to a type of explanation—the so-called covering law model—which is not applicable to the explanation of human behaviour. According to this model, 'causal explanations presuppose general laws of nature that connect the specific cause with the effect to be explained' (Hempel, 1967, p.80). These general laws may be of a strictly universal or of a probabilistic kind. The objection is that there are no general laws, not even probabilistic ones, under which human actions and interactions can be subsumed (von Wright, 1971; Ball, 1975).

We may say on this, first, that the use of causal language is often considered appropriate even where the covering law model is held not to be applicable. 'The point is that we often can give some explanation of an occurrence by saying that this or that caused it when we know of no law of which it is a case, or even think that there is none.' (Urmson, 1952, in White, 1968, p.162; see also Goldman, 1970, p.72.) According to this view, we are entitled to say that a given action was caused by the actor's motives even if we cannot refer to a general law that covers this event. But again, and more importantly, we are dealing here with power phenomena: we are trying to explain R's choice and action x by reference to some action y of another actor P. Such explanations do in many cases invoke general causal laws. For example: why did driver R stop when policeman P signalled him to do so? Answer: drivers tend to obey traffic rules when these are well enforced. That is to say, whenever a driver is (or rather: believes himself to be) in a situation to which well enforced traffic rules apply, he will tend to comply (it is highly probably that he will comply). This general empirical law, together with the 'initial condition' that P gave the appropriate signal, probabilistically implies that R stopped—that R decided to comply rather than to risk a penalty. We conclude that the driver's decision to stop was caused by P's action, and that therefore—given our definitions—P deterred R from driving on, and exercised power over him in that respect.

A related objection is that men act *in order to* conform to man-made customary, legal or normal rules (either willingly or under compulsion). Human behaviour is thus 'rule-governed', and must therefore be explained not causally but teleologically (or at least 'quasi-teleologically'; see von Wright, 1971, p.83). The last example may serve to refute this argument. We have just explained the driver's stopping by reference not to the normative rules of traffic but to the descriptive law of human behaviour that such regulations are generally being obeyed. Now, teleologists might use a counter-example such as the following. Why do MPs tend to vote as their constituents want them to? (And why are the former under the latter's power in that respect?) In order to be re-elected; and in order to achieve this goal, MPs had better conform to their constituents' wishes. Isn't this explanation based on a prudential rule rather than on a causal law? No, it is not the means—end rule that explains the MPs' voting behaviour, but the empirical law that people tend to act in ways that maximize their chance of attaining their goals. In this case: MPs generally consider pleasing their constituents the best way of getting re-elected.

Finally, that social relations generally and power relations in particular often involve multiple causation and (as we have seen) causes of a probabilistic kind is not a valid objection against defining them in terms of causation either. These features merely point up the practical difficulties often involved when attempting to determine who has power over whom with respect to what activity.

## 7 POWER AND NECESSARY OR SUFFICIENT CONDITION (1): EXERCISING AND HAVING INFLUENCE

The question still remains whether 'cause' in the defining expressions of power concepts should be interpreted in the sense of necessary condition or sufficient condition or both. A necessary condition of a given event is a set of circumstances without which that event could not have occurred. A sufficient condition of a given event is a set of circumstances such that, if they obtained, the event had to occur. Contrary to Chazel (Section 1 above), it is feasible to give the notions of necessary and of sufficient condition a probabilistic interpretation; and for the reasons given before, it is useful to do so when dealing with human interactions. Let us say, accordingly, that a probabilistically necessary condition of a given action is a set of circumstances without which the occurrence of that action would be highly improbable, and a probabilistically sufficient condition of a given action is a set of circumstances that make that action highly probably.

### 7A. Exercising influence

It is in the sense of necessary condition that most writers implicitly refer to causation in connection with exercising power in general and exercising influence in particular: 'influence is a *relation among actors* in which one actor induces other actors to act in some way they would not otherwise act.' (Dahl, 1963, p. 40.)[3] If R would have acted differently had P not intervened, then P's actual intervention was a necessary condition for R's actual behaviour. This interpretation would have the advantage of enabling us in certain cases to measure the degree of influence by the magnitude of the deviation of the respondent's actual behaviour from what he would have done without the other actor's intervention.

However, the assertion that P influenced R to do x seems to me perfectly compatible with the contrary-to-fact assumption that R would have decided to perform the same action x even if P had not intervened. 'P influenced R not to do x' implies only that P performed some action y that made it highly probable that R decided not to do x; hence, that y was a probabilistically sufficient condition for R's final choice. That the United States, by dropping the A-bomb on Hiroshima, influenced Japan not to continue the war means: given the fact that the United States dropped the bomb, it became highly probably that Japan would decide to capitulate. That is to say, the former event was a sufficient condition of the latter. It need not be the case that Japan would have continued to fight had Hiroshima not occurred. Japan might have come around on its own to give up, or the Soviet government might have persuaded the Japanese to capitulate. On the other hand, election officer P's placing R's name on the voting register is a necessary condition for R's voting, and also for R's voting Labour. Yet, surely P does not thereby exercise influence over R with respect to his voting, let alone thereby influence R to vote Labour. Registering R, while a necessary condition, is not a sufficient condition for his voting, or for his voting Labour. Thus, if P influenced R to do x, P's action y *may* have been a necessary but *must* have been a sufficient condition for R's final decision. Hence, causality as a defining characteristic of exercising influence should be taken in the sense of a sufficient condition, not in the sense of a necessary condition. This interpretation has a further advantage. Sufficient conditions are usually easier to establish than necessary ones, at least in the area of of human interaction. From the fact that the United States dropped the A-bomb (as a threat of still greater harm) one could predict fairly safely that Japan would capitulate. This was actually the prediction of the American policy-makers. The hypothesis that Japan would have capitulated otherwise is much more difficult to substantiate, and it need not be established to ascertain that the United States exercised influence and power over Japan in this instance.

## 7B. Having influence

'P has influence over R's not doing x' means that, were R to contemplate doing x, some previous action z of P would be a probabilistically sufficient condition for R's deciding not to do x. In other words it would make it highly probably that R would choose to abstain from doing x. That R keeps off P's ground may be due either to P's 'No trespassing' sign or to R's own inclination. In the latter case, P, while not *exercising* influence, nevertheless *has* influence over R with respect to his not trespassing provided that, were R to contemplate doing so, P's sign would be sufficient to deter him. Similarly, the Ministry of Transport has influence over drivers with respect to their not speeding if the enactment and enforcement of speed limit legislation has made it highly probably that drivers won't speed, even if they were to contemplate speeding.

## 8 POWER AND NECESSARY OR SUFFICIENT CONDITION (2): COERCING AND PREVENTING

## 8A. Coercion

We have seen that coercion, unlike influence, presupposes a conflict of will between P and R. For R does not merely contemplate acting in a way contrary to what P wants him to do but he actually attempts to do so. It would therefore seem that a 'requirement for a person being coerced is that he would have chosen differently had he not been threatened' (Bayles, 1972, p.19), and that P's coercive action y is therefore a necessary as well as a sufficient condition for the failure of R's attempt to do x. Similarly, according to Goldman (1970, p.217): 'S* will be said to have constrained S only if S* succeeds in causing S to perform an act which he otherwise would not have performed.' Now, in the dramatic cases that immediately come to mind, such as the gunman's coercive threats, we do indeed suppose that the victim would have kept his purse had there been no coercion. But we cannot, and need not, make this assumption in every instance. There are situations in which, even if P had not restrained R from doing x, R might have suddenly decided to give up his attempt to do x, either as a result of his own change of mind or because someone other than P influenced or coerced him not to do x. Again it would be counter-intuitive to require, as a defining characteristic of coercion or restraint, that P's action y be a necessary (as well as a sufficient) condition for R's giving up his attempt to do x, especially if we subsume threats of severe deprivation under coercion. Surely, such threats should not be interpreted differently depending on the degree of their severity. Coercion, like influence, requires only that P's action y be a sufficient condition for the failure of R's attempt to do x. Thus, while P's placing R's name on the voting list is a necessary but not a sufficient condition for R's voting, denying R's request for registration is a sufficient condition for R's not voting but not a necessary one since R might have abstained anyhow. In this case P restrains R from voting and exercises power over him in this respect.

## 8B. Prevention

'P prevents R from doing x' means that some action z of P is a sufficient condition for R's being unable to do x—that is, for R's not doing x were he to attempt to do so. In other words, were R to attempt x, then, given the fact that P did z, it would be highly probable that R's attempt would fail (or highly improbable that it would succeed). By erecting a high wall, instead of a 'No Trespassing' sign, P prevents R from trespassing. P's action is a sufficient condition for R's being unable to trespass. But P's action need not be a sufficient condition for R's not trespassing. If R does not attempt to trespass or does not even contemplate trespassing, his lack of inclination is a sufficient condition for his not doing so, and it is trivially true that he does not trespass (unless accidentally). Yet P's action y is not a necessary condition either for R's not doing x or for R's inability to do so. Indeed, even if P had not erected the wall, R might not have trespassed, perhaps because he did not attempt (and perhaps not even contemplate) doing so; and R might not have been able to trespass, perhaps because he broke his leg. All these hypothetical cases are compatible with the assertion that P made it impossible for R to trespass (i.e. prevented him from doing so) and had power over him with respect to his not trespassing.

We may now restate the definition of the concept of *control* as follows. Exercising Control: *P exercises control over R's not doing x* = $_{df}$ *P performs some action y which is a probabilistically sufficient condition for R's deciding not to do x or for the failure of R's attempt at doing x.* And having control: *P has control over R's not doing x* = $_{df}$ *P performed some action z which is a probabilistically sufficient condition for R's deciding not to do x were he to contemplate doing so, or for his being unable to do x.* Whenever such actual or hypothetical causal relationships of probabilistically sufficient conditions can be ascertained in a given situation, it follows logically—given these definitions—that P has control, and hence power, over R with respect to his not doing x.

## 9  POWER AND NECESSARY OR SUFFICIENT CONDITION (3): PUNISHING AND MAKING PUNISHABLE

### 9A.  Punishing

In all situations of exercising control, it is P's action y that constitutes a sufficient condition for R's doing (or not doing) x. It may seem that in the case of punishment causality flows in the opposite direction, from R's action (e.g. speeding) to P's action y (e.g. fining R). We have seen, however, that P's punitive action y is the causal effect not of what R actually did but of what P himself (rightly or wrongly) believes R to have done. That P punishes R for having done x means that P's belief that R did x is the cause of P's performing some action y that deprives R. The direction of causality is thus the same in all three forms of exercising power.

There is an important difference, however. In contrast to the cases of exercising control, 'cause' must be taken here in the sense of necessary as well as sufficient condition. Strictly speaking, punishment involves three such causal relationships. (i) R does something (driving) which causes P (a policeman) to form the belief that R did x (speeding). Had R not acted in a certain way, P would probably not have believed that R did x; and the fact that R acted that way made it likely that P would interpret R's conduct as an instance of x. However, this causal connection is not, and need not be, mentioned explicitly in the definition of the concept of punishment. (ii) P's belief that R did x motivates (hence causes) him to perform some action y (imposing a fine on R). (Some authors deny that motives are causes, as mentioned earlier.) Without P's belief that R did x, P would probably not have done y; and having formed that belief it became probable that he would. (iii) P's action y causes R some harm. Without P's punitive action, R most probably would not feel deprived (probably, but not certainly; someone other than P might have harmed him instead, whether or not as a punishment for his having done something, whether x or something else); and the fact that P did y made it highly probable that R would feel worse off (but not certain: some people sometimes do not mind paying a fine or are even glad to go to jail).

### 9B.  Making punishable

To say that P (the Ministry of Transport) makes it punishable to do x (to speed) is to affirm that P performs some action z (enacting and enforcing speed laws) such that, were R (any driver) to do something that some agent Q who acts under P's authority (a policeman) believes to be an instance of x (speeding), this belief would be a probabilistically necessary and sufficient condition for Q to perform some action z (imposing a fine) which would deprive R. Here we have an additional, but hypothetical, causal link, namely between P's action z and Q's action y. This is, again, a relationship of both necessary and sufficient condition. The fact that P does z makes it highly probable that Q would do y, should he believe that R did x; and Q's action y probabilistically presupposes that P did z.

This section can be summarized in two definitions. First, punishment: *P punishes R for having done x = df P's belief that R did x is a probabilistically necessary and sufficient condition for his performing some action y harmful to R.* And second, making punishable: *P makes it punishable for R to do x = df P performs some action z which is a probabilistically necessary and sufficient condition for the following: were Q (who acts under P's authority) to believe that R did x, this would be a probabilistically necessary and sufficient condition for his performing some action y which would deprive R.*

# 7

# Co-operative Negotiations and Bargaining: Some Notes on Power and Powerlessness

KNUT MIDGAARD

## 1 INTRODUCTION

Negotiation is one central method, or family of methods, of collective decision-making. This method, or family of methods, can be defined as a kind of process where explicit proposals are put forward and discussed with the official purpose of arriving at an agreement on some practical matter: the exchange or distribution of certain goods or evils, the establishment of some common good, etc. (cf. Iklé, 1964). Negotiation is consequently a kind of process the course of which may significantly influence both the total set of goods and evils shared by the actors involved and the way in which these goods and evils are distributed over them, in so far as they can be distributed at all. Negotiation is further a kind of process that can take place in highly different contexts and that may lead to a great variety of situations if it breaks down: there may be a war, or a strike or no transaction at all; or the issue may be left to mediation, arbitration, a vote or a unilateral decision.

There are several reasons for studying negotiations in a systematic way. There may be a wish to be able to describe and explain the course and outcome of negotiations that have already taken place. Similarly, there may be a wish to be able to predict the course and outcome of future negotiations or negotiations under way. Various practical interests may of course be at play, for example that of serving the interests of one's country. As to the work from which this chapter emanates, it stems partly from more general theoretical interests and from a certain fascination with this subject matter. An equally strong motivating factor, however, has been the wish to attain knowledge that might help organize and carry through negotiations in a way conducive to efficient and fair outcomes.

So, this chapter first points out some central respects in which the parties to a set of negotiations can co-operate, and introduces a set of distinctions, in particular that between co-operative negotiation and pure bargaining (cf. Barry, 1965). It then comments upon and illustrates some conditions under which co-operation in the form of open discussions aimed at reaching an efficient and fair outcome can prove difficult while tendencies towards pure bargaining can prove correspondingly likely. To understand the various dilemmas involved, however, we need to come to grips with the kinds of dynamics that can evolve if a negotiation process assumes the character of bargaining; this topic, of course, is also interesting and important in itself. Two sections therefore discuss one central model of bargaining, and illustrate its relevance and consequences. Our line of reasoning also involves ideas about the significance of images. There is therefore a section devoted to the role of images. In the final section we indicate the relevance that the perspectives of the present paper have to the analysis of power and powerlessness. This discussion takes a broad power concept as its point of departure, more specifically that of Russell (1938), the production of intended effects. It is pointed out that power and powerlessness often have to do with an actor's ability to influence the aggregate value to be enjoyed by the set of actors in question, at the same time as they have to do with the actor's ability to influence the way in which goods and evils involved are distributed. A power analysis that does not combine both dimensions will in many cases prove inadequate.

## 2 CO-OPERATIVE DISCUSSION VERSUS BARGAINING: ELEMENTS OF A THEORETICAL FRAMEWORK

### 2A. The two ideal types of negotiation, and a central type of dilemma

If a negotiation process is not to be meaningless or strained, the parties must agree on its purpose, at least officially. Suppose they do. The minimal objective that they must then set themselves, at least officially, is to arrive at an agreement that is better than no agreement. Efficiency, or Pareto-optimality, is a somewhat more ambitious but equally natural goal. Finally, the parties may, at least officially, aim at an outcome that is fair or just.

The achievement of any of these goals requires, or makes for, some kind of co-operation. They may, first, elicit a co-operative effort to identify new alternatives. In addition, they may lead to various forms of co-operation with regard to which alternative the parties should agree upon as the outcome of the negotiations; in particular, an open dialogue on what would be a fair outcome can take place.

As to efforts to identify new possible outcomes, it should be noted that these may in some cases be efforts to identify alternatives that would dominate some of the alternatives that have so far been undominated or feasible. In other cases there may be little hope of being able to do such a thing; the negotiations will primarily have to be 'distributive'. At the same time there may be a great need for identifying alternatives that can serve as 'compromises' between elements of the given set of feasible alternatives.

Suppose, now, that the parties entertain a serious preference for joint problem-solving aimed at an efficient and fair outcome. Suppose, further, that they are known to be so motivated. Then the negotiations are likely to approach a type of dialogue where the attitudes of the parties to the various alternatives presented are determined only by the content of the descriptive and prescriptive premises presented during the talks, and where the parties, in attempting to contribute to an efficient and fair conclusion, are completely attentive and open with regard to their thinking about possible alternatives, and with regard to their descriptive and prescriptive premises. As regards real-life approximations to this ideal type, it seems that deliberations among the Friends, as they are supposed to occur, could serve as an example.

To understand the dynamics of such negotiations, one has to understand, among other things, the prescriptive premises of each party. It may, in particular, be decisive whether anybody finds the utilities associated with no agreement to be relevant or irrelevant. Consider a case where the Nash criterion is adopted as a prescriptive premise, so that the outcome should maximize the product of the parties' gains over no agreement (see Luce and Raiffa, 1958). The outcome is not unlikely to be quite different from what it would be if, for example, Bentham's principle of happiness maximization were adopted or if the parties followed the principle of justice maintained by Rawls (1971): that the situation of the worst-off party should be made as good as possible.

We shall, in the subsequent discussion, use the term 'co-operative negotiation', or 'strictly co-operative negotiation', to denote the ideal type of negotiation described above. In using this term, however, we shall in particular have in mind negotiations where the utilities obtained by the parties in the case of no agreement are not considered relevant to the problem of choosing between alternatives that are better to all parties than no agreement. Negotiations where a criterion such as the Nash criterion were adopted as a prescriptive premise would therefore not belong to this class.

So far, we have presupposed that the parties are known to be completely co-operative. Some will hold that this is nothing more than a limiting case. In any event, our condition is often far from being met. Quite often a party, while paying lip-service to the idea of fairness, has a very different goal, viz. that of maximizing his own advantage. In other cases, although none of the parties would accept a grossly unjust outcome even if it were in his own narrow interest, each of them may nevertheless be primarily concerned with his own advantage. Finally, at least some of the parties may be suspected of not being fully co-operative even if all of them in fact are.

In situations like these, negotiations will easily take a course where the attitudes of the parties to alternatives presented and to their own presentation of alternatives will be rather different from those typical of co-operative negotiations. First of all, the actors may have good reasons for controlling their own presentation of possible alternatives and, similarly, for keeping back or even distorting information. Further, they may have good reasons for basing themselves on the art of brinkmanship ('Chicken') or on methods of attrition. Within this framework they may find it useful to exploit implicit or explicit commitments. They will not merely express, or give an account of, the way in which they are committed to various premises on the basis of conviction, judgement or obligation. They will, by such means as pretending certain concerns, deliberately *create* or *reinforce* commitments through utterances that can have this force (cf. Austin, 1962). These commitments, of course, must somehow be relevant to the alternatives under consideration, in particular to proposals already submitted. It should be noted, however, that an actor's commitments may link with the relevant proposals and alternatives in rather indirect ways. Finally, it should be noted that the art of *not* becoming committed in an unfavourable way (through one's choice of arguments, for example) is as important as the art of committing oneself in an appropriate way to premises and alternatives to which one ought to become more or less committed.

Negotiations can deviate from co-operative negotiations in one or more of these respects and they can do so more or less drastically. If anything is to be conceived of as the opposite of co-operative negotiations, it must be, it seems, a negotiation process which deviates drastically from co-operative negotiations in all these respects. I propose to call such a type of negotiation 'pure bargaining'; and I propose to use the term 'bargaining' to characterize negotiation processes that have much in common with this ideal type. The characteristic features of pure bargaining are accordingly as follows: (i) brinkmanship or attempts at attrition are predominant; that is to say, considerations related to the parties' possible gains and losses from standing firm determine their attitudes and positions; and (ii) the possibility of commitment is exploited fully, and arguments and other moves are used merely to improve one's position in the process of brinkmanship or attrition.

It should be borne in mind that assertions as to what is fair and what is not can be exploited for a party's egoistic purposes in pure bargaining. That is one of several reasons why negotiation studies should pay attention to the notions and problems of fairness.

It should also be borne in mind that, even in pure bargaining, if successful, there is a significant element of co-operation or tacit co-ordination. A party who wants a given set of negotiations to become strictly co-operative, in the sense introduced earlier, will of course feel far from happy with this kind and degree of co-operation. On the other hand, the possibility of being exploited by a ruthless opponent is likely to be the worse outcome to him. If he does not trust the other party or parties, he may therefore find himself in a serious dilemma. He may find that, in order to get the talks on to a strictly co-operative track, he has to make a move that is risky because it can be exploited to his great disadvantage in bargaining. The move that he has to make is for example to

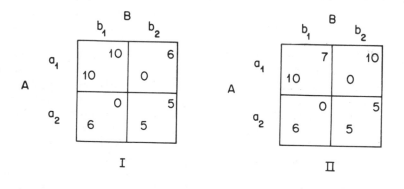

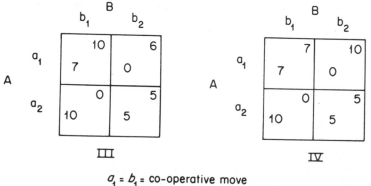

$a_1 = b_1 =$ co-operative move

$a_2 = b_2 =$ bargaining type move

release some significant information, to focus attention upon a problem or an interest that is central to him or his organization, and so on.

The situation may in fact be like this for both or all parties. Consider a two-person case. The situation may be that both parties simultaneously have to choose between a co-operative move or a bargaining-type move. The actual preference structure may then be as in matrix I in Figure 7.1, while A fears it to be like that of matrix II and B fears it to be like that of matrix III.

It seems that in such a case matrix IV in Figure 7.1 easily becomes the analytic clue (Midgaard, 1965) of the situation, which means that both choose the bargaining-type move. As the parties become aware of this problem, however, they can in different ways try to transcend the situation, or even prevent it from arising. They can divide a central problem into minor parts, close the meetings, arrange informal contacts and so on.

Such methods can of course also be useful, or necessary, to overcome a deadlock in a negotiation process that has definitively acquired the character of bargaining, although there the situation is more likely to be of the Prisoner's Dilemma type as represented in matrix IV.

If it proves difficult to get a negotiation process on to a productive, co-operative track, this need not be due primarily to unco-operative attitudes or to suspicions about others' attitudes. The reason may very well be that the parties have not done their homework sufficiently well or that they have not organized their meetings in a productive way. A discussion may come to an end because the parties have not provided sufficient material or because they have not gone through each other's points of view sufficiently carefully. In such a situation the parties may in certain cases choose to compromise out of respect for each other; but they may also end up in a bargaining process that leads to no result.

## 2B. Some more distinctions

Having established the two concepts 'co-operative negotiation' and 'pure bargaining', it may be useful to take a look at the stimulating work by Walton and McKersie (1965), where the tension between a party's interests under a distributive perspective and his interests under an efficiency perspective constitutes a central focus of interest.

Walton and McKersie distinguish two ideal types of negotiations: 'distributive bargaining' and 'integrative bargaining'. In addition they introduce a third category, 'mixed bargaining', as follows:

Distributive bargaining is the process by which each party attempts to maximize his own share in the context of fixed-sum payoffs. Integrative bargaining is the process by which the parties attempt to increase the size of the joint gain without respect to the division of the payoffs. Mixed bargaining is the process that combines both an attempt to increase the size of the joint gain and a decision on how to allocate shares between the parties. [Walton and McKersie, 1965, p.13]

These are useful concepts. Our previous discussion should make it clear, however, that they ought to be further elaborated. First, Walton and McKersie presuppose that in distributive bargaining each party is motivated by his own interest only. They do not make it clear that the negotiators can try, through a co-operative effort, to arrive at a reasonable or just solution. Second, the inventiveness that is necessary for successful integrative bargaining may also be necessary in distributive negotiations where the original set of perceived outcomes is not exhaustive and can therefore be transcended. The possibility of identifying new outcomes within a 'distributive' framework (that is, in negotiations where increased utility for one party means reduced utility for another) can call for a co-operative effort as well as for techniques specific to pure bargaining such as keeping back relevant information.

Now, let us use the term 'distributive negotiations' to denote negotiations where the distributive aspect dominates. Within this class there will of course be subsets of very different kinds, including the cases of pure bargaining and co-operative negotiations. (It should be kept in mind that the identification of new potential outcomes may be a significant element of both types of negotiations.)

Our concept 'pure bargaining', although defined somewhat differently, seems to be coextensive with Walton and McKersie's 'distributive bargaining'. As to the class of negotiations that are both distributive and co-operative, the term 'negotiations aimed at fairness' might be suggestive.

Similarly, we can introduce a term 'efficiency-oriented negotiations' to denote the kind of co-operative negotiations that take place in a situation where the efficiency rather than the distributive aspect dominates. This concept is similar to or identical with Walton and McKersie's concept of 'integrative bargaining'. (It should all the time be borne in mind that 'efficiency' is used in the sense of 'Pareto-optimality'; it has nothing to do with means—end relations.)

What about the concept of 'mixed bargaining'? Walton and McKersie emphasize the dilemma that can confront a negotiator who at the same time wants to secure his own interest and wants to contribute to increasing the joint gain. It seems that a similar dilemma can confront a negotiator who wants at the same time to secure certain minimal interests of his own and to contribute to a co-operative discussion aimed at reaching a fair solution. Spontaneity and openness may be conducive either to co-operate negotiations or to exploitation by one's opponent. So, a negotiator's behaviour may be the result of an attempt to strike a balance between the requirements of co-operative negotiations and the requirements of securing certain minimal interests of one's own in pure bargaining.

In accordance with the terminological suggestions made above, I propose to replace Walton and McKersie's term 'mixed bargaining' by 'mixed negotiation', defining the latter as negotiations containing elements of both co-operative negotiation and pure bargaining.

## 2C. On the operationality of the concepts introduced

Now, the question can be raised as to the operationality of our concepts 'co-operative negotiation' and 'pure bargaining'. Or rather: as these are ideal types one may ask to what extent it is possible to determine the kinds and degrees of deviation from either of them. Little reflection is needed to see that problems easily arise. Thus, the setup and context of the negotiations may be such that an actor who is willing to exploit all effective means to maximize his share of a given amount of goods may have to behave as if he were completely co-operative. Therefore it may be difficult to recognize, and impossible to demonstrate, to what extent he is keeping back information, or to what extent he is insincere in uttering a strong commitment to a certain principle (thereby creating a commitment rather than expressing one), and so on.

Such difficulties, however, do not mean that the concepts are useless or even meaningless. If we, as observers, have difficulties in determining how a negotiator's attitude and behaviour should be described, we may be in just the same situation as one of the actors. So, our concepts can help us to describe the latter's situation. Furthermore, in so far as we can influence the organization and course of a set of negotiations, our concepts may be of use even though it may perhaps prove difficult to tell exactly what character the talks are in fact assuming.

Thus, a negotiation process that looks very much like a co-operative discussion may contain significant elements of bargaining. On the other hand, a negotiation process that in fact contains significant elements of bargaining may do so in spite of what we might call the primary preferences of the participants. There may be a disagreement about the purpose of the talks which makes it difficult to get a meaningful discussion started. Or, as we have seen, a participant may be uncertain about the motives of the other party or parties and therefore find it necessary to use techniques characteristic of bargaining. Or, finally, the parties may have realized that they are not able to get any further in influencing each other's premises; in that case, they may, as we have seen, agree to compromise out of respect for each other, or they may invite a mediator or leave the issue to an arbitrator. The possibility also exists, however, that they may end up in bargaining.

## 3  CO-OPERATIVE DISCUSSION VERSUS BARGAINING: SOME ILLUSTRATIONS

### 3A. An historical outline for the international negotiations on the regulation of pelagic whaling, and the background of these negotiations

All the illustrations in this chapter but one are drawn from the international negotiations on the regulation of pelagic whaling. An outline of these negotiations and their background is therefore needed at this point (see Bock, 1966; Tønnessen, 1970; and Midgaard, 1973-4).

Excessive exploitation of the whale stock in Antarctica and other areas was already a problem in the interwar period, and continuous efforts were made during the 1930s to limit the catch. In 1946 a Whaling Convention was adopted that established an organization, the International Whaling Commission. This Commission was to meet annually to regulate whaling with a view to increasing the stock to its optimal level, at the same time as taking the problems and needs of the industry and of consumers into consideration. An important means to this end was the introduction of an annual global quota; within the framework of this quota competition was to be free, although subject to certain rules about the size of the whales caught, etc. The quota was at first set at sixteen thousand blue whale units. (For the uninitiated, one blue whale unit equals one blue whale, or two finback whales, or two and a half humpback whales, or six sei whales.) This figure reflected the need for whale products after the war rather than a scientific estimate of the biologically optimal catch. Although it became quite clear to biologists during the 1950s that the global quota had to be drastically reduced, whalers were not convinced, at least not officially. Owing to this fact and the interests involved, the global quota remained at about fifteen thousand blue whale units.

Within this framework, however, the capacity of the whale fleets continued to increase in spite of attempts at regulating the number of whale-catchers in operation. This was due partly to modernization and partly to the introduction of new factory ships. Thus, in the mid-fifties Holland replaced her old factory ship with a new, bigger one; Japan both modernized her fleet and added three more expeditions; and, finally, Soviet Russia announced a substantial expansion. Several factors seem to have been at work here. First, there seems to have been a desire for self-sufficiency. Second, nations with a modest share of the global catch (in contrast to Norway and the United Kingdom, which were the traditional and dominant whaling countries) apparently still found expansion to be profitable. The expansion of course reduced the profitability of the industry, and the situation was becoming very serious for Norwegian and British whalers. As a consequence, the chairman of the Norwegian Whaling Association, at the annual meeting of the Whaling Commission in 1956, warned expansionist states that Norway might withdraw from the Convention, which would mean a still heavier exploitation of the whale stock.

In 1958 the United Kingdom took the initiative in calling a conference on the establishment of national quotas. Before that, Norwegian whalers had privately suggested that three of their expeditions might be withdrawn on the condition that whaling companies of other nations joined a compensation arrangement. This proposal had been dismissed by the Japanese whalers who emphasized that they adhered to the principle of free competition. At the conference, which took place in London in November 1958, Soviet Russia accepted 20 per cent as her quota (which implied a considerable expansion). No agreement was reached between the other four countries at this conference. Before the end of the year, Norway notified its withdrawal from the Convention, and Holland and Japan followed suit.

Private talks were then held by Norwegian and Japanese whalers in February and April 1959. It seems that Japanese attitudes had now changed in the light of the new situation. There are good indications that Japan in these talks was inclined to accept an arrangement stipulating quotas of 30 per cent each for Japan and Norway with about 14 per cent for the United Kingdom and about 6 per cent for Holland, although this was not said plainly. Japan even seems to have been willing to compensate Norway in return for getting such an agreement. The Norwegian authorities found this distribution to be unacceptable. At the London conference in the preceding November, Norway had proposed the following distribution, based on the average catch of the expeditions involved during the last eleven years: $26\frac{1}{3}$ per cent for Japan, 5 per cent for Holland, $33\frac{2}{3}$ per cent for Norway and 15 per cent for the United Kingdom.

The official conference in Tokyo in May 1959, and the negotiations during the annual meeting of the Commission in London in June, did not lead to any agreement. Norway and Holland, therefore, carried out their withdrawal from the Whaling Convention, while Japan chose not to put her notified withdrawal into effect.

Various moves were made during the subsequent years. An important step forward was made at a conference in London in February 1961, but disagreement remained about Holland's share. Having originally demanded 8 per cent, Holland now insisted on 7 per cent while the other countries would not offer more than 6 per cent. It was not until the summer of 1962 that an agreement was signed, stipulating 33 per cent for Japan (which had bought an expedition, along with its quota, from the United Kingdom), 6 per cent (plus a special bonus arrangement) for Holland, 32 per cent for

Norway and 9 per cent for the United Kingdom. The 20 per cent share of Soviet Russia had not been touched. This agreement lasted until 1966 when another agreement was negotiated between Japan, Norway and Soviet Russia, which were by now the only remaining whaling nations.

It was not until after the conclusion of the agreement in 1962 that the global quota could be reduced. The reduction, however, was carried through at a much slower rate than that recommended by scientists. This seems to have been a consequence of economic interests involved, in particular the financial obligations assumed by Japanese whalers in taking over European expeditions. Today, only Soviet Russia and Japan are left in Antarctica, and their annual catch amounts to only a small fraction of the global quota of the 1950s and the early 1960s.

## 3B. Specific examples

We stated earlier that the parties to a negotiation process must agree, at least officially, on its purpose and topic if the talks are not to become meaningless or highly problematic. This kind of problem did not play a central role in the negotiations on whaling regulation. To find a good example we have to look elsewhere.

The first phase of the Paris talks on Vietnam provides us with an illustration. The representatives of North Vietnam maintained that the purpose of the talks was to decide on the unconditional cessation of US bombing and all other acts of war against North Vietnam, and *thereafter* to take up other questions of common interest. The United States, for its part, maintained that the purpose of the talks was to discuss the cessation of bombardment *together with* related questions.

It is obvious that such a disagreement makes a co-operative discussion on what would be a reasonable outcome highly difficult, or rather impossible, because the disagreement has to do with what the topic of the discussion should be. In fact, such a situation makes for bargaining of a particularly unpleasant and straining character. The negotiations may in fact acquire an element of the absurd.

Coming, then, to the whaling negotiations, their obvious purpose was to establish a quota for each of the pelagic nations. Within this framework, however, several types of arrangements could be envisaged. As the global quota was in principle changeable, and in fact needed to be reduced, any agreement, it seems, had to be in terms of percentages. Such an agreement, however, could be of different forms. What the parties agreed upon was a fixed percentage distribution (for each season up to 1966-67). More flexibile arrangements, however, are also imaginable—for example arrangements that would make it profitable for some to catch less during the initial years of the agreement so as to contribute to the growth of the whale stock. For actors with a long-term perspective an agreement of this kind might be more efficient than one with a fixed percentage distribution. Apparently, such flexible possibilities were never seriously discussed, if touched upon at all. Without going into specific technical and economic problems it does however seem that under certain conditions efficiency-oriented negotiations dealing with the exploitation of living resources ought to do so.

Interestingly enough, the whaling nations, in spite of what has been said above, tried in June 1959 to find an acceptable solution by introducing a type of agreement that would involve a higher sum of goods to the participants than would the alternatives considered previously. As it seemed impossible to find a solution within the framework of the given global quota, Holland proposed that the global quota should be expanded. This, of course, would be pointless unless a sufficient number of participants were concerned with absolute figures rather than percentages. Several countries, however, insisted on their demands in terms of percentages, so no solution was found in this way. However, this kind of solution, while presenting higher efficiency from a short-term perspective, would have represented a lower efficiency from a long-term perspective.

The historical outline of the whaling negotiations and their background does not perhaps make it surprising that the element of bargaining seems to have been quite strong. The parties did indeed defend their positions in terms of fairness and reasonableness, but perhaps more so in their declarations during meetings of the Whaling Commission than during negotiating sessions. We shall not go into the details of their arguments. What does seem worthwhile pointing out however, is that in these whaling negotiations a nation could indeed find it dangerous to present all arguments that would have weight in strictly co-operative negotiations.

Consider the case of Japan. This country had both strong long-term interests and strong short-term interests in the whaling industry. On the one hand, it was strongly interested in maintaining whaling as a lasting source of protein. On the other hand, Japanese whalers had to meet considerable financial obligations as a result of the recent expansion and modernization of their fleet. Now, the short-term interest stemming from financial obligations would constitute a strong argument in favour of Japanese demands both in co-operative discussion and in pure bargaining. The long-term interest, on the other hand, while being a weighty argument in co-operative negotiations, would in pure bargaining have the function of focusing attention on the need for Japan to avoid a breakdown in the negotiations, because a situation in which pelagic whaling continued to be largely unregulated would increase the danger of a serious depletion of the whale stock.

Suppose that the Japanese representatives really wanted the negotiations to be co-operative. They would then like to argue in terms of both long-term interests and short-term interests. However, in so far as they did not trust the other parties to adopt a fully co-operative attitude or to share their own criteria of fairness to a high degree, the Japanese negotiators would not be likely to emphasize their long-term interests, because this argument might acquire the character of a strategic clue (Schelling, 1960) working to their disadvantage. In fact, the Japanese negotiators seem to have concentrated on short-term interests during the four-way negotiations between Holland, Japan, Norway and the United Kingdom. This class of arguments, then, had to be exploited fully, to compensate for the weight of the arguments that could not be used. This again means that the Japanese had to exploit the commitment inherent in their arguments. In fact, the unperturbed way in which the Japanese negotiators again and again repeated Japan's position and arguments seems to have exerted a strong psychological pressure, or strain on other parties, in particular Norway.

Similar conditions are relevant to other actors. As was indicated in section 2, this does not mean that the types of uncertainty suggested necessarily preclude co-operative negotiations. Thus, trust may be gradually built up. It should be borne in mind, however, that, in situations like the one described, thorough preparation, talent and a very firm resolve to try to bring the negotiations on to a co-operative track may be required.

## 4 THE SOLUTION OF A BARGAINING GAME:
## THEORETICAL CONSIDERATIONS

We have seen above that an actor who would like to make a move that could be conducive to co-operative negotiations may hesitate to do so because such a move may fail in its purpose and in that case prove highly disadvantageous. If we are interested in the conditions for co-operative negotiations, we therefore have to study the dynamics of bargaining so as to get a better grasp of the significance of various types of moves in different bargaining contexts. It should also be pointed out that the dynamics of bargaining are of interest independently of the dilemmas to which the *possibility* of bargaining can give rise, even for a person who is primarily concerned with the conditions of fairness or a specific type of fairness. Thus, a good grasp of what makes for strength or weakness in bargaining ensures a better chance of seeing what can be done to favour fairness, or a specific type of fairness, even if co-operative negotiations are out of reach.

In this chapter, only a few aspects of bargaining can be dealt with. Our point of departure is on the one hand a primarily game-theoretic kind of discussion found in the literature and on the other hand reflections upon material presented as illustrations in the subsequent section.

Game theorists have discussed both normative solutions (in the sense of arbitration schemes) and descriptive solutions (in the sense of outcomes that will be reached if the parties act rationally). The latter kind of solution requires a specification of the institutional conditions of the game, as has been emphasized by *inter alia* Schelling (1960), Walton and McKersie (1965) and Ståhl (1972).

One central question is what kind of move structure the negotiation game exhibits. Is there a clear deadline? Can the parties make many moves? Do they move simultaneously or in sequence? If there is no deadline, or if the deadline is quite far off, several questions arise. In particular, will no agreement become a steadily growing evil to one of both of the parties? Will the value of an agreement, to one or both of the parties, decrease if its conclusion is delayed?

The significance of the answers to these various questions is far from self-evident. In spite of a growing theoretical literature, many questions still seem to be open. In this chapter no attempt will be made to go through the existing body of formal theories, the assumptions of which certainly require analysis. I will limit myself to some elementary considerations.

Let us look first at the question of what kinds of games can occur in negotiations with a clear deadline. It seems fruitful to focus attention on the end phase of the game. Following *inter alia* Harsanyi (1956), I will assume that, at least in many cases, this period of the game can be looked upon as a sequence of simultaneous moves (cf. Luce and Raiffa, 1958). This may seem a surprising premise. In fact, various authors (e.g. Ståhl, 1972) assume alternate moves. As two parties cannot, or should not, speak simultaneously, the latter assumption may look the more reasonable. Nevertheless, various considerations can be made in favour of the relevance of the assumption of simultaneity.

First, it may often be the case that each party can make significant decisions with regard to its position only in separate and parallel delegation meetings. In many cases, at least if no communication takes place between the delegations during their separate meetings, this fact implies that the parties make their moves simultaneously.

Second, if the negotiators are permitted to make significant decisions during the joint sessions, and express themselves accordingly, the negotiation process can be looked upon as a non-finite game. In such a situation there is no *a priori* reason to say, beforehand, that one specific party, and not his opponent, will have the move at a given point in time towards the end of the negotiations. Although the sequence of interventions up to a certain point may put a somewhat stronger pressure upon one party than upon the other, the game is not made strictly sequential until one party has made an absolutely credible, irrevocable commitment. The game that precedes such a commitment will be a game where each player has the possibility of claiming that it is now his opponent's turn to make a move, or denying that it is his own turn.

A central problem here is of course what should be understood by 'a move'. We have implicitly presupposed that not just any utterance or intervention is to be considered a move: moves have to do with making concessions, or choosing whether to do so. Now, although interventions have to be alternate, the situation may be indeterminate as to whose turn it is to make a concession, or to choose whether to do so. So, the moves can be conceived of as being simultaneous or 'quasi-simultaneous'. This again means that the two-by-two game that is constituted by the players simultaneously choosing between standing firm and giving in may acquire such a prominence as to become the 'analytic clue' to the situation.

Let us first have a look at what this game can be like in a negotiation process with a deadline. Its payoff structure may certainly vary substantially. At one stage the game may have the structure of the 'Prisoner's Dilemma'. At a later stage, however, after the players have made further concessions, it can have acquired the structure of 'Chicken'. Walton and McKersie (1965, pp.46ff.) give the latter game structure a prominent place in their analysis, introducing a game matrix of the form represented in Figure 7.2.

'Hard' in their analysis means the strategy of sticking to one's own 'target' (i.e. one's maximum objective) and 'soft' means the strategy of accepting the opponent's target. I find it more natural to focus on the two strategies of insisting on one's official demand and of accepting one's opponent's. The essential point is in both cases that tacit bargaining is required to avoid the worst outcome. As the deadline approaches, an actor's decision to stick to 'hard' may prove to be his last choice; and, as the deadline is passed, the parties may have to recognize that none of them gave in.

In some situations there will be no intermediate position between those of the two parties. In other situations there will be some or many. In both cases the question arises who has to yield. Let us look at the problem in a general form. Suppose that player A is demanding an agreement with utility payoffs $(u_a, u_b)$ to A and B, respectively, and player B is demanding $(v_a, v_b)$. Suppose further that a breakdown in the negotiations implies $(w_a, w_b)$, and that the event of both yielding means a compromise with the utilities $\frac{1}{2}(u_a + v_a) + e_a$ and $\frac{1}{2}(u_b + v_b) + e_b$ to A and B respectively. (If $e_a \geqslant 0$ and $e_b \geqslant 0$ are left out, the compromise will not necessarily be Pareto-optimal.)

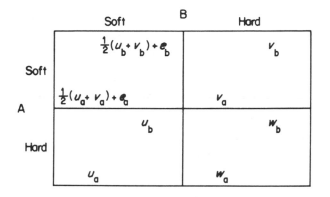

Harsanyi (1956), in his analysis of Zeuthen's bargaining game and Nash's arbitration scheme, suggests a dynamic or a principle that, in our terms, means that player A will, or 'should', make a unilateral concession if, and only if,

$$\frac{u_a - v_a}{u_a - w_a} < \frac{u_b = u_b}{v_b - w_b}$$

This principle can be formulated in the following way: A will, or should, make a unilateral concession if and only if his relative loss from accepting his opponent's proposal, instead of insisting on his own proposal, is less than that of his opponent.

Harsanyi (1956) has proved that a bargaining process that develops according to this formula leads to the outcome that maximizes the product of the two parties' gains over no agreement, that is to the Nash solution of the problem of arbitration (cf. Luce and Raiffa, 1958). This can easily be seen by choosing the breakdown point as the origin. This means assuming $w_a = w_b = 0$ in the above inequality. Under this assumption the inequality will be equivalent to

$$u_a u_b < v_a v_b.$$

This means that a party has to make a concession if its proposal entails a smaller product of the two parties' gains over no agreement than does the other party's proposal. Consequently, the bargaining process converges on the outcome that maximizes the product of the two parties' gains over no agreement.

As has been argued by Schelling (1960), various features of the situation, the players or the proposals may influence the outcome of a process of tacit bargaining. Thus, the fact that one of the proposals involves a round number or a principle of some sort may turn the corresponding equilibrium point into the strategic focal point of the game, even if Harsanyi's principle suggests the opposite. A relevant question then is how powerful a clue the feature focused upon by Harsanyi will be, in particular in a tradition where it has acquired salience.

Harsanyi's principle is equivalent to the following principle, which seems intuitively more telling and more convincing: A will, or should make a unilateral concession if, and only if,

$$\frac{u_a - v_a}{v_a - w_a} < \frac{v_b - u_b}{v_b - w_b}$$

This principle can be formulated in the following way: A will, or should, make a unilateral concession if and only if he has less than B to win, as compared with what he can lose, by insisting on his demand instead of yielding. It is easily seen that this principle, too, implies that the party whose proposal entails the smaller product of the two parties' gains over no agreement has to make a concession. Consequently, this principle too leads to the Nash solution. In our subsequent discussion, when referring to 'our model', we shall assume that the parties to a bargaining process act upon this principle.

So far, we have presupposed that the negotiation in question has a clear and definitive deadline. Quite often, however, the deadline is rather vague, and in many cases it is not definitive; there may be a more or less explicit understanding that the talks can always be resumed. Having said this, however, I would venture the assumption that negotiators tend to operate within the frame of quasi-deadlines in cases where there is no real and definitive deadline.

First, negotiations are often organized into conferences or sessions with substantial pauses in between; and the end of a conference or session is normally a kind of deadline. Second, if the talks are quasi-continuous, each party may feel it useful or necessary to divide the time ahead into periods; there may even be some common understanding as to periodization. This, again, can give rise to quasi-deadlines.

Now, our arguments in favour of considering moves as simultaneous did not presuppose the existence of a deadline. In fact, indeterminacy as to who has the move can very well occur in cases where there is no clear deadline. Moreover, if the parties can make many moves before they approach anything like a deadline, the distinction between alternate and simultaneous moves is of little consequence. Altogether, no harm seems to be done if we go on conceiving of moves as simultaneous.

Let us consider then some typical two-party situations characterized by their preference structures.

(1) Consider first the case where the value of any agreement at any point in time is independent of its time of conclusion, and where the value of no agreement is independent of time. Presupposing that the parties use the first quasi-deadline ahead as their point of reference, I suggest that the following method of establishing who must concede is not implausible. Both parties consider, for each of them, what the aggregate value of each agreement would be over time and similarly what the aggregate value of no agreement would be over time. On this basis they establish what each of them can gain and lose by standing firm. That party, then, will or should make a unilateral concession who has less to win, as compared with

what he can lose, by insisting on his demand instead of yielding. (The parties could also make their comparisons on the basis of some measure of the value of each outcome per unit of time.)

Indeed, this line of reasoning, which is identical with the one discussed above, is less compelling in the case under discussion here, where there is a quasi-deadline, than in a case where there is a clear and definitive deadline. The reason is that in the former case changes may occur if no agreement is concluded during the period in question, so an optimist might hope for an improved bargaining position. Nevertheless, the parties may find that there is no better clue to the analysis of the situation.

It should also be noted that, if one party cannot benefit from an agreement until some date in the future, and the other party cannot do so until another date, early benefit is a relative disadvantage, strategically speaking.

(2) Let us consider next the case where, for each party, or one of them, the value per unit of time of any fairly advantageous agreement declines the longer the conclusion of it is delayed. (Cf. the regulation of the exploitation of living resources.) It seems immediately clear that, the more marked the value reduction, the more similar the symmetrical situation will be to that of a clear and definitive deadline. As to the asymmetrical case, the party whose utilities decrease with a delay (or decrease most) is of course at a relative disadvantage.

(3) Finally, there is the case where the value per unit of time of no agreement decreases over time for one or both parties. (Cf. peace negotiations taking place while fighting goes on.) Here too it should be noted that, the more marked the value reduction, the more the symmetrical situation will be similar to a situation with a clear and definitive deadline. As to the asymmetrical case, the party for whom value decreases, or decreases most, will of course be at a relative disadvantage. Under certain conditions, a game of attrition will take place.

## 5 THE SOLUTION OF A BARGAINING GAME: SOME ILLUSTRATIONS

When in the preceding section we concluded that a modification of Harsanyi's account of the bargaining process is a plausible one, we did so on the basis of rather abstract reasonings about the move structure of a bargaining process and the existence of deadlines or quasi-deadlines. We shall now look at some historical material that seems to support our conclusion, viz. a couple of arguments submitted by Holland, at a late stage of the quota negotiations, in favour of her demand.

After the four-power whaling conference between Japan, Holland, Norway and the United Kingdom in London in February 1961, which broke down because Holland insisted upon a quota of 7 per cent while the other countries would not agree to giving her more than 6 per cent, Norway sent a note to the Dutch government saying that 6 per cent ought to be enough for Holland as she had only one expedition and the average per expedition for the other countries was 4.35 per cent. In its reply to this note, the Dutch government made three points.

(i) The Netherlands could not accept a quota of 6 per cent because the Dutch whaling industry, with its one expedition, could not, in case of a reduced global quota, maintain a reasonable profitability by reducing the number of expeditions.

(ii) The Dutch government was prepared to contribute to the bridging of the gap of one per cent still remaining.

(iii) 'A failure of the Vancouver meeting [to be held shortly after] would have grave and far-reaching consequences, certainly for the Netherlands but particularly for those countries that were to an even greater extent interested in whaling in Antarctica.'

Two of these points, (i) and (ii), contain arguments in support of Holland's position. Point (i) partly serves the function of establishing the reasonableness of her demand. At the same time, however, there can be no doubt that it has a bargaining function, just as does point (iii). Let us see how.

The Dutch government in point (i) suggests that a concession of one per cent on the part of Holland would involve a greater sacrifice to Holland than a similar concession on the part of the other countries would involve to them; in other words, Holland has more to gain by insisting on her demand than have the other countries. In its third point, the Dutch government suggests that a failure of the forthcoming conference would have graver consequences for the other countries than for Holland, although the consequences would be grave for Holland as well; in other words, Holland has less to lose by insisting on her demand than have the other countries. In both places, the Dutch government carries out an 'interstate' or 'interpersonal' comparison of utilties. This is an interesting fact in itself, since the interpersonal comparison of utilities is a much discussed problem in theoretical literature, not least in the theory of negotiations. We shall not go into this problem here, however. What is of particular interest to us is that the two points entail a comparison of the kind suggested in our model. In fact, the Dutch note entails a comparison to the effect that Holland has much more to win by standing firm, as compared with what she can lose by standing firm, than have the others.

The Dutch government does not draw the conclusion that the remaining gap must be bridged by the other party unilaterally. The Dutch government is prepared to accept some compromise, but it is apparently not willing to go more than halfway. On the contrary, it suggests that this is what the other party has to do. (The actual compromise was of a kind that made a direct comparison of the respective concessions difficult: Holland was to get, in addition to her 6 per cent, forty-five blue whale units if she had caught 75 per cent of her quota when 80 percent of the ordinary season had elapsed; similarly, she was to get sixty blue whale units if she had caught 80 per cent in that period, and she was to get seventy units if she had caught 85 per cent in that period.)

It should finally be pointed out that the Dutch government establishes the end of the conference in Vancouver as a quasi-deadline. Now, the long-drawn-out history of the quota negotiations might indicate that there would be a later chance even if the Vancouver meeting failed. On the other hand, still more negotiations on the remaining difference of one per cent could seem rather meaningless. The suggestion that the Vancouver meeting is something like a deadline is therefore not implausible.

Let us now turn to the significance of our bargaining model. In section 3 we discussed briefly the significance of using a country's long-term interests in the whaling industry as an argument in support of its demand for a favourable national quota in co-operative negotiations and in pure bargaining respectively. Our model, whose relevance has been elucidated above, makes a more precise and systematic analysis possible. Suppose that the negotiations develop into a bargaining process of the type described in our model. The question then is how long-term interests will affect the relationship between what the country can gain by standing firm and what it can lose by doing so. It is obvious that strong long-term interests tend to increase the loss that a country risks by standing firm, unless the essence of the long-term interests can be realized only if the country obtains a larger quota than that offered by its opponent. The long-term interests also tend to increase the potential gain, however, so more specific assumptions have to be introduced to answer our question.

The following consideration will do for our purpose. A country that has only very short-term interests in the whaling industry will hardly be risking any loss from a breakdown of negotiations. In fact it might gain from a breakdown, both in relation to its opponent's offer and in relation to its own demand. So, long-term interests seem to increase the potential loss more sharply than the potential gain, unless, for material or emotional reasons, the realization of the country's long-term interests depends wholly or essentially upon getting a bigger quota than that offered by its opponent.

We shall finally see how our model can help to explain a tendency which, according to Norwegian participants, was characteristic of the negotiations in the mid-1950s on the number of whale-catchers to be used by each expedition. The purpose of these negotiations was to improve whaling economy by having the operating season somewhat extended, or at least not further cut down. In Norway, which was still the dominant country in pelagic whaling, there was a quite common feeling that Norwegian whalers obtained less favourable terms than others (Tønnessen, 1970). We shall not inquire into the justification of this suspicion. The point to be made here is that it would not be surprising if such a suspicion proved to be true. It should first be noted that Norway had taken the initiative in these negotiations. This fact may have weakened Norway's position somewhat; the Norwegian negotiators were particularly committed to bringing about an agreement, and this had also become part of their image. The 'logic of collective action', however, seems to have been of at least equal importance. It is indeed likely that it forced the dominant actor to pay more than the other actors for the collective good in question, in this case an extended season. A significant point in our case is that a discrimination of the type suggested would not necessarily be too provocative, since the factory ships and whale-catchers were not easily comparable.

A reference to Mancur Olson Jr's work (1965) might suffice at this point. It is instructive, however, to look somewhat more closely at the consequences of the dynamics suggested in our model where one actor has a greater share of the total catch than another.

Consider a case where there are two actors: actor A, who catches two-thirds of the global quota, and actor B, who catches the remaining third. We assume that all expeditions are similar and that there are fifteen whale-catchers in each expedition. Furthermore, we assume that analyses have proved that a general reduction of the number of whale-catchers per factory ship to, say, ten would lead to a Pareto-optimum, that a unilateral reduction to this number would be unprofitable for either actor, and that a reduction to ten would be profitable to the bigger Actor A only if B reduced its number at least to thirteen.

In such a situation it would not be surprising if actor A proposed a general reduction to ten whale-catchers per factory ship, and B proposed such a reduction for A and a reduction only to thirteen for himself. So, let us assume this, and let us assume that a breakdown of the negotiations means maintaining the *status quo*.

Actor B has obviously more to gain by standing firm than has A. In fact, B's possible gain, if measured in whales caught per expedition, is twice that of A because the gain obtained by each of B's expeditions from B's proposed arrangement (as opposed to A's) is double the loss incurred by each of A's expeditions (since A's fleet is double the size of B's). It is also obvious that B has more to lose by standing firm than A, because A's proposed arrangement is better for B than B's is to A, and the *status quo* means the same to both. Now, our assumptions suggest that B's proposed arrangement is only slightly better than the *status quo* to A. It is therefore reasonable to assume that B has clearly less to gain as compared with what he can lose than has A. In so far as the bargaining process is of the type described in our model, B consequently has to yield, for example by proposing an arrangement that assigns twelve whale-catchers per factory ship to his fleet and ten to A's. Suppose that B does so far as to propose only eleven whale-catchers per factory ship for himself. It is reasonable to assume that in this case A has to yield. B's possible gain from standing firm (measured in whales caught per expedition) is still twice that of A while his possible loss is not likely to be much larger than A's.

Perhaps an arrangement assigning twelve whale-catchers per factory ship to B and ten to A would be the Nash solution, that is to say the outcome that would maximize the product of each party's gain over the *status quo*, and on which the parties would converge if they acted according to our assumption.

## 6 THE SIGNIFICANCE OF IMAGES IN BARGAINING: THEORETICAL CONSIDERATIONS AND AN ILLUSTRATION

In so far as a negotiation process acquires the character of a game, not only are the strategies, preferences etc. of the parties essential, but so also are the assumptions that the parties entertain about each other's strategies, preferences, etc., and the assumptions they make about each other's assumptions. In fact, these assumptions may decide whether the negotiations are to acquire the spontaneous character of co-operative negotiations or the calculated character of a bargaining game. It is noteworthy in this connection that, even if the parties entertain adequate pictures of each other, they may have to base their choices on partly inadequate assumptions, because for some reason or other an image (Jervis, 1970) of one of the parties or both has developed and has become the 'strategic clue' of the situation. Consequently, two parties who would prefer to negotiate co-operatively may find it impossible or difficult not to end up in typical bargaining, perhaps because one of them has acquired the image of being a smart bargainer.

The significance of images in a bargaining process like that described in our model is obvious. Thus, even if it is inadequate, an image of a party's preference structure—a 'sterotype utility function', to use Harsanyi's (1962a) expression—can easily become the 'strategic clue' to a process of bargaining where each phase can be conceived of as a game of 'Chicken'.

The international negotiations on national quotas in pelagic whaling are illustrative in this respect, too. In particular, one element of the bargaining that took place between Japan and Norway in the spring of 1959, within the framework of the four-power negotiations, is of interest. In the negotiations between Japan,

Holland, Norway and the United Kingdom, Norway based her bargaining position on her traditional share of the annual catch, and was not willing to reduce her demand on the basis of a deal with Japan on the sale or withdrawal of some Norwegian expeditions. We have seen, however, that in the preceding year, before the whaling nations had agreed to negotiate on national quotas, Norwegian whalers had proposed an internationally-financed withdrawal of three Norwegian expeditions. Japanese negotiators, who had at that time refused to consider such a scheme, because they favoured free competition, repeatedly referred to this move during the spring of 1959, declaring that the reason why Japan had agreed at all to participate in the negotiations was that she believed that Norway was interested in such a deal. The representatives of Norwegian authorities, on their side, repeatedly dismissed this possibility, referring to the interests that the Norwegian government was serving.

It is difficult to say precisely what were the Japanese assumptions about Norway's preference structure. It may look as if the Japanese negotiators wanted to strengthen the image created by the Norwegian whalers the preceding summer, so as to make it the unavoidable clue to the bargaining situation.

Now, it appeared that the four countries were not able to reach an agreement on how to divide the part of the global quota that was left for them after Soviet Russia had accepted a quota of 20 per cent the year before; in particular, Norway and Japan were not able to agree on how to divide the 60 per cent that was generally accepted as their lot. As we have seen, Norway and Holland consequently did not cancel their withdrawal, already notified, from the international whaling convention, and it was not until 1962 that a quota agreement was signed.

One may therefore ask if the Japanese position during the spring of 1959 was unrealistic. It is equally natural to ask the same question in connection with Norway's firm commitment to a position that was irreconcilable with Japan's official premises for participating in the negotiations. Norwegian authorities and Norwegian negotiators should perhaps have taken the view that it was impossible, in a few months, to eliminate or neutralize the image created in 1958 to the effect that Norway was willing to trade some of her quota demand for a financial arrangement involving the sale or withdrawal of some Norwegian expeditions.

The general lesson to be drawn from this experience is that an actor who would like to create a certain image may find that an image has already been created by other actors in his organization, and that the latter image has to be taken seriously if he is to negotiate on a realistic basis.

## 7 EPILOGUE: POWER AND POWERLESSNESS

In the preceding sections an attempt has been made, first, to distinguish two ideal types of negotiation: co-operative negotiation and pure bargaining. Further, the factors making for tendencies towards the one or the other have been discussed and illustrated. It has, in particular, been emphasized that negotiations can easily acquire the character of bargaining even if the parties have a strong wish for co-operative negotiation with its possibility of achieving a more fair and/or efficient agreement. In so far as this happens we might say that the parties experience some kind of powerlessness: it has not been in their power to conduct their negotiation in the way they wanted to. Now, one of the parties may perhaps have done quite well in the bargaining process. If this is the case, he has in one respect proved powerful. It may be, however, that both his 'objective' bargaining strength and his image as a shrewd bargainer are among the factors that precluded co-operative negotiations. It is further possible that co-operative negotiations would have made even him better off. In that case, his bargaining power has in spite of all entailed some powerlessness.

As a result of considerations like these I have come to think that it might be useful to take a look at the concept of power from the point of view of this chapter.

The term 'power' has been given both broad and narrow definitions. Broad concepts have prevailed in philosophy, while in political science there has been a need to define narrower concepts, or focus on specific types of power that are particularly relevant to the discipline. As regards the broad concepts, Hobbes's definition is of interest: 'The power of a man, to take it universally, is his present means to obtain some future apparent good, and is either *original* or *instrumental*.' (Hobbes 1960, Ch.10.) Bertrand Russell, too, defines 'power' broadly: 'Power may be defined as the production of intended effects' (Russell, 1938, p.35). He then makes a distinction between power over nature and power over men. Lasswell and Kaplan in this respect follow Russell closely. Having quoted his definition they state, 'But power in the political sense cannot produce intended effects in general, but only such effects as directly involve other persons: political power is distinguished from power over nature as power over other men' (Lasswell and Kaplan, 1950, p.75).

I should like to take as my point of departure two tendencies that are common in political science: first, the tendency to conceive of political power as exclusively or primarily power *over* other men; second, the tendency to conceive of political power as something that is exclusively or primarily *distributed* over the set of actors in question. The one tendency does not imply the other, but they are closely related. I find that these tendencies, although reflecting significant structures, can easily make us overlook equally significant possibilities and facts.

Various reasons can be given to support the view that in many cases political power should not exclusively, or even primarily, be looked upon as something that is distributed over the actors in question, if it is distributed at all. My main point is this: a group's power, defined as its ability to produce intended effects, may increase or decrease with the ability of the members to co-operate or to stimulate each other. So, a member who can be said to increase his power if he increases his ability to co-operate or to bring forth constructive and stimulating ideas need not thereby reduce some other member's power, as he would in the case of pure distribution; on the contrary, the power of each partner may be increased. Further, if the group's ability to co-operate is taken to be given, it is not perforce meaningful to conceive of this ability as merely a sum of abilities that are distributed over the members; the group's total ability, or power, may be due to the *pattern* or *constellation* of qualifications, attitudes, expectations, etc. in the group.

These considerations also suggest why political power is not necessarily power *over* other men. Suppose A's power over B in a given respect is defined as A's ability to behave so as to make B do something specific which he would not otherwise do, that is as A's ability to deliberately influence B in a certain way (cf. Dahl, 1963). Of course, people who co-operate will to some extent have this kind of power over each other; they will deliberately influence each other, by their arguments, their suggestions, their attitudes, etc. But there will probably be a strong element of creativity in their interaction, which means that the interplay of personalities and ideas ilicit ideas, suggestions and so on that are not foreseen by anybody as the intended effects of his attempt to influence another.

As already suggested, a number of significant problems are likely to attract too little attention in political research if studies of power are one-sidedly focused on its distributive aspect, in particular on cases where the distribution of goods or evils is a central problem. The efficiency aspect also has to be brought in, and above all, the two must be studied together. Thus, the ability, or lack of ability, of a political regime or a set of actors to procure a collective good or to attain efficiency in producing individual goods may depend very much upon the degree of mutual trust—trust that attempts in this direction will not be successfully exploited by actors who think primarily of maximizing some particular interest, or who might do so. On the other hand, it may be impossible to understand the power, or powerlessness, of a given actor in a competitive context if the sincere but risky efforts of other actors, or this actor, to contribute to an efficient and fair outcome are not taken into account.

The problems of peace, and the ability of various actors to exploit the risk of conflict, in particular nuclear war, of course have to be seen in this light. And so must the problem of long-term and fair exploitation of natural resources, and several other problems of our time.

It perhaps contradicts the rules of ordinary language to use the term 'power' to characterize a group's ability to secure efficient and fair outcomes through co-operation, if this co-operation does not imply overcoming the resistance of some external actor. But it does not contradict ordinary language to characterize the lack of such an ability as powerlessness. The main purpose of the above considerations, however, has not been to influence the use of the word 'power', although I find the power of words to be considerable. My main point has been to sketch a broader framework within which studies of power in narrower meanings of the term should also be seen—and carried out.

# 8

# The Economic Theory of Politics: Suggestions for   Reconsideration

FRANZ LEHNER AND HANS GERD SCHÜTTE

## 1  THE AUTONOMY OF POLITICAL SCIENCE: THE ESSENTIALIST FALLACY

Theoretical designs in political science tend to rely on programmatic perspectives which cover a broad range of basic assumptions or principles. Often, these are not explicitly formulated. Recent work in the theory of knowledge and philosophy of science has shown how various factors determine the direction of scientific arguments and restrict the scope of admissible formulations. Among these factors are ideas about method, personal experience, rules of experience, certain specific kinds of logical and mathematical schemes and general background knowledge (see Popper, 1963). All of these tend to be taken for granted. Thus programmatic conceptions easily escape any criticism as their elements remain unclear. Yet at the same time, articulating these conceptions may petrify scientific disciplines and turn them into traditions or conventions of thought that lose as much relevance as they gain 'dignity' when it comes to applying them to real problems.

The ideas that determine knowledge are rarely discussed. This is all the more of a problem for political science since it seems to be dominated by one particular perspective. There are two elements: first, the conception of political science as autonomous and second the specialized interest in the themes of power and conflict. This limitation of interest occurs not only for the legitimate reasons of scientific specialization and division of labour but also to justify the claim for autonomy of political science. This claim still remains to be cashed in. The limitation amounts to no more than the suggestion that in order to deal with a particular theme we also need a particular theory which must be differentiated from rival theories in sociology, economics or psychology.

In this context, political systems are taken to constitute their own specific reality *sui generis*. Their characteristics are then explained and explicable only in terms of the 'nature of politics'. And indeed there are plausible arguments as to why we should limit ourselves to one dominant theme. The idea of the authoritative allocation of values through the State, seen against the background of political antagonisms and the need to take binding decisions at a centre, provides a good enough reason for us to analyse the mechanisms of power. And without doubt the relations between political parties and other pressure groups can be interpreted as conflict relations. Who would question that parliaments, secret services, businessmen or mass media are capable of exercising influence and therefore constitute a theme for political science? But power and authority are exercised in other areas as well. Many of them are never analysed by political scientists. And conflict is so widespread in social life that it will not be easy to use it as a criterion.

Although this is not necessarily so, the interest in certain preferred and selected themes is often connected with the claim that political science is autonomous. This is an essentialist attitude. The question of what are genuine themes for political science is transformed into an affirmation about the *essence of politics*. It follows quite logically that the debate among scholars tends to concentrate on questions of delimiting the subject matter and on questions about the uniquely distinguishing characteristics of political objects. Since no such assertion about defining characteristics contains any information, these exercises can scarcely give rise to testable statements. Questions about the nature of essence of political objects can be answered only with an infinite regress of definitions. The information value remains nil, as nothing is said about reality.

This can be seen in typical statements about the 'essence of politics'. Usually this leads to an analytical separation of the State and society, economy, morals or religion depending in each case on the interests of the author and his public. It is not a great step to the autonomy of politics and society and to conclude that 'politics has its laws, laws that the statesman must apply' (Sartori, 1973, p.11). According to this view political sociology uses theories that fail to work for specific problems of politics. Then it is said that 'sociological reductionism flattens politics' (Sartori, 1973, p.21). But neither sociological laws nor regularities concerning the political features of society are really made explicit here. Therefore, 'reductionism' can hardly mean the logical reduction of one science to another. The relation between the 'science of the State' and the 'sciences of society or economy' remains unclear.

If we want to talk about the reducibility or the autonomy of one of these sciences we could do so provided the findings of sociology could be shown to follow logically from those of political science or vice versa. In that case one of the two 'sciences' is obviously reducible whereas the other could be said to be 'autonomous'. Alternatively, it would have to be shown that the statements of both sciences are incommensurable. In any case such a comparative analysis would presuppose that we actually had testable systems of statements, that is to say nomological hypotheses about the nature or quality of social and political conditions. But this cannot in fact be presupposed.

On top of these presuppositions the science in question would have to be shown to be autonomous also with respect to economics and psychology. And although economic laws and laws of political science may indeed differ, it would be advisable to remember that both are concerned with the same individuals. In their political framework these individuals 'vote'. In their economic context they 'consume' or 'produce'. And yet there is no convincing evidence to show that voting and consuming are determined by different laws. Until we can prove the contrary, there is a theoretical alternative to the autonomy of political science, consisting in the assumption that in both cases there are decisions to be taken and choices to be made between alternatives. Any theory capable of explaining this phenomenon adequately would also be able to incorporate both 'economic' and 'political' objectives and premises.

If we presuppose that conjectures about reality in the social sciences can be tested only by reference to the properties of individuals we can hardly justify the theoretical separation of disciplines. It would be surprising if we could identify persons who clearly belong to political systems and to no others. We should recall here the sociological platitude that in virtue of the division of labour man assumes several roles. The behaviour of a prime minister or of a voter cannot be explained in total separation from other roles such as that of consumer or producer of economic goods. All these parts are played by the same person. If we separated rigorously the different functions of one and the same agent we would have to pretend for instance that fluctuations in the value of money influence neither voters nor party programmes. This would be unrealistic to say the least. Anybody who failed to include in his calculations such factors as the movement of prices, the crime rate or the level of employment just because these belong to sociology or economics would be a poor politician. In fact, these 'laws of politics' that a statesman has to apply do not all reflect the traditional borderlines between different scientific disciplines.

The alleged autonomy of political science can be based only upon its logical independence from other sciences, or in a weaker sense on the belief that 'economic', 'social' and 'political' features of individuals relate to each other at random. Perhaps this conclusion could be avoided if an organic interpretation of the State, economy and society is adopted. Such an interpretation or explanation would pay no particular attention to the behaviour of individuals or their characteristics in the widest sense. The individual would not figure among the action units selected for explanation. But empirically this alternative scientific strategy does not appear to be very convincing (see Schütte, 1971a).

Most of the 'theories' produced within the programme of 'autonomous political science' are descriptive models, 'conceptual frameworks' or systems of classification that fail to do what they claim to do, namely to offer explanations. In as far as these supposed theories contain statements of a general nature, more often than not the statements turn out to refer to human behaviour rather than to 'the State', 'the society' or 'the economy' as wholes. Their terminological façade tends to hide reality. For in actual fact these explanations consist of assumptions about 'what normal human beings normally do'. These assumptions are then projected on to complex constellations of social and political conditions. We believe that the explanatory power of these programmatic designs is essentially based on and restricted to the class of general assumptions about behaviour which in most cases remain implicit.

Today neoclassical economics is the only social science with a sufficiently concrete programme to allow a clear view of its basic assumptions and their implications. Leaving aside some of its more problematic aspects, we can say that neoclassical economics is more open to scientific criticism than are alternative modes of explanation. We can see this in the fact that fairly general assumptions are taken as a basis for its development. A critic may say that these assumptions seem to describe a rather unrealistic *homo economicus*, but we cannot just dismiss these theoretical constructs on the grounds that their premises are unrealistic. Not only have economists explained some phenomena of competitive markets, but also an economic theory of politics is reaching more and more results that deserve the political scientist's interest (Downs, 1957; Buchanan and Tullock, 1962; Olson, 1965; Wilson, 1973).

An alternative can be recognized in the area known as political sociology. Research into voting behaviour has produced a wealth of data that not only corrects traditional judgements about the political process but also to some extent contradicts the economic explanation. (Lazarsfeld *et al.*, 1948; Campbell *et al.*, 1960.) In this case too there are general observations about *behaviour* that play a dominant role. They are basic assumptions of social psychology which do not conform easily with economic axioms. And yet the structure of the arguments is identical in both cases: conclusions are derived from a few premises which do not relate to 'economic' or 'social' objects but to human behaviour generally.[1] And they can be tested (Davis, 1966).

Many sociologists and political scientists have little confidence in such an individualistic procedure despite various indications of its trustworthiness. It is indeed understandable that a theoretical programme based upon 'psychological' principles should have been resisted by social scientists so long as psychology was defined as the science of inborn behavioural dispositions and utilitarian economics was a simplified version of hedonism. We cannot help feeling however that justified arguments of this kind became self-subsistent as time went by and assumed the function of excuses. This can be said of the dispute that Max Weber had with the psychology of his time as well as of Durkheim's critique of utilitarianism that caused him to condemn classical economics altogether. Unfortunately these arguments have not improved as time has passed and psychology has changed its basic orientation and become a behavioural science.

When we speak of assumptions about human behaviour as bases of any theory in social science we do not mean to restrict ourselves to a specific behavioural theory, such as the economic theory of rational action or those cognitive theories that dominate broad sections of experimental social psychology and microsociology. Neither do we imply any sort of reduction of political science to economics or psychology. Rather we wish to say that a general theory of human behaviour has so far been most clearly expressed in terms either of economics or of psychology. Obviously there are overlaps, complementarities and even contradictions. What counts are the possibilities of applying these theories in all fields of social science and hence in political science too. An adequate political theory has to come to terms with the basic assumptions of economics and psychology and apply them to the explanation of those phenomena that have always (although sometimes in a sense that needs to be revised) been considered political.

## 2 THEORIES AND MODELS

When we consider the widespread doubts about the 'psychologism' involved in individualist programmes of explanation, we have to realize that it is obviously impossible to understand social relations as long as we talk only about the attributes of persons. The problem here is not one of 'individual' or 'society'. Rather it is a problem of the logical vocabulary of theories. Unfortunately, the debate is dominated by a conceptual perspective that considers psychology as exclusively concerned with the *attributes of persons* on the one hand and the social sciences as preoccupied with the *attributes of collective agents* on the other hand. Two problems are mixed up in this perspective: (i) the question of the relation between general theory of behaviour and the explanation of political or social phenomena, and (ii) the question of the logical structure of theoretical statements.

The distinction between individuals and collectivities makes sense only as long as it is drawn between motivation and needs on the one hand and social classes, parties or governments on the other. Only then is there the possibility of a meaningful distinction between a theory of behaviour and a theory of society. But a theory of power or conflict cannot be built on psychic attributes of persons such as their tendency to be aggressive or their need to exercise power. The fault is not that theories of behaviour fail to work in this connection but that a classificatory logic cannot do justice to the phenomena under analysis.

Concepts such as 'power' or 'status' cannot be used in the sense of attributes that may or may not apply to persons. In both cases, we have to recognize that we refer to interpersonal relations and not attributes of single individuals. Therefore the calculus of a theory of behaviour has to refer to the logic of relations, connections and exchanges. Formal structures of this kind take into account the fact that the interaction among individuals produces effects that cannot be attributed to any single individual. Under these conditions the difference between a theory of behaviour and a theory of society shrinks so much that its only remaining legitimation is the need for a divison of labour. For it ought to be evident that, in order to explain motivations, power relations and exchanges have to be considered—that is to say, processes of a relational character.

This argument does not entail choosing an exclusively economic theory, although the expression 'exchange' may suggest this. (For 'non-economic' exchange theories, see Homans, 1961; Thibaut and Kelley, 1959.) It is merely a matter of accounting for the interdependence of human action in the sense to which 'power' and 'dependence', 'gain' and 'loss' correspond. The exchange of material commodities constitutes a special case which frequently hides the fact that symbolic communication or social recognition also constitute exchanges in a formal sense. Whether economic principles (such as the principle of diminishing marginal utility) can be applied to all these processes may remain open for the moment. We simply wish to take into account right from the start that *actions are as a rule interactions* and that hence there are *interdependencies of effects*. We also contend that in principle one theory can explain the exchange of immaterial benefits (such as information) as well as the exchange of consumer goods. We do not however deny that there are good reasons to assume that economic theory has gaps with respect to social and psychological determinants of behaviour and that economic theory therefore needs further refinement (Albert, 1967; Lehner, 1973).

We do not want to make too much of the distinction between theories and models. Certainly it cannot be merely a matter of formal structures. And yet quite generally it can be shown that the choice of certain logical vocabulary has consequences for the way in which problems are tackled in the social sciences. Classifications lead to the assumption of an independent rationale, whereas a formal scheme that takes relational characteristics into account makes it possible to recognize the mutual interdependence of events in a political model or theory. (See, on systems theory in this connection, Markl, 1972.)

When it comes to models there is a second point: the difference between general statements and singular descriptions of initial conditions. In this sense a model is a system of statements that characterizes selectively a certain section of reality. Thus we could start from a certain general theory and apply it to different sets of conditions. A competitive market in this sense constitutes a different set of conditions from a centralized organization or a small group. It is evident that identical theoretical statements together with different descriptions of intial conditions will lead to different conclusions. If for instance we analyse the behaviour of political parties in terms of a market model (Downs, 1957) we will reach different conclusions from those we would have come to had we applied an organization model (Wilson, 1961). In both cases, however, the same (economic) *theory* is applied.

The confusion of theories and models implies a confusion between nomological hypotheses and assumptions about specific empirical conditions. This methodological error may play its part in the dispute about the task and the autonomy of political science. Applying an economic theory to political phenomena does not of course mean (as Parsons, 1963c, mistakenly claims) that political processes are explained *as* economic processes. It also does not imply the reduction of political phenomena to economic facts, nor does it imply any reduction of political science to economics. Both sciences may use the same theory, but different models. It is not at all clear why conjectures about the number of parties, the character of conflicts or the basic features of the constitution in a certain type of political system (e.g. a democracy) have to be introduced as an indispensable part of a political *theory* rather than as a part of a specific *model*. Structural descriptions are required as parts of a model if and when a theory is applied. The logical status of such descriptive statements is not the same as that of the general hypotheses of a theory. The latter have to be nomological statements, the former necessarily are singular statements which are not capable of being generalized. Whenever a general theory is applied to political phenomena, explanations are joint products of theory *and* model. Attacking such explanations of specific events, we have to make clear whether the theory is assumed to be false or the model is considered to be unrealistic. Refuting the economic theory of politics by saying that Downs and other economists make use of unrealistic models does not make sense, for we might be able to formulate better explanations simply by using a more realistic model.

### 3 PSYCHOLOGY AND THE ECONOMIC THEORY OF POLITICS

We do not deny that the economic theory of politics is replete with deficiencies and that many of these deficiencies are connected with the axiom of rationality. But still we do not wish to argue that this axiom is unrealistic. We would be misconceiving the function of such axioms if we wanted to use them in order to identify rational action in individual cases. As a basis for classificatory typologies in Max Weber's sense, the application of the principle of rationality is problematic. Max Weber's typology of different types of behaviour in terms of purposive rationality, value rationality and tradition is of little significance in a descriptive sense because it defines ideal but not real types of behaviour. And as an intended theory it remains fruitless because nothing can be deduced from it. What is of real interest are the implications of statements like the principle of rationality in relation to the empirical conditions to which they are applied. Whether such a statement is valid or not depends upon its conclusions, which may be shown to be true or false. It is never determined by any observation of a pure type of rationality in an individual case. As an axiom the principle of rationality does not define rational behaviour, but postulates that any individual behaves rationally in the sense of a given definition of rationality. (See for example Riker and Ordeshook, 1973, Ch.2) And it might well be that the term rationality cannot be operationalized but must remain a purely theoretical term.

Often we find that the principle of rationality is interpreted as a logical decision rule without any informational content. A pure *logic of choice* can hardly say anything about reality. Nevertheless such a construction is often applied in a realistic sense in order to explain for example the behaviour of parties or voters. According to this construction, (i) rational individuals are able to distinguish alternatives, (ii) their alternatives are arranged in a transitive preference ordering, (iii) they always choose the most preferred alternative, and (iv) they always make the same decision and opt for the same preference in similar situations (Downs, 1957; Riker and Ordeshook, 1973). As a definition of rational decision-making this formula is of little relevance because it is a convention, and as a nomological hypothesis it is false. Psychology and plain practice tell us that individuals are quite often unable to distinguish alternatives, that a lack of transitive ordering of preferences causes decisional conflicts and that individuals quite often do not behave consistently over time. (Compare Festinger, 1964; Schroder *et al.*, 1967.)

Since we can be interested neither in analytical statements nor in false hypotheses, it might seem reasonable to drop the rationality principle altogether. But this would simply amount to a fundamentalist solution. For even if the principle of rationality often fails to come true (and strictly speaking this means it is false as a general hypothesis), it can under certain limited conditions constitute a valid and acceptable hypotheses (Lehner, 1975). This being so, it is advisable to ask for the conditions under which this hypothesis really holds true.

In a very cursory manner we can take it that traditional societies formulate, arrange and repeat clear alternatives. Similarly we can assume that we will find the same phenomenon in any cohesive group with high consensus among its members. In relation to modern societies, this means that groups with high social status (for such are most cohesive groups with high consensus) are able to articulate ordered preferences, whereas low social status is accompanied by lack of clear opinions. For we know that the consensus and cohesion of groups varies in relation to the social position (status) of their members (Schütte, 1971a, pp.129ff.). However, this conjecture is in need of further elaboration.

For instance, in the case of social mobility it does not seem to be easy to maintain the assumption of ordered preferences. There are conflicts of decision-making to do specifically with a change of social status. Beyond that, any kind of vertical or horizontal mobility (that is: any change of the social context of an individual) will affect an individual's ordering of preferences or—to use a psychological term—his cognitive structure. It can be demonstrated that only under very specific circumstances are individual preferences (individual cognitive structures) systematically related and transitively ordered. As a result of the distribution of information within society, well-educated individuals with high social status are in general more likely to develop such preference structures than members of low status groups with less education. Without going into details we can say that generally only individuals with high status, high level of information and complex but stable interactions may be expected to develop a system of differentiated and transitively ordered preferences (see Lehner, 1975).

The weaknesses of the rationality axiom in economic theory permit us only to narrow down its applicability. Consequently, the status of our explanatory principle is sharply altered. The principle itself now requires explanation because we have to look for hypotheses that help to explain the applicability of the principle of rationality as well as its failures. The reference to the dependence of rationality on status and consensus serves as a first approach to such a programme.

It does not, however, formulate a theoretical alternative yet. It shows only that preferences are not ordered by chance but depend upon social conditions. And within this pattern some classes of people seem to be more adequately described as 'rational' men than others.

Before we turn to a theoretical solution we have to emphasize that the contribution theoretical economics makes to the solution of problems of political science does not depend decisively on relativizing or refuting any particular postulate. Economics as 'the science of scarce means and unlimited ends' (Robbins, 1932, p.15) has a theoretical significance beyond some problematic features of the underlying theory of rational action. It certainly constitutes a problematic approximation to a general theory of behaviour, but we still cannot eliminate scarcity and exchange from our discussion. Conflict, co-operation, consensus, stratification and the characteristics of constitutions: none of these can be explained successfully without reference to the principle of the exchange of scarce goods.

The economic theory of behaviour in its special features is dubious (Albert, 1967). But eliminating the principles of scarcity and exchange would have much more far-reaching consequences. We insist upon an economic theory of politics not in order to spare from criticism certain assumptions about behaviour but rather in order to account for the principle of scarcity and the possibility of balancing interests through exchange. For in a world where all goods were free (and plentiful, that is freely available in unlimited quantities) there would probably be no social relations at all.

One of the central weaknesses of neoclassical economics consists in its separation from modern psychology. This has led to a situation in which economic theory seems unnecessarily limited to the construction of artificial worlds. Economic theory takes individual preferences to be independent of experience and neglects 'feedback' from the results of actions on the individual's preference structure. *Homo economicus* is taken to be incapable of learning. Behaviourist learning theory as well as different variants of cognitive theory agree that success or failure of actions in the social and non-social environment determine to an important degree whether preferences are maintained or changed. For the present purpose we want to neglect differences between various approaches in contemporary psychology. Despite such differences, the principle in learning theory of instrumental conditioning as well as cognitive theory and theories of cognitive consistency amount to saying that *the results of instrumental action and information about chances of success are important factors in the motivation for changing preferences.* Economic rationalism is to be replaced by a less narrow version of the theory of behaviour that takes into account changes of goals and preferences on the basis of personal experience as well as the rearrangements of preferences because of interferences with their cognitive balance.

For example, a psychological theory provides better indications as to the processes that can be expected to occur if the results of action are uncertain—the classical doctrine of rationality has never satisfactorily solved the problem of uncertainty (Lehner, 1975). At the same time all those phenomena come to light that would not play a part in a world of certainty. A rational individual in the sense of the economic doctrine is not in need of communication with others in order to determine his preferences. Even though economic theory is becoming more and more aware of the problem of uncertainty, it still neglects various consequences of uncertainty and social influence. It neglects important aspects of human information-processing and strategic behaviour. This results in theory with rather little explanatory power: a significant amount of behaviour seems to be 'irrational' in terms of economic theory. Many of the problems of economic theory can, however, be solved if we incorporate psychological theory. The following is an attempt at a social—psychological reformulation of the theory of rational action, that is to say as an attempt to integrate economic and social—psychological theory. It should be pointed out that the social—psychological theories we use are based by and large on similar ideas to those of economic theory, but are at the same time complementary in important aspects.

## 4 A PRELIMINARY STATEMENT OF A THEORY OF HUMAN BEHAVIOUR

A theory of human behaviour that integrates economic and social—psychological perspectives can be formulated on the bases of four assumptions. We shall confine ourselves here to stating and discussing the general features of this theory only, since a more detailed version of it has been put forward in Lehner (1973). We assume that:

(1) *Individuals choose from among a set of two or more perceived alternatives that one which is associated with the highest expected utility or, if there is no difference in expected utility, that one which is associated with the lowest costs.*

We should mention here that in our conception behaviour is a matter of actually perceived alternatives. The set of perceived behavioural alternatives does not necessarily include all alternatives that actually exist. It is possible in limiting cases that all relevant alternatives are recognized. And of course it is also possible that some alternatives are recognized or imagined although in fact they cannot be chosen and therefore constitute *false alternatives.* (For a more 'economic' analysis of this problem, see McGlen, 1974.) Analysing the alternatives that appear to be objective to the observer or scientist does not always permit predictions about individual behaviour although it may be useful in order to estimate the chances of success or failure of behaviour. The discrepancy between perceived and real alternatives is one of the conditions for correcting or changing preferences and information strategies. Apart from this we are not dealing with utilities but with the *expectation of utilities.* Our second hypothesis is based on the theory of Thibaut and Kelley (1959)[2] and relates preferences to experience and actual pay-offs of behaviour.

(2) *Individual behaviour is determined by expectations which serve as standards for the evaluation of the results of actual and intended actions. Results above the expected value are judged positive, below this value negative.*

In combination with hypothesis (3), this hypothesis accounts for the control of human behaviour through success and failure. Expectations are not fixed but variable standards that are shaped by experience and communication (see below). The assumption of transitive and connected preferences is the most far-reaching idealization of economic rationalism (see Riker and Ordeshook, 1973, pp.16ff.). It is not only false in a number of cases. It is also not very convincing once the principle is adopted that evaluations and behaviour depend on experiences. Basically, personal and interpersonal comparisons of expectations, values and results of actions disconnect, modify or change the relation between preferences, so that preference structures may be highly variable with respect to connectivity and transitivity. Therefore it makes sense to start from a principle of consistency. Following *the theory of cognitive dissonance* (Festinger, 1957) this can be formulated as follows:

(3) *Individuals behave in a way such that their cognitive dissonance is reduced to a minimum. Cognitive dissonance is defined as a psychological contradiction. Two cognitions are dissonant if the one psychologically implies the opposite of the other. The degree of dissonance increases proportionally with the importance the cognition has for the individual. Dissonance theory postulates a tendency to reduce dissonance.* (For details see Festinger, 1957.)

The relevance of this theory for the axiom of rationality can be exemplified as follows. We assume that someone has to decide whether or not a commodity is to be bought. From the viewpoint of the prospective purchaser, this commodity has a number of qualities. Some of these qualities tell in favour and others against buying the commodity: whatever decision is taken, cognitive dissonance will result. This cognitive dissonance can be reduced in many different ways. Perhaps new information is added that corrects the earlier judgement and thus facilitates the decision, or else other alternatives appear more attractive. But it could also happen that a choice is made under pressure although the cognitive structure of our individual is not consistent. Then there will be a process after the decision is taken to legitimize the choice. For instance the individual would seek reaffirmative information. The alternatives would move apart. This 'post-decisional' effect may bring about a transitive and connected order of preference (Festinger, 1964). In a similar way, of course, preferences that have been transitively ordered may become disconnected in the course of a post-decisional process. The principle of cognitive consonance explains why transitivity of preferences can be established though post-decisional effects. Because of this process the probability of repeated modes of behaviour generally increases. A person would tend to vote for one party more consistently, for instance after having adapted his preferences more and more to his experience. After each activity expectations and requirements change towards the results actually obtained. This is so as long as this result is not very unlikely in terms of previous experiences of the individual or in terms of the information that is dominant in a given social environment.

If we apply these principles to voting behaviour as a test we soon find that a reformulation of political economy in psychological terms meets a number of difficulties. For instance, it is very hard for both the voters and the representatives of political parties to set standards for success. It may be equally hard for them to recognize party programmes as alternatives and thus construct a significant party differential. And the relation too between cognitive dissonance or consonance on the one hand the voter's expectation or the actual behaviour of the government on the other can no longer be identified as easily as when these principles of explanation were applied to *direct* exchanges on markets or in social groups. Collective decisions differ from individual decisions because it is so much more difficult to say exactly what is the result of a given action and to identify the 'cause' of a certain result. This relation between action and its effect is doubtless important for the maintainance or change of preferences. In the case of the voter or in most cases of collective action this relation is not as clear as it is in the case of *quid pro quo* exchanges. In a more complex transaction it may be quite difficult to correct or re-adjust action according to its effects.

If a solution is to be found to this problem it has to be considered that under conditions of uncertainty judgements, expectations and behavioural probabilities are determined not only by success or failure but by comparison with other people. Comparisons are no longer made just by one individual between the intended aim and the actual result of his action (Festinger, 1957). They are made in social communication. As soon as there is uncertainty and thus a need for mutual communication *intra-personal* comparisons are to a large extent replaced by *inter-personal* comparisons.[3] Following Festinger (1954) we assume that:

(4) *Individuals tend to evaluate their abilities, activities and views. If there is any uncertainty, this evaluation takes the shape of social (interpersonal) comparisons.*

Recognized discrepancies between one's own plans, results and views and those of others lead to cognitive dissonance. It follows, in connection with (3), that the occurrence of discrepancies in social groups leads to the attempt to bring undesirable or undesired opinions or activities close to one's own position to understand, and eventually to accept them. Consensus is a state of affairs identical by definition with the reduction of cognitive dissonance. The direction of the process of convergence can be analysed in terms of psychological theory and of certain conditions of application. Among them are the potential for the breakdown of social relations and rank orders within a group. Persons with high status set standards. These standards initiate processes of convergence. Psychology can thus be connected in an interesting way with the theory of rational behaviour because social status constitutes a measure not only of success or failure but also of utilities and costs of behaviour.

In the following we shall limit ourselves to relating the formulated explanatory principles to problems of consensus and conflict and connected questions. (For other applications see Lehner, 1973.)

## 5 THE LOGIC AND PSYCHO-LOGIC OF INDIVIDUAL CHOICE

Before we can turn to an application of our principles to problems of consensus and conflict we have to make clear one crucial difference between our approach and a 'pure' economic approach. This has to do with the 'logic' of choice. The economist's rational man is supposed to seek maximal utility. This implies more than just choosing among a given set of behavioural alternatives the one that is associated with highest expected utility—it implies a *search* for maximal utility. Problems of search and choice normally are not separated in economic theory. Economic theory is assumed to deal with decisions in terms of choices and it involves more often than not a static analysis. It is static in that it analyses the choice among alternatives that are given at a certain moment and does not consider the possibility that alternatives may not occur simultaneously but in some kind of a sequence. And yet such a view implies the idea of a systematic search for alternatives before decisions are made: the rational individual

150

first investigates the set of all possible alternatives and then chooses the best one.

In order to clarify the differences between a pure logic of choice and a psycho-logic of choice we make use of a simplified model. If we assume transitive and asymmetrical preferences we can represent the behavioural space of an individual on a one-dimensional utility scale (Figure 8.1). For a moment we neglect point $E$. In our

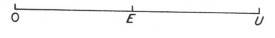

Figure 8.1

simple graph $U$ represents maximum utility. According to a pure logic of choice we can assume that an individual not only prefers every alternative that is closer to $U$ than to 0, but tries to find an alternative that lets him reach $U$. We can thus assume that the individual will not be satisfied unless he has reached $U$. For this individual, gain and loss simply mean success or failure in reaching $U$. If we turn now to the psycho-logic of choice we have to give our one-dimensional scale a second interpretation: the scale represents not only utility but also property (actually achieved utility). In this design point $E$ assumes a special significance: it indicates the individual's actual achievement *and* his level of expectation. The expectation-level ($E$) is the standard for the evaluation of outcomes and 'defines' gain and loss: any point between $E$ and $U$ is a gain, any point between $E$ and 0 is considered as loss. Whereas in a pure economic view the individual is not satisfied unless he actually reaches $U$, in a psychological model every outcome between $E$ and $U$ leads to satisfaction (see Thibaut and Kelley, 1959).

Since we cannot regard the expectation level as a given constant, a static model would not make much sense. As pointed out before, we assume that the expectation level is determined by experience and social comparison. Let us first look only to the individual's own experience and neglect social comparison. Whenever the individual gets results that differ negatively *or* positively from the expectation, cognitive dissonance will result. The 'normal' way of reducing this dissonance is the adaptation of the expectation to the actual result. This is shown in Figure 8.2. $E_0$ indicates the

```
0              E(0)   E(1)  E(2) U(1)    U(2)          U
```

Figure 8.2

basic expectation, $E_1$ and $E_2$ the adapted expectations after reaching results $U_1$ and $U_2$. As Figure 8.2 indicates, the expectation does not move to the position of the actual result but to some point between the original expectation and the new result. The expectation has to be considered as a weighted mean of all results an individual has received or learned about by social comparison (see Helson, 1963). Helson presents a rather sophisticated formula in order to determine the 'adaptation level' (expectation level). We do not need to be so sophisticated. We need to keep in mind only that expectations are some kind of a mean of results and so an expectation will not immediately change to the position of the actual result. If, however, in a sequence of behaviour our individual always received results $U_2$, the expectation would eventually become identical with that point. Anyhow, as long as each result $U_{n+1}$ of the individual is equal or higher than $E_n$ we can assume that $E_{n+1}$ will approach $U_{n+1}$. This might be different if $U_{n+1}$ were below $E_n$. The resulting dissonance could be reduced not only by changing the expectation but also by changing the behaviour. Without going into details we can formulate the following hypotheses (for details see Lehner, 1973, pp.109ff.).

(1) Success leads to an increase, failure to a decrease in expectation.
(2) The greater the success or failure, the higher the increase or decrease of expectation as long as success and failure are *not* considered by the individual as unique and exceptional (in the latter case the weight of the new result would be infinitesimally small and it would therefore not affect expectation).
(3) The more an individual's degree of success and failure differs from that of people in similar positions, with whom social comparison is made, the less do success and failure affect expectation.
(4) Failure leads to a search for alternatives whereas in case of continuing success over a long time some behavioural routine is developed.
(5) If, in case of failure, the search for alternatives also fails, the level of expectation drops until it corresponds to the result of behaviour that is actually obtained.

We will discuss the implications of these hypotheses for the analysis of consensus and conflict in the next section. For the moment we wish to return to the problem of search and choice. Our analysis clearly suggests that rational (purposive) behaviour is *not* determined by the attempt to maximize utility. Of course, an individual will —according to our basic hypothesis (1)—always choose the best alternative that is perceived. But this means much less than maximization of utility, for the latter necessarily involves a *search* for the optimal alternative. In models of rational choice it is usually assumed that the results of all *possible* alternative choices are evaluated by the actor before he reaches a decision. This amounts to the assumption that a systematic search for the alternative that maximizes utility is an essential part of rational behaviour. It is our contention however that the search for alternatives takes place only when a certain line of behaviour fails, that is when its result does not match up to expectation. If in a pure economic analysis *choice* and *search* were to be strictly separated and if the costs of search were taken into account, the 'economists' would certainly reach similar conclusions to ours.[4]

## 6 CONSENSUS AND CONFLICT: AN ECONOMIC ANALYSIS

In the general discussion of political science, very often a specific theory of conflict and power is demanded. This demand is understandable as a reaction to the dominant type of political theory. Easton's systems theory or Deutsch's cybernetic theory do indeed tend to neglect problems of power and conflict and concentrate on consensus. The demand for a theory of conflict and power is, however, nowhere matched by results. It is our contention that a *specific* theory of conflict is not needed, nor would it contradict a theory of consensus on the bases of shared values. We wish to show that the problem of conflict and consensus is not a problem of different theories but a problem of different models, that is to say a problem of differing constellations of initial conditions. This implies the postulate that one single behavourial theory is able to explain consensus as well as conflict (see Sperlich, 1971).

The assumption of the necessity of specific theories of conflict and consensus most frequently seems to be based on the conception that consensus means shared values whereas conflict indicates the absence of shared values. In this view, a conflict model applies to a society within which two incompatible alternative value systems exist. This implies the hypothesis that within any social association (a group, an organization or a whole society) conflict reaches a maximum when consensus on values reaches a minimum. However plausible such a hypothesis may sound at the first glance, it is generally false and misleading.

This can be demonstrated by constructing a simple but quite realistic model of a conflict. Let us assume two agents who both compete for the same material or non-material good. Let us further assume that the quantity of the good that each agent can receive depends on what the other one does—the more A gets the less B can get. This is the situation of a zero-sum game. A real phenomenon that corresponds to this model is for example competition between political parties for votes. A gain of votes by party A always implies a loss of votes for B. (We are here neglecting the possibility of a change in the participation rate which could lead to a gain in absolute number of votes for both parties. This is of no importance since we are interested in the relative number of votes.) Since such a conflict can be 'solved' only by one party winning and the other one losing, our model is an almost ideal model of a pure conflict situation.

Although our model describes an extreme case of conflict that might not be found very often in reality, it is worthwhile analysing extreme types because in this way the counterfactual implications of certain basic assumptions on conflict may be clarified. Our model shows that pure conflict occurs if two parties are characterized by a system of values that coincides in all points but one. Their preferences are identical and there is complete consensus with regard to the evaluation of scarce goods. What constitutes the conflict is that there is no consensus with respect to the *distribution* of the goods in question.

This amounts to the postulate that conflict requires a fairly large amount of consensus: heterogeneous evaluations and totally differing estimations of the desirability of goods or services are not likely to produce social and political relations at all and thus also no conflict relations. We admit, of course, that traditional sociological theory is completely right in postulating consensus on values as the basis for social relations and society. There is nothing wrong with that. The point is, however, that consensus is the basis not only of harmonious relations but also of conflictual relations. Harmony indicates a condition in which there is a consensus over values *and* an accepted distribution of scarce goods. It does not make sense to distinguish harmony and conflict by the presence or absence of consensus. The difference lies in the presence or absence of a 'just' distribution. And it makes even less sense to consider consensus and conflict as opposites.

Normally, consensus makes us think of a relatively harmonious condition. As we can see, however, consensus is perfectly compatible with situations that amount to zero-sum games. And these are not reputed always to be particularly conducive to peace. From this perspective, it appears not to be very sensible to differentiate between theories of conflict and theories of consensus. Consensus theories are often used to justify conservativism because they imply statements or assumptions of just distribution. Conflict theory on the other hand tends to overlook the point that differing positions of interest and property do not necessarily lead to conflict or antagonism. Correlational concepts like consensus and conflict *taken separately* often feign a 'reality' that nowhere exists (see Schütte, 1971b, pp.133ff.).

The model we just used describes an extreme case of conflict. In reality, zero-sum situations and conflicts for which there is no acceptable solution are rather rare. Even more rarely will such a conflict model apply to a whole society.

The most convincing solution of a conflict in terms of economic theory is obviously based on the assumption that the existence of more than one good allows for bargaining and exchange. As soon as the preferences of the agents engaged in a conflict situation concern more than one good or service, harmony of interest can be reached through exchange. In societies organized in terms of a division of labour, that is in a society with many goods and multi-dimensional preferences, the possibility of a bargaining solution of any conflict nearly always exists. Despite all the criticisms levelled at pure economic theories and models from the side of behavourial theory, we have to admit that the idea of bargaining and equilibrating interests through exchange frequently shows a way out of the pure conflict model and quite often constitutes a realistic analysis. In contrast to conceptions that postulate the will of a majority and of a whole people embodied in a State that solves all conflicts as an objective and neutral judge, and in contrast to élitist conceptions of a similar kind, the idea of exchange opens up valuable possibilities for realistic theories. That is why we wish to discuss briefly an economic model of conflict resolution.

Conflict relations are characterized by a discrepancy between property and preference. A given distribution of property fails to correspond to the preferences of at least one of the participating parties. We can discuss the relationship between property, preference and conflict by using an 'Edgeworth box' representing the field of interaction of two agents (parties) A and B as in Figure 8.3. The property

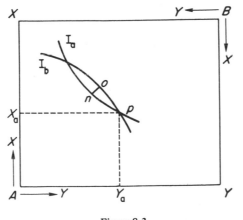

Figure 8.3

conditions are represented as follows: For A it is the field $(A, X_a, Y_a)$, for B it is the complementary field $((B, X, Y,)-(A, X_a, Y_a))$. The maximum claim A could make would be for $(A, X, Y)$. This would leave B without any property. This model might again look like a zero-sum game situation. But as soon as we assume that the commodities X and Y can be substituted the one for the other there is always a potential solution of the conflict between A and B, for we can conjecture that A would be prepared to exchange a certain quantity of X against a certain quantity of Y. In this case both parties can reach an individual optimum that depends upon the position of the indifference curves $I_a$ and $I_b$. The economic solution of the problem amounts to showing that a contract locus $(n,o)$ can be reached through exchanges and negotiations. By definition all solutions on the contract curve are Pareto-optimal (see Buchanan and Tullock, 1962, pp.100ff.). Again, we have to note that the dimensions of conflict defined by commodities X, Y coincide with dimensions of consensus.

This model is certainly relevant for political science, for even within a purely economic approach it shows the way in which interests can be brought into equilibrium. Furthermore, the model can be related to decision rules and it offers many interesting insights into political processes (compare Buchanan and Tullock, 1962). Two things, however, reduce the explanatory relevance of this construction. First, its assumptions about behaviour do not always hold true in the political context. And secondly, the specific nature of political (collective) goods that are indivisible makes bargaining more difficult.

We now introduce a model that is still based more or less on economic theory but also relates to concepts of empirical social research. The model (Figure 8.4) consists of a matrix that divides the number of individuals $(N)$ that belong to a certain society into classes according to their attributes in terms of property on two dimensions. The two dimensions $X$ and $Y$ are arguments in a utility function. For simplicity's sake they occur in the shape of dichotomous attributes $X/x$ and $Y/y$. The number of all members of the 'society' in question is $N=a+b+c+d$. If we assume that all members of society seek to maximize their utilities they would try to reach the combination $X/Y$.

Figure 8.4

Equilibrium would occur only at $N=a$. This state of affairs would correspond to that of a classless society. However, it creates a contradiction if maximization of *scarce goods* is generally assumed. Anyhow, $N=a$ ymbolizes the extreme case of a society in a state of pure harmony. The opposite extreme of pure conflict is given by conditions $N=a+d$. This corresponds to a society in which there exist two organized conflict groups that differ maximally in property—it is the model of an antagonistic class society. Neither extreme corresponds to modern society (see Dahrendorf, 1959). Rather we find that $a$ is a relatively small number (a socioeconomic élite), $d$ is a relatively large number (low social layer) and $b$ and $c$ are variable numbers of those who are characterized by 'incongruent' property conditions—the 'middle classes'. As we will see below, the existence of incongruent property relations in stratified societies has considerable effects on the political process and the communication within society (Schütte, 1971b).

Now it is easy to connect the structure of society marked by social stratification with utility theory if we simply define utility dimensions as *status dimensions* too. This relates to the usual criteria of stratification like income, property, prestige, education etc. Gain and loss of positions is nothing but *social mobility*. Mobility from *b* and *c* into *d* indicates a process of impoverishment and would contribute to the conditions of antagonistic social conflict. Mobility in the other direction (social advancement) would help to avoid social polarization. As long as *b* and *c* are not zero, conflict does not reach a maximum. This amounts to the familiar thesis that societies with more or less numerous middle 'classes' are marked by a great number of conflicts of interest but not by a generally prevailing class conflict. However, since the number of conflict dimensions and the number of possible parties to the conflict are relatively large, the number of partial conflicts increases. And yet conflict will not reach a maximum because of the prevalence of changing coalitions that eventually will tend to 'harmonize' interests to a large extent (see Riker, 1962).

## 7 DECISION AND CONFLICT: A BEHAVIOURAL ANALYSIS

We return now to the argument developed in Section 5 in order to explain further why, even in a society with sharp inequality in terms of income and property, antagonistic conflict is not likely to appear. From a rationalist point of view, a large downward mobility produces the conditions for social conflict in that two classes are likely to emerge and to confront one another. In this view a systematic failure of a large part of the lower classes to reach their goals would contribute to a polarization of society. As we have seen in Section 5, failure that is compatible with social comparison first leads to a search for alternatives and, if this search is not successful, to a decrease in the level of expectation. Success in the search for alternatives is quite considerably determined by the degree of information an individual can obtain. Since the level of information of an individual depends on his social status, we can assume that individuals with lower status are less successful in searching for alternatives (Lehner, 1975). Consequently they have to lower their aspirations. (Note that because any outcome that is equal to the expected level or higher than the expected level is satisfactory, the aspiration level coincides for us with the expectation level. We can therefore use both terms as synonymous.)

Empirical social research has confirmed the conclusion that the lower the status the lower is the level of aspiration (see Hyman, 1953). According to Lenski (1966), the distribution of scarce goods within any society is determined mainly by social status (and social power). We certainly cannot assume that this distribution meets any criteria of justice. According to the theory of social exchange, any deviation from just distribution increases the conditions for social conflict (see Homans, 1961, Ch. XII; Waldman, 1972, p.23). But even if we do not accept the economists' assumption of an harmonization of interests through exchange, but insist on the existence of an unjust distribution, we are not able to agree with the conclusion of exchange theory. Since failure makes the level of aspiration (expectation) drop and systematic failure of whole classes of people does not provide social comparison that inhibits the lowering of expectations in a situation of unjust distribution, we have to expect political apathy in the lower classes rather than politicization or polarization of the society at large. Social inequality and injustice are far from a sufficient condition for social conflict. In modern society, social inequality will rarely produce a class structure but is much more likely to produce a system of stratification with a differentiated distribution of property. In such a society there does not exist a system of shared values, but neither will there exist antagonistic conflict. Rather, we will find partial conflict, a high amount of apathy among those members of society that get least benefits and a high amount of compensation through the pursuit of satisfaction outside the political–economic sphere.

The problem we are concerned with is to a large extent connected with the problem of uncertainty, since the level of expectation (aspiration) depends on social comparison and social communication. It is therefore advisable to discuss briefly some problems of decision-making under uncertainty. As Downs (1957) has shown in his impressive analysis of voting behaviour, individual search for information can be looked at purely in terms of cost and benefit. This is an extension of the economic analysis, but it still remains in the framework of a rationalist argument. Information is understood as a scarce commodity. Its acquistion is connected with benefits but also with costs. For Downs, uncertainty is mainly a problem of the *quantity* of information an individual can get. Assuming that individuals of higher status generally obtain more information than those of lower status, Downs concludes that uncertainty varies with social status. This conjecture can be held only as long as we consider uncertainty simply as a matter of quantity of information but neglect quality of and need for information. If the problem is analysed in terms of human information-processing it can be demonstrated that uncertainty is low among individuals with low social status—despite their low quantitative level of information. This has to do with the fact that a low level of information does not allow the development of complex cognitive structures.[5] Individuals with simple cognitive structures do not *need* much information in order to make their decisions (see Lehner, 1975).

Under the conditions of simple cognitive structures, post-decisional conflicts are unlikely and therefore cognitive structures tend to be stable. Failure then leads not so much to adaptive alterations in behaviour or to a change in cognitive structure but to adjustments of the expectations and aspirations. This makes it unlikely that people will participate in conflicts: social and political conflicts always have some element of élitism. Individuals with higher status are (as Downs has shown) generally better informed about political and other problems. The higher level of information allows for the development of complex cognitive structures. This not only makes a successful search for alternatives much more probable, but is also increases the likelihood of post-decisional conflicts. Such post-decisional conflicts tend to level out different dimensions of decision. This amounts to a psychological rationalization of behaviour which involves a spread of alternatives. Individuals with high status are, thus, much more likely to develop transitive preferences as a result of post-decisional processes. Such individuals will generally be more likely to get involved in conflicts. They have the cognitive and behavioural potential that is required for exchange and bargaining as described in the economic model we presented in the last section. This leads to the conclusion that the economic model of conflict behaviour and conflict solution employed in the previous section applies much better to the behaviour of higher-status people than to that of lower-class people. This does not imply that the economic model of conflict is unrealistic, but it means that we have to restrict its applicability. It does not generally apply in the case of lower-class individuals: like the economic theory of politics the conflict model is in fact a description of middle- and upper-class behaviour. This becomes even more clear if we take into account the fact that uncertainty initiates comparison, which in turn influences expectations. The lower the degree of uncertainty, the more the level of expectation is determined by the success or failure of instrumental action exclusively, and the more behaviour will become similar to the economist's conception of rational behaviour.

Our analysis of consensus and conflict makes it quite clear that pure conflict and pure consensus models of society hardly correspond to any social or political reality. The consensus model fails if we are not in a position to assume that some kind of generally accepted just distribution exists within a society. If this is not the case (and there is no evidence that it is the case in modern capitalist society), consensus increases conflict rather than producing some kind of harmonious state of affairs. And yet we cannot assume that antagonistic conflict results. Rather we have to expect partial conflict with an élitist feature and a large amount of apathy among the lower class. This leads to the 'paradox' that individuals are the less likely to participate in activities against a given society, the lower the utility is that they receive from that social system.

## 8  COLLECTIVE BEHAVIOUR: COALITION AND CONSENSUS

Consensus models not only play an important role in the dominant sociological and political theory, but also they are contained implicitly in some aspects of economic theory. Economic theory of politics as well as the theory of the firm generally tends to consider parties, interest groups, organizations and firms as varieties of consensus group, in other words social associations that share values and preferences. Furthermore the idea of a social welfare function indicates a similar view of a consensus society.

Arrow's (1951) fascinating analysis of the problem of collective choice made it clear that, despite rationally ordered individual preferences, collective decisions may be cyclical, intransitive and hence irrational. This is of crucial importance for the problem of majority and minority in democracies. The traditional theory of democracy is based largely on the idea of majority rule. The assumption is that this majority is related in some fairly unprecise fashion to the idea of public interest. Behind this assumption we might well find the idea of a 'volonté générale'. At least it implies the idea that majority and minority agree in relation to the 'best' alternatives and that collective decision-making leads to consensus. A theoretical foundation for this view is available only in the theory of small groups and in mocro-sociology (see Schütte, 1971b). As soon as the assumption of consensus and majority is analysed more closely we will find that in fact there does not exist a real consensus among majorities and minorities but some rather unstable 'aggregation' of individual preferences that by no means indicates a consensus or a unified will of the majority and the minority (see Arrow, 1951; Buchanan and Tullock, 1962; Riker and Ordeshook, 1973).

The recognition of this problem leads to the conclusion that in almost any case of a collective decision there exist potentially many possible majorities and that the actual majority is nothing but an unstable coalition. Consequentially, political decision-making in terms of votes and elections represents a process of changing coalitions that never allows for a stable majority. This makes clear that we have to stop the naive use of the notions of majority and minority that characterize so much of political science (and of course the speeches of politicians and very often the interpretation and application of law by courts).

The economic coalition model of collective decision-making is certainly much more realistic than traditional democratic 'theory'. However, it involves serious fallacies in so far as it concentrates upon coalitions and neglects the possibility that bargaining and coalition formation might well lead to processes of convergence and consensus formation. Paradoxically, economists concentrate on bargaining and coalition formation but very frequently treat the result of such processes as a consensus group as soon as the coalition is organized. Consequently, economists tend to confuse coalitions and consensus groups. As we shall show below, the behaviour of coalitions and consensus groups differs in important aspects—but it also differs from the predictions of the economic theory of politics.

If there is a lack of general consensus (that is to say, if there exists only a partial consensus) the formation of a temporary coalition always produces post-decisional dissonance among the individual participants in the coalition. Again, in a post-decisional process individuals may rearrange their preferences, and if the coalition is successful they may reach some kind of convergence. If the interaction of the individuals (and groups) involved in the formation of the coalition continues over time, an increasing consensus can result and the coalition can become more and more a consensus group. It is of course clear that, although bargaining always involves processes of communication and persuasion that tend towards bringing about dissonance reduction and consensus formation, consensus groups result from this process only if there is continuous interaction and co-operation over time. Under conditions of frequent and rapid change of coalition partners, consensus groups will rarely be formed.

The condition of continuing interaction is quite often reached in small social associations. In small decision-making bodies, a problem of collective rationality that produces changing coalitions is unlikely to occur. For as soon as numerous decisions have to be made over an extended time period within a small association, consensus groups are built that are characterized by homogeneous preferences. It does not follow from our argument, though, that convergence processes are universal and that the assumption of a general social consensus can be theoretically justified. On the contrary, since the formation of consensus groups is bound up with certain conditions of communication and interaction that are never reached in large social associations and certainly not in whole societies, our argument contradicts any consensus model of society.

The formation of consensus groups is always a size problem: consensus groups are possible only within rather small social associations that allow for intensive and continuing communication. If we keep the size argument in mind, we can conjecture that in general small minorities of people sharing a particular and specific interest are more likely to be organized as consensus groups than large numbers of individuals sharing less specific and less particular interests. This amounts to the thesis that in general the particular interests of upper-class groups are more likely to be organized in consensus groups than the much less particular interests of lower classes: upper-class organizations will generally be consensus groups whereas lower-class organizations are no more than large coalitions with serious problems of organizational structure, participation and efficiency. (See Olson, 1965; Schütte, 1973.)

This is certainly relevant to the discussion of an adequate model of modern society. The most important feature of such a model is the existence of many particular conflicts carried out predominantly by middle- and upper-class organizations that are generally quite efficient consensus groups, while at the same time the lower classes participate only indirectly through their organizations, which in general are coalitions. Our model would differ in important aspects from the model of a pluralistic society, mainly because we cannot derive any justification from our theoretical argument for the existence of a process of countervailing power leading to distributive justice. Rather, our model would have to point to the existence of social inequality and to the lack of distributive justice, to an élitist structure of conflict and widespread absence of class consciousness among those who gain the least benefit from the society.

As we said above, the economic theory of politics generally understands collective choice as a coalition process, yet paradoxically it quite often ends up by conceptualizing coalitions as consensus groups as soon as the coalitions become organized. Economic theorists quite frequently consider organizations as monolithic blocs and neglect their internal structure. In this view organizations like parties or firms are perfect consensus groups. In terms of our analysis such ideas are untenable because large parties or firms can never become consensus groups.

The Downsian theory conceptualizes all political parties as consensus groups that seek to maximize votes (see Barry, 1970, pp.147ff.). Downs obviously assumes that the higher the consensus among the members of a party, the more the party will behave rationally in terms of vote maximization. This assumption sounds plausible but it is nevertheless false. As soon as we analyse the communication structure of the party and the distribution of preferences among its members we come to the opposite conclusion: the higher the consensus among the members and leaders of a party, the less the party will be able to adjust its programme and behaviour to changing preferences among the voters and the less successfully it will pursue the goal of vote maximization.

Within consensus parties the process of social comparison systematically reinforces and integrates the political attitudes of members and leaders. The party develops a cohesive 'Weltanschauung' and an elaborate and consistent ideology. If a change in preferences among a significant part of the electorate necessitates a reorientation of the party programme, cognitive dissonance emerges among the members and leaders of the party. Suggestions for reorientation are then taken as deviant behaviour and correspondingly met with negative sanctions. Any demand for reorientation leads to serious conflicts within the party (see Festinger et al., 1956). Within coalition parties with loosely connected wings, such reorientations produce much lower internal costs. Since no strong and cohesive ideology is produced by the process of internal communication, the party can change its programme according to the requirements of vote maximization. Furthermore, the reorientation can be organized by changing the faction providing the leaders of the party—changes in the voters preferences might affect the distribution of power within the party. Although this may lower the party's efficacy, a coalition type of party is much more successful in terms of vote maximization than a consensus party (see Lehner, 1973, pp.197ff.).

None of this applies if the goal of a party is not to compete for votes (with the object of ruling) within a given system but to replace the system as a whole. In this case the advantage lies with consensus parties because they depend less on external success and failure. If a coalition is confronted with a series of failures it is likely that it will alter its level of aspiration because there is hardly any internal commitment to a shared ideology. A consensus party on the other hand can maintain its level of aspiration much longer, because discrepancies between aspirations and external benefits are reduced internally—the party's ideology provides plausible explanations for failures with the political environment, at least for a certain time.

Our argument leads to the conclusion that the Downsian theory based on the idea of vote maximization applies only to party systems whose elements are coalitions. Since, however, in most modern democracies the political parties are in fact coalitions, his theory provides a fairly realistic model of modern democracy, which fits well into the general model of modern society that we outlined above.

# 9

# On Some Problems of
# Political Theory

JOHAN K. DE VREE

## 1 INTRODUCTION

To write about the writings of others, as is the task before me, poses problems of
omission and of commission. That the several contributions to the present volume
should be variations and improvisations on one common theme, 'Power and political
theory'—not a very simple, transparent, or brief one!—isn't very much of a limitation
to the number and variety of problems raised. My task, then, involves an acute
problem of selection, it being obviously impossible to deal with all the problems raised
by all the essays concerned.

Rather shamelessly indulging my own interests and inclinations, I shall mainly
discuss the following problems: those of a more philosophical nature that concern the
relationships between concepts and empirical theorizing (in Section 2); that of
individual behaviour (Section 3); the problem of the political process, including that
of linking the human individual to collective actions (Section 4); and, finally and
briefly, those concerned with power and influence (in Section 5). These problems
would seem to cover at least substantial parts of the several individual contributions,
while they are at any rate of central political importance.

At the risk of adding pedantry to insult I will make some effort to criticize
'constructively'. That is, going beyond merely noting what would seem to be weak
points in the analyses, I shall try to advance alternative interpretations or solutions
that may carry the argument forward in a perhaps more promising direction.

## 2 ON EMPIRICAL THEORY

If by 'philosophical problems' are here meant those of a rather formal and
non-empirical, perhaps even speculative, nature, concerned with how to develop
(scientific) knowledge, then philosophical problems play a relatively prominent part
in the essays under discussion. In part this is surely due to the circumstance that we are
in a relatively early stage in the development of political science. Articulate empirical
theories of some proven applicability and validity are still largely lacking. In the
absence of solid substance, then, argument and discussion almost inevitably develop,
or degenerate, into 'philosophy'. But on the other hand, and much more honourably,
the prominent role of philosophical problems equally testifies to the fact that we are
concerned with inquiry of a fundamental nature. To put it somewhat bombastically:

operating at the frontiers of knowledge inevitably raises basic problems with regard to the nature of the enterprise itself.

Thus, attempting to build a political theory of some scope and rigour where none seems to have existed before to serve as a sort of model naturally raises the question of what a theory actually is or should be, and how it relates to 'reality'—a notion that is elusive enough in itself! To some extent, the importance and relevance of these matters is indeed reflected in the essays in this volume, and, more generally, by the problematical status of the term 'theory' itself—as manifested by the flowering of such expressions as 'approach', 'framework' and 'scheme' ('conceptual' or 'analytical'), 'pretheory', 'frame of reference' and 'paradigm'. Such expressions are used alongside with or even in lieu of the term 'theory' itself. In all cases they designate rather loosely defined intellectual structures of a definitely weaker, less elaborate and less rigorous nature than theories properly so called.

Generally speaking, their relevance to our knowledge of the empirical world is unclear and ambiguous. And instead of constituting strictly defined systems of propositions about observable phenomena, they amount to little more than complicated vocabularies. It is hoped that real theories will eventually come to be expressed in such terminologies, but they do not as yet contain or represent such theories themselves. They seem to be produced by a more or less Aristotelian prejudice that knowledge resides primarily in definitions, and that inquiry should start with definitions—if not worse. Sometimes, too, and progressively more now than in the past, one meets with fairly complicated and sophisticated research which applies methods and languages of a mathematical or quantitative nature. Again, though, such research often leaves us in doubt as to what has actually been investigated, and what its relevance is to our understanding of empirical reality. Here, too, the main problem is concerned with 'theory' or the theoretical status and import of concepts and research. These are no mere matters of scientific folklore or fashion; they crucially affect our knowledge or understanding of the world. For it is precisely this—to explain observable reality—that it is the central function of a theory to serve. A theory is merely a set of interconnected propositions that is to explain reality, that is to say to produce propositions about observable reality from other propositions about observable reality. And, conversely, if one does try to do this, to explain reality, one thereby *ipso facto* engages in theorizing—accordingly a very common activity, not restricted to the doings of professional scientists only.

A theory, then, is to *explain* reality, not to 'picture' or 'reflect' it. In fact, one cannot even say there *is* something to be thus 'reflected' or 'pictured', which would exist independently from the mirror or painter and about which we would be able to say something outside of any theory. For philosophical inquiry brings to light the point that there is a close interaction between, or rather a mutual determination of, any theory and the empirical reality that it is to explain. For ultimately reality can be known only in and through some form of theory as embodied in some language, natural or artificial. In other words, what we call 'reality' already implies some theoretical construction, even though perhaps of a rather primitive and informal nature (cf. De Vree, 1968/9a, 1968/9b and 1972a, Ch. 2).

As has been intimated a moment ago, to explain reality is to derive propositions about observations from other propositions about observations. This does not, however, mean that such observations could be conceived of as the independently given building-blocks of reality and theory construction. For what has been said with regard to theory and reality fully applies to observations, too. That is, even though we may have to take their mere occurrence somehow for granted, their precise form and contents, i.e. *what* we observe, is again determined by the theoretical structure that we apply and within which such observations have or are to have a status, role, and position—a meaning, in short.

The upshot of all this is twofold. In the first place, a concept or term, its introduction and eventual meaning, are ultimately determined solely by the way in which they are to serve in a large structure, the theory within which we choose to view reality. In other words, one can speak intelligibly and meaningfully about terms and concepts only in the context of a *theory*. In the second place, terminology and definition are matters of secondary interest only.

For a theory, whether scientific or common-sense, is no mere chain of words and definitions. Explanation requires rather more than definitions, notably certain ideas, laws, presuppositions or axioms as to how things actually 'work' and people behave. One can only derive propositions about observables from other such propositions about observables—so much is implied by the logical nature of derivation or deduction. At the bottom of a theory, then, are to be found certain 'primitive' notions about relationships between observables: the axioms or postulates of the theory.

Of course, such axioms have to be expressed in words or other symbols, and a theory will employ some terminology or vocabulary as a matter of course. But the point is that such terms and their definitions are entirely conventional and theoretically barren. They do not allow for any proposition or deduction to be made about the empirical world. They are indeed mere matters of words—tools of secondary importance only. The axioms and assumptions just mentioned, on the contrary, *are* theoretically 'creative'; that is, they do allow for taking deductive steps from one region of the observable world to another. Again, one cannot explain the world unless one does have some ideas about that world, something that is not provided by mere definition, i.e. terminological convention.

It should be noted, incidentally, that this does not mean that every notion and proposition in a theory could or should be linked directly to observables. Often, it will be convenient or even inevitable to introduce a greater or lesser number of concepts and assumptions about things that, in and by themselves, are *un*observable. This does not really matter so long as such theoretical constructs are, indirectly and via others, eventually linked to observables—at the edges of the theoretical structure, so to speak.

In this connection, then, it will be clear that the construction of vocabularies and terminologies is an activity that makes sense only if and inasmuch as it is embedded in a set of creative empirical assumptions or axioms. But if this is indeed the case, if a set of such axioms as to how people behave or interact has indeed been recognized and formulated explicitly (in the social sciences at least) then the quest for formal and explicit definition loses much of its attraction and importance. This is not to deny the importance of clear and precise definition for the sake of using the language in question consistently. But, to put it somewhat differently, it is less from such formal definition than from the way in which a concept is actually used in scientific explanation that we discover the creative basis upon which it rests as well as its meaning. If, on the other hand, the concept is not embedded theoretically and there is no link to an articulate theory, an investigation into its meaning reduces to scholastic or grammatical analysis and debate which, while entertaining at times, will not advance insight very much. It is as if, in a different realm, one were to attempt a definition of 'temperature' without referring to certain empirical assumptions—creative ones!—as to how bodies behave when heated.

Unfortunately, much of political science is bedevilled by just this practice. And it is herein that resides the main weakness, often even futility, of past and present attempts to define such notions as 'power', 'influence', 'politics', 'legitimacy', 'democracy' and 'imperialism'—to mention merely a few of the better-known ones. Similarly, in such 'approaches' and 'frameworks' as 'systems analysis', 'cybernetics', 'communication theory' or 'functionalism', inasmuch as these are applied to politics and social life, one meets with little except more or less elaborate vocabularies: they represent chains of words, but how to build sentences from them remains rather unclear. Or, rather, the creative ideas, the empirical axioms and assumptions that underlie these vocabularies lie too deeply buried beneath the terminological surface and remain too implicit to play the role they deserve. Moreover they remain too deeply hidden to be noted, exposed and criticized or disciplined in research. Above all, they lie too deeply buried to advance our understanding of the political realm appreciably beyond the level of common sense. And much the same applies to the more or less sophisticated classifications, schemes and sets of indicators as well as correlational analyses that are to be found in pieces of more advanced research.

In contrast to this, it seems to be precisely the chief merit of the 'rational' or 'economic' approach to politics (with its kin, 'exchange' theory), which figures so largely in the individual pieces of this volume, that it does indeed introduce some specific empirical axioms about politics and human behaviour. These assumptions may be the wrong one, they may be applied inconsistently, they may be too crude and shallow, and the approach itself may be narrow-minded and may distort reality. But even if the works adopting such an approach did indeed contain all these, and more, defects, they do contain an argument and tell us something definite about the world. And it is precisely thereby that they themselves allow for the detection of such defects, errors and weaknesses, thus contributing essentially to their eventual improvement and to the advance of knowledge—which is not the least merit a scientific theory may have!

## 3  HUMAN BEHAVIOUR

In so far as the several contributions to this volume are concerned with the explanation of the political process, as are those by Birnbaum, Barry, Midgaard and Lively in particular, they all employ as their starting point some notion about what is essentially individual human behaviour. And indeed it is difficult to see how it could be otherwise. For, ultimately, social and political life is made up of human individuals; social and political life processes consist ultimately of (inter)acting human beings; and even the largest, most comprehensive and long-term historical process is actually produced by, and is nothing more than, more or less complicated configurations of individuals behaving in certain interrelated fashions. That they may do so unwittingly and without being conscious of what they eventually produce does not really make a difference. Indeed, most social and historical processes considerably overstep the measure of the single individual, in both place and time, in the sense that they result from or are made up of complex *patterns* and *configurations,* of *sets* and *systems,* or human actions, stretching over more or less extended areas and periods of time. They cannot, accordingly, be said to be 'produced' by man in the same sense as that in which man engages in individual actions to reach individual goals. Still it is such actions that are somehow to be found at the bottom of the collective outcomes and patterns mentioned.

There is no denying, then, the fundamental and profound difference between the realm of individual action and that of collective behaviour and processes. Nevertheless it is difficult to see how one could explain the latter without any ideas, without postulating some notions, as to how individuals behave and interact. And ultimately it would seem to be from such ideas and notions that insights about larger political systems and occurrences are to be derived. It may with some justification be said that it is precisely in this way and through this sort of theorizing that the fundamental differences between the sphere of the individual and that of the collectivity become most clearly visible. Roughly, collective occurrences appear to be produced by what are for all intents and purposes to be conceived as political processes. And while these are to be explained from certain assumptions about individual behaviour, the individual assumptions do not apply directly to such political processes and outcomes: it is a matter of *derivation*, not of *identity*!

In fact, it seems to be one of the main weaknesses of the theories mentioned and discussed in this book that they rather indiscriminately apply their basic behavioural assumptions both to individual and to collective actors, thus ignoring the fundamental differences that exist between these. But one cannot, and one should not, attempt to explain the 'behaviour' of a collectivity (even the term 'behaviour' itself is suspect in this sphere!) such as a state, a political party, an interest group or an institution, along the same lines as individual action. Such collective behaviour is to be conceived as the outcome of a political process, which is generically different from individual action even though it is ultimately based upon it.

Of course, one could take a fundamentally different approach to the matter by starting with the collectivity and the system instead of with the individual. Sometimes this is pretended to be the essential contribution of such 'approaches' as systems analysis and (structural-) functionalism. However, inasmuch as these can indeed be said to represent theories at all, and inasmuch as they do indeed explain something, closer scrutiny invariably reveals that what makes them 'work' is precisely some relatively crude ideas about human behaviour. It is on these ideas that the centrally important explanations appear to be modelled: explanations of why units make political demands and lend support to political objects, or why they occupy certain functions and roles and perform certain functions or how the system acquires legitimacy. That no distinction is made between the realm of the individual and that of the collectivity is, while important enough in itself, merely a minor point in the present context.

Much ink has been spilled about the issue of 'individualism' and 'atomism' *v.* 'holism'. It is a distinction that does not seem to be very useful with respect to the sort of theory discussed here. For, far from necessitating and implying a so-called 'individualistic' conception of society and of the collectivity, process and system, it is precisely this sort of theorizing that provides us with the means to recognize and identify the differences between the two spheres as well as to connect them—even though some actual applications may in fact ignore these problems.

Now, what *are* these ideas about individual behaviour that are applied in or seem to underlie the several contributions to this volume? The fact that a relatively great number of different terms are used in this connection presents us with some difficulties. Thus one meets with such notions as 'rewards' and 'punishments', 'costs' and 'benefits', 'gains' and 'losses', 'rationality' or 'self-interest' and 'utility', all of which are meant to explain individual human behaviour. Generally speaking, such notions are not very sharply articulated and are elaborated only to a limited extent. But the general direction of the argument would seem to be clear enough as well as intuitively plausible: individual behaviour is postulated to be a matter of choosing among alternatives that are ranked in terms of some such notion as 'utility' or 'attractiveness'. That is to say, individuals are assumed to 'choose' that behavioural alternative with the highest 'utility', the most 'attractive' one. Or, in probabilistic terms, some choice, that is some behaviour, becomes more probable the higher its utility is estimated to be. Now this idea would seem to be quite plausible and fruitful, provided several things are clearly and firmly kept in mind.

First of all it should be recognized for what it is: merely the very first beginnings of a theory of human behaviour, not amounting to much more than a mere convention as to how, in what terms, to study such behaviour. It fixes the terms in which we are to phrase it, but does not yet have any empirical contents at all. For, contrary to what Professor Birnbaum seems to think, the meaning of the axiom's most central term 'utility' has not at all been (pre)determined. 'Utility' here can refer to anything from supernaturally inspired ideas to vulgar self-interest expressed in monetary terms only. On the other hand, at this stage in the analysis it may mean nothing more than 'that which renders particular behavioural choices more probable'. This amounts to a convention to call this property (or, rather, complex of properties) 'utility', thereby at the same time clearly identifying the next problem for inquiry. For to make the axiom really work in explaining human behaviour, we clearly need further assumptions as to what alternatives, in which situations, will be ranked in what ways by what individuals. In other words, what is utility?

Going somewhat beyond the papers discussed here, with the partial exception of Barry's, one may venture a further extension of this reasoning by linking the notion of utility to those of preference and probability, as is commonly done in 'decision-making theory'. That is, one may further postulate that utility is determined by the preferences and the probability judgements that the individual forms with respect to the outcomes that he associates with each of the several alternatives 'before' him. Thus one may assume that, if such an associated outcome is a *benefit* (i.e. if its occurrence is preferred to its non-occurrence), then the utility of an alternative increases with any increase in the estimated probability of that outcome's occurring as a result of the alternative. If, on the other hand, such an outcome is a *sacrifice* (i.e., if its non-occurrence is preferred to its occurrence), then utility increases with an increase in the magnitude of preference as well as with a decrease in its estimated probability. In sum: greater and surer benefits as well as smaller and more remote sacrifices increase the utility of the actions concerned. (See for a more precise and elaborate development De Vree, 1972b and forthcoming.)

Thus having carried the implicit definition of the notion of utility one step further by relating it to preference and (subjective) probability, the problem now obviously becomes that of saying something definite about actual human preferences and probability judgements. In the papers under discussion this problem is hardly dealt with in any systematic fashion. Here, as in common sense, the problem is 'solved' by assuming, mostly implicitly at that, a number of general human preferences, as for life, for self-preservation and security, for monetary values and productive resources—and by ignoring the problems posed by the notion of probability.

Even without any deeper discussion of the notions involved, it is apparent that they represent grave and difficult problems of crucial importance to the further development of the kind of theorizing with which we are concerned here. Clearly, too, the common solution of directly introducing some general propositions about such probability and preference judgements will not always work. For in view of the enormous differences that characterize human tastes and insights, in view also of the infinite variety of situations to which these are to apply, such general assumptions cannot but be of a highly abstract nature and, as a consequence, applicable only with difficulty.

What is needed, then, is a separate though related theory about the *growth* and *development* of the judgements concerned, about the formation of tastes and the processing of information, in short a theory of the process of human learning. It would be the task of such a theory to determine what sort of judgements would be made by what people in what situations, and, not least, to determine the relative 'weight' that several possibly conflicting judgements would acquire in concrete behavioural situations. This does not mean that one could really dispense with at least *some* direct and general statements about probabilities and preferences. But a theory of the sort indicated would serve as the mechanism for connecting such generalities to the concrete situations in which people actually find themselves. There is no question that such a theory does not yet exist. But if the theorizing discussed is ever to become relevant to our understanding actual human behaviour, the problems of learning theory cannot be ignored.

With this we arrive at a second observation concerning the axiom of utility under discussion here, namely one regarding its generality. As it stands—that is, without any stipulations as to the actual human preferences and probability judgements allowed—the axiom is empirically empty. By the same token, it is also completely general in that it allows for any kind of motive, interest, degree of ignorance or information, judgement or prejudice on the part of the choosing individual. Accordingly, it refers to each and every sort of human behaviour. Thus it is not *a priori* limited to situations of 'free choice' (whatever that may mean) or to those of a peaceful or voluntary nature only—a point especially important in discussions about the limits of 'exchange theory', as the preceding chapters bear out. For, even when one is forced at gunpoint to give up one's wallet, the axiom in all its empty generality still fully applies.

What actually happens in such a situation is determined by, roughly, the fact that a man generally prefers his life to his death and to the relatively small amount of money he ordinarily carries in his wallet. This, together with some information about the physical properties of guns and bullets and an assumption about the robber's determination to fire the gun as well as about his chances of actually scoring a hit if he fires (all this being plainly a matter of probability estimates!), generally allows us to predict that the utility to someone of actually giving up his wallet in such situations will be higher than that of alternative actions, such as fleeing, counter-attacking, crying for help and so on. But it should be clearly recognized that all this is a matter of additional information, of facts and assumptions to be fed into the original axiom to make it work and yield the normally accurate prediction that (or explanation why) the probability of compliance when thus threatened will generally be higher than the probability of non-compliance. The application of force, then, does not mean any departure from the sort of analysis here discussed.

In this connection, it should also be mentioned that the theory perfectly allows for people choosing to die (as Mr Lively observes by way of criticizing a similar notion) out of the feeling *'dulce et decorum est pro patria mori'*. Likewise, the axiom is not, as Birnbaum suggests, biased in any specific normative direction. In fact, the main difference between the conception found in Bentham and nineteenth-century utilitarianism on the one hand and the present conception on the other is that the former *was* an essentially normative conception being concerned with a particular idea of justice and specific policy proposals, while the latter is merely concerned with *explaining* individual human actions.

The conception under discussion is, in the third place, often called 'rational' or 'rationalistic'. Even supposing it possible that one could agree on the meaning of the term 'rational', it is doubtful whether this would represent an adequate characterization of the theory. For in itself this theory does not prohibit any silly or self-damaging actions or preferences, does not prevent people from having odd notions about the world and the alternatives open to them, and does not guarantee the factual correctness of their estimates and expectations. Again, therefore, any actions can in principle be explained by the theory, both 'rational' and 'irrational' ones. In this connection it is of fundamental importance to realize that, according to the axiom, human preferences and information can in principle be distilled only from actual behaviour—which prohibits any *a priori* limitation as to their scope and nature that might imply that behaviour itself is to be treated as given.

To be sure, the axiom seems to suggest a sort of calculative rigour, with businesslike computation and comparison of the costs and benefits of all alternatives, and to imply highly conscious deliberation and action. But the axiom does not pretend to describe what goes on in the individual's head, to represent the way in which he conceives or rationalizes his actions himself. It is a mechanism to *explain* such actions. And in this respect it does not really matter at all whether or not people actually 'calculate' or are really 'aware' of the alternatives before them or whether they precisely compare the pros and cons of their actions. Nothing of the sort has to be presupposed in order actually to apply the axiom.

This axiom also has a definite 'economic' flavour. And in fact it is in the science of economics or 'political economy' that we meet with its historically first and most elaborate application. It is no coincidence, then, that the approach that most consistently and openly rests upon this axiom is often referred to as the 'economic approach' to politics, not least because many of its adepts were originally trained as professional economists. While the term 'economic approach' can thus be explained as a matter of *historical* precedence, this does not imply *theoretical* precedence.

For, speaking purely theoretically, the relationship between economics and political science, or, rather, between the utility axiom as applied in economics and in political science, is rather the reverse. That is, the former is much narrower than the latter, and the latter can be seen to include the former as a special case. For, with the significant exception of welfare economics, the axiom in its economic interpretation is rather stringently limited by the presuppositions about what preferences actually govern human behaviour (roughly those for more monetarily expressed value to less) that are exemplified by the famous 'economic principle' thought to underlie the behaviour of 'economic man'. Clearly, no such sharp restriction of human tastes can be admitted in political science where many more preferences are of immediate relevance, such as those for survival, power and influence, votes, individual or national honour, peace and security and so on. For, after all, political transactions are not limited, as in the economic case, to buying and selling and their derivatives.

In fact, then, the economic interpretation of the utility axiom is but a special case of the political one. And, as will appear in the next section, the economic process and economic transactions can be actually conceived as special cases of political processes and transactions.

Finally, not the least of the merits of the axiom is that it provides us with a basis for meaningful discourse about processes of power and influence between people, or, more generally, about human interaction, in which capacity it is clearly visible in so-called exchange theory. For, obviously, if we have some theory about how people behave, even if it be merely the very first beginnings of it, we thereby also have a (perhaps rudimentary) tool for explaining and predicting the effects of the actions of others upon us, and a starting-point for a theory about the political process. The crux of the matter in analysing interaction and politics is that *my* actions may represent *outcomes* associated with the *behavioural alternatives of others,* and that, conversely, the several *behavioural alternatives of others* represent *outcomes* with respect to which *I* may form preferences and probability judgements.

Thus, the basic idea of 'exchange theory', as developed notably by Homans and Blau and discussed in some of the preceding contributions, is clearly entailed directly by the axiom already stated. A interacts with B—provides him with certain goods or performs certain actions while abstaining from others—to the extent that B provides him with (positive or negative) incentives for doing so. And B can make A behave in some specific fashion only to the extent that he is able to increase the utility of the action in question while decreasing the utility of other actions. The means employed by B to make A conform to his wishes obviously depend upon B's own estimates of the utility to him of A's behaviour, that is to say upon his preferences and probability estimates with regard to A's actions. All this, however, is clearly a matter of a relatively straightforward application of the axiom discussed.

Here, however, we touch upon the problem of the political process which is to constitute the subject of the next section.

## 4 THE MECHANISM OF POLITICS

With the exception of Dr Lane, none of the authors discussed here provides an explicit definition of what politics is about. Nevertheless, it would seem, we do need some means of identifying the problems with which we are to deal. As is well known, the solution of this problem has been sought for in a variety of directions—in such notions as 'authoritative allocations of values', 'binding decisions', 'governmental policies', 'power' and 'influence', the 'control' of human behaviour, etc. Again, and as is illustrated by Lane's contribution, the problem is mostly discussed outside of the context of any well articulated theory. As has been argued in the second section of this chapter, however, one should be wary of the formal and explicit definitions that result from such an approach. For they cannot generally be much more than rather arbitrary terminological conventions whose theoretical status and relevance are quite unclear. And, not being cast in terms that figure in a true explanatory theory, nothing guarantees the solubility of the research problems that such definitions identify. Far from producing any knowledge about the political world, a definition of politics merely serves to define what sorts of problems that world poses. And the solution of these problems clearly involves developing a substantive theory about that world.

As we have seen, the several essays in this volume do provide at least the first beginnings of such a theory. The problem now is obviously that of developing an adequate notion of the political in terms that this theory employs. And this does indeed seem to be possible.

Thus, the authors, in their different ways and employing different terminologies, all seem to be concerned in one way or another with the process through which people or groups of people get other people or groups to do certain things and to abstain from doing other things. So much, incidentally, also seems to underlie such notions as 'authoritative allocations of values' and 'binding decisions', as well as others that have been mentioned. In all these and similar cases the crucial problem of politics is always reducible to processes and patterns of 'influence' or 'control'. In terms that have been used in the preceding discussion: politics is apparently concerned with the process through which the choice of some behavioural alternatives by certain people is made more probable and the choice of others less probable. Or, more generally still, politics is the process through which people try to establish or change a particular set or configuration of behavioural probabilities in sets of other people.

After some reflection, it will be clear that such typically 'political' outcomes as the adoption of a government tax policy or foreign policy, the execution of a law or decree, the delimitation of constitutional positions and competences and the determination of spheres of influence or territorial boundaries are all particular instances of rather complicated sets of what are ultimately individual behavioural probabilities, or *behavioural distributions,* as I will call them.

Collective actions such as those by states and political parties, interest groups and coalitions, administrative organizations and organs, are instances of specific behavioural distributions. 'Action' by such a collectivity (consisting of greater or lesser numbers of individuals who perform different task and occupy different positions) is a matter of its individual members behaving in different though related ways. It is like an orchestra whose 'performing' a piece of music dissolves into its members performing a great variety of quite different things, albeit, one hopes, in a well co-ordinated fashion.

Such distributions of behavioural probabilities do not generally come about automatically. Rather, they normally represent the outcomes of processes in which several people and groups actually try to achieve some such result. They occur as a result of the fights, struggles, debates and negotiations between those concerned. Or, as I shall put it, such behavioural distributions result, if not automatically, from the participants to the political process directing *demand behaviour* at one another, that is to say actions designed to bring about certain (changes in) behavioural probabilities in others. And a political process occurs, accordingly, when some actor engages in demand behaviour *vis-à-vis* some other actor. Incidentally, it is here that lies the chief difference between individual and collective behaviour. For, whereas the former is a matter of the (relative) probability of choosing one from among a set of behavioural alternatives, the latter concerns the growth and development of *configurations* of such behavioural probabilities. And whereas the former is a matter of 'choice', the latter (for which the term 'behaviour' is already misleading) is generally an outcome of political processes.

It may be observed, incidentally, that a conception of the political process such as has just been sketched, and which seems to define the core of what the several authors mean by it, is a particularly wide one. According to it, political processes will occur in almost any human group or encounter; virtually all social interactions involve some sort of mutual behavioural adaptation and the growth of more or less stable patterns of behaviour—in short, the occurrence of certain behavioural distributions. And indeed, such a wide conception of the process is precisely what is contained in Barry's paper in particular, there being nothing at all inherent in the argument that should restrict it to, say, the 'official' governmental sphere only.

Obviously, a full discussion of this matter is out of place here. Suffice it to mention a few pertinent observations.

In the first place, the fact that this conception would cover such things as family or even love relationships does not mean that these were 'nothing but' political phenomena. It would be absurd to suppose that political science, with a theory like the one sketched here, would ever fully cover the essential characteristics of such relationships. But this does not mean that, say, a love relationship does not have certain important traits in common with warring states or parties bargaining in a coalition. It merely means that such relationships or phenomena are political in some, but not in all, respects.

In the second place, and related to this, to define such relatively uncommon (at least viewed from current practice in political science) phenomena as (partly) political does not really force us actually to investigate them. It may be scientifically advantageous to do so, as certain political phenomena may be more accessible in the setting of small groups than in say, governmental negotiations. It may sometimes even be necessary to do so, namely when occurrences in these spheres have a bearing upon more centrally relevant phenomena—as is the case with political socialization research. But no real obligation can be deduced to make such phenomena the centre of one's professional interests. The generality of this conception is a benefit without any strings attached.

In the third place it may be mentioned in passing that (as has been intimated already in the preceding section) such typically economic transactions as buying and selling can also be viewed as instances of political processes. For here, too, parties direct demand behaviour at one another so as to increase the likelihood of A's parting with some of his money and of B' providing certain goods. And the economy as a whole, or rather its state at any particular moment, can be conceived as a behavioural distribution—though not one that is produced in a fully conscious way, at least in economies that are not centrally directed. This again suggests that part at least of economics is to be viewed as a special case of politics.

To return to the development of the theory itself, then, the question that presents itself rather naturally at this point in the analysis has to do with the central mechanism of the political process. To explain the occurrence of a behavioural distribution as being influenced by or as being a result of political processes is in fact the problem of why people's behaviour is or can be changed by the actions of others. Or, why and how is demand behaviour successful, and to what extent? In other words, as it will be called here, what determines the *weight*? It is this problem that is clearly and centrally involved in such common notions as power and influence, and it seems to be this that they seek to express—though note that we are here concerned with properties of certain *behaviour*, not with those of *actors* or *relations between actors*!

172

So far as this volume is concerned, it is in particular 'exchange theory' and the 'economic approach' that are centrally concerned with this matter. The weaknesses of this sort of theorizing have been elucidated by Barry and Lively in particular. But at any rate they definitely do provide the instruments to solve this fundamental problem, at least in principle. For, according to them, or to what has been concoted from them here, people can be influenced (i.e. demand behaviour can be successful) only if and to the extent that it attaches valued outcomes to the other's alternatives so that the relative utilities of these alternatives change. In plain words: behaviour can be made to change only by linking 'rewards' to some alternatives and 'punishments' to others.

Of course, in some cases one can influence behaviour also—as is mentioned, though in different terms, by Barry and by Mokken and Stokman—by (physically) increasing or decreasing the range of alternatives from which people may choose. It is not too difficult to see, however, that this always comes to either causing some outcome to be linked (with some positive probability) to a certain alternative where previously this probability was zero (in other words, where that alternative was previously an impossible one) or the other way round. Impossible alternatives can be conceived as members of the sets of alternatives from which people choose (their *behavioural sets*), provided the probabilities attached to them are to be treated as minimal, and, accordingly, no utility estimates can be made with regard to them. As a consequence, *changes* in such probabilities can be accommodated by the theory, including changes from impossible to possible and *vice versa*. And, since the manipulation of such probability values (or, rather, expectations) is one of the fundamental aspects of any demand behaviour, it can clearly be seen, even without pursuing the analysis any more deeply, that increasing or decreasing the number of alternatives before the other party does not really constitute a departure from the theory's main line of analysis.

What the 'rewards' and 'punishments', the 'carrots' and 'sticks' that have been mentioned, will actually look like is of course undetermined as yet: they completely depend upon people's actual preferences and are accordingly sensitive to individual and cultural idiosyncrasies and differences.

Seen in this light, the tendency of exchange theory in particular to concentrate upon peaceful political processes and to ignore violence and coercion is completely arbitrary, and it is rightly criticized for that. For, as we have already seen, the axiom on individual behaviour upon which the present reasoning rests is in no way restricted to peaceful behaviour. Consequently, neither can a political theory built upon it be so restricted. Similarly, the emphasis on 'reciprocity' and 'voluntariness' so characteristic of exchange thinking is completely unwarranted. If the axiom on individual behaviour as discussed here is indeed accepted, there is no way around the conclusion that influence is wielded (i.e. demand behaviour acquires weight) only to the extent that people are offered certain benefits or threatened with certain sacrifices—as these are determined by their preferences and their information. Conversely, if people have certain preferences, such as for life, happiness, money, truth, honour, social approval and so on *ad infinitum*, then affecting and manipulating such outcomes is inevitably a means of changing behavioural probabilities.

At this level of the analysis, then, it is completely immaterial whether people 'freely' and 'of their own accord' participate in political processes or whether they comply with the wishes of others. It is immaterial whether or not they have the feeling (rightly or wrongly) that they all come off equally well or badly and whether or not their preferences are more or less complementary or congruent. Obviously such things do make an important difference to the actual nature of the political process and its outcomes, as well as to the fate of the participants! But the important point here is that all such differences can easily be accommodated within the theory as sketched thus far, and that they do not represent any departures from its fundamental ideas.

All this makes the theory, a sort of generalized 'exchange' or 'economic' conception, one might say, quite attractive. But, as in the case of the underlying theory of human behaviour, it owes this attractiveness in large measure to its relative emptiness. It provides an admirably general and rigorous account of the fundamental mechanism of politics. But, here too, in order to make it work at a somewhat less august level, and to make it do any duty in concrete instances of political processes, one would need a much more elaborate and refined set of notions.

To begin with, one would need a rather precise knowledge of the outcomes at stake between the participants as well as their preferences with regard to them, including (among other things) each party's evaluation both of his own and of his counterpart's alternatives. And it would not be merely a matter of knowing A's preferences with regard to 'his' outcomes—something that is difficult enough in itself as we have seen already—but, rather of knowing how the parties' preferences *relate*. Thus it obviously makes a great deal of difference whether, as in the case of a 'zero-sum game', the judgements concerned conflict sharply (a gain for A implying a loss for B and vice versa) or whether A's joys are for that reason also B's joys, as may occur in a love relationship.

It hardly needs emphasizing that these problems are vastly difficult, the more so since they generally concern complex bundles of outcomes involving larger or smaller sets of individuals. It would also seem to require rather advanced types of measurement as, for example, of the relative magnitudes of preferences and the degree of complementarity or congruence existing between them. At present all such knowledge—a much more adequate (refined and elaborate) behavioural theory—is conspicuous only by its absence. Mostly, as in the papers under discussion here, the problems are not even recognized at all. Nevertheless, it cannot be seen why the solution of the problems raised should be *a priori* impossible. And, accordingly, they do not seem to impair the validity of the theory outlined so far in any fundamental sense.

Similar problems can obviously be raised with regard to the second component of the utility notion: probability estimates. These, too, must be among the determinants of the course of political processes and their outcomes—we have met them already in our discussion of the physical extension or reduction of the sets of alternatives before people as a means of exerting influence. More generally, whether and to what extent some individual will engage in some political action (that is to say, the extent to which he will invest in demand behaviour) depends partly upon his estimate of its chance of success—that is to say, it depends on the (subjective) probability estimate of the action's realizing the outcomes for which it is undertaken. And, viewed from the other side of the game, the result of such demand behaviour is determined partly by the estimate made by the recipient of the demand of the chance that the demanding agent will indeed associate the relevant outcomes to his own action by carrying out his threat or fulfilling his promise. It is especially this factor that has traditionally been recognized in such expressions as 'prestige' and 'credibility'.

Surely, it is one of the scientifically most valuable aspects of the present conception that it does raise such problems for further inquiry, in theoretically meaningful and relatively precise terms. Yet, even if their eventual solution could be taken for granted, we should still have to solve the main problem for which the theory was developed in the first place, namely that of the occurrence or change of behavioural distributions. What has been done in fact so far is merely a preliminary step, namely to sketch a mechanism explaining the effect of demand behaviour upon people.

The problem that is to be raised at this point, however, is: how do *sets* of demand behaviour (together and in interaction) produce an outcome, in the sense of a new behavioural distribution? For normally politics is not a matter of party A unilaterally directing his demand behaviour at B who in turn merely passively responds by revising his utility estimates—although perhaps not sufficiently so in relation to A's wishes. Rather, B will normally respond by defending himself against A's actions or by trying at least to make A pay for his compliance so as to gain something from the process, too. That is, B, too, will engage in some demand behaviour of his own—not necessarily with respect to the same sort or category of outcomes as is involved in A's demand behaviour. It is from the interaction of these two demand behaviours, most commonly from a *chain* of such interactions during a certain period of time, that an outcome, a (new) behavioural distribution, will eventually result. And, more often than not, there will be more than two participants to the process, who all feed their demand behaviour to one another, a situation that rather complicates the analysis.

This, then, is another of the more centrally important problems raised by the sort of theorizing under discussion, although it can hardly be said to have received full and clear recognition. It is out of the question to discuss this problem adequately here. Nevertheless, and if only to show some of the potential of the line of reasoning sketched, it may be useful to pursue it briefly in relation to this crucial problem. It would indeed seem that the problem does allow for a solution—at least in general and abstract terms.

For, apparently, some outcome of a political process is reached when the several behavioural probabilities involved do not *change* any more, that is when they settle down at a new and, momentarily at least, stable level. Incidentally, this does not at all mean that the political process thereby also comes to an end. Quite to the contrary, most political outcomes and (momentarily) stable behavioural distributions are produced by continuing processes, and exist precisely by virtue of the fact that the partners continue to feed demand behaviour of some intensity to one another. Such incidental and isolated transactions as buying and selling *end* by being concluded; that is, parties stop trying to influence one another when the goods are delivered and the price is paid. Important outcomes such as, for instance, state boundaries, spheres of influence, constitutional law and practice and positions of relative power and competence, in contrast, exist precisely by virtue of those involved continuing their efforts to influence one another's behaviour. And should any one participant really stop his demand behaviour, the previously existing outcome would immediately shift to another level—generally and naturally to the detriment of the one who tries to leave the game.

Now it follows from the theory developed so far that behavioural probabilities change to the extent that some demand behaviour with some weight is addressed to them. Conversely, such probabilities stop changing when the (total) weight of demand behaviour(s) addressed to them stabilizes. In other words, a momentarily stable outcome among a set of individuals is reached when all the participants stop trying to change their demand behaviour in order to change the weight of such behaviour. And, according to the theory's central axiom, this will happen only if all the participants judge that the costs of trying to change the currently reached outcome by changing their demand behaviour are too high in relation both to the relative attractiveness of that outcome and the probability of their attempts meeting with success.

Obviously, this does not imply that the eventual outcome should really be attractive to all the participants, still less that it should be *equally* attractive to all of them. Certainly, this may occur, and an outcome will then be reached because it satisfies all concerned. Generally speaking, though, it will be a function of the relative magnitudes of the benefits and sacrifices the participants are able to manipulate, of their relative strength and of their ability and willingness to apply sanctions to deter one another from further attacks upon the outcome attained. To attain such a result may be conceived as involving the building (either tacitly and unintended, or expressly recognized and intended) of a sort of coalition able to mobilize enough demand weight to maintain that outcome, comprising those for whom the outcome is sufficiently attractive to make them resist changes in it.

I will not pursue this line of analysis any further, or discuss the many problems it obviously involves. The argument presented suffices to show that this kind of theorizing seems perfectly capable of dealing with the problem of the production of political outcomes from sets of demand behaviours.

In this connection it may be useful to return briefly to the problem of collective 'action'. For, as we have seen, such collective action should generally be explained as just such an outcome of a political process. And to be able to speak about such 'action' or 'behaviour'—as we often do, and inevitably so!—accordingly requires us to predict accurately the outcome of such a process, or the result of the 'equilibrium' condition derived above. Such speech, then, presupposes a quite advanced type of knowledge!

In practice, though, we often do have enough knowledge to enable us to speak about collective 'behaviour' with some confidence, and, what is more, to allow us to treat it along the same lines as individual behaviour. In particular this occurs when the 'key' to such collective action, say the foreign policy of a state, resides in the actions of some particular individual such as the foreign secretary, the prime minister or the head of state. For often we can take the compliance of the rest of society with respect to such individually decided actions for granted. Sometimes, too, we know that all those involved have roughly identical alternatives and evaluate them in similar ways. Or we have such knowledge with respect to a dominant and stable coalition in the collectivity in question. In such cases, too, we may confidently predict the nature of the collective actions concerned and even assimilate collective action to individual behaviour.

But it will be clear by now that such prediction in all cases rests upon some, usually implicit, knowledge about the political process in the collectivity concerned. And while in some cases we happen to have such knowledge (usually of a rough and simplifying kind), we do not have it in others. Both in order to estimate more precisely the conditions under which we may speak about collectivities in simplifying individual terms, and, more generally, to explain collective action, there is no way of escaping a detailed analysis of the political processes involved.

Obviously, what has been sketched here is no mere 'exchange' or 'economic' conception of the political process. It is not even a mere summary and critical discussion of the several contributions to this volume. But it does seem to preserve and generalize the strong and substantive elements to be found in them. The present argument surely demonstrates that the sort of approach that is to be found in the preceding chapters, inasmuch as it is concerned with the development of political theory, lends itself to further elaboration and development.

## 5 THE NOTION OF POWER

It remains to deal with the notion of power, which, to judge from ordinary discourse, the title of this volume and several of its individual chapters, is of central importance to our understanding of politics. Power, and its inevitable companion 'influence', do indeed seem to be virtually unavoidable notions in political science, and much discussion of them has taken place and will surely continue to do so. Yet it cannot be said that until now these notions have received anything more than a marginally satisfactory definition and analysis. And the same applies with even stronger force to their measurement.

Let us begin with the latter aspect: the unsatisfactory status of the concept as well as of virtually all analyses and attempts at measurement. The explanation would seem to reside chiefly in the generally rather non-theoretical nature of such attempts and analyses. That is, the notion is not related to an articulate and elaborate behavioural theory resting upon 'creative' axioms about how people behave. In the absence of such a theoretical connection, as we have already seen, the analysis of the notion of power becomes a mere linguistic exercise, and its measurement a matter of the development of measurement technology but not of advancing our understanding the (political) world.

Of course, power and influence refer to something that is real and important enough: the process of making others behave in a particular fashion according to one's interests or desires and the chances of meeting success therein. 'Power' most commonly seems to refer to those properties that make for success in such actions, in the sense that, the more powerful one is with respect to another, the greater the likelihood of the other complying with one's wishes. And this is a problem that is of crucial importance in the political process—whatever the terminology one uses to express it. Clearly, too, it is this that accounts for the seemingly unavoidable character of these notions.

It should be clearly recognized, though, that the notions of power and of demand weight are not identical. The differences between them are fairly obvious. To begin with, demand weight is unambiguously related to a relatively articulate theory about behaviour and politics, while power is not or is hardly so. In this connection, too, the notion of demand weight clearly refers to an attribute of some specific demand behaviour, while the reference of the concept of power is not so clear.

At any rate, power would seem to be defined most commonly in relation to the *actors* between whom political processes occur, not to *behaviour*. Thus it is sometimes viewed as an *attribute* of an actor, or as a *relation* between actors—and some controversy and debate actually centres around this issue. (The issue of attribute *v.* relation does not seem to be too meaningful in view of the fact that the attribute in question can hardly be defined otherwise than in *relation* to other actors, whereas, conversely, power as a relation will surely involve certain *attributes* of the actors concerned.) Perhaps, then, power could be conceived as the complex of attributes that renders the demand behaviour of an actor with respect to a set of other actors especially (or, rather, relatively) weighty. But as soon as one defines such a notion in relation to *actors*, one makes it cover a relatively extensive number of different demand behaviours, behavioural situations with their attendant differences as to the preferences and probabilities involved. Throwing all this into one bag, it is difficult to see how the result could be anything else but a hotchpotch, serving no useful theoretical purpose at all. And much the same considerations would apply to conceiving power as a sort of generalized demand weight of an actor with respect to some or all of the other actors with whom he engages in political processes.

These considerations, then, clearly bring to light the inadequacies of such a generalized notion as power—and, again, such generalization (over a number of behaviours and situations, that is) is a direct consequence of its definition in relation to actors instead of behaviour. Nevertheless, the *problem* to which the notion of power apparently refers is a real one, namely: what makes for the relative weight of demand behaviour? It may be useful to deal with this problem at modest length at this point again, in order to uncover the highly involved problems raised by this (or for that matter any other) notion of power.

As we saw in the last section, demand behaviour will be successful in changing behavioural probabilities only if and to the extent that it attaches benefits and/or sacrifices to the alternatives involved. We have also seen that (physically) changing, extending or reducing the alternatives before people (a possibility discussed by Barry and by Mokken and Stokman) is also to be reduced to manipulating relative utilities. In this connection it should also be mentioned that, since such utilities and their manipulation ultimately rest upon human evaluations and human information, one can conceivably change human behaviour also by changing these elements. In fact this is what is attempted in propaganda and education: to change people's attitudes and beliefs in the hope that this will eventually result in changes in actual behaviour.

There are good reasons, however, to ignore this 'method' here. In the first place, it involves a rather different sort or level of theorizing, namely that of human learning. For, as has been indicated already, it is this that is concerned with the growth and development of preferences and probability judgements, or attitudes and beliefs. In the second place, and in relation to this, processes of human learning generally involve more or less extended periods of time and they are, partly for this reason, difficult to manipulate on short notice. Accordingly, their application is out of the question in most actual and immediate political situations. Finally, there is reason to think that processes of human learning ultimately are also based upon the manipulation of concrete benefits and sacrifices, even if only in an indirect fashion and over more or less extended periods of time. The process of influencing human behaviour, and of giving weight to demand behaviour, then, will here be treated as being simply a matter of manipulating benefits and sacrifices to change the relative utilities of the alternatives involved.

It is important to see that, in A's demand behaviour *vis-à-vis* B, what counts is what B considers to be benefits and sacrifices as well as B's estimates as to the probability with which certain outcomes will be associated with his choices. Clearly, if I do not care about my life or about money, threats to kill me or offers of bribes will remain ineffectual. And someone else's firm resolve to carry out a threat does not help him if I do not believe him. In other words, whatever A may invest in demand behaviour, it is B's preferences and probability estimates that have sole importance in explaining A's demand weight. And estimating the demand weight with respect to some given demand behaviour would require us to develop some sort of 'mirror utility' notion with respect to the outcomes manipulated by the demand behaviour. Let us call this *demand force*, using it to denote B's utility estimate with respect to the outcomes involved in A's demand behaviour. Obviously, then, demand weight will vary with demand force.

But some demand behaviour of a given force can be effective only if and to the extent that B does indeed associate the relevant outcomes to his behavioural alternatives. In other words, if I do not know or perceive that someone else is threatening me with what I normally consider to be great sacrifices, such threats cannot be effective. And, of course, an important part of demand behaviour, a significant proportion of its costs to the demanding agent, may consist—and often does consist—of merely guaranteeing that certain outcomes will indeed be associated with the relevant alternatives of the addressee. Such costs need not stand in any direct proportion to the actual effect attained: to threaten your neighbour involves less costs than threatening some distant country, but such costs are completely immaterial to the addressee. In many cases this problem can surely be ignored and taken for granted, as in some face-to-face relationships and negotiations. But in many others it cannot: witness the differing 'costs' incurred by different people in establishing such associations as have been mentioned: for example, the difference between the ordinary citizen and the king's or president's mistress, or the difference between an ordinary American and his president with respect to, say, the Russian leadership. The actual (political) behavioural consequences of such differences are pretty obvious!

There is reason, then, to introduce another notion referring to this phenomenon, namely that of *demand access*: the probability that demand behaviour will indeed succeed in associating the outcomes it manipulates with the addressee's alternatives. The term 'access' has been used here, because it seems to be this notion that is most centrally involved in the common conception of that term and notably in that of David Truman. Clearly, demand force results in weight only if and to the extent that there is demand access. In this connection the importance becomes clear of possessing information and of controlling its processing, as in the command of channels and means of communication. (This is strongly emphasized in Mokken and Stokman's contribution.) It serves to establish efficient access and provides the opportunity for manipulating what will be considered benefits and sacrifices.

It should be emphasized that so far we are concerned only with attributes of demand behaviour. Since the notion of power generally refers to actors, however, there is reason to see whether the present analysis allows us to say something about this too, that is to say about (the relations between) actors. In fact, three sets of factors appear to be relevant in this context: the relative *strength* of actors, their relative *position*, and their (mutual) *dependence*. It can easily be seen that these aspects of the relations between actors also involve what is normally discussed under the heading 'the bases or sources of power'.

To begin with the last-mentioned aspect, *dependence*, it refers to the extent to which for A to achieve his outcomes it is necessary for B to act in specified ways: that is, the extent to which A cannot reach his goals without B's 'co-operation'. Accordingly, B's actions will come to constitute more or less highly valued outcomes for A. And this makes it more likely that A will try to bring them about (or to avoid them), in other words will engage in demand behaviour *vis-à-vis* B. For B, conversely, it means that his actions represent benefits or sacrifices for A which may increase the weight of his demand behaviour.

In relation to this, furthermore, demand force is constituted by the extent to which the outcomes manipulated by A are valued by B. But this also means that the political relation between A and B, the relative demand weight that they can mobilize with respect to one another, is co-determined by their relative *strength*, that is to say by the extent to which each 'disposes' of outcomes valued by the other. Roughly, the stronger A is with respect to B, the more he can invest in his demand behaviour and the greater his demand weight will be. But, also, the smaller will the negative value of a given investment be to A and the more readily he will in fact perform such an investment. And this effect will be strengthened by the relatively high chances of success of A's actions, which will again make them more likely.

The relative *position* of the actors refers to such things as geographical and social distance, the place they occupy in a political system and the extent to which they command channels of communication. These are of central importance in determining relative demand weight since they determine demand access. In particular they are related to the strength of parties since they co-determine the costs of establishing access.

Relative position, strength and dependence thus refer to politically central attributes of, and relations between, actors. It is this range of problems that appears to be involved in most analyses concerned with the sources and bases of power. And although the notions used so far can surely not be said to be unproblematical, calling as they do for much more intensive elaboration and development than could be undertaken here, the preceding argument does seem to demonstrate the fruitfulness in this respect of the conception discussed here.

Again, and more generally, this is what I have been aiming at throughout this essay: instead of merely summarizing and criticizing the contributions to this volume, to see whether and to what extent they contain or contribute to a theory of the political process, and to suggest reformulations and extensions where these seemed to be called for.

# 10
# Constructing a City in Speech: Planning as Political Theory

HERMAN R. VAN GUNSTEREN

*'Come, now,' I said, 'let's make a city in speech from the
beginning. Our need, as it seems, will make it.'* [Plato, 1968,
369c]

## 1 THE CONCEPT OF PLANNING

Almost everyone plans. Planning is an activity that is as old as human history.
Someone says: 'I plan to go skiing in January'. By saying this he is not only giving
information, he also commits himself or has done so before. He directs his own
activities, both in the present and in the future. Others in turn can orient themselves
to his plan. The plan to go skiing in January is a focus around which other actions and
decisions can be arranged. The speaker makes reservations for hotel and train, buys
clothes and sunglasses, makes no appointments for the time he is away, pays his bills
before leaving, etc. His plan brings a certain order in his own life and his interactions
with others.

Planning, like promising, guaranteeing and expecting, is a conventional activity by
which we create order and certainty. By way of conventions we try to make the future
into a calculated and controlled field of action. We try to bridge the gap of uncertainty
that is inherent in the course of nature and spontaneous Hobbesean human
interaction. We know that we cannot always succeed here. The lack of one hundred
per cent success is part of the grammar of words like promising, guaranteeing and
planning. Conventions that are never violated are not conventions. When the outcome
of our actions is absolutely certain we speak of technical manipulation or of
inexorable fate. We have recourse to conventional activities like promising, holding
someone responsible and planning when we see that the sense and success of our own
actions depend in part upon actions of others which cannot be completely controlled
by us. We speak of planning when we order a series of actions in time; in particular,
when we or others must act *now* in order not to get stuck in the future.

Planning, like speaking, is a variable but universal activity. We cannot do without it.
Government planning, however, has been attacked as a failure and quite a few authors
have argued for its abandonment. Since there cannot be any question of doing away

with planning altogether they must be arguing for the substitution of new kinds of planning for orthodox public planning.

Traditionally, tradition has provided the main orientation for action under uncertainty. When change is faster and man is seen as the maker of his own history there is a change of emphasis from tradition towards promises and contracts as conventions that structure our fields of action. (Examples: contract theories in the seventeenth and eighteenth centuries; the development of Roman law towards an open system of contracts.) In the twentieth century, when networks of interdependencies grow wider and cut deeper, isolated promises, contracts and interventions are no longer sufficient. In order to direct our activities effectively a number of interdependent promises and interventions is needed: planning. 'We will speak of planning and planned thinking (*planen*),' says Mannheim, 'when man and society advance from the deliberate invention of single objects or institutions to the deliberate regulation and intelligent mastery of the relationships between these objects.' (Mannheim, 1966, p.152.) At present it is becoming less and less likely that this kind of orthodox planning can provide the right kind of orientation. This is so because our (planning) actions are part of complex networks that are subject to rapid multiple and unforeseen changes. Orthodox planning in this context results in solving yesterday's problems. It provides rigidity where learning and flexibility are needed. Therefore a number of planning theorists are trying to design new kinds of planning. In this chapter I shall examine some of their writings and point out striking similarities between their work and that of the traditional political theorist. I distinguish between different kinds of planning as follows: (i) everyday-life planning, including operational planning, e.g. the planning needed for building a bridge, for withdrawal of troops, for skiing in January; (ii) orthodox planning; (iii) new planning (I shall distinguish three varieties of this later on).

Whereas everyday-life planning is a context-bound activity, orthodox planning claims to be a general method. It is said to be a comprehensive and superior way of making and implementing policy that has, like mathematics, a general use; i.e., it is transferable from one area of government concern to another. Orthodox planning provides the means by which we can realize our substantive and common goals. It can be characterized as control of complex networks of interdependencies on the basis of scientific knowledge by way of big formal organizations. This kind of planning can work only when there is a reliable basis of knowledge, when the field of application (task environment) is relatively stable and when the plan is sustained by considerable power and consensus. It is becoming rare that these conditions are met. Planners have to do their work under conditions of rapid and often unforeseen change. Their task environment is often unstable, insufficiently known and not responsive to their control. Moreover, politicians often fail to provide the power and consensus that are needed to implement the planners' rational proposals. I have shown elsewhere that this failure can be explained and that politicians may have good reasons to refuse to go along with the planners (van Gunsteren, 1974). Orthodox planning lacks the variety that is needed to cope with turbulent and unforeseen change.

A number of planning theorists have tried to repair the flaws of orthodox planning while leaving intact its overall structure and conception. Their revisionist theories cannot stand scrutiny and will not be investigated here. Instead I turn to those theorists who do not want a revision but a new conception of planning.

## 2  THE NEW PLANNING

Let me begin by setting out characteristic differences between orthodox and new planning.

**Style of thought**

| *Orthodox planning* | *New planning* |
|---|---|
| Mechanistic | Cybernetic |
| Causality | System dynamics; micro-causal processes (physical, social—psychological) are subordinate and often unknown (and they need not be known) |
| Means—ends scheme | (Sub-)system functions |
| Consistent goals | Conflicting goals |

**Vision of social systems that are object and context of planning**

| *Orthodox planning* | *New planning* |
|---|---|
| Simple models of social systems (mechanistic or homeostatic models) | Social systems are highly complex, probabilistic, self-regulating and self-organizing |
| Planning system has external position; is separated from social system which is object of planning. | Planning is open sub-system of social system within and on which planning operates; continuous interaction and communication between planning system and social system. |
| Thinking in terms of closed systems | Thinking in terms of open systems |

**Vision of planning process**

| *Orthodox planning* | *New planning* |
|---|---|
| Linear programming | Tuned to complex system-dynamics |
| Planning results in changes within given systems structure. | Planning aims also and in particular at structural change of sociopolitical system (design of new system structures). |
| Planning aims at changing the environment. | Planning aims also and in particular at changing values and institutions. |

| | |
|---|---|
| Planning is programming the future. | Planning provides a matrix within which, according to circumstances, different programmes can be generated and implemented. |
| Planning concerns resources and behaviour. | Planning concerns in the first place information and communication structures; only later on, *ad hoc* and at subordinate levels, are resources and behaviour considered. |

## Strategies

| *Orthodox planning* | *New planning* |
|---|---|
| Direct control | Indirect field control; direct control of complex systems is disastrous because it destroys adaptive capacities and thereby diminishes the chances of survival for the system. |
| Imposed control | Control *is* the structure of the system; control by way of entropic movements of sub-systems; making use of on-going mechanical and homeostatic processes. |
| Fixed course, straight ahead toward given ends | Flexibility, learning, zigzag courses |
| Eliminate uncertainty (enemy) | Reckon with and profit from uncertainty (friend or unavoidable companion) |
| Reduce and kill variety | Design system within which at the right time and the right place requisite variety can be generated |
| Organizations and people as operating units | Organizations and people as semi-autonomous sub-systems |
| Planning creates order and system | Order *is* there already. Self-organizing systems. Hierarchical control should tune in with this order and not, like God, try to create order out of nothing. |
| Hierarchical co-ordination | Market-type co-ordination is fundamental. Formal and |

| | hierarchical co-ordination is tip of an iceberg (but therefore not unimportant). |

Eliminate inefficiency; avoid duplication, overlap, redundancy; long means—ends chains.

Redundancy and short chains of dependence make system reliable and flexible; semi-autonomous and functionally overlapping subsystems needed.

### Relations between planning and politics

*Orthodox planning*
Ends 'given'

*New planning*
Determination of goals and norms part of planning process

Planning neutral with regard to politics

Planning *is* politics; normative planning

The planner predicts; the politician chooses.

Planning is inventing and willing the future.

Planning takes place within the limits set by political choice and the constitution.

Planning involves political choice and constitutional design.

Criterion for success: realization of goals

Criterion for success: system survival, ecological balance

This scheme is ideal-typical and intended for initial orientation only. Of course, not all the characteristics mentioned here can be found in each new theory of planning. At first sight it is remarkable how openly the new planners are involved in politics—and not only in issue politics or party politics, as were the orthodox planners without being able to admit it, but also and primarily in system-politics. The theorists and practitioners of the new planning are constructing cities in speech just as political theorists like Plato, Machiavelli, Hobbes and Rousseau used to do. Let us look at theories of the new planning in more detail to see whether this first impression is accurate.

There are at least three kinds of new planning: systems-rational planning, bio-cybernetic planning and communicative planning. Systems-rational planning substitutes systems thinking for linear-causal thinking, but still holds to the idea of central rationality and control. It assumes that our analytical models of the systems we want to steer are reliable. Representatives of this line of thought are Jantsch, Ozbekhan, Forrester and Luhmann.

Bio-cybernetic planning on the other hand acknowledges that in most cases our analytical models are inadequate. From this it follows that it is foolish to base the making and implementation of policy on such models. The analytical models lack requisite variety and the same is true therefore of steering based on them. Where analytical models cannot work we must develop radically different techniques and concepts of policy-making and control. Insights from neurophysiology and neurocybernetics are helpful here. Representatives of this line of thought are Beer and Chadwick.

Communicative planners insist that the most urgent problem of planning is not the improvement of controls and central intelligence, but the raising of civic consciousness, the formation of a societal subject (*gesamtgesellschaftliches Subjekt*), the creation of communication structures. The plan constitutes a language within which rational and reasonable discussion and decision-making concerning our common future can take place. Communicative planners have no objections against systems thinking as such. In fact they often use systems language. They criticize systems-rational planning and bio-cybernetic planning on the grounds that they reify the system and make thinking about plans into an élite activity. This results in dangerous gaps between plan and implementation; between initiators, problem-solvers, implementators, clients and beneficiaries; between theory and praxis. Representatives of this line of thought are Habermas, Churchman and Foster.

A warning: the new planning has seldom been practised by governments. And in any case the results of this practice are not available to me. My argument must therefore be theoretical. And when objections against the new planning are stated they are of a theoretical and provisional kind because they cannot be directly confirmed by planning practice, as can objections to orthodox planning.

## 3 SYSTEMS-RATIONAL PLANNING

### 3A. Jantsch

The ideas of Erich Jantsch can be found in his *Technological Planning and Social Futures* (Jantsch, 1972). He emphasizes three features of the new planning (Jantsch, 1972, p.14).

(1) Planning is normative, 'futures-creative', non-deterministic. Prediction is but a means that helps us to invent and will possible futures.

(2) System design is the central concern of planning. Planning is non-linear; that is, it works upon structures, not upon single variables of a given system. That this implies a new politics and even a new ethics is emphasized. As Jantsch writes:

Whereas currently the tasks of forecasting and long-range planning may still be looking for a place in existing structures, it will increasingly be the long range perspective on society's future which will determine organizational forms. [Jantsch 1972, p.135.] [One wonders on what evidence this prediction itself is based.] Perhaps, if we better understood what Churchman calls the 'ethics of whole systems'—which evidently runs counter to much of the individual ethics in which we believe by tradition or naive choice—we might acquire the courage to engineer the world system by restructuring what we now consider 'non-negotiables'. But a new political process would be needed to do that. The democratic process of bargaining over 'negotiables' to achieve some incremental steps, obviously cannot do it. [Jantsch 1972, p.211.]

(In other words, only if the world were totally different from what it is now would planning *à la* Jantsch be feasible! What kind of planning would enable us (who?) to bring about such a new world?)

(3) There are three levels of planning: 'Normative or policy planning (ought), strategic planning (can), tactical or operational planning (will)—in whose interaction the 'new' futures-creative planning unfolds.' (Jantsch 1972, p.14.) At each level there are various planning phases. Those divisions, which should also be worked out in institutional form, are needed in order to bring about the indispensible combination of flexibility and integration, of 'decentralized initiative and centralized synthesis' (Jantsch, 1972, p.135). Decentralization is needed for flexible learning, centralization for coping with widespread interdependencies. This last requirement results in the demand for a still more comprehensive and abstract approach: 'Integrative planning, ideally, will attempt to go again to a higher level of abstraction and to gain control over the interplay of the functions.' (Jantsch, 1972, p.37.)

Jantsch admits that his conception of planning is at present no more than a non-operational wish, a rough guideline for future action. He writes:

New approaches to systemic forecasting and planning are gradually emerging, but are yet in a primitive stage of development, making long-range planning an art rather than a set of rigorously prescribed and logical procedures. [Jantsch, 1972, p.2.] [Immediately the question arises: why should we entrust ourselves body and bones to these artists?] It must be said right here that we are far from being sufficiently advanced to have a planning methodology to deal with the total area embraced by 'ecological engineering'. [p.38.] [How far away are we?] There is no escape, at present, from using increasingly partial information as a base, the higher and the more integrative planning becomes. [p.38.] Our perception of the evolving necessity to establish 'futures-creative' planning . . . is still primarily intellectual and still basically lacking the realistic angle of view which could give us a clear concept of desirable institutional changes. [p.138.]

Let me state some objections against Jantsch's conception of planning.

(1) The objection concerns the feasibility of this kind of planning. The planning techniques are not yet operational, a matter of art rather than of method. Moreover, the worldly conditions under which these techniques can be practised are not met. The techniques are not ready and the world is not ready. Jantsch's ideas seem not to be made for our historical epoch.

Let us assume however for a moment that this planning system is desirable and that it will be practicable some day. Then we still face the following question: can it be made operational soon enough, before it is too late to deal with the urgent problems that Jantsch mentions in his book? For him this question does not make sense because he assumes that there is no alternative. It is planning à la Jantsch or doom. Doesn't Jantsch fall victim here to a thought block, to the Western European assumption that problems can be handled only by way of rational control of self and world? (See van Gunsteren, 1976.) Alternatives are not examined in Jantsch's book. He simply assumes the necessity of planning.

The only empirical evidence he adduces is the supposed success of the Planning Programming Budgeting System (PPBS). But here he is mistaken. On the contrary, the experience with PPBS confirms the impossibility of planning conceptions as advocated by Jantsch. Not even the staunchest defenders of PPBS maintain that PPBS has *had* the intended success. The most they dare say is that success will now soon be there and/or that PPBS has had favourable secondary consequences (unintended results) (van Gunsteren, 1975).

It follows that there are no good reasons for us customers to buy this planning conception at this moment, the more so because there are reasons to expect that the product will never be of practical use. (Further, the product is also expensive.)

(2) Jantsch is right to insist that planning must be flexible and that therefore a multi-echelon planning structure is needed. But how can flexibility be combined with an effective comprehensive approach? Jantsch speaks about a central synthesis, but this constitutes a verbal solution only. In his book he does not indicate *how* the integration of, or articulation between, levels and phases of planning takes place. Therefore his remarks on integration and flexibility, on keeping a straight course and learning, are nothing more than restatements of an old problem: how can one plan comprehensively while avoiding dangerous rigidity and blindness?

'Reduction of complexity versus requisite variety' is one great dilemma of planning. Limited human capabilities make reduction of complexity imperative. Thus the comprehensive steering centre will not have sufficient variety to cope directly with numerous novel situations. Semi-autonomous sub-units are in a better position to do this. The weakness of sub-units, however, is that they have insufficient knowledge of the interdependency networks within which they function. Therefore a comprehensive steering centre is needed. The weakness of this centre is that the models it uses are often hopelessly out of date. They have not been adapted to novel situations because the centre lacks requisite variety. Of course one can say that the sub-units should process variety and forward relevant information to the centre. The trouble is however that the centre will be flooded with information and therefore will have to reduce complexity. It will admit only information that is relevant. And what information is considered relevant? Only information that appears to be relevant within the outdated models that the centre has available. And thus the centre confirms, unknowingly, its own prejudices and shortcomings. A *real* improvement of the methodology of planning would enable us to take into account more relevant variety than we are able to do now. Jantsch does not offer such an improvement.

(3) It is unlikely that many politicians and other power-holders will accept Jantsch's conception of planning. Moreover, what would happen to political rationality when this conception of planning had been accepted? Political rationality fulfils vital functions. It enables us to address, and sometimes to change peacefully, structures of power and co-operation. Jantsch's planning model does not contain functional equivalents for this.

## 3B. Ozbekhan

The theories of H. Ozbekhan can be found in *Perspectives of Planning* (Jantsch, 1969), a volume that contains a report and papers from the well known Bellagio planning conference. Ozbekhan presents an incisive critique of the dominant technological conception of rationality. Orthodox planning, which dominates in practice and is even gaining more influence, is based on this conception and must therefore fail. In the present circumstances it is impossible to cope with social problems by way of technological strategies. Orthodox planning tries in vain to remain outside the so-called domain of values. Values and goals, however, are neither purely subjective nor given. And the implementation of the plan is not a neutral activity: '... the necessity of controlling the environment so that the forecast actions occur in the manner established by the plan ... leads to what might be called authoritarian planning.' (Ozbekhan in Jantsch, 1969, p.120.) Ozbekhan's criticism of orthodox planning is appropriate. However, he goes further and attempts to construct alternatives.

The new planning must involve and promote value changes. Planning is willing the future. Orthodox planning is '. . . problem solving rather than planning. Its main results are to insure continuity of non-integrated solutions that attain momentary stability through series of sub-optimizations.' (Jantsch, 1969, p.119.) The new planning takes a broader view. Sector planning must be integrated. This implies a different relation between planning and politics. Planning is no longer the servant of politics, has indeed never really been able to play this role: '. . . it seems necessary to see planning not as the handmaiden of policy making but as the larger framework of decision and action processes of which policy making . . . is an intrinsic phase.' (Jantsch, 1969, p.139.) That is, planning is constitution-building, designing the political system within which politics can take place. Policy-making becomes a function of normative planning. And the basic norm is no longer love, objectivity or utility, but ecological balance (Jantsch, 1969, p.140).

Just like Jantsch, Ozbekhan admits that the new planning is no more than a pious desire and that in practice orthodox planning is dominant. And against his conception of planning the same objections can be made as against Jantsch. His conception of planning is anti-political, still more abstract and comprehensive than orthodox planning, and in the present world not operational.

## 3C. Forrester

Jay Forrester too criticizes orthodox planning which, according to him, does not differ from other policy-making strategies (Forrester in Jantsch, 1969, p.237). Orthodox planning identifies a problem and designs a plan as a remedy for it. The systems on which orthodox planning operates, however, are complex, that is they are 'counter-intuitive', 'insensitive to changes in many system parameters' and they 'counteract redirections in policy' (Jantsch, 1969, p.240). It is understandable that orthodox planning is so often ineffective. Curing symptoms cannot provide permanent solutions.

But what then? How can we bring about change in complex systems? The answer is: 'Planning, instead of dealing with problems and their solutions, could deal with the design of social systems to produce systems less likely to generate problems.' (Jantsch, 1969, p.237.) The strategy is the following. Make a model that generates the problems. Find the critical pressure points in it. These are the moments of effective intervention, the points at which different paths can be chosen. Planning is not concerned with remedying problems, but with removing their causes.

Obviously Forrester's conception of planning is more modest than that of Ozbekhan and Jantsch. He leaves ample opportunity for self-regulation and self-organization of the planned system. Forrester writes:

Good planning based on a deep insight into the behaviour of complex systems will attempt to release the internal power, initiative, driving force, enthusiasm, and human potential of the people in the system. It will do this instead of heaping more work, more discipline, more repression, and more coordination on them in an effort to push back a social system that is still trying to go in the wrong direction. [Jantsch, 1969, p.245.]

The role of planning is a modest but essential one: at the right moment giving the right touch in the right direction.

The question remains, however, whether the system models are reliable enough. Whether again and again unexpected events do not take place that make the model useless and which can only *a posteriori*—when it is too late—be incorporated in a new model. In the final analysis Forrester also puts his trust in the superior analytical insight of an élite as the basis for planning.

Moreover, one wonders what help Forrester's planning conception can give to public servants who have to operate in the present world. There is not much use telling us that we have missed so many 'critical pressure points' in the past unless there are similar critical pressure points ahead that can be identified in time.

### 3D. Luhmann

Niklas Luhmann did not attend the Bellagio conference but his theory of planning is sufficiently similar to those just mentioned to be treated under the same rubric. From Luhmann's rapidly growing published work I consider only *Zweckbegriff und Systemrationalität (Goal Concept and Systems Rationality)* (1973) and *Politische Planung (Political Planning)* (1971). A general exposition of Luhmann's ideas goes beyond the subject of this paper. Such an exposition could, not withstanding Luhmann's amazing productivity, be short because Luhmann is a hedgehog who knows one thing well: reduction of complexity is essential and without systems theory we cannot accomplish this. (The notion of the hedgehog is taken from Isaiah Berlin (1957, p.7), who quotes the Greek poet Archilochus as saying 'The fox knows many things, but the hedgehog knows one big thing.')

Luhmann's ideas about planning are interesting and bring important innovations, though mainly in details that will not be considered here. Luhmann also gives us incisive criticism of orthodox planning. Planning should not be conceived of in terms of means—ends but in term of systems. The functions of planning are reduction of complexity, circumscribing (programming) of sub-systems and testing whether the sub-systems fulfil meaningful roles within the total system. Luhmann provides a number of ingenious ways to alleviate the dilemma of 'requisite variety versus comprehensive steering'. Of particular importance is his insight that reduction of complexity, with all the risks this involves, must of necessity take place both at the centre and in sub-systems.

Good planning designs and attends to a system within which sub-systems are semi-autonomous. That is, their internal processes are neither planned by, nor known to, the centre. The higher unit determines only the decision-making premises of the sub-system. And different sub-systems use different decision-making premises, decision-making models and criteria of success and failure. The sub-systems have their own tasks and problems, their own rationality. Direct orientation on the general plan is impossible. 'Das Ideal ist zu weit entfernt, um für kleine Schritte der Annäherung ausreichende Orientierung zu bieten.' (The ideal itself is too far away to provide sufficient orientation for small steps leading toward it.) (Luhmann, 1973, p.277.) One should not aim at an optimum combination of sub-systems, such that in one sub-system an optimum decision can only be determined and taken when the same happens in all other sub-systems. A sub-system should be designed in such a way that the correctness of decisions taken within this sub-system depends as little as possible upon the correctness of decisions, in particular future decisions, taken outside the sub-system itself.

Does this not lead to dangerous sub-optimization? To actions that are rational in terms of the rationality of a particular sub-system, but which, in combination with actions of other sub-systems, are disastrous for the wellbeing of the total system? Luhmann recognizes this danger and postulates as a remedy a central controlling unit which sees to it that what the sub-systems are doing makes sense in terms of the overall system. So planning does two things: (i) programming sub-systems (determining decision-making premises) and (ii) controlling whether these programmes continue to make sense as a whole. (Of course this is totally different from control in the sense of ensuring the faithful execution of given programmes.)

Fundamental objections can be made against Luhmann's theory of planning.

(1) We just saw that a central unit for control and correction is needed to avoid the dangers of sub-optimization. But who and what is this unit? Does it possess sufficient knowledge and power to fulfil its task? I do not think so.

According to Luhmann the central controlling unit should make its analyses independently of existing programmes. This must be so because it is the meaningfulness of these very programmes that is being examined. It does not make sense to use the languages of the programmes under consideration here. This would not constitute an examination but a certain confirmation of programmed prejudices which we wanted to identify in the first place. But Luhmann's own arguments show such a programme-independent analysis to be impossible. The job is too complex. Without a programme there is no reduction of complexity and therefore no meaningful and intelligent human action.

So in fact Luhmann's programmed system remains uncontrollable. It cannot be evaluated with regard to its meaningfulness as a whole. His central controlling unit is a *deus ex machina* which, according to his own previous analyses, is an impossibility. Moreover, apart from lack of knowledge it is doubtful whether the controlling unit would ever have enough power to impose its own insights effectively.

Just like the planning theorists mentioned earlier, Luhmann appears to put an unwarranted confidence in the analytical powers of an élite, and to be building his planning model on it.

(2) In Luhmann's system the majority of the people play limited roles only. They are operating units which cannot be held responsible in terms of the total system. According to Luhmann, people do not want more responsibility than this. Be that as it may, in any case this conception conflicts openly with the idea of citizenship and is therefore anti-political.

Moreover, Luhmann does not make clear why the view of the whole, which the central controlling unit is said to possess, should necessarily be lacking in other sub-systems and citizens. In politics we find different 'sub-systems' which each bring their own vision of the whole polity into the debate and the struggle for power, which compete with each other and often reach compromises that contain programmes for common action. In politics we characteristically do *not* find one super-intelligent controlling unit that, on the basis of its superior insight, authoritatively settles conflicts. One would even have to say that the word 'politics' is out of place where such a superior and authoritative controlling unit exists. Luhmann's conception of planning is indeed anti-political.

(3) Luhmann solves the problem of 'following a straight course *versus* flexible learning' by generally holding on to the straight course and letting learning take place at the top only. (In the sub-systems learning takes place, but only within the limits set by the decision-making premises.) It is questionable whether the top, which has so few direct contacts with 'reality', is the most appropriate place for learning. And even if learning does take place at the top level this is not enough in times of rapid and unforeseen change. Learning and responsibility are needed at *all* levels or the polity. Opportunity for semi-autonomous learning is not only a demand of citizenship and human dignity, but also a necessary condition of meaningful and effective government.

(4) There are similarities between Luhmann and Hobbes. Hobbes was obsessed by fear, Luhman by complexity. Both derive from their obsessions the necessity of an order that is programmed from above. And, just like the state of nature, absolutely unreduced complexity is not a historical fact but an analytical construct—an indication of tendencies and dangers that are to be avoided. And with both Hobbes and Luhmann reification of analytical constructs leads to a neglect of tradition.

In whatever situation we find ourselves, complexity *is* always already more or less reduced. Consider for instance the development of children, which cannot be interpreted as a continuing reduction of complexity. On the contrary, it looks more like increasing differentiation and complexity. It is true that the particular reductions of complexity, within which we are situated historically, could have been different from what they are. We might have had another mother tongue, system of law, economy, etc. But from this it does not follow that we are capable of choosing and bringing about these alternatives now. I might have had a different mother tongue, but from this it does not follow that I can *choose* a different one. Our society might have been a non-capitalist one, but from this it does not follow that we can get rid of capitalism just as we can take off our coat. From the fact that our forms of life could have been other than the ones we happen to live in, it does not follow that we can change them at will. Forms of life, tradition and culture are historically variable but nevertheless often can not be manipulated by us. They constitute the indispensable non-rational basis for any kind of rationality and reduction of complexity. The necessity of reduction of complexity varies historically and is not such a fundamental and universal problem as Luhmann thinks. From the insight that tradition and forms of life could have been different from what they are now, we cannot infer the degree to which they can be changed by conscious human intervention.

## 3E. Conclusions

Let me draw some conclusions concerning the theory of systems-rational planning.

(1) Systems-rational planning wants to be still more comprehensive than orthodox planning. The declaration that was made up at the end of the Bellagio conference states: 'The need is to plan systems as a whole, to understand the totality of factors involved and to intervene in the structural design to achieve more integrated operations.' (Jantsch, 1969, p.8.) But wasn't holism one of the big problems of orthodox planning? Doesn't systems-rational planning make on a bigger scale the same mistake of 'overreaching'?

(2) Success of systems-rational planning depends upon the superior analytical insight of an élite. At present it is unwise to base our plans exclusively on such insight. The system models are often inadequate or simply do not work. (Or is it that we silly people lack competence to make them work?) They are too global and often outdated before they can be used in practice. They contain insufficient variety. They lead to systems myopia. Too often they cannot cope with unexpected but important events.

(3) Systems-rational planning ignores or suppresses other rationalities than its own (e.g. political rationality) which are essential for our living together in (relative) peace and dignity. And neither does it provide functional equivalents for those other rationalities. The deeper cause of this mistake is the failure to appreciate the meaning and character of tradition, common-sense understandings and forms of life that constitute the given basis for any form of rationality and interaction.

(4) The basic value of systems-rational planning is system survival or ecological balance. But it is not clear what kind of survival of what kind of system *is* at stake. Survival of the steering system?

(5) Just like orthodox planning, systems-rational planning aims at technical control of social systems. The technique is systems-theoretical instead of causal-mechanistic. But what difference does that make? Human beings and sub-systems are still treated as operating units, as mute and obedient executors of the plan, although in the systems approach they have a little more elbow room. The fundamental contradiction, however, persists that people are treated as things while at the same time dedicated and intelligent behaviour is expected from them.

(6) This contradiction appears also in the ambiguity with regard to participation and democracy that one finds in the writings of systems-rational planners. On the one hand they see that widespread support and dedication are indispensable, on the other hand they are afraid of these. In the Bellagio declaration it is said for instance that planning should take place at the '. . . lowest effective level [which is quite high] to make possible a maximum of participation in the planning itself and in its implementation,' (Jantsch, 1969, p.8). There is little confidence in processes that have not been designed by the planners themselves. 'All large, complex systems are capable of some degree of self-adaptation. But in the face of immense technological, political, social and economic stresses, they will have to develop new structures. This can easily lead to grave social disturbances if the adaptation is not deliberately planned, but merely allowed to happen.' (Bellagio declaration in Jantsch, 1969, p.8.) What a mistrust speaks through the word 'merely'. Unlike 'leftist' planning, this planning is not designed to help the underprivileged. It aims at system survival and at those changes that are necessary to accomplish this. The planners are constitution builders and Platonic philosopher—kings.

And it is painful to see how the systems-rational planners, like so many before them, show up with the well tested would-be solution for real political problems and contradictions: The *Leader*. In the report of the Bellagio conference one reads: 'The necessity to take all social planning directly to the people, and the impossibility to do so because of the time-lags involved [is that the only difficulty?], finally led to the discussion of leadership.' After which we hear the lame conclusion: 'There was no agreement as to who should be called a leader . . .' (Jantsch, 1969, p.31). No, I am glad there was no agreement yet.

(7) Systems-rational planning is not operational. Not even on paper: '. . . the discussions [at the Bellagio conference] , alas, never arrived at a sufficiently clear view

of institutional requirements for carrying out and implementing planning in the fullest sense.' (Jantsch, 1969, p.25.) This alone is sufficient reason to hold off from attempts to practise systems-rational planning on any grand scale. But there is more.

It is highly unlikely that systems-rational planning can ever be operational on any grand scale. Systems-rational planning demands not only new planning techniques but also a different context (another world) in which this kind of planning can take place. The conditions that are necessary for systems-rational planning to be effective are not met in the present world. Bringing about those conditions would imply a profound transformation of existing patterns of interaction. But in order to effect this controlled transformation we need, according to the systems-rational planners, systems-rational planning. But, again according to those very same planners, systems-rational planning can only work after the required transformation has taken place. Who will create the new political structures and political will? Who will sufficiently control systemic interactions to prevent them from deviating too much from the superior systems-models of the new planners? The *Leader* will have a difficult job. And finally: what are the costs of this (attempted) transformation?

With all this I do not want to suggest that the writings of the systems-rational planners are worthless. On the contrary, they contain many fascinating and important insights. But their theories are not of such high quality that we can hand ourselves over to them body and bones. It seems to me that it is impossible to develop a theory that on theoretical grounds alone can justifiably claim our total allegiance. It is always people who must use and justify theories in historical practice. Therefore the implicit claim of systems-rational planning, that on the sole basis of superior systems insight it has the right to direct society, must be rejected on principle.

#### 4 BIO-CYBERNETIC PLANNING

Both Stafford Beer and George Chadwick use systems language, but there is an essential difference between their approach to planning and that of the systems-rational planners. Bio-cybernetic planners openly admit that the available analytical models of the social systems we want to plan are absolutely insufficient as a basis for external control of those systems. The analytical models presuppose a strategy of goal maximization. Such a strategy, however, is often a danger to the survival of complex systems. The analytical models presuppose consistent goals. But complex systems with conflicting goals have better chances of survival and intelligent adaptation. And worst of all, the analytical models contain insufficient variety. Action that is taken on the basis of these inadequate models is either ineffective (the lesser evil) or effective in the sense of constituting a danger to the survival of the planned complex system. Beer and Chadwick both reject the use of analytical models that do not contain the requisite variety and the use of external, imposed and mechanistic controls. Chadwick says: 'The idea of "steering" human activity systems is thus ludicrous: their characteristics are not amenable to this kind of approach.' (Chadwick, 1971, p.370.)

But what then? Isn't all this purely negative? I do not think so. The admissions by the planners themselves that for a long time they have been trying to do the impossible is in itself a step forward. But bio-cybernetic planners have more to say.

Beer makes an important innovation by developing a control system that is not based on models of insufficient variety but which is capable of generating *ad hoc* the requisite variety (for details see Beer, 1966). A summary description goes as follows: make a structural model of the situation you want to control. State parameters. Let this model (with parameters) interact by way of a black box (computer) with a sample from the situation to be controlled. Order the resulting ratios in sets. (The statistics are not complicated but cannot be given here.) Repeat this operation regularly so as to remain aware of structural changes in the situation you want to control. In order to predict one must determine to which set an event belongs. The sets that result from the statistical ordering are unconventional and cannot be understood analytically. But the predictions based on them are reliable.

Bio-cybernetic planners say that instead of imposing order from outside we must trust, and make use of, order that is there and is constantly being recreated. Complex systems are self-regulating and self-organizing. They work because they consist of networks of feedback processes which result in homeostasis (self-regulation) and also in the generation of new criteria for homeostasis (self-organization). Multiple and conflicting goals of sub-systems are not an evil. On the contrary, they are essential for the functioning of feedback processes that result in learning and 'intelligent' or 'functional' behaviour of complex systems. However, the words used here are misleading. They suggest an intelligent steering centre. But complex systems seldom work that way. Beer writes as follows:

In thinking about control, it seems, people have been too mechanistic and too introspective. Ideas have been mechanistic, because in engineering we do not achieve results unless the parts of a system operate in an entirely preordained way: the infrastructure of a workable machine must be fully specified. Ideas of control have been introspective, because the most impressive natural system in a man's eyes is himself, and he is controlled by a brain. Hence if a system is under control, being organized, we tend to look for the box that contains 'the works', 'the programme', 'the computer'. But the big lesson of cybernetics is that most commonly in nature there is no such thing. Natural systems organize themselves over a period of time to be what they immanently are. To the observer, who determines the criteria by which the end result is called organized, this process looks like learning or, in general, adaptation. In fact, it is a process of entropy. [Beer, 1966, pp.359-60.]

Complex systems cannot be controlled by determining general goals and designing a 'machine' for their implementation. But they can be controlled by changing their structure so that the entropy of the sub-systems moves in the desired direction. Hierarchical control can be effective only as long as it does not conflict with the implicit controls of the system on which it is being exercised.

Thus the role of planning is reduced to more modest proportions. The rationality of planning leaves room for other rationalities. The planning system is no longer being reified. 'Thus scientific method, system theory, cybernetics, may be used as "ideal" rational constructs, not because the "real world is like that", but because we may begin to understand, and to manipulate, the real world through them . . . .' (Chadwick, 1971, p.336.) The role of planning is twofold: (i) avoiding ruin-paths, and (ii) enlarging the matrix of choice. This is a low-variety task which does not exceed the capabilities of planning at a general level: to create a framework within which high-variety responses can be generated at lower levels. (See Chadwick, 1971, p.368.)

Some comments follow.

(1) Beer says that the plan should not try to counteract the self-organization of the system it wants to control, but must make use instead of its entropic movements (homeostasis). But how do you know what the system is doing, what its 'spontaneous' entropic movements are, and how these can be used to serve the goals of the plan?

(2) What should one do when the self-organization of social systems seems to be moving towards disaster?

(3) Beer has done pioneering work. Not as an outsider but as a management consultant, he has been able to tear himself away from mistaken confidence in the superior analytical insight of an élite. But at the same time, and rightly so, he does not reject all technical and intellectual novelties like cybernetics, systems theory, computers, etc. He uses these novelties intelligently and draws conclusions which make a marked contrast with the exaggerated cries of the systems-rational planners. However, Beer's approach also has its shortcomings—or more precisely, his theory is not wrong but incomplete. Beer does not pay attention to problems of co-operation, power and the raising of civic consciousness and competence. His approach is not anti-political but non-political. He keeps silent about political questions. That this is a weakness is confirmed by events in Chile. I have heard that Beer was an adviser to the Allende government. But in his control system there was no place for guns, strikes, demonstrations, deceit and intimidation. (I do not know whether he is still working in Chile.)

## 5 COMMUNICATIVE PLANNING

Communicative planners maintain that we have already enough control techniques. What is needed in the first place is more civic consciousness, motivation, formation of political will, emancipation (*'Emanzipation zur Mündigkeit'*), without which rational government is impossible. The planners have mistakenly assumed that technological steering can bring about civic consciousness etc. or provide functional equivalents for these. They confound theory and praxis, making and acting (Arendt), *'Verfügen'* and *'Handeln'* (Habermas), control of natural systems and the governing of sociopolitical systems.[1]

Die Irrationalität der Geschichte ist darin begründet, dass wir sie 'machen', ohne sie bisher mit Bewusstein machen zu können. Eine Rationalisierung der Geschichte kann darum nicht durch eine erweiterte Kontrollgewalt hantierender Menschen, sondern nur durch eine höhere Reflexionsstufe, ein in der Emanzipation fortschreitendes Bewusstsein handelnder Menschen befördert werden. (The irrationality of history is based on the fact that we make history without being able to do so consciously. Therefore we can make history more rational, not by increasing our powers of control, but only by moving toward a higher level of reflection, by the conscious actions of people which steadily move toward emancipation.) [Habermas, 1971, p.328.]

This does not imply that planning techniques are worthless. But it is an error to think that scientific planning techniques can make political processes superfluous. Planning as a comprehensive steering system is nonsense. A plan makes sense if it provides (or improves) a language, a communication structure, within which citizens can discuss the present, the future and their relations and thereby arrive at common and rational decisions.

This conception of planning cannot be worked out here. It is sufficiently clear, however, that, with the advent of communicative planning, planning is brought back to realistic proportions and politics finally resumes its rightful place. Problems of rational living together can only be 'solved' *in* historical praxis, not by implementing a theoretical blueprint.

How this dialogue between theory and practice can take place is not yet very clear. Research and theorizing is badly needed here. And perhaps we are looking for an impossible kind of clarity. Isn't it logically impossible to determine *a priori* and in theory the details of this dialogue? Dialogue is a practical historical task.

## 6  CONCLUSION: PLANNING AS POLITICAL THEORY

Orthodox planning implied a theory of political decisionism (political decisions are subjective and non-rational). In the new planning the place of decisionism is taken by: (i) the planners (systems-rational planning; wrong), or by (ii) practical political discourse and decision-making which has its own rationality (communicative planning; right). Beer, the bio-cybernetic planner, occupies a middle position. He offers techniques that help to make political communication more relevant and rational.

The new planning can no longer be separated from politics and policy-making in general. Thus the new planning constitutes a return to everyday-life conceptions of planning. The extreme division of labour that was required by orthodox planning has been abandoned. Planning is a context-bound activity and is one component of evolving patterns of interaction.

Important differences exist within the new planning. The systems-rational planners are afraid to acknowledge the implication of their own insights, namely that the intelligent and responsible participation of many people is indispensable. They retreat to a hazy notion of 'The Leader' and a mistaken confidence in the superior analytical insight of the few. The communicative planners are more consistent: political emancipation and decision making are now more important than new analytical and managerial techniques.

All the new planners, with the exception of Habermas, fail to pay sufficient attention to power structures. (Or if they pay attention to them they do not incorporate them into their systematic analyses.) They say that variety is indispensable. But it is a historical fact that power has often been a functional equivalent for variety.

Thus none of the three varieties of the new planning is immune to criticism. All three pay insufficient attention to power and tradition. Bio-cybernetic planning and systems-rational planning fail to see the importance for rational government of political emancipation and participation. And systems-rational planners are mistaken to rely on the so-called superior analytical insight of an élite.

If one compares the new planning with traditional political theory one notices striking similarities. One can say that the new planning constitutes a rediscovery by the planners of politics and political theory. The new planners are constitution builders; they design new political systems, frameworks within which adaptation can take place. They turn to quasi-juridical principles of order (failure planning, avoiding ruin-paths). They turn to politics and recognize the importance of creative political thought and will. They see that intelligent participation and political emancipation are crucial to rational government. In short, the new planning needs politics and is a form of political theorizing. The new planning takes place at the intersection of managerial and organizational techniques, political theory and political praxis.

It is comic and sad to see how the new planners, with the exception of Habermas, ignore the available tradition of political thought while they are doing the same kind of work that political theorists used to do. As Schelsky says: 'Das Dilettantische vieler "Kybernetiker" besteht geradezu darin, in einer neuen Begriffs- und Fachsprache Probleme und Gedankeninhalte zu präsentieren, die in der Geistesgeschichte oder in anderen Disziplinen längst bekannt und abgehandelt sind.' (The dilettantism of many 'cyberneticians' consists in their presenting, in a new conceptual and professional language, problems and thoughts which have for a long time been known and worked through in the history of thought or in other disciplines.) [Schelsky in Schäfers, 1973, p.406.]

Thus one can say that the new planning is political theory equipped with the latest techniques. It is interesting to note that the planners have come to political theory not by reading Plato or Marx, but by thinking about techniques and their practical use. This shows how vital and necessary political theorizing is. The danger of this approach is that the discussions will remain too technical and uninformed by the available tradition of political theory. This situation calls for interdisciplinary work. Political theorists can learn from planners about problems and possibilities of big organizational networks and managerial techniques which seem to be unavoidable parts of present-day political reality. Political theorizing that ignores those realities can hardly be called relevant and contemporary. Planning theorists, on the other hand, may recognize that they are doing what traditional political theorists used to do. In their work they might begin to draw upon the rich tradition of political theory. The convergence of modern planning and traditional theorizing may bring a revival of the old vocation of 'constructing cities in speech' and of the political theorist as an impatient adviser of political actors.

# 11

# The Comparative Method and its Neighbours

EVERT VEDUNG

## 1 THE PROBLEM

During the last decades there has been a remarkable upsurge in scholarly concern with social science methodology. Considering the vast body of methodological literature from the viewpoint adopted in this chapter, two features are particularly salient.

First, there are, of course, numerous books, pamphlets and journal articles which, at least to some extent, deal with the history and logic of comparative method.[1] There is, then, undoubtedly an international controversy about the problems of comparative research. The more surprising is it then to discover that a great many renowned methodological works do not present even the slightest attempt to single out any specific comparative method (Leege and Francis, 1974; Kerlinger, 1973; Gregor, 1971; Galtung, 1969; Selltiz *et al.*, 1959).

Maybe this reflects a fundamental insight that comparison is a constituent part of all scientific work, so that it is impossible, inappropriate or at least problematic to treat it as a specific research instrument. This impression is further strengthened by the second noticeable feature: the obvious conceptual variety to be found in that part of the methodological literature which really comprises comprehensive discussions of the problems of comparative method. The sets of properties devised to characterize the expression are indeed profuse and sometimes even bewildering. Thus, it must be stated that those researchers who have decided to view comparative method as something particular, as opposed to social science methodology in general, have failed to reach a general agreement about what should be meant by such a specific research procedure.

This vividly illustrates the fact that 'comparative method' is a highly problematic concept. There is ample justification, therefore, for starting this chapter with a semantic assessment of various prescriptive definitions and ordinary usages of "comparative method". Apart from "comparative method" the expressions "comparative approach", "comparative analysis", "comparative research", "comparative inquiry", "comparative studies", "comparative perspective", "comparative procedure" and "comparison" are included in the inquiry. Expressions like "comparative politics" and "comparative government" are left out, because, in my view, they do not in the main connote a research strategy but a substantive field within the discipline of political science.

The principal objective of this section is to decide whether it is at all reasonable to delimit "comparative method" as a specific research instrument in contradistinction to social science methodology in general. The purpose is to make a definition of my own which fulfils the criteria of (a) reasonable unambiguity and (b) reasonable conformity with ordinary scholarly language and lexicographic usage. In addition, the expression should be (c) practical to employ and (d) fruitful for the wider purpose of clarifying the methods of social science.

The last criterion is the crucial one. To be fruitful a usage must point to something of interest that would otherwise remain unnoticed or be considered of secondary importance. This amounts to saying that the subject matter of the controversy about comparative method is decisive when it comes to defining the concept proper. The concept must be delimited in such a way as not to exclude from discussion very interesting problems in the controversy about the comparative method. The implications of this statement will we hope become evident in the subsequent exposition.

The mode of procedure to be used in the paper is, following a commonly accepted proposal by Carnap (1950, pp.1ff.), referred to as explication. It is relatively well known to philosophy (Tarski, 1944, pp.341ff. is a famous example; see also Heeger, 1972, pp.307ff.), but, so far, employed rather rarely in the social sciences. As yet, it has not been applied to the subject of comparative method. Explication is concerned with expressions whose meaning in scientific discourse is more or less vague (such as "truth", "probability", "power"—to mention some typical objects of explicatory study) and aims at giving those expressions a new and precisely determined meaning, so as to render them more suitable for clear and rigorous discourse on the subject matter at hand. But the definitions proposed by explication are not arrived at simply by an analysis of customary meanings. To be sure, the considerations leading to the precise definitions are guided initially by reference to customary scientific usage; but eventually the issues become so subtle that a study of prevailing usage can no longer shed any light upon them. Hence, the assignment of precise meanings to the terms under explication becomes a matter of rational reconstruction rather than of merely descriptive analysis. An explication does not simply exhibit the commonly accepted meaning of the expression under study but rather proposes a specified new meaning for it (see e.g. Hempel, 1952, pp.11ff.).

The second objective of the paper is to locate the comparative method within the context of the family of social science methods in general. The best way of throwing light upon the comparative method seems to be to compare and contrast it with its closest neighbours: the experimental, the statistical and the case study methods.

The literature to be discussed mostly derives from the period after 1945. However, a few classical statements are also included.

## 2  THE GENERAL FORMAT OF "COMPARATIVE METHOD" DEFINITIONS

A penetrating scrutiny of current and classical literature on comparative research reveals that all, or nearly all, serious attempts at prescribing or merely delimiting the connotation of expressions like "comparison" and "comparative method" seem to have been made with regard to at least one of three different aspects. Comparison is usually considered to be (i) a mental activity or, more specifically, a process of observation and thinking centring upon (ii) some particular object or aspect of an object and (iii) aiming at a goal, end-product or outcome, which is always some sort of knowledge. All definitions of "comparative method" appear to be cast in the same general format, involving at least one but usually two and sometimes all three of these aspects. It seems reasonable, therefore, that our critical review of various definitions and usages would be pursued with regard to each of these in turn.

Furthermore, the topic will be expounded in a systematic way, which means that all definitions will be bunched together and dissected aspect by aspect and sub-aspect by sub-aspect. Consequently, the reader will not find a comprehensive overview of each individual definition in its totality. As one of the present purposes is to decide which aspect and sub-aspect ought to be subsumed under our own final stipulation, the former approach is to be preferred.

### 3  RESTRICTIONS IMPOSED ON "COMPARABLE METHOD" WITH REGARD TO THE MENTAL ACTIVITY INVOLVED IN COMPARISON

An examination of the restrictions made with regard to the mental activity involved in comparison displays the basic difficulty with 'comparison' as a methodological concept. In common usage, very frequently employed by scholars as well, "comparison" seems to denote an extremely general human activity. This makes it very difficult to give the term a more specific connotation which would be particularly fruitful in a methodological perspective.

It is exceedingly usual for "comparative method" to be regarded as a thought operation of a very general and fundamental kind. In those very few cases where "comparison" is defined in ordinary dictionaries or encyclopedias of philosophy or social sciences, this specific content is sometimes attributed to the term. In the *Dictionary of Philosophy*, "comparison" is defined as 'the act of discerning or describing the common properties possessed by two or more objects' (Benjamin, 1942, p.60; see also Stout and Baldwin, 1928, p.202).

In the literature of comparative politics or social science in general there are at least some definitions in use which, roughly, have this extraordinary width of content. In his *Politics and Social Science*, the political scholar W.J.M. Mackenzie appears to look upon "comparison" or "comparative method" as a necessary tool of discovery for every man—indeed, even every animal. 'One cannot *not* compare', he declares in a revealing formulation, and 'when we begin to study government with curiosity, at the same instant we begin to "compare"' (Mackenzie, 1967, pp.310ff.).[2]

From what he maintains it appears that any assertion about two states of being is comparative, e.g., 'Denmark is smaller than Sweden'. Furthermore, his pronouncement on the sheer impossibility of not comparing might be interpreted as implying that comparison is involved even in statements such as 'Denmark is small', because they presuppose an implicit comparative frame of reference like, for instance, 'in comparison with other nation-states in Europe'. To Mackenzie and other authors who share his view, comparative method, obviously, denotes a very wide range of activities of the mind. To put it rather bluntly: 'to compare', roughly means 'to think' or 'to observe'.

Admittedly, expressions like "comparative analysis" might properly be given this same extremely extensive connotation. Comparison may well be perceived as a generic quality of human thought, pervasive in all concept formation, qualitative classification and quantitative measurement as well as in the elaboration of judgements and drawing of conclusions. In certain situations and for certain purposes there is, evidently, a great need for such a concept. The fact that comparison is conceived as a process of the mind, however general, enables the researcher to differentiate it from such phenomena which, at least to some extent, involve non-mental activities as well. Hereby, it becomes possible to distinguish comparison from, for example, social action or behaviour. But then it is virtually impossible to grasp which mental activity would not be regarded as comparative. Obviously, the conception is diluted to a point where it loses all its discriminating power with regard to the activity aspect. This objection is absolutely crucial, if we want to arrive at a definition that singles out comparative method as a particular methodological mode of procedure in contradistinction to social science methodology in general.

Thus, the various extremely wide or *general* conceptions of comparison are entirely unrewarding for the present purpose. In our view, the activity at stake would be better referred to by such expressions as "to think" or "to observe" than by the term "to compare".

To avoid such an unjustified stretching of the concept, most methodologists have therefore ventured to designate "comparative method" more particularly as a methodological device in the arts and the social sciences. This conception is rather patently manifested in such a classic work on comparative political science as Edward Freeman's *Comparative Politics* (1873, pp.1ff.) or in modern authoritative accounts of the matter composed by, for instance, Adam Przeworski and Henry Teune (1970, pp.36ff.), Shmuel Eisenstadt (1966, pp.187ff.), and Stein Rokkan (Duijker and Rokkan, 1954, pp.8ff; Rokkan *et al.*, 1969, pp.119ff.; Rokkan, 1970, pp.645ff.; see also Scarrow, 1969, pp.4ff.; Galtung, 1967, pp.1ff.; Murdock, 1957, pp.249ff.).

But even these authors make no effort at all to draw an accurate line of demarcation between 'comparative method' as a research instrument and as a tool of thinking and observation in general. In the greater part of the contributions to the controversy over comparative method, where people are adopting the position that comparative method is something specific, there seems to have been no attempt made to distinguish comparative analysis as a specific research procedure as opposed to some other scholarly technique that is not labelled "comparative".

Consider, for instance, the article by Eisenstadt on comparative study in the *International Encyclopedia of the Social Sciences*. There he argues, 'that the term "comparative approach" does not, as has sometimes been claimed, properly designate a specific method in social research . . . In principle, therefore, the methodological problems involved in these studies are not distinct from those of any other type of sociological (or behavioral) investigation.' (Sills, 1968, p.423.)

But why then even talk about a comparative approach to sociology or politics when apparently referring to the methodology of social research in general? Of course, one can avoid specifying the concept with respect to the mental activity involved and make the specification with respect to the subject matter towards which it is directed or the goals which it is assumed to be designed to promote. As will be shown in later sections, this has certainly also been the case. But disregarding that, as far as the mental activity aspect is concerned it would seem more to the point simply to talk about the scientific method or social science methodology. Again, the concept is diluted to such an extent that it tends to be deprived of all its potential discriminating power.

There are a handful of writers, however, who, regarding comparative research as an activity of the mind, try to stake their claim for it a bit more narrowly. In their view, the comparative method is the social scientist's closest equivalent to the *experimental method* of certain branches of natural science. These attempts at identifying a *specific* comparative research method in deliberate juxtaposition to the experimental method are very interesting and are worthy of further consideration.

The authors in question seem to take as their point of departure the matter of scientific explanation. Such an explanation, it is asserted, consists of two basic elements: (i) the establishment of general empirical relationships between given dependent and independent variables, and (ii) the simultaneous control of all other conceivable independent variables. One cannot be sure that an explanatory relationship is a true one unless the influence of other potential independent variables is controlled or held constant. The relationship must, in other words, be valid *ceteris paribus,* that is, under otherwise similar circumstances (Lijphart, 1971, p.683).

Now, it is apparent that the control aspect cannot be considered a constituent part of an explanation proper but merely a prerequisite for reaching a valid explanation. Let us, however, ignore this lapse and continue expounding the main line of argument. According to this, different scientific procedures may be ordered with respect to the way in which they differ in solving the problem of establishing explanatory propositions or, weaker, propositions about concomitant variations valid *ceteris paribus.* Most powerful in this respect is the experimental method. When making an experiment, the researcher deliberately introduces certain changes into a process and makes observations or measurements in order to evaluate and compare the effects of different changes. In the classical experimental situation the investigator is able to hold all influencing factors but one under control. The latter's effect on the dependent variable can thereby be measured with the greatest possible precision and accuracy.

In social science, experimentation is usually conducted by establishing two groups—the experimental and the control group—which are equivalent in respect to all known sources of variation. In the classical experiement, the subjects are selected by random sampling and assigned to the groups by a random procedure, as well. The conditions shared by the two groups can now be treated as parameters, that is, assumed not to vary. With regard to the operative condition under investigation, the experimental group is stimulated, the control group not. Even this administering of stimuli can be made in an entirely random way. Now, if the dependent variable changes in value as the independent variable is manipulated, then it may be asserted that there is a relationship between the two. This conclusion is made possible because the *cetera* and *paria;* i.e., the groups are alike in all aspects but one. If the experimenter were to allow a number of other extraneous variables to operate in the experimental situation, it would not be possible to arrive at any such distinct finding. The distinguishing feature of the experimental method is precisely that it enables the research worker to vary one variable at a time, holding all other conceivable independent variables constant. As the groups are deliberately created by the investigator, he is able to manipulate them according to his scientific purpose. Thereby, he can produce a primary source material of good quality (Smelser, 1973, pp.45ff; Lijphart, 1971, pp.683ff; Martindale, 1959, p.58; Cox, 1958, pp.5ff., 70ff.).

The counterpart of experimentation is non-experimentation or *ex post facto* research. The literal meaning of *ex post facto* is 'from what is done afterward'. It implies that events can be investigated only after they have actually happened. Some drawbacks are associated with this mode of procedure. Admittedly, even in *ex post facto* research the research worker can select his subjects at random. But he is not able to assign subjects to groups at random or to administer treatment to groups at random. This is because the variations in the independent variable or variables have already occurred. This amounts to saying that he cannot start by manipulating an independent variable and note the effect on the dependent one. He must instead start with observations of some dependent variable. A retrospective search for possible independent variables then ensues. This is the significance of the act of studying events only after that they have come about. (For a good treatment of these problems, see Kerlinger, 1973, pp.314ff. and 378ff.)

According to one line of reasoning, all methods of science that do not make use of experimentation are somewhat loosely summarized under the rubric of 'comparative method'. This would mean that every procedure that does not imply the artificial induction of variation in phenomena is comparative. A considerable number of authors seem to concur entirely in this usage, the most well-known being the psychologist and philosopher Wilhelm Wundt, and the social anthropologists S. F. Nadel and Edmund R. Leach (Wundt, 1921, pp.62ff.; Nadel, 1951, pp.222ff.; Leach, 1968, pp.339ff.).

It must be readily acknowledged that the distinction between experimental and non-experimental methods is reasonably clear and significant. To be able to manipulate variables directly and immediately in a controlled situation is something qualitatively different from scrutinizing their impact in their natural surroundings only *ex post facto*. In the natural sciences, the differentiation seems to be of a considerable practical significance as well. In physics, chemistry, biology and physiology, experimentation is commonly used, whereas in astronomy, geology and meteorology it is for obvious reasons usually out of question. Even in some of the social sciences the demarcation is of some moment. Education as well as psychology makes rather frequent use of experimentation. Even in anthropology, sociology and political science, experimentation is more and more often put to use, particularly in the form of simulation. In addition, experimentation might be employed even more if the research workers were able to come to grips with certain practical and ethical impediments.

But in political science and comparative government, experimentation is still relatively rare as compared to non-experimental methods. More often than not, the explorer of the political realm must be satisfied with data produced by the political and social process itself and not by controlled experimentation. Consequently, there is a certain tendency in the present conception of 'comparative method', if not in theory yet in practice, to be equated to the methodology of political science in general. Still, it appears to be a bit too wide for the current purpose. That is one reason why the search for some further criterion of demarcation should be continued.

By looking at the demarcation line from a somewhat different angle, we may advance another reason for this search. Granted that the comparative method is a non-experimental technique, is it really reasonable to paste the label 'comparative' on *all ex post facto* modes of procedure? In the first place, it might well be stated that comparison in no way is confined to the non-experimental field. On the contrary, it might be argued that this is an inherent characteristic of experiments as well, because in an experimental situation one must perform numerous comparisons, e.g. between various aspects of the experimental and the control group (see e.g. Fisher, 1942, pp.56ff., 132f., 136f., 199ff.; Cochran and Cox, 1957, pp.70, 75ff.). This has induced at least one author to talk about 'comparative experiments' (Cox, 1958, p.4). Once again, the tendency to use the term in its most general meaning causes us some trouble. Nevertheless, this particular connotation must be entirely disregarded if we are ever to arrive at a conception of comparative method that will be fertile from a methodological point of view. Therefore, in my opinion, the current objection is not a very weighty one.

Yet, if we keep within the bounds of non-experimentation, it does not seem altogether justifiable to label all *ex post facto* research 'comparative'. It is doubtless perfectly all right to examine one case in ludicrous detail without opening up any comparative vistas at all. This may be taken as a second reason why the search for some further criterion of demarcation must be pursued.

In the light of these facts, the attempt to narrow the connotation of the phrase even more and to single out a specific *statistical method* from the realm of comparison is currently attracting a particular interest. This noteworthy deviation from the scheme adopted by Wundt and the two social anthropologists can be found in two very interesting articles, one written by the sociologist Neil Smelser, the other by the political scientist Arend Lijphart.

These two authors distinguish between experimental, statistical, comparative and case study methods. Two lines of demarcation concern us here: that between experimentation and statistics on the one hand and that between statistics and comparison on the other.

According to Lijphart and Smelser, the crucial difference between experimentation and statistics is that the former solves the problem of holding constant or cancelling out sources of variation by means of situational manipulation, whereas the latter tries to attain the same goal by conceptual manipulation. In applying the statistical method, the scientist attempts to control for influence from other factors than the one he is primarily interested in by means of partial correlations. Take, for instance, a political scientist who studies relationships between political affiliation and religious creed. He may find it wise to control for influence of occupation, because there may be proportionally more manual workers among Catholics than among Protestants in his data. This may be done by partialing—dividing—the sample into a number of different occupational groups and looking at the correlations between political affiliation and religious creed within each separate occupational group.

The weakness of this procedure compared with an experimental design where the groups are created by deliberate randomization is that in the latter case the investigator knows with a high degree of probability that all other factors are controlled, whereas in the former case he can control only those key variables that are known or suspected to exert influence (Lijphart, 1971, p.684; Smelser, 1973, pp.47ff.; cf. Holt and Turner, 1970, pp.7ff. and Martindale, 1959, pp.58ff.).

As to the second boundary, that between the statistical and the comparative methods, the latter method resembles the former in all respects except one. The crucial difference is that the number of cases the latter deals with is too small to permit systematic control by means of partial correlations. It should be resorted to when the number of cases available for analysis is so small that cross-tabulating them further in order to establish credible controls is not feasible. Thus, the comparative method is held to be a weak substitute for both the experimental and the statistical method of the efforts to develop explanations (Lijphart, 1971, pp.684f.; Smelser, 1973, pp.47ff.).

Lijphart's and Smelser's attempts to shrink the aura of vagueness surrounding 'comparative method' and, simultaneously, to circumscribe the expression in an entirely new way are very estimable and suggestive. They constitute, as far as I can judge, the most interesting examples of their kind in the literature so far considered. As yet, their efforts have not gained any wider acceptance in the scholarly community. In our view, there is at least one weighty reason why such a wait-and-see policy should be abandoned immediately. Here, for the first time, we face a concept that considers comparative method as something truly specific. It is held to be a subdivision within the general methodology of social science. It is a method among other conceivable methods to be used in social research.

Having said this, it must also be emphasized that their description of the method gives birth to a number of difficulties of which they themselves seem, at least to a considerable extent, to be fully aware.

One important criticism can be levelled against the suggested borderline between experimentation and statistics. As was readily admitted above, one is quite entitled to draw a line of demarcation between experimental and non-experimental scientific procedures. Nevertheless, that does not justify a sharp distinction between experimental and statistical methods. Whatever meaning is attached to the term 'statistics', it seems obvious that statistical methods can be used in experimental as well as in non-experimental research. In a classical experimental situation, subjects are sampled randomly, all characteristics concerned are randomized over the experimental and control groups and treatments are administered to groups in a random way as well. Statistical procedures of sampling and randomization are in other words brought into play even in the stage of designing an experiment.

But even the data obtained by an experiment thus designed are perfectly susceptible to statistical analysis. Let us make the latter statement a bit more concrete. It may many times be difficult to tell whether the dependent variable values for one group are higher or lower than the values for the second group simply by looking at the unorganized raw data. Hence, the experimenter must try to reduce his data to numbers that can be reasonably handled, by resorting to some simple measures of descriptive statistics. For example, he may compute the mean, the median, the standard deviation and the variance for both the experimental and the control group. However, these descriptive statements do not carry him very far. Assuming that the experimental group has a higher mean score than the control group, he may ask himself if the difference is a real one, owing to the impact of the independent variable, or if it is only an accidental one, owing to pure chance. This is a problem of induction from the sample to the population. To obtain a solution to that, the experimenter must make use of any of a number of statistical tests of significance. These tests will indicate whether the difference is statistically significant or not. In addition, the research worker may also try to estimate the true values in the population under consideration. These operations of significance testing and estimation can be considered the principal contributions of statistics to the interpretation of experimental results (Cochran and Cox, 1957, pp.1ff., 45ff., 96ff., 107ff.; Fisher, 1942, pp.2ff., 13ff.; McGuigan, 1960, p.10).

In conclusion, to recognize experimentation as fundamentally separate from statistics stands out as highly unwarranted and misleading.

Another equally important criticism points to the fact that no reasonably unequivocal boundary between the statistical and the comparative method is within sight. The former, it is held, can be applied to many cases, whereas the latter can be brought to bear upon relatively few but at least two. But where is the boundary between few and many? So far, this question has received no satisfactory answer (Smelser, 1973, p.53; Lijphart, 1971, p.684). Furthermore, one of the strategies of improving the comparative method, recommended by Lijphart, involves maximizing the number of cases for investigation. This amounts to implying that statistical procedures will be used to analyse these cases. The comparative method is then nothing but the statistical method used under relatively unfavourable, but improvable, circumstances (Lijphart, 1971, p.686; that Lijphart himself is fully aware of the difficulties may be seen on p.684 and in his paper from 1973, p.3).

Another shortcoming of lesser moment concerning the statistical—comparative boundary is that the distinction is very closely associated with non-experimentation taken in the meaning of *ex post facto* research. It will be recalled that *ex post facto* research means research in which the variations in the independent variables have already occurred and in which the research worker starts with the observation of a dependent variable. He then studies the independent variables in retrospect for their possible relations to, and effects on, the dependent variable (Kerlinger, 1973, p.379). As far as comparative government is concerned, however, non-experimental inquiries may also be conducted for purely descriptive purposes. The researcher may be concerned not at all with relations between variables, but merely with description of singular variables. Our point, then, is that non-experimental research can be divided into explanatory (*ex post facto*) and descriptive research and that the demarcation of Lijphart and Smelser pays attention only to the former.

Actually, it seems to be very closely related to a specific kind of *ex post facto* research: that which employs the technique of partial correlation. In ordinary statistical language, partial correlation is a parametric statistical technique. Upon closer inspection it becomes evident, however, that Lijphart does not use the term in this ordinary meaning. As may be seen from the summary given above, partial correlation includes for him the non-parametric technique of cross-tabulation as well. To designate all this 'partial correlation' is perhaps a bit confusing. From the substantive point of view of defining a particular statistical method, however, the inclusion is well motivated. Undeniably, even cross-tabulation is a method of studying relatioships between variables, holding all other variables constant. But still, the definition is a bit special, because even multiple regression analysis, path analysis, two-way analysis of variance and related techniques are such methods and they are apparently not included in 'partial correlation'.

The attempts at specifying a particular statistical method are thus less successful and may be safely ignored. More fertile are, on the other hand, endeavours to mark off a comparative method from a case study method.

At first sight, the suggested boundary between a comparative and a *case study method* would seem quite natural. It seems rather plausible to assume that the concern about a comparative method has developed as a reaction against a state where research into single cases was the rule, and that, as a corollary, the former should be put in contradistinction to the latter. Furthermore, for purely linguistic reasons alone, the comparative method seems to be a device for studying at least two cases.

Consequently, it seems appropriate to argue that the comparative method deals with two or more cases whereas the case study method deals with only one.[3]

Upon searching examination, however, this seemingly clear boundary turns out to be somewhat ambiguous. The intricacies are of two different kinds. First, it might be argued that the purpose of the scrutiny of one single case, or, alternatively, the way the investigation is actually carried out, has to be taken into consideration when it comes to deciding whether the case study method is employed or not. The quandaries associated with this line of reasoning can best be illustrated by reference to the extensive treatment of the case study method in Lijphart's article mentioned above.

Lijphart introduces a very imaginative sixfold typology of case studies. The first ideal type, the a-theoretical case study, is entirely descriptive. It moves in a theoretical vacuum. It is neither guided by established or hypothesized generalizations nor motivated by a desire to formulate general hypotheses. Consequently, it is regarded as a pure case study without any moment of comparison in it, be it with guiding theories or theories as end-products (Lijphart, 1971, p.691).

The remaining five types of case studies, however, occupy a ground somewhere in between an ideal, a-theoretical case study and a fully fledged comparative investigation. Closest to the a-theoretical case study is the interpretative one. Even that is motivated by an interest in the case *per se*. To that end, however, established theoretical propositions are explicity made use of. A generalization is applied to a specific case with the aim of throwing light upon the case rather than of improving the generalization in any way. It cannot be denied, then, that a comparative moment sneaks into the study because of the use made of generalizations. It might well be said that generalizations are compared to specific cases (Lijphart, 1971, p.692).

In the other four types, a single case is investigated for the purpose of theory-building. Hypothesis-generating case studies are meant to develop theoretical generalizations in areas where no theory yet exists. They start out with a more or less vague notion of possible hypotheses, and attempt to formulate definite hypotheses to be tested subsequently among a larger number of cases. Here, as well, there is a touch of comparison involved in the preliminary observations designed to find out whether the presuppositions actually fit the data at hand.

Still more evident is, according to Lijphart, the comparative feature in the theory-confirming, theory-infirming and deviant case studies. The first two types are tests of established generalizations which may turn out to be confirmed or infirmed by them. Deviant case analyses are studies of single cases that are known to deviate from established generalizations. In all three cases the relationship between theory or generalization and empirical case data constitute the comparative element (Lijphart, 1971, p.692).

To sum up Lijphart's argument, in so far as the examination takes a substantive theory or hypothesis as its point of departure or aims at coming up with such a theory or hypothesis, it will involve a comparative feature. Thereby, it immediately becomes an intermediary case between a comparative investigation and a case study. Lijphart even goes so far as to admit that these types of inquiries may be considered as implicit parts of the comparative method (1971, p.693).

Some authors are willing to go even further and maintain that single-case studies are 'comparative' granted that the analysis is conceived and reported within a conceptual framework that makes comparisons readily possible. According to a not-unreasonable interpretation, Howard A. Scarrow in his *Comparative Political Analysis* appears to follow this line of thought. In brief, he declares, a perspective is 'comparative' if the description of the particular is cast in terms of classifications, typologies and broadly applicable analytic constructs (Scarrow, 1969, pp.2 and 7; see also Lijphart, 1971, p.691 and Smelser, 1973, pp.56ff.).

Certainly, there is an element of comparison involved in all the operations here outlined by Lijphart and Scarrow. But 'comparison' must then be taken in a very general and vague meaning. Such a wide connotation is, as we may recall, not very suitable for us since we want to find a more specific conception of comparative method. The reason is that it would discriminate too little. The usage suggested by Lijphart would decisively single out simply and solely so-called atheoretical case studies as real examples of the application of the case study method, whereas all other inquiries into single cases would be deemed 'comparative' or 'semi-comparative'. Concerning the practical implications of such a usage, even Lijphart has to admit that almost any analysis of a single case is at least guided by some vague theoretical notion, even if it lacks theoretical aims. Therefore, he has to concede that an actual instance of an a-theoretical case study is very rarely to be found. In fact, he could have added that there is in the real world no such thing as an a-theoretical presumption in order to make some selection from among the myriad of facts surrounding us (see e.g. Hempel, 1966, pp.10ff.). Thus, Lijphart's argument about the boundary between the case study and the comparative method ends up with the actual conclusion that there are no real case studies to be found. And the usage of Scarrow implies roughly the same but stated in a different way: that every study is "comparative".

It seems much more to the point, therefore, to stick to the original idea that a comparative study deals with at least two identifiable cases. But what, more exactly, do we mean by a 'case'?

Obviously, it is not the number of registrations of variations in an actual or potential independent variable that is decisive here. Thus, the number of explanatory factors taken into consideration has nothing to do with the question of whether it is a case study or not. A study of the formation of the British Labour government in 1945 would be a case study, even though it were to contain comparisons of numerous causal explanations of why it came to look like it actually did.

Consequently, the number of different registrations of variations in the principal dependent variable is the determinant of whether the investigation is a case study or not. A survey of the causes of the variations in voting turnout in country A and country B at the same point in time is obviously comparative. But so is also a study that tries to answer the question why there is a change in voting turnout figures in country A from one election to another. True, in the latter case the investigator deals with the same dependent variable in the same social unit but at different points in time. However, I suggest that registering values on the same variable at two different points in time is identical to scrutinizing two separate cases (cf. Warwick and Osherson, 1973, p.8; Lijphart, 1971, p.689; Smelser, 1973, pp.63ff.; Galtung, 1967, p.1).

But suppose we register variations in voting turnout continually over a longer period of time. Is such a study also comparative? Of course, if voting turnout is the fundamental dependent variable. If, however, the variable under consideration is the process of change itself, then the study is a case study. Only when two processes of change in voting turnout are compared with each other will such an investigation become comparative.

Thus, despite all difficulties, it seems very sensible to differentiate comparative examinations from case studies. It ought to be underlined, however, that the distinction is made from a logical point of view. By no means does it imply any rank ordering of the two methods on substantive grounds.

Now, the time has come to summarize the usage so far attained. On the highest level of generality we encounter the scientific method, common to all social and natural sciences. In the present context, we need not dwell upon that very extensively. On a somewhat lower level of abstraction we can differentiate between experimental and non-experimental modes of procedure. Now, as to comparisons, in the most general meaning of the term, they can be resorted to in all scientific situations and for all scientific purposes. They may be put to use in experimental as well as in non-experimental research. Such a usage can be designated the *general conception of comparison*, or more properly the general conceptions of comparison, because there are several of them. The meanings of these expressions come very near those of "to think" or "to observe". Obviously, they are far too wide to be of any particular use in a methodological context. Therefore, the term has to be circumscribed a bit more. For the time being, we suggest a *specific conception of comparative method* to be defined as a non-experimental, scientific mode of procedure which is resorted to when at least two instances or cases of the basic unit of analysis are taken into consideration.

The usage so far adopted can be viewed as an elaboration of suggestions put forward by Lijphart and Smelser. It is also in general accordance with ideas held by other authors, for example Robert Holt and John Turner (1970, pp.5ff., 13, 15).

Before proceeding to the second and third aspects—the object and the goal—of the general format of the comparative method definitions, one further delimitation with regard to the mental activity aspect will be considered. In an article by Arthur L. Kalleberg, measurement according to the rules of the *ordinal scale* is singled out as the true comparative method, in conscious contrast to mere classification, on the one hand, and quantitative measurement proper at the level of interval and ratio scales on the other. As a matter of course, the classes of a rank order must be both jointly exhaustive and mutually exclusive; that is, they must satisfy the logical conditions of a valid classification. But furthermore, it must be possible to order the elements of the classes according to their having more or less of the characteristic in question. Rank ordering means attributing ordinal numbers to the elements in order to show their relative position on a particular variable. This is the operation equated by Kalleberg to comparative method (Kalleberg, 1966, pp.72ff; cf. Hempel, 1952, pp.54ff.).

It is not very difficult to realize that Kalleberg is not applying the same principles of division as Wundt, Lijphart, Smelser and others, whose suggestions for a clear and fruitful usage we have dealt with earlier this section. From one point of view, it is a definite strength to associate, as Kalleberg does, comparison with the language of measurement. It gives the concept an outstanding lucidity, one very seldom encountered in the literature. No one can be in a state of uncertainty as to where the limits of comparative method in this case actually are drawn. Moreover, comparative method is equated to something specific in the domain of discourse.

But this conception also suffers from some definite drawbacks. It appears to be all too limited in its scope. Any research problem specifically connected with quantitative measurement as well as qualitative classification is by definition left outside the discussion. Furthermore, it is not in accordance with common scholarly usage; on the contrary, Kalleberg is its only proponent in our selection of literature. All this implies that Kalleberg's conception must be put aside.

By that, every possibility of restricting the concept with reference to the mental activity supposed to be performed in comparison seems to be exhausted. But many authors are still very dissatisfied with the demarcation of the concept thus arrived at. One conceivable solution left for them is to search for this more specific delimitation with regard to one property or more in the subject matter, towards which the mental activity at stake is assumed to be directed. Let us now examine the diverse efforts in this direction.

## 4 RESTRICTIONS IMPOSED ON "COMPARATIVE METHOD" WITH REGARD TO THE OBJECT TOWARDS WHICH IT IS DIRECTED

In the literature considered here, most definitions and usages in effect take at least one aspect of the subject matter into account in the definiens proper. This is actually a rather remarkable discovery. It is at variance with a long tradition in social research of distinguishing very carefully between method and subject matter. From a logical point of view, questions of technique and questions of substance are entirely distinct and different. A method is a way of working, be it a mode of collecting, processing or analysing data. The substance, on the other hand, is the concrete material to be worked upon. Now, there is nothing that forces one, by logical necessity, to study a particular kind of political reality by means of a definite type of technique. From a logical vantage point, one is free to study whatever substantive area with whatever method happens to be at hand. The selection of tools for analysis depends upon the theoretical purposes of the current investigation, not upon some compelling logical relationships between data and technique. Of course, this by no means implies a denial of the evident empirical fact that some kinds of data are more susceptible or suitable to certain kinds of methods rather than to others. But for the time being, we are concerned with logical, not empirical, relationships.

This general argument alone is sufficiently strong to warrant the rejection of all attempts at defining comparative method in terms of a definite subject matter. However, in order to demonstrate clearly some of the more specific intricacies of this approach to comparative method definition, I shall devote a few lines to a couple of the most common concrete proposals for suitable object delimitations.

One of the aspects of the subject matter to which theorists of comparative method pay attention is the *kind of units of analysis* to be compared. Widely divergent positions seem to be opted for. However, the most common units associated with the comparative method seem to be culture, society, polity and nation. This amounts to maintaining that the comparative method in one way or another by definition is connected with cross-cultural, cross-societal, cross-polity and/or cross-national research.[4] Let us single out the final example for a brief discussion.

First, it is apparent that 'nation' is a highly ambiguous concept. In fact, there is a century-long controversy about the meaning of "national" and "nationalism". One crucial point in this great debate is whether 'nation' ought to be conceived as pertaining to something falling essentially within the cultural sphere, such as a common language and a common culture, or to something within the sphere of politics such as a territorial state. In this respect, some modern authors on comparative research demonstrate a marked tendency to waver between the two connotations (Rokkan *et al.*, 1969, pp.120ff.; Duijker and Rokkan, 1954, p.9; Rokkan, 1970. p.647; Loewenstein, 1944, pp.540ff.). For the argument to be developed here, however, this ambiguity need not bother us very much. Therefore, let us simply assume that "cross-national" means 'across the borders of at least two separate nation-states'.

Now, in most cases cross-national research is conceived as merely one type of research, in which the comparative method is a constituent part. It is, in other words, regarded as a sufficient but not a necessary condition for comparative method (Holt and Turner, 1970, pp.5ff., 13, 15). Obviously, there is nothing to disagree with in such a line of reasoning. Provided 'cross-national analysis' implies the study of at least two cases, it seems quite justified to designate such a study " comparative". It may even be argued that cross-national investigations are the most interesting and important instances of the applications of the comparative method.

But if cross-national analysis is equated entirely to comparative research, then the issue is altered. The implication would be that boundaries between nations are more important from a methodological point of view than any conceivable boundary within nations or above nations on an international· or global level. To say the least, it is difficult to discover any reasonable justification for this train of thought. True, some practical and even theoretical reasons may be advanced to sustain the boundary. Thus, it may be argued that the nation-state still is the most salient unit of political life. It may also be maintained that data-collection is more exacting to carry out within a cross-national context than with an intra-national, because of the burdens that difficulties in culture and language impose upon the cross-national researcher. But this by no means implies any methodological differences. The dissimilarities, if any, are at the most in degree, not in kind. Within-nation investigations across a large number of spatial units, such as the fifty states of the United States, must come to grips with the same methodological problems as cross-national inquiries across fifty nation-states. To sum up, from a methodological point of view, the argument that comparative method ought to be equated to cross-national method appears entirely unwarranted.

Similar intricacies are encountered when using the second boundary criterion with reference to the subject matter: the *level of the subject* towards which the analysis must be directed. In the main, attention is paid to the level in two different ways. In the first place, the cases of the unit selected, whether cultures, nations, societies or states, must be treated, it is said, in the main as integrated wholes, if their study is to qualify for the label of "comparative research". Not only must investigations be carried out on the level of national political systems or on still higher levels, but the phenomena under investigation must also be treated as mutually interdependent and interrelated wholes. Should these conditions not be fulfilled, then the studies are not to be counted as "comparative" (Hopkins and Wallerstein, 1967, pp.25ff.; Wittram, 1958, p.50).

In the second place, it is asserted that a study must be focused at all events on two levels of analysis in order to be considered "comparative". In their penetrating volume on the logic of comparative social inquiry, Adam Przeworski and Henry Teune suggest a definition of this kind. "Comparative research" is explicitly and distinctly defined as inquiry in which more than one level of analysis is possible and the units of observation are identifiable by name at each of these levels. Thus, a study of local leaders sampled from local communities in a single country is comparative, since research can proceed at both the individual and at the community levels. But if supranational regions are not identifiable, then according to this definition a study conducted exclusively at the level of countries is not comparative (Przeworski and Teune, 1970, pp.36ff.).

It would seem that no one is willing to deny that the level of analysis represents a crucial problem in comparative government or in social science in general. And yet, many cogent criticisms can be levelled against the inclusion of some statement about the level of analysis in the proper definition of comparative method. The principal point, however, is that such an inclusion would make the conception too narrow, specific and strange. Numerous investigations which should reasonably be considered "comparative" would be excluded, according to such a definition. Take, for instance, an investigation across ten nation states, dealing with only one level of analysis. It would not be labelled "comparative", whereas a study of only one case, if conducted at various levels, would be included without much further ado. But such a usage seems to conflict too much with ordinary scholarly usage. I shall not therefore include anything about the level in my definition of "comparative method".

## 5  RESTRICTIONS IMPOSED ON "COMPARATIVE METHOD" WITH REGARD TO THE GOALS PURSUED BY COMPARISON

At least a few advocates of "comparative method" do not look upon it merely as a mental activity focused on certain kinds and aspects of substance. In addition, they also insert in their definitional statements sub-sections about goals, aims or products towards which the employers of the method are presumed to strive.

In some of the lexicographic definitions referred to at the beginning of section 3, "comparison" is taken to be an activity by which similarities and differences among diverse kinds of units are elicited, apprehended or discerned. From these pronouncements, comparison may be construed as something falling entirely within the context of discovery (Stout and Baldwin, 1928, p.202; see also Santinello, 1957, p.1192, and Gould, 1964, p.116).

No doubt, this circumscription is too narrow for the present purpose. Aiming at a discussion of the goals of comparative method in both context of discovery and context of justification, and perhaps particularly in the latter, we do not wish to exclude the most important of them by a definitional decision.

Other authors seem to include both context of discovery and context of justification in their definitions. Accordingly, comparative method is held to be a technique of generating as well as testing hypotheses. Nevertheless, this usage is too narrow because other qualifications are added. It is thus argued that the purpose of comparison is to find out and test resemblances. Sometimes, it is even specified what sort of similarities it must be. In his first article, Lijphart defines "comparative method" as one of the basic methods of identifying and establishing general empirical propositions, in the main of an explanatory kind (Lijphart, 1971, pp.682ff.). We nevertheless do not wish to restrict the method to the purpose of obtaining similarities, be it general descriptions or general explanations. We wish the definition to be neutral with respect to the goals of generalization and individualization. Therefore, the above position must be rejected.

Last but not least, evolutionary hypotheses or theories are also included in the definitions proper of "comparative method". Whether it be done for the sake of discovery or of testing, "comparative method" is said to imply the arrangement of social, cultural or political conditions observed in different political surroundings into a series that is then taken to represent a process of evolution. The purpose of the method is, by definition, to describe the course and direction of change from the simple and primitive to the higher and more complex (Bock, 1965, pp.269, 275; Hoenigswald, 1963, pp.1ff.).

This curious association of "comparative method" with evolutionary theory can be found in current literature (Easthope, 1974, pp.106ff.), although it is considerably more common in works from the period before the First World War. 'The establishment of the Comparative Method of study has been the greatest intellectual achievement of our time. It has carried light and order into whole branches of human knowledge which before were shrouded in darkness and confusion.' With these proud words Edward Freeman initiated his pioneering lectures on comparative politics, delivered before the University of Oxford more than one hundred years ago. A scrutiny of Freeman's line of argument displays that he indubitably assumed that an evolutionary purpose should be a self-evident component part of a comparative study of politics. The comparative method should be directed at exploring differences and likenesses and explaining the latter by a theory of a common derivation from a common origin (Freeman, 1873, pp.1ff., 18ff.).

That this inclusion of an evolutionary goal in the definition proper makes it too exclusive is altogether patent. Such a usage would turn nearly all social scientists of today who regard themselves as comparativists into non-comparativists.

This review of various attempts to insert goals into definitions of "comparative method" leads us to the conclusion that goals should not be included in our definition at all. We wish to keep it open which goals can be pursued by the application of the comparative method. This position is entirely in accordance with ordinary scholarly usage, most scholars inserting nothing about goals in their definitions (Rokkan, 1970, pp.645ff.; R. M. March, 1967, pp.5ff.; Sjoberg, 1955, pp.106ff.; Przeworski and Teune, 1970, pp.36ff.; Payne, 1973, pp.13ff.).

## 6 DEFINITION OF "COMPARATIVE METHOD"

The expression "comparative method" can now be formally defined as *a scientific, non-experimental mode of procedure, implying that at least two instances of the basic unit of analysis are taken into consideration.*

This definition can be elucidated by the tree of classification illustrated in figure 11.1. The specific conception of comparative method outlined in the figure must be carefully distinguished from another, more general conception of comparison. Being nearly synonymous with "to think" or "to observe", comparison in this broader sense is a constituent part of all methods of research. It sneaks into the experimental as well as the case study method. Regarded as a more specific research instrument, however, comparative method is a mode of procedure that can be differentiated from the experimental and the case study method.

Thus, the comparative method is something specific in relation to a more general phenomenon called "comparison". But it is also, in its turn, something general in

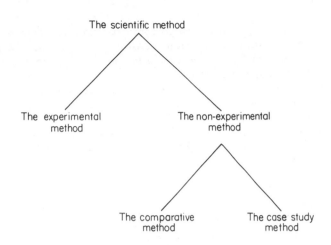

Figure 11.1. The position of the comparative method among other methods of social science

relation to other, more specialized techniques. For those modes of procedure indicated in the figure ought to be regarded as broad-gauged or middle-gauged general methods. In this respect I am entirely in agreement with Lijphart when he argues that the comparative method is a basic research strategy rather than a narrow, specialized technique (1971, p.683). Instances of these narrow-gauged techniques are statistical methods such as regression and correlation, text-critical methods, the interview method, the methods of content analysis, source criticism and participant observation. They might be resorted to in experimental as well as in comparative and case study research. As they in principle belong everywhere, there is no reason why they should be specifically mentioned in Figure 11.1.

One fundamental line of division in the chart is that between the experimental and the non-experimental method. Experimentation implies the direct and immediate manipulation of variables in a controlled situation. The distinguishing feature of the experimental method is that it enables the researcher to vary one variable at a time, holding all other variables constant. Thereby, he can create his own source material. The non-experimental method, on the other hand, implies that events necessarily are investigated only after they have happened. The research worker cannot produce his own sources in controlled circumstances, but has to be satisfied with studying what has already occurred.

The second basic boundary is that between comparative and case study method. A comparative study is one where at least two empirical instances of the principal unit of analysis are taken into consideration. Assume that the nation-state is the principal unit of analysis and that the size of the public sector is the dependent variable under study: then an examination of the public sector in two countries at the same point in time is comparative. But so also is a survey of the volume of the sector in a single country at two, three or more different points in time. Now, let us assume that the unit of analysis is changed and that instead of size we are concerned with the process of growth of the public sector. Then, the expansion of the sector in Sweden between, say, 1965 and 1975 may be taken as one instance of growth, although in computing the figures showing it the researcher has to consider—and even compare—the same figures of size as in the last example. This demonstrates that the line of demarcation between the case study and the comparative method is dependent upon what is conceived to be the focal unit of analysis.

The present stipulation seems to be in tolerable accordance with the criteria of adequacy outlined at the beginning of the chapter. It is reasonably unambiguous and it is not entirely out of touch with common scholarly usage. The definition also fulfils the criterion of practicality. It other words, it is not awkward to apply. This amounts to saying that there is no need to undertake unduly extensive and laborious empirical investigations in order to be able to decide whether an examination is to be classified as comparative or not.

And finally, the definition is, I make bold enough to claim, scientifically fertile. It is sufficiently narrow to single out a particular comparative method from other conceivable modes of procedure in social science. But it is also sufficiently wide not to exclude entirely or skew partly a discussion of some interesting problems usually associated with the method. But these problems must be dealt with in another connection.

# 12

# On the Use of the Word "Political"

JAN–ERIK LANE

## 1 INTRODUCTION

A semantic study of the word "political" as used in scientific language can be pursued along different lines. At least three problems are relevant, and these should be kept distinct since the answers to them have quite different conditions of validity. The first is: (P1) What are the explicit or implicit definiens expressions in the use of "political" by various authors? (P1 is a problem for empirical semantics and can be answered by language descriptions of the following type: (LD) According to the group G the sentence "x is a political behaviour/action/system/etc" is synonymous with the sentence "x has the properties (A), (B), (C), etc." It goes without saying that it would be useful to have an exhaustive list of (LD)s, arranged according to the degree of precization of the definiens sentences with the aid of the methods of empirical semantics (Naess, 1966). In most definitions, "political" occurs in connection with other words. The term can be used about quite different types of objects: behaviour, action, relation of influence, corporation, etc. This state of affairs may give rise to partial definitions of "political", excluding a general comparison between different (LD)s. For example, in $(LD_1)$ it may be a matter of defining "political" in connection with "action", but in $(LD_2)$ in connection with "corporation", without there being any indication as to what are the common properties in the definiens sentences in $(LD_1)$ and $(LD_2)$.

Thus, in order to make definitions of 'political' comparable, the various (LD)s must be broken down into non-partial definitions. This will be done by rendering the definiens sentences of the (LD)s into stipulative definitions of the following type:

(SD)     "x is political"          $=_{df}$    "x has the properties (A), (B), (C), etc."

Of course, the existence of different (LD)s, $(LD_1)$, $(LD_2)$, . . . $(LD_n)$, cannot without more ado be regarded as evidence for the presence of conceptual diversity, since in several (LD)s the same concept may occur. That is, it does not have to be the case that to each (SD) belongs one and only one (LD). Consequently, it is possible to answer a second type of semantic problem: (P2) What concept of political is implied in an (LD)?

For all (SD)s it must be the case that: (i) the range of entities among which the variable "x" may take its values is the same; and (ii) the set of possible values of "x" must be as general as possible, i.e. behaviour or action. A necessary condition for the fulfilment of these two requirements is that the terms with which "political" occurs in combination in partial definitions can somehow be reduced to each other. If these terms ("behaviour", "action", "power", "corporation", etc.) could be introduced exactly in a taxonomy, it would be possible to state the level of each (LD) and by substitution to render them into (SD)s. Furthermore, a structuring of terms for types of entities in the social world is a necessary condition for a fruitful comparison between different (SD)s. If such a taxonomy is created it can be shown for each (SD) at what level of complexity the property political is introduced and what structure the entities in the set of political phenomena have. This problem of taxonomy will be dealt with below in connection with the discussion of Weber.

As in all conceptual analyses, the analysis of (SD)s has two objectives: (i) specification of meaning and (ii) specification of reference.

(i) *Specification of meaning*. It is often maintained that there are a number of different concepts of political denoted below by "$PC_1$", "$PC_2$", . . . "$PC_n$". Provided that the (SD)s fulfil the usual criteria of adequacy, it would thus be possible to have a basic set of (SD)s, each different from the other in at least one property. This basic set of (SD)s could then be structured in a logically exhaustive way, from which it would follow exactly how one concept, $PC_1$, differed from another, $PC_2$.

The presence of conceptual diversity as regards the term 'political' on the level of meaning cannot be taken as conclusive evidence for the existence of separate references of the word. It may well be that different concepts, $PC_1$ and $PC_2$, delimit the same set of entities. This empirical question can only be settled by comparison of the sets belonging to each concept. Only if referential diversity prevails does the term "political" become ambiguous.

(ii) *Specification of reference*. This implies for each (SD) an empirical specification of the set of entities referred to by the concept of political in an (SD). The result will be a number of sets $S_1, S_2, \ldots S_n$ corresponding to a number of concepts $PC_1$, $PC_2, \ldots PC_n$. It is then possible to state the set-theoretical relations between these sets. This gives our third problem: (P3) Given the presence of referential diversity, is it possible to introduce an explication of "political"? (P3) presupposes the presence of a number of concepts $PC_1, PC_2, \ldots PC_n$ with different references. And (P3) asks for an explicans, *the* concept of political, which fulfils the criteria of adequacy for explication. An explication sentence may have the following form: (ES) According to criteria $C_1, C_2, \ldots C_n$, x is to be called "political" if and only if x has the properties (A), (B), (C), etc.

What are the *criteria of adequacy* that are relevant for an (ES)? We can say that at least the following four criteria must be met:

$C_1$ : A concept of political must fulfil the standard rules for the introduction of concepts.
    (i) It is neither the case that the definition is circular explicitly or implicitly, nor is it the case that the definiens term is ambiguous or more unclear than the definiendum term or that it is redundant.
    (ii) It is not the case that everything in the domain of discourse is political under the definition.

(iii) It is not the case that nothing in the domain of discourse is political under the definition.

$C_2$ : A concept of political must not be too wide or too narrow in relation to what is considered political in scientific language.

$C_3$ : A concept of political must be theoretically fruitful both in the construction of concepts and in the specification of sentences.

$C_4$ : If more than one concept of political (e.g. two separate partial definitions) is introduced then the sets corresponding to these concepts must be mutually exclusive.

The relevance of $C_1$, $C_2$ and $C_3$ for (ES) need not be discussed. The importance of $C_4$ lies in the fact that if $C_4$ is not fulfilled it is possible to require a more exact statement of the relationships between the different concepts.

This paper will contain a first attempt to approach these problems (P1)–(P3). The emphasis will be put on analyses of a few definitions which are the result of theoretical work oriented towards the problem of defining "political" and which have had a central place in the concept formation of political science. The objects of analysis are (LD)s given by Max Weber, by David Easton and by Harold Lasswell and Abraham Kaplan. More specifically, the objective will be to discover whether the (SD)s that can be constructed out of these authors' (LD)s satisfy the criteria $C_1$–$C_4$ for an (ES).

## 2 WEBER

Weber introduces explicit definitions of "political corporation", "political action" and "politically orientated action" in his list of general concepts for the social sciences in "Soziologische Grundbegriffe" (Weber, 1964a, pp.3–41). (This was first published in *Wirtschaft und Gesellschaft* (1922) and later translated into English in Weber, 1964b, pp.87–157 and Weber, 1968). Thus, Weber does not give one definition of "political", but three rules that govern the use of the term in connection with other terms. One problem is to investigate the relations between these partial definitions in order to find out if one of them is a complete definition of "political" to which the others are reducible, or if more than one (SD) can be constructed out of these (LD)s.

When the (LD)s drawn from Weber have been broken down into (SD)s, the next problem is conceptual analysis of these (SD)s: we ask what properties an entity must have in order to have the property political and what there is in the set of political phenomena.

However, the discussion of Weber will start with the more general problem of structuring terms for types of entities in the social world. The objective will be to break down Weber's list into a deductive taxonomy. Such a taxonomy will not only clarify Weber's (SD)s, but will be used in the comparison of different authors' (SD)s.

### 2A. The Weber taxonomy

According to Zetterberg, Weber's list of concepts is '. . . the most successful attempt so far to provide a taxonomy for sociology' (Zetterberg, 1965, p.43). It is true that Weber starts from simple terms and progresses towards more and more complex terms, as Zetterberg (1965, p.44) points out, but Weber's list does not satisfy the usual criterion for an adequate taxonomy: it is not built up deductively. An attempt will now be made to do this. As the objective is the systematic introduction of terms,

220

Weber's definitions will not be followed in every respect, but whatever changes may be necessary from the point of view of deductive simplicity will be made.

    I.    Primitive terms
- (a)    Non-logical terms
  - (i)    Minimum terms: "behaviour", "orientations", "neutrality", "approval", "responsible", "rule", "violence", "binding", "obedience", "staff"
  - (ii)    Borrowed terms: "human being", "territory", "physical", "worldly", "condition"
- (b)    Variables: "x", "y", "z" and "w" (where "y" and "z" take as their values an actor or a group of actors, and where $y \neq z$)
- (c)    Logical terms: the standard logical terms, i.e. first order predicate logic with identity

    II.    Defined terms

(DF1)    "x is an action by y"    $=_{df}$    "x is an oriented behaviour by y"

(DF2)    "x is an activity by y and/or z"    $=_{df}$    "x is a set of actions by y and/or z"

(DF3)    "y is an actor"    $=_{df}$    "y is a human being with activity"

(DF4)    "x is a social action by y with regard to z"    $=_{df}$    "x is an action by y, oriented towards z"

The term introduced in (DF4) "social action", sets the limit of the possible range of entities belonging to social reality. A necessary and sufficient condition for an entity to be a social entity or part of a social entity is that this word can be used about it. The rest of the taxonomy introduces terms for different types of or sets of entities in the social reality on the basis of properties of these social entities or of sets of such entities and properties of these properties etc. "Social action" will be called a *"basic term"*: it is true of each and every social unit, when analysed into its basic parts. The term in (DF4) introduces a basic property and stands for a set of basic units, which constitute the *domain of discourse*.

(DF5)    "x is a social relation between y and z"    $=_{df}$    "x is an activity by y and z and where y is oriented towards z and z is oriented towards y"

In (DF5) a term of the *first order* is introduced. The emphasis in Weber's taxonomy lies on social relations and their properties and the combination of these properties into more complex and thus higher order properties.

    The definiens in (DF5) is vague, because it is not specified how many actions are to be included in an activity for an activity to be a social relation. However, the number of actions is a function of the type of social relation. Some types of relations consist by definition of several actions (e.g. friendship) while other types contain only a few actions (e.g. recruitment). A necessary restriction on (DF5) is that it should be empirically possible to distinguish between the existence and the persistence of a social relation.

| (DF6) | "y and z are members of a social relation x" | $=_{df}$ | "x is a social relation between y and z" |
|---|---|---|---|
| (DF7) | "x is complementary to w" | $=_{df}$ | "x is a condition for w" |
| (DF8) | "x and w are complementary" | $=_{df}$ | "x and w are orientations where the realization of x is complementary to the realization of w and vice versa" |
| (DF9) | "x is a one-sided relation between y and z" | $=_{df}$ | "x is a social relation between y and z, and the orientations of y and z are neither of the same type nor complementary" |
| (DF10) | "x is a two-sided relation between y and z" | $=_{df}$ | "x is a social relation between y and z, and x is not one-sided" |

In the case of two people hating each other the orientations are of the same type and in the father-son relation the orientations are complementary. In (DF9) and (DF10) terms of the *second order* are introduced: terms for properties that consist of first order properties and their properties.

| (DF11) | "x is an endogenous condition" | $=_{df}$ | "x is a condition for membership in a social relation, which condition is orientation only towards action in the relation" |
|---|---|---|---|
| (DF12) | "x is an exogenous condition" | $=_{df}$ | "x is a condition for membership in a social relation, which is not an endogenous condition" |
| (DF13) | "x is an open relation" | $=_{df}$ | "x is a social relation, which has no exogenous conditions" |
| (DF14) | "x is a closed relation" | $=_{df}$ | "x is a social relation, which has exogenous conditions" |

As types of examples of closed relations Weber mentions the family, the emotional relation, the religious association and the monopoly. The market under conditions of free competition is an example of an open relation. Over time, some social relations hover between these two extremes.

| (DF15) | "x is a communal relation between y and z" | $=_{df}$ | "x is a social relation between y and z, whose condition is y's approval of z and z's approval of y" |
|---|---|---|---|
| (DF16) | "x is a relation of interest between y and z" | $=_{df}$ | "x is a social relation between y and z, whose condition is neutrality by both y and z" |

"Communal relation" stands for relations like relations of deference and erotic relations, whereas "relation of interest" refers to market relations, voluntary corporations and the like. Obviously, the terms in (DF15) and (DF16) are terms for two types of *co-operation,* one based on mutual feelings and the other based on shared interests or compromise of interests. As Weber points out there are seldom social relations that have only one of these two properties.

(DF17) "x is a relation of solidarity between y and z as regards w" $=_{df}$ "x is a social relation between y and z, where y and z are responsible for w by y or z"

(DF18) "x is a relation of representation between y and z as regards w and y represents z" $=_{df}$ "x is a social relation between y and z, where z is responsible for w by y, and x is not a relation of solidarity with regard to w"

The property solidarity is most usual among communal and closed relations like the family and the tribe. Representation occurs in rationally instituted corporations and mostly in organizations.

In (DF13)–(DF18) are specified the meaning of other *second order* terms. However, none of these terms are key terms in the definition of "political" in Weber's taxonomy. There is thus no logical reason why an entity should be political and have one and not another of these properties in so far as the latter are not mutually exclusive. With the aid of the definitions given so far, other definitions can be made which contain key terms for "political".

(DF19) "y has authority over z as regards w" $=_{df}$ "between y and z there is a social relation in which z is in obedience to y as regards w"

The second order term in (DF19) is of central importance for the definition of "political": a social relation is political only if it is an authority relation. Weber's term for the property specified in (DF19) is of course "*Herrschaft*" and he treats this term as synonymous with the term "*Autoritat*" (Weber, 1964a, p.157). The definition in Weber is equivalent to that of (DF19): 'Herrschaft soll heissen die Chance, für einen Befehl bestimmten Inhalts bei angebbaren Personen Gehorsam zu finden' (Weber, 1964a, p.38). And in the translation of Weber into English the same concept is specified: ' "*Imperative control*" (Herrschaft) is the probability that a command with a specific content will be obeyed by a given group of persons' (Weber, 1964b, p.152).

According to Blau, Weber meant his concept of authority (DF19) to be a sub-category of his concept of power (Blau, 1974, p.40). Thus, if Blau is right, power must be a component of the concept of political in Weber's taxonomy: political implies authority which implies power. But is Blau right? In order to settle this problem we turn to the definition of power in Weber.

(DF20) "x is a relation of selection between y and x as regards w" $=_{df}$ "x is a relation between y and z in which either y or z has/does or will have/will do w but not both"

(DF21)  "x is a relation of conflict        $=_{df}$  "x is a relation of selection
         between y and z as regards            between y and z as regards w,
         w"                                  and x is a social relation in
                                                     which y orients towards
                                                   selection for y whereas z
                                                   orients towards selection for
                                                   z"

(DF22)  "x is a relation of competition  $=_{df}$  "x is a relation of conflict
         between y and z as regards w"        between y and z as regards w
                                                   in which there is no physical
                                                   violence"

Weber distinguishes between biological and social selection and considers selection to be a fundamental property of every social relation. Conflict is the contradictory to co-operation as it involves a clash between opposite orientations in a relation of selection. Weber distinguishes between different types of conflict relations like competition and regulated conflict.

(DF23)  "y has power over z as regards  $=_{df}$  "there is between y and z a
         w"                                  social relation in which y
                                                   realizes his orientation as
                                                   regards w at the expense of
                                                   the possibility of z realizing
                                                 his orientation as regards w"

Thus a power relation is such a social relation in which one party carries through his will against the will of the other party. If the definitions (DF19) and (DF23) are compared, it is obvious that the concept of authority and the concept of power are not logically related in the way asserted by Blau. A relation of authority can be a relation of power and a relation of power can be a relation of authority. How these matters stand is an empirical question and cannot be decided by investigating definitions only. A person can obey a command by another person and at the same time realize his orientation; and a person can have power over another person without obtaining obedience to his commands. A social relation can be a relation of authority and at the same time not a relation of power. Consequently, authority is not a sub-category of power for Weber and a political relation is not by definition a power relation.

Blau makes conflict a part of Weber's concept of power (Blau, 1974, p.40). The same thing is also done in Talcott Parsons's edition of Weber (Weber, 1964b, p.152). This is not correct. The property in (DF23) can occur in combination with the property conflict in (DF21), but whether or not it does is an empirical question. There can be a relation of power without there being a relation of conflict—for example, when there is a relation of authority that is also a relation of power. One can carry through one's will against the will of another person without resistance from the latter.

In his comment on Weber's concept of authority Blau furthermore claims that the concept of legitimacy as specified by Weber is a part of the concept of authority (Blau, 1974, pp.41, 50). If this were the case a political relation would always be legitimate.

Is this really so for Weber? This problem can be decided by introducing a few definitions containing terms that occur in the definition of "political".

| | | |
|---|---|---|
| (DF24) | "x is legitimate for y" | $=_{df}$ "in y's orientation x is binding for y" |
| (DF24') | "x has legitimacy for y" | $=_{df}$ "x is legitimate for y" |
| (DF25) | "x is a system of norms" | $=_{df}$ "x is a set of rules, in terms of which action is oriented" |
| (DF26) | "x is a legitimate system of norms for y" | $=_{df}$ "x is a system of norms whose rules are legitimate for y" |
| (DF27) | "x is a system of norms, guaranteed by the actions w by w" | $=_{df}$ "x is a system of norms towards the rules of which there is obedience, and a condition for the obedience is the actions w by y" |

It can now be shown that the concept of authority does not imply the concept of legitimacy. It is an empirical question whether or not a social relation having the property specified in (DF19) also has the property specified in (DF24). As Weber states, a person can obey a command from many different motives, where one is a belief in the command as binding, that is to say legitimate (Weber, 1964a, p.157). If Blau were right, Weber's theory of authority would be a tautology, since it states a relation between authority and legitimacy, as we shall see.

On the basis of the definitions of "authority", "power", "conflict" and "legitimacy" in Weber, it is clearly possible to make distinctions between basic concepts in political science. Of these concepts, only that of authority and that of conflict are logical opposites in the sense that they are contraries. It is an empirical question whether or not a relation of authority is legitimate, whether a relation of authority is a power relation or not, and whether a relation of power is a relation of conflict or not.

After this digression on the relation of authority to other concepts it is possible to proceed with the introduction of the definition of "political". An entity is political only if it is a social relation and a relation of authority. Now, what are the other conditions for the application of "political"?

| | | |
|---|---|---|
| (DF28) | "y is a leader for z as regards w" | $=_{df}$ "there is between y and z a relation of representation as regards w, and y represents z" |
| (DF29) | "x is a corporation" | $=_{df}$ "x is a social relation with a system of norms guaranteed by the leader(s) or the staff of x" |

The term in (DF29) is a *third order* term: a term for a property that consists of second order properties and their properties. Thus, a corporation is the combination of three properties: social relation, system of norms and guarantee by leader(s) or staff. As examples of corporations Weber mentions the family, the organization, the State and the Church. The concept of corporation has a central place in Weber's taxonomy. It is a necessary part of the concept of political: an entity is political only if it has the property specified in (DF29). And, on the basis of this property, Weber introduces other important concepts.

(DF30)  "x is a system of norms,   $=_{df}$  "x is a system of norms,
which governs the action(s)         which y obeys in the action(s)
w of y"                    w"

(DF31)  "x is an administrative action  $=_{df}$  "x is either an action by the
in a corporation w"            leader(s) or the staff of a
corporation w, which is
oriented towards the
guarantee of the system of
norms of w, or an action by
the members of w for which
the leader(s) or the staff of w
is/are responsible"

(DF32)  "x is a regulated action in a  $=_{df}$  "x is an action by the
corporation w"                 members of a corporation w
which is not an administra-
tive action in w, but which is
governed by the system of
norms of w"

(DF33)  "x is an introduced system of  $-_{df}$  "x is a system or norms in a
norms in a corporation w"         corporation w, which comes
into existence through action
by the leader(s) or the staff
and the members of w
oriented towards that state of
affairs"

(DF34)  "x is an imposed system of  $=_{df}$  "x is a system of norms in a
norms in a corporation w"         corporation w, whose introduction is conditioned by the
authority or power of the
leader(s) of w over the
members of w"

(DF35)  "x is a system of norms    $=_{df}$  "x is a system of norms in a
voluntarily agreed to in a       corporation w, whose intro-
corporation w"                duction is conditioned by the
approval of the members of
w"

(DF36)  "x is an administrative system  $=_{df}$  "x is a system of norms
of norms"                   which governs administrative
action"

(DF37)  "x is a regulative system of  $=_{df}$  "x is a system of norms
norms"                      which governs regulated
action"

In his comment to these concepts Weber points out that a *laissez faire* state would be a corporation with a minimum of administrative action and a maximum of regulated action, whereas a communist state would imply the exact opposite. The distinction between an administrative and a regulative system of norms is a generalization from the distinction between public and private law. Further, some relations between a corporation and its environment can be analysed on the basis of these concepts. A corporation is *autonomous* or *heteronomous* depending on whether or not its system of norms is introduced by the corporation itself or imposed from the outside. A corporation is *autocephalous* or *heterocephalous* depending on whether or not the recruitment of its leader(s) is decided by the corporation internally or decided externally. These dichotomies give a 2×2 table and the possibility of defining a corporation as *part* of another, if it is heteronomous and heterocephalous.

Weber introduces not only terms for properties of corporations but also terms for types of corporations. Whereas a political entity may have all the properties specified in (DF30)–(DF34) and in (DF36) and (DF37), a political unit must be of a certain type of corporation. It remains to specify this type.

(DF38) "x is a territorial corporation" $=_{df}$ "x is a corporation whose system of norms governs the actions of the corporation only within a territory"

(DF39) "x is an organization" $=_{df}$ "x is a corporation which is a relation of interest between the members of x"

(DF40) "x is a compulsory corporation" $=_{df}$ "x is a corporation in which the system of norms of x governs the members of x whether or not they approve of being thus governed"

(DF41) "x is a voluntary corporation" $=_{df}$ "x is a corporation in which the system of norms of x governs the members of x in so far as they approve of being thus governed"

(DF42) "x is an authority corporation" $=_{df}$ "x is a corporation whose system of norms governs a relation of authority"

The properties specified in (DF38)–(DF41) are not necessary nor sufficient conditions for the applications of "political". It is thus an empirical question whether or not a social relation that is political is voluntary or compulsory or whether or not it occurs within an organization. Matters are different with regard to the property specified in (DF42). This term, "authority corporation", is a *fourth order* term adding the property specified in (DF19) to the property specified in (DF29). And for Weber a social relation is political only if it is an authority corporation. The property in (DF42) is a necessary but not sufficient condition for the definition of "political". The problem is, of course, to specify the property or properties that distinguish political authority corporations from non-political authority corporations.

(DF43) "y makes a threat against z" $=_{df}$ "y does a social action towards z, which is oriented towards a relation in which y

has power over z, and which
is oriented towards future
action by y of which z
disapproves"

(DF44) "x is a political corporation" $=_{df}$ "x is an authority corporation, whose system of norms
is guaranteed within a territory by physical violence and
threat of physical violence by
the leader(s) or the staff of
x"

The word "political" is thus a *fifth order* term. The sufficient conditions for an authority corporation to be political are that its guaranteed system of norms has the properties of *territory* and *physical violence.* The basic principle is that the use of "political" about a unit requires a certain structure, a combination of properties in a set of basic units. The word does not stand for all the units in the domain of discourse. It requires of a unit a type of structure specified as a combination of five properties in order to be a political unit. Only those basic units that are part of such a unit having these five properties in the combination specified are political units. The hierarchy in Weber's taxonomy can be rendered in Figure 12.1.

| Ist<br>level | 2nd<br>level | 3rd<br>level | 4th<br>level | 5th<br>level | 6th<br>level |
|---|---|---|---|---|---|

Figure 12.1. The structure of a political unit

It is now clear what properties a social relation has if and only if it is to count as political. Of course, it would be possible to introduce the term at a lower level. (DF44) would then be a partial definition. However, this is not done by Weber. (This point will be discussed in the following section.)

Weber defined other terms of central importance, especially for his theory of authority ("*Herrschaft*").

(DF45) "y has a monopoly on w in a      $=_{df}$      "y has w, and for all z it is
   set of the persons y and z"                the case that z does not have
                       w and there is at least one z"

(DF46) "x is a state"      $=_{df}$      "x is a political corporation
                 and a compulsory corporation
                 and the leader(s) or the staff
                 of x guarantee(s) the system
                 of norms of x by a monopoly
                 on legitimate physical
                 violence"

The word "state" is a *sixth order* term and is to be used about political corporations. Though every state is a political corporation, it is not true that every political corporation is a state, or that the two concepts are identical. In contemporary theoretical works on political systems and their properties it is usual to make some distinction between a concept of the political system and a concept of the state in order to be able to speak of the politics of stateless societies. Sometimes such distinctions start from the distinction between (DF44) and (DF46). However, the result is often a confustion of these definitions. (See for example Almond and Coleman, 1960, p.5, Almond and Powell, 1966, pp.17-18, Eisenstadt, 1969, p.5, and Schapera, 1963, pp.94-134.) Accordingly, since the concepts refer to different entities, the result is confusion as to what is a political system.

(DF47) "x is psychic violence"      $=_{df}$      "x is non-physical violence"

(DF48) "x is a hierocratic      "x is an authority corpora-
   corporation"      $=_{df}$      tion, whose system of norms
                is guaranteed by psychic
                violence of a non-worldly
                nature"

(DF49) "x is a church"      $=_{df}$      "x is a hierocratic corporation
                and a compulsory corporation
                and the leader(s) or the staff
                of x has/have a monopoly on
                legitimate psychic violence
                of a non-worldly nature"

(DF50) "x is a regularity among y"      $=_{df}$      "x is a type of social action or
                social relation for which it is
                true that there are several
                values of 'x' by y over time or
                there are several values of 'x'
                among y at the same time"

The definiens expression in (DF50) contains vague terms and the probability of intersubjective agreement on the application of the word is not great. But it can be used to describe phenomena that neither are only a single particular action nor constitute an uniformity (i.e. law) of action. To Weber, the social sciences have as their object the explanation of regularities, not particular actions. Weber has the following division of regularities:

(DF51) "x is a usage among y"  $=_{df}$  "x is a regularity among y, whose condition is a great number of values of 'x' among y"

(DF52) "x is a custom among y"  $=_{df}$  "x is a usage among y, whose condition is orientation by y towards the fact that there are values of 'x' over a long time"

(DF53) "x is a fashion among y"  $=_{df}$  "x is a usage among y, whose condition is orientation by y towards the fact that there are values of 'x' over only a short time"

(DF54) "x is a state of interest among y"  $=_{df}$  "x is a regularity among y, and the values of 'x' are relations of interest"

(DF55) "x is a valid order among y"  $=_{df}$  "x is a regularity among y, whose condition is orientation by y towards the system of norms of x as legitimate"

(DF56) "y has a relation of dis-approval towards z"  $=_{df}$  "y does not approve of z and y is not neutral to z and y is oriented towards z"

(DF57) "x is a convention among y"  $=_{df}$  "x is a valid order which is guaranteed by approval or disapproval among y"

(DF58) "x is a law among y"  $=_{df}$  "x is a valid order among y which is guaranteed by violence by a leader or several leaders or a staff"

The words defined in (DF50)–(DF58) are key words in Weber's theory of the property of stability of social relations and thus also of political corporations (Weber, 1964a, I, p.3 and II, pp.8-9). The two basic sentences in this theory are: (S1) it holds generally that a valid order is more stable than a custom, which is more stable than a state of interest; and (S2) it holds generally that if a political corporation has stability, then it is a valid order. Weber's theory of authority is based in the hypothesis that the set of political units that have stability is included in the set of valid orders.

Hitherto the discussion has been oriented towards a solution of a general theoretical problem, viz. the deductive specification of words for types of entities in the social world, among which "political corporation" occurs. Perhaps Weber's taxonomy contains the most fertile attempt to deal with this problem.

## 2B.  Weber's (SD)s: "territory" and "physical violence"

As mentioned above, Weber defines the term "political" in connection with two other

230

terms, "corporation" and "action", and he distinguishes between "political action" and "politically oriented action". The three definitions can be rendered in the following (LD)s, constructed on the basis of the German original (Weber, 1964a, pp.39–41):

> (WD1) For Weber the sentence "x is a political corporation" is synonymous with the sentence "x is an authority corporation, whose system of norms is guaranteed within a territory by the use of and threat of physical violence by the leader(s) or the staff of x".
>
> (WD2) For Weber the sentence "x is a political action" is synonymous with the sentence "x is an action which is part of a political
> (WD3) corporation".
>
> For Weber the sentence "x is a politically oriented action" is synonymous with the sentence "x is an action which is oriented towards the influence of political action".

The relation between these three (LD)s is the following: the definition of "political action" is completely reducible to the definition of "political corporation"; and "politically oriented action" is partly through the definiens of "political action". Thus, since the definiens sentence in (WD2) is defined in terms of the definiens sentence in (WD1), and the definiens sentence in (WD3) in terms of the definiens sentence in (WD2) and thus in terms of the definiens sentence in (WD1), we can say that (WD1) in fact contains a complete definition of "political". There is no action that is political that is not part of a social relation that is political. The basic (SD) in Weber is:

> (SDW) "x is political" $=_{df}$ "x has the properties (a) social action that is part of a social relation that is (b) a relation of authority with (c) a system of norms guaranteed within (d) a territory by (e) use and threat of physical violence"

To this definition can be added another important (SD) in Weber, namely

> (SDW') "x is politically oriented towards y" $=_{df}$ "x is not political, but x has the property (a') orientation towards the influence of y, which is political"

These two, (SDW) and (SDW'), are the two fundamental (SD)s to be treated below. (SDW) is the basic one, but (SDW') has independent status, since it is not conceptually or referentially reducible to (SDW).

We begin with specification of meaning. Both the concept of political and the concept of politically oriented are complex and they require quite a number of properties of an entity for it to be political. With these properties it is possible to sort out from the set of political units some types of entities. How far could this division proceed? Let us take first the SDW political and then the SDW' politically oriented.

According to (SDW) an entity x is political if and only if x has the following properties.

*(a) Social action that is part of a social relation.* A political entity is an entity or part of an entity including at least two persons between whom there is a particular relation,

namely that their actions are both oriented towards each other. If this orientation component is missing the term is not applicable. A non-oriented behaviour, a behaviour oriented towards non-actors or a social action that is not part of a social relation can never be political.

(b) *Authority*. With this property Weber separates from the set of political entities all one-sided social relations and all conflict relations. Though an authority relation cannot be a conflict relation, it may be a relation of co-operation or a relation of power—these being empirical questions. Thus, the fact that there is a power relation is neither a sufficient nor a necessary condition for the application of "political". The concept of power is not a part of the concept of political, since authority does not imply power. The property authority may be combined in different ways with the property power. In a social relation both properties may occur at the same time or at separate times. A person who obeys a command against his will would be an example of the last case. However, the properties may also be causally related. A person may base his authority on his power, exclusively or otherwise, and a person may rest his power on his authority.

(c) *Guaranteed systems of norms*. The concept of political requires not only intentional behaviour, but behaviour oriented in terms of rules which are enforced by a leader or staff. According to Weber it is important to distinguish between sociological rules and juridical ones. A rule is a sociological rule if and only if there is at least one action that is oriented towards the rule—either towards its preservation or towards its neglect. A juridical rule may also be a sociological rule, but the two are by no means conceptually identical, nor do they always go together empirically. It is easy to distinguish between a political entity and a number of other types of social relations on the basis of (c). For example friendship relations do not usually have this property. With the aid of (c), Weber separates from the set of political entities all social relations that are authority relations but are not corporations. Simple exchange relations involving authority would fall outside the scope of political by this criterion, as would all types of regulated actions (DF32).

(d) *Territory*. There are social relations that are authority relations with a guaranteed system of norms (that is to say, authority corporations). Examples are family relations or economic corporations. But not all of these authority corporations are political according to Weber. In order to make this distinction between authority corporations that are political and those that are not Weber resorts to two criteria, territory and physical violence. Can they serve this end? According to Weber, one distinguishing mark of a political corporation is not only that it has a guaranteed system of norms but also that this system of norms is guaranteed within a territory. Political corporations are territorial corporations in the terms in which this property is specified in (DF38). For any political corporation it is thus always possible to tell for what geographical area its system of norms holds. What is the distinguishing power of this criterion? Weber does not observe that this property territory may be specified in a way which makes it trivial and useless as a criterion. If the geographical area is specified by disjunction ("or") then certainly the criterion loses all distinguishing power. If the geographical area is delimited as that area within which the authority corporation occurs then the same thing happens. A necessary restriction on this property is that such applications are prohibited—but Weber makes no restrictions. The property territory is introduced in order to qualify the property (c), a guaranteed system of norms. And the combination of (c) and (d) gives a property that Weber believes to be fundamental to political units, *the principle of territoriality*, as follows. If a unit, of whatever kind it is, is political, then it has a system of norms, which is guaranteed within exactly one nontrivially specified geographical area. However, this will not do what Weber wants it to do. If only there were enough knowledge of a family relation, the principle of territoriality could be applied to it. And in the case of certain economic corporations it is actually possible to apply it. Furthermore, for many political corporations it is not possible to state the borders exactly. The property specified in the principle is not a distinguishing mark in the way that Weber believes it is.

(e) *Use and threat of physical violence.* There are entities that have the properties $(a')$, that is orientation towards the influence of such a structure. According to (SDW) an action is political only if it is part of a type of social relation. This is by no means necessary as regards (SDW′). The term "politically oriented" is a term of the *first* violence. It is the fact that the system of norms is guaranteed by this means that is the final distinguishing mark of political corporations. Now, will this property do the trick, separating those authority corporations that are political from those that are not? What does this criterion of physical violence imply? The *criterion of physical violence* runs as follows: 'If a unit, of whatever kind it is, is political, then its system of norms is guaranteed by the leader(s) or the staff of the unit by the use and threat of physical violence, actually or hypothetically.' But why could not any family relation, economic corporation, organization like a workers' association or an employers' association satisfy this criterion? If the criterion of physical violence is to have any distinguishing power it has to be interpreted to mean that the leader(s) or the staff of the unit themselves guarantee the system of norms by physical violence. Alas, this would turn many political corporations like government bureaux and local administrative units into non-political units.

We thus conclude that (SDW) is not satisfactory. Two of the properties specified in (SDW) lack distinguishing power. They are in fact redundant. Weber does not achieve his end, namely to make a fundamental distinction between types of authority corporations. While the property (e) does weed out a few units, those that do not use physical violence or the threat of physical violence, it in no way accomplishes what it is meant to accomplish. The property (d) is redundant.

Let us now turn to the (SDW′) politically oriented. This concept presupposes (SDW) and it admits of application on a unit even though this unit does not have a complex structure of the properties (a)–(e). The concept requires only the property $(a')$, that is orientation towards the influence of such a structure. According to (SDW) an action is political only if it is part of a type of social relation. This by no means necessary as regards (SDW′). The term "politically oriented" is a term of the *first order*: an entity need be only a social action for the property politically oriented to be relevant. For this concept no such requirements as hold for political can be stated: an entity is politically oriented if and only if it has a certain type of orientation—no matter what other entities it is part of.

After specification of meaning we move to specification of reference. The word "political" refers to those social relations in which there is authority having a system of norms guaranteed within a territory by physical violence. The set of entities that have these properties will be denoted "(WS1)". What types of entities are there in (WS1)? In (WS1) there are at least the following types: (i) states; (ii) local administrative units like different types of communes; (iii) social relations like patriarchy, patrimony, decentralized authority based on legal privileges (*"ständische Herrschaft"*) and feudal relations; (iv) primary groups like villages, clans, tribes and families; not all may be political as the property (*e*) may be lacking; and (v) corporations: parties, interest organizations and factories. Though the definition of "political" satisfies criterion $C_1$ set out in Section 1, it is very questionable whether it satisfies $C_2$. The set of political units is very inclusive with regard to scientific usage. The failure of the properties (*d*) and (*e*) explains why the concept is too wide.

The word "politically oriented" refers to those actions that satisfy the definiens conditions in (SDW'). Let "(WS2)" denote the set of such actions. A central problem concerning the set (WS2) is its set theoretical relations to (WS1): can an entity E be both political and politically oriented? (SDW) and (SDW') explicitly forbid this: thus, the sentence "An entity E is political and politically oriented" is a contradiction. If this were not the case, there could be two referentially non-exclusive concepts and according to $C_4$ it would then remain to inquire for the exact relations between the entities that are political and politically oriented and those that are not.

In WS2 there are entities of all types in the social world with the exception of those entities that are in (WS1): actions that are not part of social relations like certain assassinations, one-sided social relations like deceit, conflict relations like war or competition, non-authority power relations like coercion, authority corporations that lack of property (*e*).

For (WS1) and (WS2) the following hold:

    (i)    $(WS1) \neq \phi; (WS2) \neq \phi$.

    (ii)   $(WS1) \cup (WS2) \neq V$ (V = the domain of discourse, namely the entities in the social world)

    (iii)  $(WS1) \cap (WS2) = \phi$.

## 2C. Weber's (ES)

The conceptual analysis of (SDW) and (SDW') has shown that these (SD)s are not quite satisfactory from the point of view of the criteria $C_1 - C_4$. The cause of the difficulties lies in (SDW). It can be argued that (SDW) does not satisfy $C_1$ (i) or $C_2$. Weber needs some criterion to separate authority corporations that are political from those that are not, but the properties introduced to this end will not do. As a consequence, the concept becomes unclear and too wide. Thus, we can say of Weber's definitions: (ESW) According to criteria $C_1 - C_4$ there is no satisfactory definition of "political" in Weber.

## 3 EASTON

### 3A. Easton's (SD)s: "authoritative", "society" and "allocation"

Easton has dealt with the problem of defining "political" in a number of works (Easton, 1953, pp.125-48; 1965a; 1965b, pp.17-33). Easton's explicit definitions can most readily be found in *A Framework for Political Analysis* (1965a), which contains a discussion of the central concepts of his theory of the persistence of political systems, among which the concept of political is a key concept. I have constructed the (LD)s and the (SD)s on the basis of this book, which will be referred to as *FPA*.

Three (LD)s may be distinguished.

(ED1) To Easton the sentence "x is a political system" is synonymous with the sentence "x is a set of interactions, through which values are authoritatively allocated for a society" (Easton, 1965a, p.57).

(ED2) To Easton the sentence "x is a parapolitical system" is synonymous with the sentence "x is a set of interactions, through which values are authoritatively allocated for a social system that is not a society" (Easton, 1965a, pp.50–6).

(ED3) To Easton the sentence "x is a political interaction" is synonymous with the sentence "x is an interaction predominantly oriented towards a political system" (Easton, 1965a, p.50).

It is possible to break down these (LD)s into (SD)s. An elimination of terms that occur both in the definiendum and the definiens in (ED1)–(ED3) gives three (SD)s:

| | | |
|---|---|---|
| (SDE) "x is political" | $=_{df}$ | "x has the properties $(a)$ allocation of values which is $(b)$ authoritative for $(c)$ a society" |
| (SDE′) "x is para-political" | $=_{df}$ | "x has the properties $(a)$ allocation of values which is $(b)$ authoritative for $(c')$ a social system that is not a society" |
| (SDE″) "x is political" | $=_{df}$ | "x has the property $(a')$ predominant orientation toward a political system" |

(SDE) and (SDE′) are independent of each other, whereas (SDE″) is dependent on (SDE). Consequently, (SDE) and (SDE′) are fundamental. (SDE″) will not be discussed at any length here, since the use of "political" in this sense makes the concept of political ambiguous. There are entities that have the property $(a')$ but not the properties $(a)$, $(b)$ and $(c)$ and consequently there are at least two concepts of political in *FPA*. The same term is used for the concept of a legitimate allocation for a society and the concept of an orientation towards such an allocation. The exact relation between these two concepts is not stated and not possible to state on the basis of *FPA*. The combination of (SDE) and SDE″) does not satisfy criterion $C_4$ set out in Section 1.

We now take up the specification of meaning. According to (SDE) and (SDE′) the following properties are key properties in the concepts of political and parapolitical.

*(a) Authoritative.* Easton gives the following definition sentence for "authoritative": 'An allocation is authoritative when the persons oriented to it consider that they are bound by it.' (Easton, 1965a, p.50.) In this the meaning of "authoritative" is identical with the meaning of "legitimate" in Weber's taxonomy (DF24). A consequence is that political systems are always legitimate systems and thus one of the basic sentences in Weber's theory of authority—(S2) in Section 2A—becomes trivial. However, Easton's us of "authoritative" is not consistent. Sometimes "authoritative" means the same as "legitimate" in Weber (Easton, 1953, pp.132–3; 1965a, p.50; 1965b, pp.29–30). Sometimes the word stands for all types of command-obedience relations (Easton, 1965b, pp.207–8), so that it means the same as "authority" in Weber. The concept of authoritative is fundamental in Easton, but it is not possible to decide unambiguously whether it is a question of the concept of legitimacy (DF24) or

of authority (DF19). Of course, only as used in connection with legitimacy does the word give any indication of the way in which political allocations differ from other types of allocation.

The status of the concept of authoritative in relation to the concept of political is not exactly stated. Easton writes as if the concept of authoritative allocation is a necessary as well as a sufficient component of the concept of political: 'But regardless of the particular grounds, it is the fact of considering the allocations as binding that distinguishes political from other types of allocations in the light of the conceptualization that I shall be using.' (Easton, 1965a, p.50.) If this were the case, (SDE) and (SDE$'$) would be reducible to one basic (SD):

$$(\text{SDE}^0) \quad \text{``x is political in y''} \qquad =_{df} \quad \text{``x allocates values authoritatively for a society y or a social system y that is not a society''}$$

(SDE) and (SDE$'$) and consequently (SDE$''$) would then be versions of this definition (SDE$^0$) by changes of the values of the variable "y". Of course, the term "political" in (SDE) would have to be replaced by something like "political 1".

Against (SDE$^0$) it can be argued that it is not clear why the fact that an allocation is legitimate should separate a political allocation from a non-political one such as certain economic allocations, or why the fact that an allocation is non-legitimate should by definition make it non-political. If the two criteria $C_2$ and $C_3$ are applied to (SDE$^0$), it can be maintained that (SDE$^0$) does not satisfy them. As Easton states, the property political according to (SDE$^0$) occurs in all types of social entities (Easton 1965a, pp.50–2). Then the problem remains: which of these are political and which are not? It is not theoretically advantageous to introduce a concept of political that is so wide as to include all legitimate allocations. The concept is also too narrow, since it is obviously relevant to use the word about other types of entities than legitimate allocations. For the property specified in (SDE$^0$), there already exists an expression "legitimate allocation". The problem is to specify when a legitimate allocation is political and when not political, and this problem is not one of definition if the criteria $C_2$ and $C_3$ are adhered to. Consequently, according to $C_2$ and $C_3$ the property ($a$) is neither a necessary nor a sufficient component of the concept of political.

It is perhaps Easton's intention that (SDE) and not (SDE$^0$) should be the complete definition of "political". The property society would then presumably make the concept more discriminative. However, this solution is inadequate because the concept of para-political then falls under the concept of non-political. It then remains to specify what it is about para-political entities that makes it necessary to speak about the property (para)political.

(b) *Society*. In both (SDE) and (SDE$'$) "society" is a key term. It is a necessary condition for the application of "political" about an allocation that it is authoritative for a society. And the term is used to distinguish between para-political and political entities. One explicit definition of the term in *FPA* is: 'To put this in a formal and more general sense, in the way I am using the term here society encompasses the social behavior of a group of biological persons, conceived in their totality.' (Easton, 1965a, p.38.) This is inadequate, since it is obvious that not every group of persons is a society. How is the distinction between (SDE) and (SDE$'$) to be upheld?

Another sentence—definition or empirical sentence—is the following: 'Society, as the most inclusive social system, is the only one that encompasses all the social interactions of the biological persons involved.' (Easton, 1965a, p.47.) This is also inadequate, because no distinct units can be specified by using this description. By the relation of inclusion between sets it is possible to put together social systems into increasingly wide social systems. But the basic question is, of course, when it is adequate to stop the inclusion. And that question is a question for Easton's definitions of "society". The term "society" must be defined with properties that specify when the inclusion has reached a level where it is adequate to stop. And these properties should unambiguously delimit a set of definite entities in the social world. This is never done by Easton. For example, what properties delimit the American society from the Mexican society or from any other society between the members of which there is a certain amount of interaction? It is to be hoped that Easton will not fall back on properties like political boundaries. How could the word "society" as Easton wants to use it be defined without the word "political" or some sort of principle of territoriality as implicit in such concepts as the nation or the state? Against the use of the word "society" as a definiens term of "political" in (SDE) and (SDE') it can be argued that on the one hand the term is not at all satisfactorily introduced. On the other hand, it is probable that the term "society" requires "political" and not the reverse, which would render all Easton's definitions circular. On the basis of $FPA$ it is not possible to state of what nature the property $(b)$ is.

*(c) Allocation.* A necessary condition for a unit being political or para-political according to (SDE) and (SDE') is that it has the property allocation. Apart from the fact that the meaning of "allocation" cannot be exactly stated on the basis of $FPA$, it is not intuitively clear why a concept of political should contain a concept of allocation. 'An allocation may deprive a person of a valued thing already possessed; it may obstruct the attainment of values that would otherwise have been obtained, or it may give some persons access to values and deny them to others.' (Easton, 1965a, p.50.) On the basis of this it is difficult to see in what way 'allocation' differs from 'social action' in Weber's taxonomy (DF5), and thus to state the nature of the property $(c)$. If a term "allocation" is to be introduced, it must be possible to separate those social actions that are allocations and those that are not. The sentence quoted does not permit this. Furthermore, the connection between "interaction" and "allocation" is not clear in (ED1) and (ED2). Is a political system those interactions that are also allocations with certain properties? Or is a political system those interactions that result in allocations with certain properties? On the basis of $FPA$ it is not possible to decide this problem. Obviously the definition is inadequate.

We now turn to specification of reference. The terms "political" and "para-political" in the fundamental (SD)s are *third order* terms. A social action is political/para-political if and only if it has the property part of a social relation that has the property legitimate that has the property for a society/for a social system that is not a society. The term "political" in (SDE'') is a *first order* term.

Let (ES1) be the set of entities that have the properties in (SDE), (ES2) the set that have the ones in (SDE') and (ES3) the set that have the ones in (SDE''). Then the following set theoretical relations hold:

(i)     $(ES1) \neq \phi; (ES2) \neq \phi; (ES3) \neq \phi$

(ii)    $(ES1) \cup (ES2) \cup (ES3) \neq V$

(iii)   $(ES1) \cap (ES2) = \phi; (ES1) \cap (ES23) \neq \phi; (ES2) \cap (ES3) \neq \phi$

## 3B. Easton's (ES)

The discussion of the definitions of Easton, $(SDE^0)$, $(SDE)$, $(SDE')$ and $(SDE'')$, can be summarized as follows: they do not satisfy the criteria $C_1-C_4$. As was stated above, they do not fulfil $C_2$ and $C_4$. While they satisfy $C_1$ (ii) and (iii), this is not so for $C_1$ (i), since 'society' is not introduced in an adequate way. The application of $C_4$ to Easton's definitions results in the following destructive dilemma:

$$(1) \quad \text{If p, then q, and if r, then s}$$

$$\frac{(2) \quad \text{Not q or not s}}{(3) \quad \text{Not p or not r}}$$

Where:   p  =  (SDE) is applied
   q  =  all allocations which are not authoritative for a society are not political
   r  =  $(SDE')$ and $(SDE'')$ are applied
   s  =  all allocations which are authoritative for a social system that is not a society or oriented towards a political system are (para)political

There is thus an inconsistency between the definitions and it can be stated generally about these definitions: (ESE) According to criteria $C_1-C_4$ there is no satisfactory definition or combination of definitions of "political" in Easton.

## 4  LASSWELL AND KAPLAN

There are in *Power and Society* (1950) a number of partial definitions of "political". Here, the analysis will start from the following (LD)s:

(LKD1) For Lasswell and Kaplan the sentence "x is a political interaction" is synonymous with the sentence "x is constituted by a pattern of influence and power" (Lasswell and Kaplan, 1950, p.53).

(LKD2) To Lasswell and Kaplan the sentence "x is a political process" is synonymous with the sentence "x is a shaping, distribution and exercise of power (in a wider sense, of all the deference values, or of influence in general)" (Lasswell and Kaplan, 1950, p.75).

Though these (LD)s are not equivalent in any way, they both relate "political" to "influence" and "power" in some way. At least two (SD)s can be constructed out of the (LD)s, one of which (according to Lasswell and Kaplan) is wide, and one of which is narrow.

(SDLK) "x is political"        $=_{df}$  "x has the property $(a)$ influence"

(SDLK') "x is political"        $=_{df}$  "x has the property $(a')$ power"

The problem concerning these (SD)s is to specify the meaning of the definiens terms "influence" and "power". Only if this is done can the above problems under (P2) be solved. Now, the terms "influence" and "power" are introduced in a definition structure starting from the most general social science concepts. This structure is quasi-systematic or quasi-deductive (Lasswell and Kaplan, 1950, p.4). One objective here will be to set out the general structure of this series of definitions in order to state where the word "political" becomes relevant. Another objective will be to point out certain deficiencies in this definition series, which makes it difficult to render it into a taxonomy. A third objective will be to analyse the concepts of power and influence and thus the concepts of political.

## 4A. The Lasswell-Kaplan taxonomy

Given an unspecified number of words borrowed from the non-social science and the standard logic, the taxonomy starts from the two minimum terms "act" and "actor". With the aid of these a possible world consisting of actors in types of environments who react in different ways with different relations between their acts is describable. By adding "symbol" and "statement" it is possible to turn the actors into egos and selves, thus to describe a world with persons having personalities, that is to say behaviour regularities and identifications. This world is very meagre, as it is not possible to state anything about the types of symbols and statements of the persons. By adding the words "value", "valuation", "sentiment" and "sentiment symbol", terms such as "demand", "expectation", "interest", "faith", "loyalty" and "perspective" are defined. There is now a world of an elementary social nature, containing properties of actors and of simple relations. However, this world is still meagre.

Possibilities for more interesting descriptions open up when the word "group" is introduced. The world now contains more complex units like organizations, associations, interest groups, cultures, institutions, societies, mores and social orders, as well as properties of such entities as opinion, consensus and morale. No doubt complexity has increased, but, from the fact that the word "political" is not yet relevant for predication on to the units of this world, it follows that it still has a low order of complexity.

To make "political" relevant the taxonomy needs new primitives "welfare value" and "deference value". By defining the words "value pattern", "value position" and "value potential", concepts for influence and class are introduced. The world is now increased as regards processes and structures. There are not only social processes and class structures, but also more refined terms for interactions like "policy" and "exercise of influence". According to (SDLK) "political" is now definable: the world needs no more properties for the property political to be analysable in terms of these. However, according to (SDLK'), there is more to political than mere influence. The introduction of the concept of power takes place through the definitions of "decision" and "decision-making process", which require of political more properties than those involved in (SDLK). The world of the Lasswell-Kaplan taxonomy (LKT) is then further augmented by the introduction of words for types of symbols, types of functions, etc. However, for the purpose of the analysis of the concept(s) of political in (LKT) it is adequate to stop here in the definition series.

Compared with Weber's, this taxonomy shows a number of deficiencies. If the terms are arranged deductively on the basis of those primitives explicitly mentioned, it is easy to show that the number of primitives is too small and that in fact certain definitions require quite a few new minimum terms. As regards parsimony, Weber's taxonomy is to be preferred to that offered by Lasswell and Kaplan. Furthermore, certain definitions are inadequate since they are either too wide or too narrow. An example of this will be given below in the analyses of the concepts of influence and power.

## 4B. Lasswell and Kaplan's (SD)s: "influence" and "power"

We begin with the specification of meaning. Let us recalled Lasswell and Kaplan's (SD)s:

| | | |
|---|---|---|
| (SDLK) "x is political" | $=_{df}$ | "x has the property $(a)$ influence" |
| (SDLK$'$) "x is political" | $=_{df}$ | "x has the property $(a')$ power" |

Clearly, these make the properties influence and power key properties of the concepts of political. Thus, the fertility and clarity of the concepts of political in *Power and Society* depend on the nature of these properties. To deal with this problem presupposes in turn that the meaning and reference of "influence" and "power" are known. This problem will be treated below, since it is by no means clear what properties these words stand for in the Lasswell and Kaplan taxonomy.

*(a) "influence" (SDLK)*. The term "influence" occurs explicitly with two meanings in LKT, on the one hand as a word for social actions that are part of social relations, and on the other hand as a word for a type of causal relation.

| | | | |
|---|---|---|---|
| (DI) | "x is influence" | $=_{df}$ | "x is a value position and value potential" (Lasswell and Kaplan, 1950, p. 60) |

The definition of "value position" is non-controversial, since it is based on two primitives "value" and "pattern". The definition of "value potential" is as follows: 'DF. The *value potential* is the value position likely to be occupied as the outcome of conflict.' (Lasswell and Kaplan, 1950, p.58.) This exemplifies the deficiencies mentioned above. The taxonomy assumes that there are other relations between acts than those of conflict but then it must be unsatisfactory to restrict the definition of "future value position" to "conflict". Such positions may be the result of non-conflict relations.

This concept of influence is a very general one, since for each actor there is at least one position as regards several values. More specific is the other concept of influence:

(DI$'$) 'DF. The *exercise of influence* (influence process) consists in affecting policies of others than the self.' (Lasswell and Kaplan, 1950, p.71.)

One key term in (DI$'$) is "affecting". One possible interpretation of (DI$'$) is that "influence" is a term for all types of causal relations in which one actor's policy or several actors' policies are affected by another actor. However, in the commentary to (DI$'$) there is a precization and (DI$'$) can be replaced as follows:

| | | | |
|---|---|---|---|
| (DI$''$) | "x exercises influence over y with regard to z" | $=_{df}$ | "x's possession of influence affects the policy(ies) z of y" |

240

Now "influence" stands for those causal relations where an actor's policy(ies) are affected by the possession of influence (according to (DI)) of another actor. However, not even this interpretation is adhered to. Out of the commentary a further precization can be constructed:

(DI″)  "x exercises influence over y  $=_{df}$  "x's possession of influence
with regard to z"  affects the policy(ies) z of y
on the basis of anticipated
reactions of y"

That is, "influence" is a concept for those causal relations where y's policy(ies) are affected by y's anticipations concerning the behaviour of the actor who possesses influence. In (DI‴) the concept of influence is a specific concept for a type of causal relation, whereas in (DI) it is a general concept for a social action that is part of a social relation. These concepts are not hierarchically related in such a way that one falls under the other. It is not conducive to conceptual clarity when "influence" stands for different types of properties, just as the distinction between "exercise of influence" and "influence" is not maintained. When "political" is defined by "influence" the result is, of course, at least two concepts of political. When is it a question of "political" as defined by (DI) and "political" as defined by (DI′) or (DI″) or (DI‴)? One specific concept of political is not specified in (SDLK). It would be possible here to continue with the analysis and maintain that these definitions have deficiencies, that alternative concept formations are more fruitful and in accordance with linguistic usage. However, it will suffice to have shown that (SDLK) does not satisfy the criterion $C_1$. On the basis of the taxonomy it is not possible to state the nature of the property (a) unambiguously.

(b) "Power" (SDLK′). The exact definition of "power" reads as follows: 'DF. Power is participation in the making of decisions: G has power over H with respect to the values K if G participates in the making of decisions affecting the K-policies of H.' (Lasswell and Kaplan, 1950, p.75.) Out of this quotation a definition can be constructed, and this will be analysed:

(DP)  "x has power over y with  $=_{df}$  "x participates in a decision-
regard to z"  making process, which affects
the policy(ies) z of y"

(DP) is adequate only if the meaning of the key terms in the definiens either is intersubjectively given in linguistic usage or can be stated in the taxonomy through other definitions. Key terms are "decision" and "policy". Given a common-sense interpretation of the definiendum and the definiens in (DP) it can be shown that it is deficient. Suppose that A commands B to do C and B refuses to obey, which causes A to do C himself voluntarily. Take A as a value of "y", B as a value of "x" and C of "z". Then the definiendum is false, whereas the definiens is true—given the same substitution for the variables. Consequently, the definiens is not an adequate definition of the definiendum.

Let us consider the definition of "decision". 'DF. A decision is a policy involving severe sanctions (deprivations).' (Lasswell and Kaplan, 1950, p.74.) This definition exemplifies a deficiency in the taxonomy pointed out above. The definition of "sanction" is not made in terms of the primitives or the defined terms. (DP) can now be replaced by:

| (DP') | "x has power over y with regard to z" | $=_{df}$ | "x participates in the making of a policy involving severe sanctions, which affects the policy(ies) z of y" |
|---|---|---|---|

One of the key terms of "power" has now been reduced to the other key term. In order to know what is meant by "political" one must know the meaning of "power", which presupposes that also the meaning of "policy" is clear. Let us therefore look at "policy". 'DF. *Policy* is a projected program of goal values and practices: the *policy process* is the formulation, promulgation, and application of identifications, demands, and expectations concerning the future interpersonal relations of the self.' (Lasswell and Kaplan, 1950, p.71.) This explicit definition is followed by the following commentary: 'Projected action may be either private or social: it may concern either the actor alone or his relations with other persons. A course of action in relation to others we call a "policy" of the actor. The field of policy is constituted by interpersonal relations.' (Lasswell and Kaplan, 1950, p.71.) Taken together, these two quotations exemplify the inadequacy of the Lasswell and Kaplan taxonomy. In Weber's taxonomy, by contrast, the rules that govern the use of key terms are unambiguous and the meanings of "policy" can be rendered in terms of the words in the taxonomy. Here, "policy" first means orientation, then it means social relation or at least it stands for some type of interpersonal relation. Next, "policy" means social action, and then it means social relation. Of course, this makes it impossible to state exactly what is the meaning of "policy" and consequently to arrive at the meaning of "political" in (SDLK).

However, as the meaning of "policy" I will choose one of the proposed definiens terms, viz. "social action", in order to show other deficiencies of (DP). As "social action" is the basic term it cannot be maintained that it is too narrow.

| (DP'') | "x has power over y with regard to z" | $=_{df}$ | "x participates in a social action involving severe sanctions, which affects the social action(s) z of y" |
|---|---|---|---|

It is now clear that the explicit definition of "power" in (DP) takes the word as referring to a type of casual relation between social actions involving severe sanctions and social actions. Given a wide meaning of "casual relation" the reference of "power" is great, but the word is not ambiguous. Correspondingly the field of political is great.

The analysis of (SDLK) and (SDLK') has given the result that neither of them satisfies $C_1$ since both key terms are ambiguous. Instead of one concept of political there are at least three: at least two in terms of "influence" (DI) and (DI''') plus one in terms of "power" (DP). Before these are analysed in relation to the criteria, a few comments will be made on a sentence in Lasswell and Kaplan about the relation between the concepts of influence and power. Now it is obvious that only the relation between exercise of influence in the sense (DI''') and power in the sense of (DP) is a problem. Lasswell and Kaplan maintain that: 'Power is a special case of the exercise of influence: it is the process of affecting policies of others with the help of (actual or threatened) severe deprivations for nonconformity with the policies intended.' (Lasswell and Kaplan, 1950, p.76.)

This main sentence about the relation between the concepts can be formulated as follows: (S1) Every relation of power is a relation of influence, but not every relation of influence is a relation of power. (S1) states that the concept of power implies the concept of influence but not the other way around. Now, suppose that A affects a social action of B by a decision, for example by assassination of a friend of B. Then there is a relation of power according to (DP), but there is not a relation of influence according to (DI‴). The relation between the concepts of influence and power is not thus stated exactly by Lasswell and Kaplan.

Let us now move on to specification of reference. The analysis of *Power and Society* resulted in three definitions of "political":

(D1)  "x is political" $=_{df}$ "x is a social action that is part of a social relation"

(D2)  "x is political" $=_{df}$ "x is a causal relation in which an actor's possession of influence affects a (several) social action(s) of another actor on the basis of antici-pated reactions"

(D3)  "x is political" $=_{df}$ "x is a causal relation, in which an actor participates in a social action involving severe sanctions which affects an (several) action(s) of another actor"

"Political" in (D1) refers to social actions of a certain type and is thus a *first order* term. In (D2) and (D3) the term refers to causal relations of certain types. In (D2) it is a matter of a *third order* term, whereas the term in (D3) is a *second order* term.

To each of these definitions there corresponds a set of entities. Let "(LKS1)" stand for the set that has the properties in (D1), "(LKS2)" those in (D2) and "(LKS3)" those in (D3). Then the following set-theoretical relations hold:

(i)    $(LKS1) \neq \phi; (LKS2) \neq \phi; (LKS3) \neq \phi$

(ii)   $(LKS1) \cup (LKS2) \cup (LKS) \neq V$

(iii)  $(LKS1) \cap (LKS2) \neq \phi \ (LKS1) \cap (LKS3) \neq \phi; (LKS2) \cap (LKS3) \neq \phi$

## 4C.  Lasswell and Kaplan's (ES)

The main objection against the concept formation in *Power and Society* as regards "political"—(SDLK) and (SDLK′)—is that it does not satisfy $C_1$ (i). Of the three definitions (D1)–(D3), which is *the* definition of "political"? Against each of the definitions objections can be raised. Not one of them satisfies $C_2$, and probably none satisfies $C_3$. Furthermore, the definitions do not satisfy $C_4$ (as stated in (iii)).

Consequently, it can be stated: (ESLK) According to $C_1$–$C_4$ there is no satisfactory definition or combination of definitions of "political" in *Power and Society*.

## 5  CONCLUSION

A comparison between the concept formations of Weber, Easton and Lasswell and Kaplan concerning the concept of political confirms the assumption that there is little agreement on the use of the key term of political science.

*(a) Meaning.* There are few common properties in the concepts:

| Weber | Easton | Lasswell and Kaplan |
|---|---|---|
| authority | allocation | social action that is part of a social relation (D1) |
| guaranteed system of norms | legitimate | types of causal relations that satisfy (D2) and (D3) |
| territory | society | |
| physical violence | | |

The discrepancy between Weber and Easton is smaller than that between Weber and Lasswell and Kaplan on the one hand and that between Easton and Lasswell and Kaplan on the other. But in any case the differences are profound. Weber approaches the problem by a definition of a word for a complex structure, which he supplements by a word for an orientation towards such a structure. Easton starts with social relations and proceeds to the property legitimate for a society in the attempt to

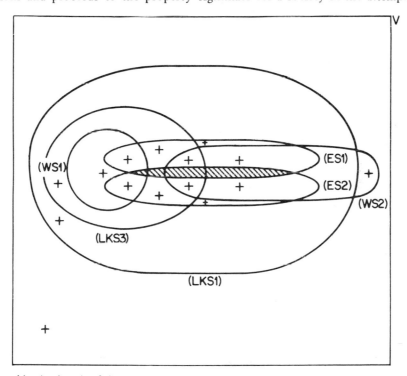

V = the domain of discourse, i. e. social actions.
+ = there is at least one entity in this set.
ℵ = empty.

Figure 12.2

discriminate within the set of basic units. Weber requires neither legitimacy nor such a social entity as society. On the other hand Easton requires neither authority nor physical violence. Lasswell's and Kaplan's concepts contain on the one hand properties for general types of social entities, (D1), and on the other hand properties for certain types of causal relations in the social world, (D2) and (D3).

*(b) Reference.* The set-theoretical relations between the sets distinguished are schematically represented in Figure 12.2.

*(c) Explication.* Of the definitions investigated in this chapter none satisfies the criteria of adequacy for turning the definition into an explication. Weber is unclear about the nature of territory, and the property physical violence will not serve the end Weber thinks it is a means to. Easton uses the word "authoritative" ambiguously, defines "society" inadequately and ends up in confusion about the relations between his concepts. Lasswell and Kaplan give several definitions of the same word and do not indicate which is *the* definition.

There are some words that may be designed as the fundamental terms of political science, like "political system", "state", "society", "nation", "authority", "power", "conflict" and "cooperation". To introduce precise, clear and fruitful definitions of these words is the basic task of political theory as I conceive it. Unquestionably, that part of political science has a tremendous task to fulfil.

# 13
# Some Conceptual Problems in Political Theory

JON ELSTER

## 1 INTRODUCTION

Sections 2–4 below relate directly to the other papers. Instead of commenting upon each paper individually I have preferred the method of associating rather freely on the cues provided. Agreement or polemics wil be implicit rather than explicit. The last two sections have a more tenuous link with the other papers, though I hope that the general interrelatedness of all problems of political theory will make for some relevance. More than the other sections they reflect my academic background, which is in philosophy and not in political science. They should be seen as an attempt to demonstrate the relevance of two rather abstract philosophical systems—the Hegelian theory of self-consciousness and the recent developments in modal logic—for our understanding of political phenomena.

## 2 CONCEPTS OF 'POLITICS'

Nothing, I suspect, is really a waste of time, but discussing 'What is Politics?' might seem a good approximation. Papers dealing with this question tend to have constructive parts that are incomprehensible, trivial or arbitrary, with destructive parts that may be valuable contributions to theory by throwing up counter-examples to previously proposed definitions. This process of cumulative negation is essential in science, but my contribution will be somewhat half-hearted as I shall content myself with some critical remarks and cautiously abstain from the dangers of positive thinking. I shall discuss the subject matter of political theory from three points of view: structural differentiation, causal autonomy, and substantive versus formal defitions.

### 2A. Structural differentiation

From Marx to Parsons, the sub-system approach to society has pervaded most of social science. The consensus has not, however, extended to the nature of the sub-systems. The main reason may be that different societies require different approaches, so that the 'general theory' is impossible rather than just difficult to construct. In some societies the distinction between (say) the economic and the political sub-systems is a distinction between sets of *persons,* in other societies a distinction between sets of activities or *roles* of persons, in a third category of societies a distinction between *aspects* of activities of persons. Societies in the first category include nineteenth-century England and classical Greece. The English workers, of course, neither voted nor governed; the capitalists did vote, but preferred to leave the actual government to the landed aristocracy. Marx (1956b, p.342) saw this as a diabolically clever move on the part of the capitalist class: Whig rule in England (as well, he thought, as Bonapartism in France and—according to recent Marxists—Fascism and Nazism) can be explained on the postulate that the capitalists prefer a mildly anti-capitalist government to one that would visibly be the direct extension of their economic exploitation. Cole (1955, pp.65, 84) suggests, less conspiratorially and more plausibly, that the entrepreneurs were happy to concentrate upon business as long as the government gave a reasonable weight to their interests. Thus political and economic decisions were placed in the hands of two different sets of people, which is not, of course, to say that the actual or anticipated decisions of the one did not influence the decisions of the other. The point is that for the government the profit of the capitalist class was a constraint rather than the maximand. In classical Greece neither slaves nor merchants were citizens, so that here again the distinction between the economic and the political sub-systems could be made largely in terms of persons (Finley, 1970).

In societies of the second category all or most persons participate in both economic and political activities. Institutions and sub-systems are then defined as sets and sets of sets of interrelated activities or roles. This conceptualization is the obvious one in a society where workers do vote and occasionally govern, where members of parliament do engage actively in the pursuit of profits. (An intermediate category between the first and the second is made up of societies that are stratified according to age: each individual at a given point of time engages in one kind of activity only, but over the whole of his life he successively takes on and sheds all possible role masks.) The important feature common to both this second concept of sub-system and the first is that they both permit causal relationships between various sub-systems. This, on the other hand, is not the case for societies of the third category, where it is at most possible to distinguish between the economic and political *aspects* of an action. The highly integrated societies described by social anthropologists often have this multifunctional character, as do also the bureaucratic societies of antiquity and today. Tax collection in the ancient empires was simultaneously a means of revenue and a means of control.

This concept of an aspect, however, is problematic, for why bother about aspects at all? Why not take the indivisible action as the unit of social life? One reason seems to have been the wish for a universal theory that would permit the same distinctions to be made in all societies. If no manifest differentiations are universally found, one has to accept latent differentiation (i.e. 'aspects') as a poor second best. (An almost caricatural example of this approach is Almond and Powell, 1966.) This tautological procedure is harmless if it is only a question of pigeon-holing, but it is confused and confusing if used as a foundation for *causal* analysis. An action can be the cause of another action, a set of actions the cause of another set of actions. An aspect of an action cannot be the cause of anything at all. This difficulty is especially acute in Marxism, where the distinction between base and superstructure is not simply a matter of taxonomy (as in the innumerable Parsonian schemes), but a basic tool for dynamic analysis. If kinship relationships are simultaneously part of the base in their economic aspect and of the superstructure in their ideological aspect (as stated in Suret-Canale, 1967), does one then have to say that the first aspect causally determines the second? This, it seems to me, is Ptolemeic Marxism. Lukács (1923, pp.229ff.) leant over backwards in order to avoid such double-talk and adopted instead the heroic solution of saying that historical materialism just does not apply to pre-capitalist societies. In this he is followed by Finley (1973a, p.50), who refers curiously to Lukács as a 'most orthodox Marxist'. It seems to me, however, that a less radical way out can be found. If the *two* distinctions that are basic to Marxism—between forces of production and relations of production, between base and superstructure—are made to collapse into *one* general distinction between man-nature relationships and man-man relationships (A. Cohen, 1969, p.219), the term 'materialism' may be understood in the sense of a causal primacy of the first over the second, regardless of the internal distinctions that may be made—or may not be made—within the second.

## 2B. Causal autonomy

Given a society of the first or second category, with a minimum of manifest structural differentiation so as to permit causal interaction between the economic and the political sub-system, how does this interaction affect the possibility of an autonomous political science? Or in Marxist terms: can there be a science of the superstructure? In the background of this question there lurks a totally inappropriate analogy with epiphenomenalism and the mind—body problem, compounded by the equally confused architectural metaphor, which in its turn has a curious inverse relationship to the *moral* connotations of 'high' and 'low'. These analogies are misleading because there is, of course, a mutual causal influence. The most formalized concept of this two-way causality is found in input—output economics, which is nothing but a more elaborate version of the Marxian reproduction schemes. Marx himself hinted at the extension of the concept of reproduction to the macro-sociological level (Marx, 1956e, Part 1, pp.363–4), an idea that has recently been worked out in great detail by Bourdieu and Passeron (1970). In this perspective it is merely a platitude to point out that the political sub-system receives inputs from the economic one while providing inputs to that sub-system at the same time. Any partial equilibrium analysis (as in the Easton/Deutsch approach) will focus upon the inputs and outputs of one part of the circular chain, leaving the details of the feedback loop to other disciplines. This focus is just a matter of analytical convenience and does not permit us to state that the part studied is more 'fundamental' than the other parts. In an economic context capital goods produce consumption goods that produce workers that produce capital goods; in a more general context priests produce religion that produces the workers that produce the surplus that produces the priests. Once we agree to play these nursery games, nothing is more or less 'important' than anything else (except possibly in the sense of Haavelmo, 1944, p.24). 'Erst kommt das Fressen, dann kommt die Moral'—it just ain't true.

The asymmetry—because I believe there is one—between economic and political sub-systems must be sought in the study of change, which I conceive of as the study of unintended consequences of human actions. Unintended consequences—*counterfinality* in Sartre's terminology—are ubiquitous, but their importance and permanence are not the same in all sub-systems. The causal primacy of the economic over the political sub-system is due, in my opinion, to the higher degree of *irreversibility* of the unintended consequences produced in the economic sphere. Irreversible destruction or entropy production (as found in erosion, pollution, species extinction) and irreversible accumulation (of scientific and technological knowledge) are found almost exclusively within the economic sphere. Thus one can talk about economic or scientific development, but hardly about political development, except in a secondary sense. Once quantum mechanics has been invented, it is irrational not to use it, but there is nothing irrational about not using Western democracy, statements to the contrary notwithstanding. (There *is* a place for the irreversibility concept in political theory, as shown in Section 6 below, but in a much weaker sense.) Not all economic counterfinality is irreversible, as may be seen by comparing the Marxian and the Keynesian theories of the contradictions of capitalism. Marx linked his theory of the falling rate of profit to the irreversible process of technical change, whereas Keynes stressed the possibility of the demand crises, which can indeed be reversed by suitable political action (Elster, 1974).

## 2C. Generalized concepts of politics

Some time ago Karl Polanyi (1957) initiated a methodological discussion of the proper subject matter of economic history and economic anthropology. He argued for a distinction between two concepts of 'economic': a formal concept, stressing maximization, economizing, choice, scarcity and ends–means relationships, and a substantive concept, stressing interaction with nature, production and satisfaction of material wants. All societies, he stated, have a substantively economic sub-system, but not all proceed in a formally economic manner. One of his pupils (Dalton, 1961) later pointed out that the formal concept also applies to substantively non-economic domains, e.g. war and voting. Thus neither of the two concepts includes the others, each applying to some situations where the other is inapplicable. The first part of this theory has been much criticized, but I believe that the criticism loses its force if the theory is reformulated in terms of the predominance of lexicographic preference structures in pre-capitalist societies. As these structures—corresponding to hierarchical wants and qualitative levels—cannot be represented by a numerical utility function (Debreu, 1954), economies where they predominate cannot be analysed in terms of utility maximization (Georgescu-Roegen, 1954), not even in the 'as if' sense. The other part of the theory is less controversial: later developments have amply confirmed the extremely general applicability of the formal concept of 'economic' action. The relevant point is of course the revolution produced in political theory by the introduction of the formal techniques of economics. Is it possible to generate a counter-revolution by introducing a generalized concept of politics that might regain the ground lost? For reasons given below, I do not think it is. Still it seems worth while to look at some trends towards a partial generalization. I shall discuss first the concepts of *exit* and *voice* introduced by Hirschman (1970) and then proceed to the distinction made by Sartre (1960) between the *series* and the *group*. Both of these distinctions seem to me to be generalizations of different aspects of the traditional distinction between economics and politics; at the same time they both cut across this substantive dichotomy.

Hirschman's theory gives only a very partial generalization, as it is intended as a conceptualization of 'responses to decline', a very small subset of social actions.

Within the economic sub-system the typical response is *exit*: the anonymous reaction of the consumer who responds to a decline in quality by switching quietly to another brand. In the political sub-system the actor typically responds by *voice*: an articulated protest intended to bring about an improvement in the quality of an institution to which he is tied by loyalty. The originality of Hirschman's approach is to abstract these two patterns of behaviour from their original settings, to see them as alternative or complementary reactions that may arise in *any* context. This restructuring makes it possible to conceptualize institutions that are economic at one end and political at the other; where members react primarily by exit while leaders are aroused primarily by voice or vice versa. Numerous examples are given by Hirschman and in a recent book by Kenneth Boulding (1973) very similar in spirit.

The basic recipe of Hirschman's approach is the following: take a problem, look at the traditional economic and political solutions, try the economic solution in the political context and vice versa, see what happens. A good catalyst is needed, e.g. a subtle and forceful mind like Hirschman's. Applying the same recipe to the problems of counter-finality and suboptimality, it is well known that the economic and political solutions typically are quite different. The economic reaction is the method of individual adjustment: if individual price anticipations are mutually incompatible and lead to a cobweb cycle, learning will take the form of a lag effect in the individual anticipations, which may or may not solve the problem by damping the cycle (Allen, 1966, p.197). The political reaction on the other hand is one of joint adjustment or coalition-forming. (Sartre uses the terms *series* and *group* to describe the two patterns of behaviour; in medieval logic a similar distinction was made between the distributive and the collective senses of plural nouns.) Following the recipe we than get the economic theory of democracy and the theory of economic collusions. Economics in this generalized sense deals with sets of maximizing individuals, politics with maximizing sets of individuals. Or again: politics is the study of ways of transcending the Prisoner's Dilemma. It is worth noting that economics in this generalized sense would include much of biology—another science that has been revolutionized in recent years by the introduction of economic concepts (Levins, 1968). On the other hand biology and politics are mutualy exclusive, at least if we side with the majority of biologists who think that natural selection works only on individuals and never on groups (Williams, 1966). In animal societies there is no way out of the Prisoner's Dilemma. It is not at all surprising that economics in this generalized sense should intrude upon the traditional fields of political and biological theory. Formal economics is a mathematical structure that finds application in all cases where the concept of a maximizing individual can be defined. (It should be stressed, however, that there is no tendency in evolution to go beyond local maxima, in contradistinction to the specifically human capacity for searching out global maxima.) Formal politics require the added notion of group maximization and will thus have a smaller extension, which excludes the possibility of a *wholly* successful counter-revolution of political science.

## 3 POWER

The notion of power would seem to be the most important single idea in political theory, comparable perhaps to utility in economics. The theory of power is in a poorly developed state, as was the theory of utility fifty years ago. At that time no one was very clear about the ties between the (absolute) notion of utility and the (relational) notion of preferences, as today there is no consensus on which comes first, the absolute notion of power *tout court* or the relational notion of power *over someone* (or something). The analogy stops here, if it ever arrived there. There are no substantial similarities or structural analogies between power and utility, no reason to think that we shall witness a clarification of the theory of power comparable to the advances in our understanding of utility.

Let me state what I see as the main questions that must be answered by a theory of power. In addition to the problem of the absolute versus the relational concepts of power, the following difficulties must be faced. (i) The relation between power and causality: the intentional aspect of power must not be overlooked. (ii) The 'chameleon' problem and the appeal to counterfactuals: we must avoid a theory that would make a person powerful just because he always sides with the majority, which means that we must admit statements about what would have happened if he had wanted differently. (iii) Closely related to this is the 'Law of anticipated reactions' (Friedrich, 1950): how to distinguish between a person who never needs to use his power because he is supremely powerful and a person who never uses his power because he has none? (iv) This problem leads to a question put by March (1966): should the use of power be compared to consumption (use leading to depletion) or to investment (use leading to increase)? (v) How can we relate the notion of an individual's power to the notion of the power of society as a whole? Complete and interrelated answers to all these questions would constitute a full theory of power, which I am not prepared to put forward. I shall concentrate mainly upon the problem of absolute versus relational power, and then add brief remarks on some of the five questions above.

The most elaborate theory of power given up to the present is probably the one proposed by Coleman (1973). While not wholly general in application, the precision and transparency of its structure make it very suitable for the purposes of local analysis. The basic concepts of the theory are those of actors and events, which are linked in two different ways: actors control events and have interests in events. Given the interest and control matrices, Coleman is able to define the power of one actor over another, the all-round power of an actor in the system and the total power of the system. Thus the relational notion of *power over something* is taken as basic, the relational notion of *power over someone* and the absolute notion of *all-round power* are derived notions. Important features of Coleman's notion of *power over someone* are the following: the power of A over B is mediated by A's control over the events that interest B; the power of A over B admits of degrees; a positive amount of power of A over B is compatible with a positive amount of power of B over A. This is all in sharp contradistinction to the Marxist theory of power as a binary all-or-nothing phenomenon. A variation on the Marxist theme is the theory sketched by Kemeny *et al.* (1966, pp.384ff.), who start from an all-or-nothing notion of dominance (or power over someone) and then go on to define a notion of all-round power, without making any appeal at all to power over something. A fourth theory is proposed by Parsons (1963b), who—as far as I understand what he is doing—starts from the notion of all-round power and then goes on to define the relational notion of 'more power than'. Thus we must distinguish three 'relational notions of power':

A has some power over B          (1)

A has power over B                                             (2)
A has more power than B                                        (3)

The logical relationships between these three relational notions is the main subject of this section. A first approach is through the standard questions of relational logic, looking for reflexivity, symmetry, transitivity and completeness. Coleman's approach is the only one where the relational notion of power, as symbolized in (1) above, is not anti-reflexive. The amount of power of A over himself is measured by the amount of control he has over the events that interest him; this power (or *autonomy*) may be zero, but may also be a positive amount. The relational notion (1) is also the only one that is not anti-symmetric: A and B may both have some power over each other, though this is not necessarily the case, so that (1) is not symmetric. The graph-theoretic representation of the power structure given by Coleman (1973, p.76) shows immediately that notion (1) is neither transitive nor complete. At the other end of the spectrum is the relational notion (3), which is anti-reflexive, anti-symmetric, transitive and complete—properties that follow immediately from the basic structure of the real number system.

The most interesting notion is probably (2), which we shall show to be intransitive and incomplete (as well as being anti-reflexive and anti-symmetric). In order to demonstrate these properties it is useful to introduce some further notions:

A exploits B                                                   (4)
A is richer than B                                             (5)

I believe that there is a very close analogy indeed between notions (2) and (4) as well as between (3) and (5), so that in the discussion below I shall give examples indifferently from the economic and the political domains. This analogy also implies that the Marxian theory of classes, based upon (4), is much closer to the theory of Dahrendorf (1959), based upon (2), than to the theory of C. Wright Mills (1963), based upon (5). It is even farther from the theory of Parsons, based upon notion (3). The logical reasons underlying the analogy will be given below. As to the incompleteness of (2) and (4), Cole (1955, p.91) acutely remarks that the 'middle classes' of classical capitalism were not in the middle of anything. Ossowski (1963, pp.79ff.) makes the same point when he refers to a 'trichotomous scheme without an intermediate class'. The *petite bourgeoisie*, on the other hand, does stand between the workers and the financial capitalists (Marx, 1956a, pp.38ff.), so that here the exploitation relationship is complete. Slave societies have usually had two lower classes—slaves and non-slaveholding free—neither of which has been 'over' the other in an economic or political sense. These three examples of trichotomous class structures show that all the logical possibilities are in fact realized: two upper classes and one lower class; an upper, a middle and a lower class; one upper class and two lower classes. As only the second structure is complete, this property cannot be a general feature of the relationships (2) and (4).

Intransitivity may seem more paradoxical: is not a class exploited by the class that exploits its exploiters? Well, it is and it isn't. It is certain, for a beginning, that the existence of B between A and C makes for a different relationship between A and C compared with what it would have been had B not existed. In public administration nepotism and corruption may be avoided or reduced by imposing a rule that forbids orders being given two steps below in the hierarchy. In the history of jurisprudence one often finds curious facts, such as a slaveowner not having the same relation to his slave as to the slave of his slave (Pauly-Wissowa, 1958), or a landlord the same relationship to his tenant as to the tenant of his tenant (North and Thomas, 1973, p.63). It is further clear that indirect exploitation of the workers by capital through the intermediary of the small masters is a different relationship altogether from the direct exploitation of workers by industrial capitalists; the 'sweating system' and the labour aristocracy may also be cited in this connection. A last example is the difference between direct investment and portfolio investment in foreign countries, the first being a one-step and the second a two-step relation. The general ideal is that the exploitation and power relationships (2) and (4) have the logical structure of fatherhood and not of ancesterhood, while the notions (3) and (5) have the structure of neither, but rather of biggerness and fasterness. A grandfather may have a 'paternalistic' attitude towards his grandchild, but he *is* not the father of his grandson; a slave-owner certainly has a master-like relationship to a *vicarius*, but he *was* the master only of his *ordinarius*. Given a concept with the logical structure of fatherhood, it is always possible, as shown by Frege, to construct a corresponding concept of ancesterhood, but the relevance of power ancestry is not always obvious.

As a first approximation to the second approach we may say that the notions (2) and (4) express internal relations, while (3) and (5) correspond to external relations. These are famous but nebulous concepts; no consensus seems to exist upon their definition or even upon their usefulness. Following recent work on Leibniz's theory of relations (Hintikka, 1972; Ishiguro, 1972) I shall propose the following definition: 'Rab' *expresses an external relation if it can be deduced from some (not necessarily unique) conjunction of two non-relational statements* 'Fa' *and* 'Gb'. Notion (3) above can be deduced from the conjunction of (6) and (7):

A has 3 units of power (6)
B has 2 units of power (7)

It would therefore seem that (3) does indeed express an external relation between the two actors. A similar argument can be given for (5). This analysis, however, neglects the fact that (6) is non-relational only in its grammatical surface structure, while having a relational deep structure. This is so because the very notion of having power implicitly refers to other people (of whom B is one). A logical analysis of (6) would unmask a hidden reference, by means of quantifiers and bound variables, to the whole social system as the *range* of these variables. The precise analysis would depend upon the theory of power chosen, but following Hintikka (1972) the following three-step analysis may be taken as a simplified paradigm. Even if 'Rab' can be deduced from 'Fa & Gb', 'Fa'—and similarly for 'Gb'—in its turn reduces to '$(x)(R'ax)$', where $R'$ is not an external relation. I propose to call the theories that neglect the last step *generalized fetichist theories*. Marx's theory of commodity fetichism is a direct prolongation of Leibniz's theory of hidden relations: the property of being a commodity appears to be a non-relational predicate, but a logico-political analysis brings out the hidden reference to a society of commodity producers (Marx, 1956d, p.86). In this sense Parsons can be said to have a fetichist theory of power. It should be clear that (5) above is an apparently external relation, which presupposes, however, an internal relation like (4) with bound variables instead of one of the individual constants. To bring out the generality of this approach, we may finally look at the following statements:

B ranks A higher than himself                                                          (8)
A has more prestige than B                                                             (9)

The relational statement (9) is similar in logical structure to (5) and (3); it must be analysed in terms of the relation (8), again with bound variables replacing one of the individual constants (see Fararo, 1973, p.364). In the analysis of social structure interaction is basic, comparison is secondary. Comparative statements, in terms of predicates that do not have a hidden relational structure, are trivial from the point of view of social science, with some exceptions like age differentials and socially relevant biological properties. It can also be shown that social *contradictions* arise only in the case of predicates with hidden relational structure (Hintikka, 1972; Elster, 1974).

A third approach to the problem at hand is more substantial: when should we take the notion (1) as basic, and when is (2) preferable? It is obvious that (2) is just a special case of (1), so that societies where power is an all-or-nothing phenomenon can formally be analysed in terms of one actor having total control over all the events that interest another. This, however, seems to me to be an artificial procedure. In a slave society the total power of the slaveowner over the slave is the basic fact, not the control over events or resources. To put the matter differently: in modern societies it may sometimes be the case that one person (e.g. a local employer) has a *de facto* monopoly over all the resources that are of importance to another, even if the latter is formally free to starve to death rather than comply with the wishes of the former. This is indeed a case of total power, which is, however, derived rather than basic. Both personal power and mediate power may be cases of total power, but a universal adoption of Coleman's model would not permit the differentiation between the two. The anonymous relationship of the market and the highly personalized and polarized hierarchies of pre-capitalist societies are so different that a theory of power that encompasses them both runs the risk of excessive generality. Among the other problems mentioned at the beginning of this section, I shall comment briefly upon what seems to me to be the two outstanding difficulties: the counterfactual aspect of power and the notion of collective power (and powerlessness). As stressed by Goldman (1972), the notion of power over an event must include the power to make that event take place and the power to prevent it from taking place. If we say that Nixon had the power to end the Vietnam War, this statement has little interest if the war would have been ended no matter what he did; the statement has substance only if Nixon could have made the war *continue* had he so wanted. Now this counterfactual—if Nixon had wanted the war to go on, it would have gone on—raises two problems. In the first place we must ask whether the antecedent is a meaningful or legitimate hypothesis; if we find this to be the case, we must ask whether the consequent is true (i.e. compatible with or implied by certain lawlike generalizations), given the antecedent. In the example the first and most fundamental problem can probably be answered in the affirmative: there is nothing known about Nixon that would make it inherently improbable that he could have wanted the war to go on. Take, however, the power of the French Gaullist party to keep communism at bay. The counterfactual aspect of this power implies that communism would have been victorious if the Gaullists had wanted it to be—which *is* a counterfactual with an absurd antecedent. The point may be brought out more clearly by an analysis of the famous counterfactual put forward by Fogel (1964) that if the railroads had not been invented, this would not had any large impact upon the development of the GNP of the United States in the nineteenth century. In order to determine the truth of the consequent (given the antecedent) we should have to know (among other things) if the internal combustion engine would have been invented earlier; in order to answer this question we should need a theory linking socioeconomic conditions to technological change, but this theory might very well have the unhappy side effect of being incompatible with the antecedent, so that the question can be put legitimately only if it cannot be answered. This delicate balance needed for a successful counterfactual—we must assume sufficient theoretical knowledge to permit us to determine the truth value of the consequent, but not so much as to endanger the legitimacy of the antecedent—constitutes a major unresolved problem in the logic of the social sciences. It is interesting, but not surprising, to see that it appears also in the analysis of power.

On Coleman's analysis it is impossible to define a notion of collective power or power of the social system. It turns out that the total power is zero if there are equal and opposite interests associated with each issue; total power is maximal if on each issue all interests go in the same direction. On the probabilistic decision rule used by Coleman, zero total power implies that each issue is decided by chance, which may indeed be seen as a form of powerlessness. On the other hand there may be reasons for attributing less-than-maximal total power to society even when all interests are identical on all issues: externalities and public goods are well-known sources of this impotence (Olson, 1965). Here—as in all cases of the Prisoner's Dilemma—powerlessness is due not to different interests, nor to lack of information; the inability to generate the optimal solution is due only to the isolation and lack of trust between the actors. (The problem of power as a variable-sum game may also be raised in this connection.) A satisfactory theory of power should be able to integrate these two sources of powerlessness: inability to reach the Pareto-optimal states and a low welfare level of the Pareto-optimal states. A powerful society would be a society where there are both a consensus of interests making for satisfactory Pareto-optimal states and a mutual trust making it possible to realize Pareto-optimality. I realize that this way of putting the matter is somewhat lacking in precision, but the general distinction made seems clear enough.

## 4 PLANNING

In this section I shall discuss two important problems in the theory of planning: the conflict between values and the inconsistency of single values. The approach is taken more or less wholesale from microeconomics, with the characteristic stress on maximization. Planning—and politics in general—have to take into account a truly enormous number of values, not all of which lend themselves easily to quantitive treatment. Here I shall deal exclusively with four values that all relate to income in various ways: mean income, minimum income, equality of income (as measured by the Gini index or in one of the other ways discussed by Sen, 1973) and total income. Mean income and total income are maximized simultaneously only if population size is constant; where population size, by the logic of *raison d'état*, is an end in itself, the two values diverge. Maximizing minimum income is not the same as maximizing income equality, as the first is an individual and the second an aggregate quantity. In a capitalist economy the simultaneous maximization of mean income and equality of income is usually thought to be impossible, either on the grounds that the different savings propensities of workers and capitalists link optimal saving (maximizing steady-state mean income) with an unequal distribution of income or on the more general sociological grounds that differential incentives are necessary for the optimal use of differential talents (Davis and Moore, 1945). Thus we can state fairly safely that the four values do conflict, either because of technological incompabilities (diminishing returns to labour make it impossible to maximize simultaneously mean income and total income when population is permitted to vary) or because of incompabilities that are specific to the social system in question.

Now there seem to be three and only three methods for combining or weighing different values: firstly, the method of changing all the goals but one into constraints; secondly, the technique of indifference curves (or indifference surfaces, hypersurfaces, etc.); thirdly, the method of lexicographic ordering of values. The first method corresponds perhaps best to what actually goes on in a mixed economy of the modern type, but it should be stressed that the goal which is taken as maximand is not necessarily seen as 'more important' than the goals that are transformed into constraints. If the constraints are sufficiently strong, very little leeway may be left for the maximand. Thus a mixed economy like the Norwegian one may appear to give much power to private capitalists by permitting them to maximize profits, but the effective range of choices available to entrepreneurs may be rather limited. Actions in general may be conceived of as *choice in the feasible set*, and there is no reason for giving less importance to power over the feasible set than to power over choice within the set, just as there is no reason for giving less importance to power over the agenda of a meeting than to power over the decisions that result from the meeting. In Section 6 below I return to the notion of a feasible set. Here I shall just add the following three comments. (i) In some cases it would seem that *all* the goals are transformed into constraints, so that the role of the decision-maker is to find *one* feasible alternative rather than the *best* feasible alternative (Simon, 1955). (ii) It may then be argued that such behaviour ('satisficing') really is a form of maximizing, because the expected costs of obtaining the information necessary for the choice of the best alternative are so high that the more opportunist method actually is the more rational one (Riker and Ordeshook, 1973, pp.21ff.). (iii) To this it must be added that not *all* cases of apparent irrationality are really a form of higher-order rationality, that it is not *always* true that 'le plus grand degré de finesse est de ne vouloir point du tout user de finesse' (Descartes, 1897ff., p.357). People sometimes act stupidly out of stupidity.

The method of indifference curves has been used extensively in recent political theory (Barry, 1973, p.6n.). The method demands the establishment of two functional relationships between the value variables in question. The first relationship is graphically expressed in the indifference curves (surfaces, hypersurfaces), each of which is the locus for all equally valued combinations of the variables. The second relationship gives the feasible combinations, as determined by technical and social constraints. The actual choice is then determined by finding the feasible combination that lies on the 'highest' indifference curve. The elegance of this approach is vitiated by a number of empirical and conceptual problems, well known from the econometric study of demand (where the indifference curve approach originated). The phenomenon of hysteresis (Georgescu-Roegen, 1971) is particularly important. This effect is due to the fact that, from the point of view of the planner, most or nearly all of the possible combinations are untried and hypothetical, so that the indifference curves (and the underlying social welfare function) reflect only his more or less imaginative evaluations of fictional situations. If (on the basis of indifference curve reasoning) one of the previously untried combinations is chosen and actualized, he may find that the *ex post* appreciation differs considerably from the *ex ante* view, so that a change in the whole indifference map may be induced. In somewhat imaginative language this means that a movement along an indifference curve may cause a shift in the curve, a possibility that is rather destructive for the whole approach.

As actual experience modifies my evaluation of the combinations, planning choices may acquire an irreversible character (Haavelmo, 1944, p.17) in the following sense: if the external constraints x lead me to choose combination X and a change in the constraints to y makes me shift to combination Y, a reversal to x does not necessarily bring about a reversal to X, because the experiences acquired in Y may change my evaluation of the various alternatives. This may also be rephrased by stating that the choice problem is not uniquely determined by state variables, so that any prediction of the planner's behaviour would have to take into account not only his present environment, but also his past history of choices. A further consequence is that not only the outside observer, but the rational planner himself should take this possibility into account when making his choice. This in turn may be done in two different ways. In the first place the planner should realize that his lack of imagination may lead him to evaluate hypothetical situations differently from what he will do when they are actualized. This should give all planning a bias towards caution and piecemeal approximation—a bias with the same effect as the bias that results from the unpredictability of the consequences of our actions. We may be unable to bring about the big change that we intended to make, and even if we are able to bring it about we may find that it was not quite what we wanted after all. In the second place the planner should be able to predict in some cases *how* (and not only *that*) the evaluation of the alternatives will change as a result of the choice between them. In individual choices this is obvious indeed: I may be indifferent now between two houses and still be able to predict that after some time I will prefer the one that I actually buy—or perhaps the other, if I am a perverse kind of person. This possibility makes for a difficult ethical problem for the planner. If he knows that the population now prefers alternative I to alternative II, but feels certain that it will come to prefer II to I if II is actually chosen, can he then claim the right to go through with II? The problem has an analogy in consumer theory: if consumers' wants are very heterogenous, thus making rational and large-scale production impossible, would it not seem ethically justified to try to change their preferences so as to be able to give them more of what they want? (Haavelmo, 1972, pp.7ff.) The reader should not commit 'the aristocratic fallacy' of automatically giving negative answers to these questions. The third method for resolving the conflict between values is that of the lexicographic ordering of ends. It may be said quite generally that hierarchical phenomena should be given a more prominent place in the social sciences than has usually been the case. This is so not only on the level of substantive wants, but also on the level of formal methods of decision. A lexicographic democracy is realized when the chairman's vote counts double in the case of equal numbers of votes, *but only in that case*. A lexicographic dictatorship (I forget where I read this example) is the following: if the dictator has a definite preference, this will be realized; if he is indifferent between all alternatives, the preference of his wife will be decisive and only if she is indifferent also will the choice be made by the people in a plebiscite. The following fact may be significant: just as lexicographic preferences cannot be represented by a numerical utility function, so a lexicographic democracy cannot be represented by the Shapley—Shubik power index. We have already referred to the first part of this proposition; the second part can be shown as follows. Suppose that the four voters, x,y,z,w have respectively 1,1,1 and 3 votes, with z as the chairman whose vote counts double in case of equality. Shall we then say that z is pivotal in the permutation xyzw? We just don't know, because he is pivotal only if w votes against the proposal, whereas the very idea of the pivotal member is that he should be identified independently of the votes of the members that follow him in the permutation. A third example can be found in juridical sentences, where the lexicographic precedence of prison over a suspended sentence makes it impossible to construct a numerical representation of the degree of severity of sentences.

For the planner a strict lexicographic ordering will seldom seem very attractive. Even it it may seem reasonable to give absolute priority to minimum income (Rawls, 1971) in situations where the struggle for subsistence is the dominant fact, no planner—I think—could accept this priority in more affluent societies, where the mean income must be given a more important role than just the function of regulating the choice between two alternatives that are equally and maximally good on the minimum income count. A similar relationship may be valid for the problem of mean income versus equality of income (but see Sen, 1973, p.70). These examples point to the need for a modified lexicographic preference structure (Georgescu-Roegen, 1954) including a threshold beyond which the hierarchy of values is reversed (or beyond which the indifference curve method takes over).

Values may conflict, but even a single value may be inconsistent. I shall deal here only with the problem of intertemporal inconsistency, first raised by Strotz (1955-6). He discussed the optimal consumption pattern for an individual possessing at $t_0$ a given amount of goods that should be entirely consumed between $t_0$ and $t_1$. This problem is important in planning (how to use resources that exist in limited amounts), but it has traditionally been overshadowed by the problem of investment versus consumption. I focus here upon the latter problem, in order to be able to make the distinction between cases I and II below, a distinction that would not be meaningful on Strotz's terms. In allocating the net product between investment and consumption, the planners may act according to one of the three following patterns of behaviour, the last of which is further subdivided in two cases.

(I) The planners maximize total consumption over the time period, which typically leads to heavy investment at the beginning of the period followed by heavy consumption towards the end. With initial standards of living near subsistence this may give grossly inhuman results because one unit of consumption under conditions of hunger is not equivalent to one unit under conditions of relative satiety.

(II) The planners maximize total utility over the time period. Typically this will

258

give a consumption pattern more evenly distributed in time, but with a less-than-maximal total.

(III) The planners maximize present value of total utility over the time period. Whereas the second criterion involves a discount factor upon future consumption, the third criterion involves a discount factor on utility itself. Future consumption counts less (or more) just because it is future. In the case of individual planning a pure time preference is rational, because the individual knows that he may die before $t_1$. (Note, however, that the negative discount of the miser is not rational.) For social planning philosophers from Ramsey (1928) to Rawls (1971, §45) have rejected pure time preference, because it implies an ethically unjustifiable sacrifice of later generations for the benefit of our own. I am not quite happy with this argument, because another way of not sacrificing the yet unborn is to let them stay unborn: that is, future population size is not an independently given variable, but a quantity that is subject to present planning. Preferring the present over the future may lead to fewer persons in the future enjoying the same consumption rather than to the same number of persons enjoying lower consumption. Be this as it may, economists and planners do use extensively a pure time discount (Sen, 1968).

Now Strotz introduces the distinction between consistent and inconsistent time preferences, the former being such as do not necessitate later revisions of the plan. Revisions may of course become necessary, but the plan should not at the moment of inception be such that revisions can be foreseen. Using techniques from the calculus of variations, Strotz shows that consistent time preferences must be based upon an exponential discount function. He arrives, however, at this result by admitting the possibility of coninuous reconsideration, so that each decision is followed up through an infinitesimal part of time only. By using the more realistic assumption of periodical reconsiderations, his result may also be proved by the following elementary method. Putting $f_i(j)$ for the discounted value in year $i$ of a constant amount of utility experienced in year $j$ the condition of a *constant* discount function can now be formulated as follows:

$$\frac{f_n(n)}{f_n(n+1)} = \frac{f_p(p)}{f_p(p+1)}.$$

This means that as the present moment—the *now*—moves along in time, my relative evaluation of this year's and next year's utility never changes: once a spendthrift, always a spendthrift. In addition we now impose the condition of a *consistent* discount function:

$$\frac{f_n(p)}{f_n(p+1)} = \frac{f_p(p)}{f_p(p+1)}.$$

This means that my relative evaluation of two successive years in the future does not change when the first of these years actually arrives. As my allocation of resources is determined by this relative evaluation, a consistent discount function implies that no reconsideration or reallocation will ever be needed, except of course for exogenous reasons. The two conditions jointly give the desired conclusion:

$$\frac{f_n(n)}{f_n(n+1)} = \frac{f_n(p)}{f_n(p+1)}.$$

This means that from a given present all pairs of successive years are valued at the same discount rate relatively to each other, which is just the discrete-time version of Strotz's result. In individual planning there are good reasons for thinking that the discount function is neither constant nor consistent: it is not constant, because as I grow older the chance that I may die before next year increases; it is not consistent either, because the probability that I shall die before the age of seventy is not the same at sixty-nine as it is at the age of twenty. Thus reconsideration and reallocation is an inescapable (and indeed welcome) feature of *la condition humaine*. In the case of social planning these reasons do not apply, so that here it should be seen as desirable to plan consistently. If time preference is in itself irrational, because it makes me regret my past decisions, inconsistent time preferences are the height of irrationality, because I continually find myself unable to stick to my past decisions.

A fascinating aspect of Strotz's paper is his discussion of the possible counter-strategies to inconsistent time preferences. If I know that I will be unable to stick to my present decision if I get the chance to reconsider, I may either make myself unable to reconsider (as with Ulysses being bound to the mast) or I may look for the optimal inconsistent behaviour. The second possibility is extensively discussed by Strotz (whose solution is criticized in Pollak, 1968); to my mind it is rather esoteric, as it presupposes a degree of rationality that should have prevented the problem from arising in the first place. The first, however, is highly important in the theory and practice of planning. Examples from everyday life of this strategy of precommitment could be the buying of an annuity that cannot be reconverted into cash, or the case of the man who tells all his friends that he is going to give up smoking, so as to make reconsideration very costly in terms of prestige. In economic planning one may note that heavy investments have a degree of irreversibility that makes reconsideration very unlikely; this may induce in the planner who fears being disowned by his successors (or by himself) a bias towards investment over and above what would otherwise have been the case. There also exist numerous political institutions that have the effect (one hesitates to say the function) of preventing too frequent reconsideration of decisions. In modern societies periodic elections separated by stretches of apathy have been seen in this light (Hirschman, 1970, pp.31-2). The equivalents in classical Greece were ostracism and the institution called *graphe paranomon*, a procedure whereby a man could be indicted and tried for making an illegal proposal in the Assembly, even when the proposal had been passed by the Assembly (Finley, 1973b, pp.267). The economic and political instability of contemporary China may be due to the absence of such devices that protect society against itself. The Chinese de-emphasizing of heavy investment is well known, as is also the use of the Paris Commune, where representatives could be recalled at a moment's notice, as a model for the Cultural Revolution. On the other hand one should not overlook the possibility that the creative energy released by these unorthodox methods may be so great as to compensate for the inefficiency with which it is used. Lest any should think this argument a case of special pleading, I would like to point out that the classical justification of capitalism by Schumpeter (1961, p.83) has identically the same structure.

## 5 ECONOMICS AND POLITICS: A MICRO-POLITICAL APPROACH

In Section 2 above I argued that in some societies the sharp distinction between economic and political behaviour is an artificial one. Here I would like
to substantiate this proposition by a study of 'micro-politics', viz. the relationship
between master and slave as analysed by Hegel (1952) and Genovese (1965). It will
be seen that in this relationship power, production and consumption are but
different facets of one complex structure, so that not only the distinction between
economics and politics, but also the distinction between consumption expenses and
costs of production tend to collapse. It should be clearly stated at the outset that
what follows is a conceptual exercise and not an empirical study of American
slavery. The recent work of Fogel and Engerman (1974), even if very far from
perfect (David and Temin, 1974), has at least shown up the multiple errors of most
or all earlier work on the subject, not excluding Genovese's. Still it would seem
important to criticize Genovese for the right reasons and not for the wrong ones. I
shall argue that both the vulgar neoclassical analysis of slavery (Conrad and Meyer,
1958) and the more subtle neoclassical theories (Fogel and Engerman, 1971) fail to
grasp the conceptual intricacies of the master—slave relationship. It is out of place
to analyse slavery in terms of profits, just as it is inadequate to conceptualize the
personal aspects of the master—slave relationships by saying that slaves are
consumption goods.

I shall briefly recapitulate the main features of the Hegelian master—slave
dialectic in the *Phenomenology of Mind*. The extreme density and opacity of the
original make all paraphrase seem flat, so that I shall reproduce here a key passage
from the text. As the English translation is very misleading, the reader will have to
struggle with the original German.

Der Herr bezieht sich *auf den Knecht mittelbar durch das selbständige Sein*; denn
eben hieran ist der Knecht gehalten; es ist seine Kette, von der er im Kampfe nicht
abstrahieren konnte, und darum sich als unselbständig, seine Selbständigkeit in der
Dingheit zu haben, erwies. Der Herr aber ist die Macht über dies Sein, denn er
erwies im Kampfe, dass es ihm nur als ein Negatives gilt; indem er die Macht
darüber, dies Sein aber die Macht über den Andern ist, so hat er in diesem Sclusse
diesem Andern unter sich. Ebenso bezieht sich der Herr *mittelbar durch den Knecht
auf das Ding*; der Knecht bezieht sich, als Selbstbewusstsein überhaupt, auf das
Ding auch negativ und hebt es auf; aber er ist zugleich selbständig für ihn, und er
kann darum durch sein Negieren nicht bis zur Vernichtung mit ihm fertig werden,
oder er *bearbeitet* es nur. Dem Herrn dagegen *wird* durch diese Vermittlung die
*unmittelbare* Beziehung als die reine Negation desselben oder der Genuss. [Hegel,
1952, p.146.]

In the fight for recognition between the two consciousnesses one ends up by
yielding, preferring a life in subjection to death in combat. As the slave he has
identified himself with brute matter, whereas the master—waging his life in the
fight—has transcended natural existence and demonstrated his absolute liberty. The
result is that the master is doubly powerful. Through the slave he has power over
the material objects of consumption, which he can enjoy without having to work
for them. Through the material objects the master enjoys power over the slave, for

by the arbitrary and conspicuous consumption of these objects he demonstrates his power over the being that has produced them. Still it turns out that the master is caught in a trap, for he can get no real satisfaction from his power over a being that he treats like a thing. The very concept of unilateral recognition is contradictory, as can be seen by thinking through the farcical idea of a nation being diplomatically recognized by one of its own colonies. To the extent that the master treats the slave on par with cattle, he gets no non-economic satisfaction from his power; to the extent that he treats the slave like a human being, he has no power over him.

These very general concepts have been given a fairly operational meaning in the work of Genovese on the ante-bellum economy of the American South. Genovese stresses especially the heavy consumption of the planters and the low degree of mechanization of the plantations. The planters preferred consumption to investment, and when they invested it took the form of capital widening (investment in more slaves) rather than of capital deepening (investment in machinery, fertilizers, etc.). (A similar analysis of classical slavery is found in Finley, 1965.) Both of these facts follow immediately from the Hegelian model: consumption and possession of slaves contribute to the master's *Selbstgefühl*, which is not the case for the profit-maximizing investment in machinery. The schizophrenic psychology of the planter, with the sudden switches from sentimentality to brutality, also finds a Hegelian explanation in the view of the master as striving to realize the self-contradictory end of a unilateral recognition.

An important part of Genovese's approach is his refusal to analyse slavery in terms of profits, capital, investment, etc. Slavery according to him was a way of life, not an object of investment; slaves had a relationship to the planters that went

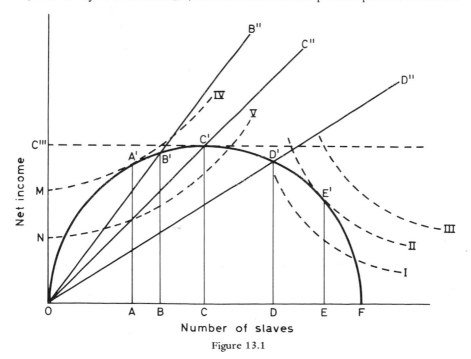

Figure 13.1

far beyond the relationship of a piece of machinery to its owner. This latter proposition has been the object of an operation of trivialization by Fogel and Engerman (1971, pp.313-4), who restate it by saying that the slave was simultaneously a production good and a consumption good for the planters. Thus *if* planters ever diverged from rational capitalist behaviour (which is not admitted), this must have been due to the twofold benefit drawn from the slaves. This suggestion may be put more formally by indifference curve analysis. Measuring number of slaves and net income along the two axes in Figure 13.1, we may construct the following two relationships. First the curve $OC'F$, which gives the set of feasible and efficient combinations. With no slaves, the planter does not get any income; with too many slaves, diminishing marginal productivity also prevents him from getting any (net) income. Somewhere between the two extremes there exists an optimal number of slaves ($OC$) that maximizes net income. Secondly one may draw a family of indifference curves, I,II,III, each of which is the locus for all equally valued combinations of slaves and net income. The idea is that the planter draws satisfaction from his slaves in two ways: both from the income they give him and from the very fact of possessing them. A reduction in net income may then be offset by an increase in the number of slaves, which explains why the indifference curves I–III are drawn as backward-sloping. The planter will then seek the feasible combination of slaves and income that lies on the highest indifference curve; on the figure this is the combination $E'$, corresponding to $OE$ slaves. A capitalist with no emotional investment in the possession of slaves will have horizontal indifference curves (like $C''' \, C'$ on the figure) and therefore choose the income-maximizing combination $C'$ with the optimal number $OC$ of slaves. Not it seems to have been the case that the profits that could be made in slavery (i.e. $CC'$) were larger than the profits that could be made on the same investment outside slavery. Fogel (in conversation) has suggested that the persistence of this anomalous fact must have been due to a negative conspicuous consumption, i.e. to an aversion to slave-holding (indifference curves like IV and V on the figure) in outside investors. This idea may be interpreted on one of the two following lines. In the first place an investor might choose the combinstion $A'$ as being the feasible combination that lies on his highest indifferent curve. Now if the normal profits to be made outside slavery were higher than $AA'$, this would keep outside investors away even if the normal profits were smaller than $CC'$. In the second place one might suggest that outside investors would invest in slavery only if the indifference curve that intersects the vertical axis at the income level that corresponds to normal outside profits, also intersects the line $CC'$ below $C'$. This would be the case for normal profits equal to $ON$, but not for normal profits equal to $OM$. This explanation assumes that investors either would not invest in slavery at all or would do so in a maximally efficient way (with the optimum number $OC$ of slaves), whereas the first explanation assumes that they might invest in a less than maximally efficient way.

I have dealt in some detail with this point because it seems to me that the Fogel–Engerman model just might be adequate to explain why non-planters did not enter slavery or entered it in an inefficient manner, whereas it clearly is inadequate to explain why and how planters stayed there. The planter was *not* the negative mirror of the outside investor, with backward-sloping rather than forward-sloping indifference curves: he was a different kind of character altogether. There is no continuum that goes from the aversion to slaves to the preference for slaves, through the neutral attitude expressed in the horizontal indifference curves. The dialectic of slavery is more complex. Thus Genovese (1965, Appendix) stresses that the concept of net income or profit did not have any subjective meaning for the planters as they did not make the distinction between business costs (to be deducted before profits) and personal costs (to be deducted from profits). Part of Genovese's statement—as the idea that education for planters' children and their expensive vacations should be seen as costs of production—have been met with badly disguised sneers in the profession (Conrad, 1967, p.520; Fogel and Engerman, 1971, p.321), but I think a case can be made for saying that they faithfully reflect the Hegelian notion that consumption is but one aspect of the exercise of power over the slaves. In Figure 13.1 this is represented by the straight lines $OB'B''$, $OC'C''$ and $OD'D''$, each of which stands for a possible relation between the number of slaves used in production and the amount of consumption. The underlying idea is that in the power—prestige aspect of slavery possession of slaves and conspicuous consumption are linked together: the one increases with the other. Possession of slaves gives power only if accompanied by large-scale consumption, but on the other hand consumption alone does not give power in a slave society. If we assume that no reinvestment takes place, the number of slaves and the volume of production will then be determined by the point of intersection between the curve of feasible combinations and the consumption line; such points are $B'$, $C'$ and $D'$.

This model shows that the treatment of planters' consumption as a cost of production can be justified analytically, because the amount of consumption is a function of the volume of production and not of the volume of profits. To some extent it may be the case also in capitalist firms that the pattern and level of the managers' consumption depend upon the size of the firm and not only upon the size of their income, but in all the standard models of consumer behaviour under capitalism the use of income is considered separately from the origin of income. In the present model this obviously is not so: use of $OA$ slaves gives the same income as use of $OD$ slaves, but the consumption out of income is very different in the two cases. Thus income is not a state variable (hysteresis effect). This conceptualization goes against the grain of neoclassical theory; it also has one implication that seems to have been overlooked by Genovese himself. On the Fogel—Engerman approach *and* (it would seem) on Genovese's theory, the number of slaves will always be more-than-optimal, to the right of $OC$, at least if we study the behaviour of the typical planter and not the outside investor. On the present approach, however, there does not seem to be any *a priori* objection to a consumption line that intersects the production curve to the left of $C'$, as in the case of $OB'B''$ on the figure; we may even get the pure capitalist behaviour if the consumption line should happen to intersect the production curve in $C'$. I leave to the reader the task of constructing an analytical or geometrical representation of the last aspect of the Hegel—Genovese theory, viz. the idea of the schizophrenic and inconsistent behaviour of the planter. The basic idea would seem to be that the planter's satisfaction (*Befriedigung*) can be conceptualized as a multiplicative function of his power over the slave and his recognition of the slave, each of these latter variables being in turn a function of the consumption level of the slave. The goal of the master is to achieve the level of satisfaction that corresponds to the product of the maximal values of these two variables, but as these variables attain their maxima for different values of the consumption level—power being a decreasing function and recognition an increasing function of the slave's consumption—this is a case of trying to have your cake and eat it. Adding a suitable dynamic assumption a cyclical model of planter behaviour may be generated.

## 6 MODAL LOGIC AND POLITICAL POSSIBILITY

Politics is the art of the possible, modal logic is the science of the possible, and never the twain have met. In this section I shall take a small step towards a reunion of the two fields, elaborating upon a hint by Ernst Bloch (1954) at the relativization of the concept of Utopia. As the relativization of the concept of possible worlds is exactly what has turned modal logic from a mathematical curiosum into one of the most active and exciting fields of philosophy, the relation seems worth exploring. It turns out, however, that the field of politics is basically ambiguous in a way that cannot be captured by a logical scheme; still the following analysis may have some limited classificatory interest.

An intuitive motivation may take off from the concept of the feasible set. An economist typically asks the question of the best member in the feasible set, a sociologist wants to determine the most probable member, a structuralist might want to know the number of members if the set is finite. A modal logician asks about the logical structure of the feasibility relation. It is not often stressed in social science that feasibility is a relation rather than an absolute attribute, but a moment's reflection suffices to show that this is indeed the case. Given the existing capital equipment and population size, what is the feasible set of combinations of capital equipment and consumption that may be realized tomorrow? Given the existing political constellations, which are the proposals that have any chance of being adopted? Given a state in a Markov chain with stationary transition probabilities, which are the states that may be reached in one step? In any number of steps? (Fararo, 1973, pp.146–7, 276ff.). The last example is important, as it shows that even in probabilistic contexts the question of pure possibility (non-zero probability) is relevant. The most striking example is probably a linguistic one: given a finite-state model for language we may ask either the probabilistic question of how *often* a given sentence will be produced or the possibilistic question of whether it is grammatically correct or not (cf. Chs. 12 and 13 in Luce, Bush and Galanter, 1963, vol.II).

Turning now to the modal concepts of possibility (M) and necessity (L), these were for a long time interpreted according to the Leibnizian idea that necessity is truth in all possible worlds and possibility truth in some possible world. These are, it should be noted, absolute and not relativized concepts. *The* feasible set is just the set of all possible worlds. The basic problem in this interpretation is that it does not make semantic sense out of what gives to modal logic a syntactical substance, viz. the iterated modalities (LL, MM etc.) and the mixed modalities (LM, ML etc.). The various axiomatizations of modal logic adopted different axioms as to the relations between mixed, iterated and simple modalities, but only one system (S5 in Lewis and Langford, 1932) made all modalities collapse into simple modalities, which makes for a rather trivial system. But if syntactical considerations make it imperative to keep the mixed and iterated modalities, semantic considerations seem to make it equally imperative to keep them out, for how should a phrase like 'LMp' be understood on the Leibnizian interpretation? 'It is true in all possible worlds that p is true in some possible world' does not seem to state anything over and above the proposition that 'p is true in some possible world'. The revolutionary way out of this problem was found by Kanger, Hintikka and Kripke around 1960: it consists essentially in the relativization of the set of possible worlds, being now defined as the set of worlds that are *accessible* from the world where the statement in question is made. For any world there exists a set of worlds that are accessible to it; necessity in that world means truth in all accessible worlds; possibility means truth in some possible world; a phrase like 'LMp' means that for each world accessible to ours there is some world accessible to that world in which p is true; and so on for all mixed and iterated modalities.

This means that the logical properties of the accessibility relation became crucially important. It turns out that all the systems of modal logic proposed previously can be classified according to the restrictions they impose upon this relation. I return to the more important of these restrictions below. Here I shall just point out that the concept of accessibility or relative possibility was largely an algebraic device that did not lend itself easily to intuitive understanding. The concept of a possible world is in itself a bit mind-boggling, but to talk about possible worlds being accessible or inaccessible to each other seems to be a piece of sheer (and rather bad) science fiction. Attempts have been made to interpret the accessibility concept, but as far as I know all interpretations proposed up to now either have nothing to do with modal logic proper or make us lose all the ground gained. Interpretations of the first type are deontic logic (with ethical desirability as the accessibility relation) or temporal logic (with succession in time). Interpretations of the second type are those that see accessibility as logical, conceptual or causal possibility (Snyder, 1971, Ch.VI); the last, for example, means that a world is accessible to ours if it works according to the same physical laws. The difficulty with this approach is the essential use of the word 'same' in the definition of accessibility, because this implies that the relation is in this case an equivalence relation, inducing a partition of the set of all worlds into a set of mutually disjoint subsets, each of which behaves exactly as the original Leibnizian set of possible worlds. Thus mixed and iterated modalities break down again. It is easy to impose the condition that the accessibility relation shall not be an equivalence relation, but is more difficult to find strictly modal and non-trivial interpretations that satisfy this condition.

I submit that the concept of political possibility offers such a non-trivial and properly modal interpretation. The basic assumption in this approach is that for any given state of society (as described by a finite number of variables) *there exists* a set of politically feasible states. The set may be empty, but it should not be fuzzy. At the end of the discussion I shall raise some basic objections to this assumption, but first I want to show what may be worked out if we adopt it.

*(a) Economic feasibility and political possibility.* It would seem reasonable to impose the condition that the set of politically feasible states should be a subset of the set of economically feasible set ('ought implies can'); in the interesting cases it would be a proper subset (as in Samuelson, 1969, p.419). For some purposes, however, we might want to do without this condition. For some years it was politically impossible for all political parties to say openly that full employment, economic growth and stable prices were ends that could not be realized

simultaneously within the framework of a capitalist economy: all political programmes had to state economic impossibilities as political possibilities. If, on the other hand, we intend our formalization to reflect what it is politically possible to bring about, and not only what it is politically possible to get people to accept, some kind of economic feasibility condition is needed.

*(b) Political modalities as sentence operators.* 'It is politically possible that p' means that there is a politically possible state where p obtains. 'It is politically necessary that p' means that p obtains in *all* politically possible states. Every politician has his attention constantly upon such 'p's. It should be stressed here that it is only by the introduction of the necessity operator that we are able to get some insights out of this approach; possibility in itself does not bring us very far. In the feasible-set approach in economics one never (as far as I know) focuses the attention upon features that are common to all feasible states, except, of course, the fact that they are all feasible (i.e. satisfy all the constraints). The set of constraints is a proper subset of the set of necessary features: given budget and calory constraints upon the consumption, it may be the case that all baskets of goods satisfying the constraints also taste rather bad, which is then a necessary feature without being a constraint.

*(c) Iterated modalities.* 'It is politically possible that it is politically possible that p' means that there is a politically possible state of affairs relatively to which p itself is politically possible. Unless the accessibility relation is assumed to be transitive (see below), it does not follow that p itself is possible. Iterated necessity is interpreted in the obvious manner. A typical political problem is the following: given Lnot-p, is it the case that LLnot-p or rather that MMp? In words: if a given proposal is politically impossible, is it possible to bring it about by first advancing another proposal that is politically possible or are all such two-step operations politically impossible also? This leads to the concept of a minimal chain of iterated possibilities: which is the smallest $n$ such that $(M)^n p$? What are the properties of the set of 'p's such that there exists an $n$ such that $(M)^n p$?

*(d) Mixed modalities.* 'It is politically possible that it is politically necessary that p' means that there is a politically possible state whose politically possible states all contain p. It may be politically impossible to bring about p, but politically possible to bring about a state from which all roads lead to p. Budget politics (Wildavsky, 1964b, pp.111ff.) illustrate this idea: creating precedents, using irreversible investment to commit future generations, exploiting hidden complementarities or bottlenecks all come under this heading. The case of LMp means that there is no way of getting p out of the system: whatever you do, p rests a possibility. Right-wing regimes seem incapable of rooting out the revolutionary potential; social democrats are unable to eliminate the possibility of Poujadism.

*(e) Time.* The mixed and iterated modalities bring to the forefront the problem of situating the states in time. Continuous time does not have any meaning here; as for discrete time the simplest case is found in periodical elections. Much of politics, however, does not have this regular rhythm. An 'analysis of the situation' that concludes by stating that revolution is possible (or impossible, as the case may be) does not give a definite time limit. The conceptual problem involved may be brought out by an example. The former state of affairs in Greece (this was written in March 1974, when it was the present state) was a military dictatorship. The political possibilities included revolution, introduction of limited democracy, return

to monarchy and continued military dictatorship. (What actually happened was something not quite covered by any of these possibilities: see *(g)* below.) An iterated modality could be the possibility of a return to monarchy as a step towards a limited democracy; mixed modalities could be the impossibility of a return to monarchy after a successful revolution or the impossibility of a revolution after introduction of limited democracy. But what about the following proposition: a continued military dictatorship will also make the revolution impossible? In contrast to the preceding examples, this does invoke some kind of time limit, though not a very specific one. This seems to point to the need for a more general concept than the notion of state; thus we may define the notion of a *situation* as including the state with the set of possible states. A change in the situation may be a change of the state or a change of the set of possible states only; the political time structure would then be punctuated not only by the visible changes of state, but also by the invisible changes of situation. I am not very happy with this solution, but it has at least the merit of highlighting the notion that in politics it may be an event that nothing happens.

*(f) Quantification.* A full-blown modal logic must go beyond sentence variables and introduce individual variables with quanitification. Quantified modal logic raises some rather esoteric problems concerning reference, existence and negation, which may be resolved in one of several ways fully covered in the technical literature. I believe that some of these problems have a political interpretation, but lack of space makes it necessary to concentrate upon more elementary questions. A classical example of quantification in political modal logic is 'You can fool all the people some of the time and some of the people all the time, but not all the people all the time.' Actually I think that in politics the opposite problem is more important, i.e. the political impossibility of doing something to some individuals without doing it to everyone. Thus the universalism inherent in modern societies may constitute an obstacle to the realization of political goals, viz. the indivisible benefits that for technical reasons must initially be made available in large amounts to some rather than available in small amounts to everyone, because it is economically impossible to make them simultaneously available in large amounts to everyone.

Consider now the following propositions:

In a monarchy it is necessary that $(\exists x)(x$ is a monarch$)$        (1)
In a monarchy $(\exists x)(x$ is necessarily a monarch$)$        (2)
In a republic it is necessary that $(\exists x)(x$ is president$)$        (3)
In a republic $(\exists x)(x$ is necessarily a president$)$        (4)
$(\exists x)($it is politically necessary that $x$ is monarch$)$        (5)
It is politically necessary that $(\exists x)(x$ is a monarch$)$        (6)
$(\exists x)($it is politically necessary that $x$ is president$)$        (7)
It is politically necessary that $(\exists x)(x$ is president$)$        (8)

(Read '$\exists x$' as 'there exists an x such that'.) It should be seen here that a statement to the effect that (1) implies (2)—and similarly for the other three pairs of propositions—would be fallacious; it would indeed be formally equivalent to the fallacy of composition, if that fallacy is taken as the deduction of

'It is possible that all x are F' from 'For any x it is possible that x is F' (Elster, 1974). In 1936 it was politically impossible to abolish monarchy in England (i.e. (5) was true), but it was politically possible to change monarch (i.e. (6) was false). If in (1) to (4) necessity is interpreted as logical or conceptual necessity, (1) and (3) come out true and (2) and (4) false. If on the other hand we use the notion of metaphysical necessity found in recent philosophical work (Kripke, 1972, pp.312ff.; Dummett, 1973, pp.129ff.), then (2) comes out true. According to this notion the only properties that are essential (or metaphysically necessary) to an object—i.e. the properties without which it would not have been *that* object—are those that are linked to the way it came into being or to the stuff out of which it was made. As this is indeed the case with monarchhood, as distinct from presidenthood, (2) is vindicated. In this sense the essentialism of the Middle Ages can be understood in the light of a political system that makes political properties appear as necessary.

Having made a case—or so I hope—for the *prima facie* interest of the political modalities, I now proceed to a closer examination of the logical properties of the accessibility relation, singling out for analysis the seven properties used in a recent textbook (Snyder, 1971, p.210) to classify various systems of modal logic.

(g) *Existence.* For every state of society there is some state that is a politically possible state relatively to it. Assuming non-reflexivity, the problem of existence is not a trivial one. Under certain historical conditions—China at the end of the Han dynasty, France in the fourteenth century, *The Lottery* by Borges—it may be impossible to *bring about* any state at all, even if of course a new state will eventually *come about*. The distinction made here corresponds to a distinction between power as causality and power as intentional production of desired ends. The fact that the actions of an agent have consequences does not mean that he has power over these consequences, for we may imagine situations where all attempts to bring something about intentionally are systematically thwarted (Goldman, 1972), so that all consequences are unintentional and undesirable. In a similar manner political situations may be blocked and credibility rot away, leaving nothing but sound and fury. (A standard argument against the possibility of non-existence would be by appeal to some fixed point theorem, in a manner analogous to Simon (1954), but it is doubtful indeed whether the continuity and convexity assumptions needed would be fulfilled.)

(h) *Limited reflexivity.* If a given state has any politically possible alternative at all, then it is a politically possible state relatively to itself. Or (disregarding trivial readings): if change is politically possible, then conservation of the *status quo* is also possible, a proposition certainly lacking in universal validity. In modern industrial societies it seems that immobility is impossible and that the only politically possible options are moderate versus radical and left-wing versus right-wing change. 'Regrediamur nisi progrediamur, quia stari non potest.' (Leibniz, 1947, p.94.)

(i) *Reflexivity.* Every state is politically possible relatively to itself. This is excluded by the immediately preceding remarks.

(j) *Transitivity.* What is politically possible relatively to a state of affairs that is politically possible relatively to the present, is also politically possible relatively to the present. This is a most controversial statement, acceptance of which may be said to constitute the essence of the Utopian approach to politics. Utopianism says that what can be done in two steps, can always be telescoped into one. There are (at least) two different refutations of the Utopian approach. Firstly one may argue on the analogy with a visual horizon (Bloch, 1954; Hughes and Cresswell, 1972, pp.63ff.): in order to see what is beyond the next hill, you have to get there first. This was, I think, the line taken by Marx (1956c, p.343) when he argued that the workers will themselves be so completely changed by the revolution that they cannot foresee what will be the range of alternatives open to them. Secondly one may argue in a more Leninist manner that, even if the political élite know what will be politically possible after the revolution, the rank and file may lack the political maturity to skip the intermediate step.

(k) *Limited symmetry.* If a given state is politically possible relatively to itself, then any politically possible alternative to that state has that state as a politically possible alternative. Or (disregarding trivial readings): if the *status quo* is a viable option, then every change is reversible. This is a proposition whose plausibility has to be decided on empirical evidence; I cannot myself think of any obvious counter-examples.

(l) *Symmetry.* Every state is a politically possible alternative to the states that are politically possible relatively to itself. Or: every political change is reversible. This is certainly false. The apparent symmetry of the notions of revolution and counter-revolution is not a real one, for the goal of the counter-revolutionaries is certainly not to create a society where revolution is politically possible. ('Il n'est pas question de revenir à la situation d'avant 1968, d'abord parce que la situation d'avant 1968 comportait les conditions qui ont créé 1968'—*dixit* Giscard d'Estaing, *Le Monde*, 8 January 1975.) Thus the present situation in Chile is a reversal *beyond*—and not *to*—the pre-Allende situation, as Eduard Frei found out too late. In this sense there is an irreversibility of political development: history and experience often make it impossible to return to a state of innocence. A neutralist country must prepare for war, but if the war comes a return to neutrality after the war may be impossible.

(m) *Quasi-equivalence.* All politically possible alternatives to a given state are politically possible alternatives to each other. This might be part of the definition of a parliamentary regime, because in the absence of this condition a losing party of an election would just have to go out of business, which is, of course, exactly what the losing party in a revolution usually has to do.

I personally have found this conceptualization useful as a means for generating hypotheses and putting well-known facts in a slightly different light, but I certainly do not claim that substantial insights can be acquired by this piece of rabbit-pulling. The main difficulty of the approach is, as stated at the beginning, the assumption that there exists a well-defined (even if possibly empty) set of political possibilities. One may indeed say that politics in the weak sense (*la politique politisée*) is a struggle about which of the states in the politically feasible set—on whose members all actors and observers are in perfect agreement—shall be realized, but politics in the strong sense (*la politique politisante*) is a struggle about what *is* possible. In all situations some actors and in some situations all actors do agree upon the borders of the possible, but sometimes there is fight over just where the frontiers should be drawn—and this fight, even if less frequent than the former, is certainly more fundamental. (Cf. what was said in Section 4 about the power over the agenda versus power over the results.) To this problem may be added the tangle of difficulties inherent in the notion of political time.

It is useful, I think, to discuss a possible way out of this problem. Even if we distinguish politicized politics and politicizing politics (or 'rule-governed creativity' and 'rule-making creativity' (Chomsky, 1964, p.59)) it might be argued that the latter activity also is subject to logic, be it a higher-order one (as rule-making also may be subject to rules). This could then be formalized by relativizing the already relativized set of possible worlds; by attributing to each state not only a feasible set, but a set of feasible sets. It is clear, however, that this approach only leads to an infinite regress.

Substantially the same point can be made by appeal to the Marxist notion of 'the unity of theory and praxis', which I take to mean that theory can have an immediate impact upon the world, changing it by interpreting it and not interpreting it instead of changing it. To publish 'an analysis of the situation' may bring about a change in the situation; by saying that the situation *is* revolutionary one may contribute to making it revolutionary. Still revolutions cannot always be made possible by this kind of self-fulfilling prophecy, and if one could know *when* it is possible to make a revolution possible by saying that it is possible—a situation where this is the case may be called a *pre-revolutionary situation*—then we of course have to ask when a situation can be made pre-revolutionary by our saying that it is pre-revolutionary. As this can go on for ever, I conclude that the 'unity of theory and praxis' is not itself a theoretical concept; any attempt to lift yourself up by the hair by constructing a theory of the relation of theory to action runs into an infinite regress.

A third way of making the same point is by a refutation of a famous argument of Simon (1954), briefly referred to above. The starting point for Simon was what is sometimes called 'the problem of self-reference' in social science: by the very act of putting forward a theory of society or a description of the state of society, one brings about a change in society and can therefore no longer claim to describe it faithfully. The paradigm case is the publication of opinion surveys before an election. Simon solves the problem by invoking Brouwer's fixed point theorem. In order to do this some rather formidable assumptions—which are admitted here only for the sake of argument—must be made: it must be possible to impose a metric upon the set of possible states, the set of possible states must be convex, the function giving the real outcome $f(x)$ as depending upon the predicted outcome $x$ must be a continuous one. With these assumptions the Brouwer fixed point theorem tells us that there exists a state $\bar{x}$ such that $f(\bar{x}) = \bar{x}$, which means that if $\bar{x}$ is predicted, $\bar{x}$ will come about. This requires, however, not only that the scientist knows the shape of the function $f(\bar{x})$, but also that he keeps this knowledge to himself. There is every reason to believe that, if people were told how they react to predictions about how they will behave, they will react differently, just as they behave differently when told how they will behave. But if successful prediction is contingent upon secrecy, then the simplest method is clearly not to publish the prediction in the first place.

# Acknowledgements and Notes

## CHAPTER 2

### Notes

1. On Bentham's political conceptions as the authority on 'English radicalism', see Halévy (1901, II, pp.187ff.). On Bentham's absence of history, see Shakankiri (1970, p.313).
2. On Durkheim's criticism of theories of utilitarianism, see Parsons (1966, pp.346–7).
3. See also Rudolph Heberle (1966, p.275) and Spykman (1966, pp.11, 20).
4. In this connection, see also Runciman (1973, pp.30–1).
5. P. Sorokin (1956) notes that Homans presents an even more individualistic and atomistic conception of the internal system in both *Social Behaviour* and *The Human Group*. In any case, the connection between the two systems is never established.
6. See also Homans (1950, p.272); Mulkay (1971, Ch.6).
7. See Clark (1972, pp.285–6); Dahlström (1966, p.261).
8. C. B. Macpherson (1973, p.26) also shows how Bentham analyses only the consumption of merchandise, not the production of it. John Plamenatz (1973, p.18) writes, 'if a utilitarian theory is bourgeois, it is so by virtue of assumptions which are not in themselves utilitarian'. What is of interest here is not the more or less bourgeois aspect of the theories of utilitarianism but the fact that they separate the internal system from the external system. This could equally well characterize other types of theory.
9. Homans (1961, p.247) writes that the just or unjust character of the relationship between the owner of a corporation and its workers remains difficult to evaluate; he concludes, 'such things are not capable of proof: they are matters of taste'.

## CHAPTER 3

### Acknowledgements

This paper is an abstract of a chapter of a book, *Graven naar macht*, *(Traces of power)* by H. M. Helmers, R. J. Mokken, R. L. Plijter and F. N. Stokman (with collaboration of J. M. Anthonisse), on an analysis of interlocking directorates in big business and government in The Netherlands (Van Gennep, Amsterdam, 1974). Acknowledgement should be made to The Netherlands Institute for Advanced Study in the Humanities and Social Sciences (NIAS) at Wassenaar, where one of the authors was enabled to work out his contributions to this paper. A version of this paper was presented at the Joint Sessions of the European Consortium for Political Research (Workshop on Political Theory) 28 March–2 April 1974.

## Notes

1. See, for instance, Schumpeter (1961), Riesman (1950), Hunter (1953), Mills (1956), Dahl (1958, 1961), Schattschneider (1960), Polsby (1960, 1963), Kornhauser (1961), Bachrach and Baratz (1962, 1963, 1970), Domhoff (1967, 1971) and Merelman (1968).

## CHAPTER 5

### Acknowledgements

The paper given at the Workshop was based on two earlier drafts, and benefited from discussion of these at the Universities of Durham, Edinburgh, Essex, Manchester and Warwick, and at a conference on 'Power in Non-Voting Groups' organized by the Institute for Higher Studies, Vienna. I should like especially to acknowledge the comments of Robert Axelrod (Michigan).

This chapter is a completely revised and substantially extended version of the Workshop paper, and diverges in many respects from it. The changes stem partly from attempts to rework points that had worried me all along but owe even more to the many perceptive criticisms to which the paper has had the good fortune to be subjected. These include the discussion at the meeting of the Workshop in Strasbourg, and comments received when the paper was read or circulated to seminars at Columbia University, New York, at Oslo University and at Oxford University. In addition, William Ascher (Johns Hopkins), John Enos (Magdalen College, Oxford), John Flemming (Nuffield College, Oxford), Robert Goodin (Strathclyde), John Maguire (Nuffield College, Oxford) and Peter Morriss (Manchester) have offered acute critical comments, for which I am grateful. I should like especially to acknowledge my debt to Robert Goodin, for a fundamental criticism of my earlier treatment of threats that I have attempted to meet by the formulation in sections 8 and 9 of the present chapter, and to Peter Morriss for forcing me to think harder about the relation between power and the gains and losses arising from its exercise. The results of this appear in sections 10 and 11 of the present chapter.

The paper presented at the Workshop has been published in *Government and Opposition*, 9 (1974), 189–223 under the title 'The Economic Approach to the Analysis of Power and Conflict' and in an Italian translation in the *Rivista Italiana di Scienza Politica*, IV (1974), 247–86 under the title 'Potere, Scambio e Conflitto'.

## CHAPTER 6

### Acknowledgements

Most of this paper was written while I was a resident fellow at the Netherlands Institute for Advanced Study (NIAS) in the Humanities and Social Sciences at

Wassenaar. My thanks go to NIAS, as well as to Carl G. Hempel for his critical comments on sections 7–9.

## Notes

1. As do many contributors to the *Nomos* volume on Coercion. E.g., 'Coercion . . . in the wide sense . . . is the result of any threat of evil' (Gert, 1972, p.33). 'A coerces B when A uses or threatens to use deprivations . . .' (Wertheimer, 1972, p.222). 'Coercion is best defined broadly as the use of sanctions to influence the behavior of others' (McIntosh, 1972, p.270; see also Bayles, 1972, p.17). According to Barry, too, A is coercing B 'when A is threatening to do something that B doesn't like unless B does what A wants' (p.000 above).

2. I did so myself: 'To have power is to be capable of exercising power' (Oppenheim, 1961, p.100). Similarly: 'Power is the ability to exercise influence' (Riker, 1964, p.347). Power 'is a capacity to cause someone to do something he would not otherwise do' (Held, 1972, p.49). 'To be powerful, is, then, to have a generalized potentiality . . .' (Benn, 1967, p.426). Power 'renders somebody able to do, capable of doing something' (Pitkin, 1972, p.276). Power is 'the possession by one actor (A) of the means of modifying the conduct of another actor (B) . . .' (Barry, p.000 above). 'Power is most plausibly defined as the capacity to hurt' (p.000 above; see also Lively, section 4 above).

3. Similarly: 'Presumably, we observe the influence of A over B by noting the differences between the way B actually behaves and the way he *would* behave if A were not present' (Simon, 1957, p.66). 'A, by his power over B, . . . [made] B do b, which B would not have done but for A's wishing him to do so . . .' (Benn, 1967, p.424). Power is 'the capacity at one's own discretion to get people to do what they would not otherwise do . . .' Barry, p.000 above; see also Held, quoted in n3, p.000).

## CHAPTER 7

### Acknowledgements

I should like to thank Ole Berg and Arild Underdal (University of Oslo) and Erik Floyd for useful comments on the manuscript of this paper.

## CHAPTER 8

### Acknowledgements

We are much indebted to Karl-Peter Markl for his efforts to translate our arguments into English; he also helped us with many substantial comments. We also wish to express appreciation to our colleague Uli Widmaier to whom we owe many stimulating ideas from numerous discussions.

### Notes

1. Davis (1966) has demonstrated that many results of empirical social research can be deduced from very few hypotheses that are based on psychological consistency

theory. Since the latter (mainly Festinger's theory of cognitive dissonance) itself is based on similar principles to economic theory this opens up a large set of possibilities to integrate social science in the framework of a reformulated 'economic' theory.

2. Thibaut and Kelley use two standards which they call 'comparison level for alternatives'. The first relates preferences to outcomes; the second is some standard for comparing the expected outcomes of alternative behaviour. Since we use a modified principle of rationality (hypothesis (1)), the second standard seems to be superfluous (see Lehner, 1973, pp.89ff.). Instead of comparison level we speak of expectation or expectation level. This does not amount to a real difference in theory. Similar concepts to expectation are the concepts of 'adaptation level' (Helson, 1963) and 'aspiration level' (Lewin *et al.*, 1944).

3. Of course, the conditions for social comparison are not always present. What counts here is the degree of social isolation and the formation of groups and organizations. The marginal case in which someone is isolated is usually connected with a collapse of the system of norms and values that determine his action. And yet *anomie* and alienation have remained concepts foreign to economic thought with the almost exclusive exception of the Marxist tradition.

4. Downs's (1957) analysis of the search for information in terms of cost—benefit analysis demonstrates that rational individuals do *not* seek the maximum amount of information, but rather attempt to get the optimal amount of information taking into account the cost of information and its expected utility when used to guide behaviour.

5. The term 'cognitive structure' is more general than that of 'preference structure': preferences are specific cognitions and as such they are part of an individual's cognitive structure. The theory of cognitive structure is described and discussed in detail in Schroder *et al.* (1967).

# CHAPTER 10

## Notes

1. 'Theorie, die sich noch auf Praxis im genuinen Sinne Bezog, begriff die Gesellschaft als einen Handlungszusammanhang von sprechenden Menschen, die den sozialen Verkehr in den zusammenhang bewusster Kommunikation einholen und sich selbst darin zu einem handlungsfähign Gesamtsubjekt bilden müssen—sonst mussten die Geschicke einer im einzelnen immer strenger rationalisierten Gesellschaft insgesamt der rationalen Zucht, der sie um so mehr bedürfen, entgleiten. Eine Theorie hingegen, die Handeln mit Verfügen verwechselt, ist einer solchen Perspektive nicht mehr fähig Sie Begreift Gesellschaft als einen Konnex von Verhaltensweisen, in dem Rationalität einzig durch den Verstand sozialtechnischer Steuerung, nicht aber durch ein kohärentes Gesamtbewusstsein vermittelt ist, eben durch jene interessierte Vernunft, die allein durch die Köpfe der politisch aufgeklärten Bürger hindurch praktische Gewalt erlangen kann.' (Habermas, 1971, p.309.)

## CHAPTER 11

### Acknowledgements

This is the first chapter of a planned research report with the preliminary title, 'The Comparative Method in the Study of Politics'. Many people have contributed advice and criticism on earlier versions of the paper. Sverker Gustavsson, University of Uppsala, has shared with me all the planning of the project. He has always been unusually generous with ideas, fresh suggestions and encouragement. I have also received valuable comments from Stefan Björklund, Mats Bäck, Walter Carlsnaes, Barry Holmström, Gunnar Jansson, Lennart J. Lundqvist, Ulf Olsson, Olof Petersson, Lars Rudebeck, and Dag Sörbom of the University of Uppsala, Bent Hanson of the Oklahoma State University, James A. Caporaso of the North Western University, and H. M. A. Schadee of the University of Liverpool. Brian Barry made it possible for me to have my paper discussed at the ECPR workshop on political theory in Strasbourg in April 1974. Leif Lewin provided me with the same opportunity at a seminar arranged by the Department of Political Science, University of Uppsala, at Södergarn, also in April 1974. Carl Nelson, Uppsala, has read the draft and corrected my English.

To all these persons I wish to express my thanks. Thanks are also due to the Swedish Council for Social Science Research which has supported my research financially.

### Notes

1. In this chapter, we shall distinguish between (*a*) linguistic entities such as words, expressions and sentences; (*b*) conceptual entities such as propositions expressed by sentences or connotations designated by expressions, and (*c*) reference, i.e. what the linguistic or conceptual entities are referring to in the real world. In keeping with semantic convention, we enclose (*a*) in double quotes, (*b*) in single quotes and refer to (*c*) without any quotation marks at all.
2. For the interested reader, a whole catalogue of similar definitions may be found in Eisler (1930, pp.391ff.) In addition, Santinello (1957, pp.1112ff.), Lewis (1956, pp.50ff. and 74), Warwick and Osherson (1973, p.7), Eisenstadt (1968, p.421), Swanson (1971, pp.141ff.) and Rokkan (1970, pp.645ff.) may be consulted.
3. Among the authors who very clearly assert that comparative analysis must involve at least two cases are Rokkan (1966a, pp.79ff., esp. 86), Rokkan *et al.* (1969, p.120), Rokkan, (1970, pp.645ff.), Eisenstadt (1968, pp.421ff.), Galtung (1967, p.1). See even Stout and Baldwin (1928, p.202), Benjamin (1942, p.60), Santinello (1957, p.1112).
4. Concerning "cross-cultural", see Leach (1968, pp.339ff.) and Murdock (1957, pp.249ff.). With respect to "cross-societal", see March (1967, pp.5ff.), Andreski (1965, p.66), Eisenstadt (1968, pp.421ff.), Payne (1973, pp.13ff.), Holt and Turner (1970, pp.5ff., 13, 15). As to "cross-policy", see Scarrow (1969, p.6) and Banks and Textor (1963, pp.2ff.).

## CHAPTER 12

**Notes**

1. The symbol "—" is used in the paper to speak of *words*, whereas the symbol '—' is used to speak of *concepts*. Concepts themselves are used without quotation marks.

# List of Books and Articles Cited

Abrahamsson, B. (1970), 'Homans on exchange: hedonism revived', *American Journal of Sociology*, 76, 273–85.

Agger, R.E., D. Goldrich and B.E. Swanson (1964), *The Rulers and the Ruled: Political Power and Impotence in American Communities*, Wiley, New York.

Albert, H. (1967), *Marxstsoziologie und Entscheidungslogik*, Luchterhand, Neuwied-Berlin.

Alker, H., K. Deutsch and A. Stoetzel (eds) (1973), *Mathematical Approaches to Politics*, Elsevier, Amsterdam.

Allen, R.G.D. (1966), *Mathematical Economics*, Macmillan, London.

Allison, G.T. (1971), *Essence of Decision: Explaining the Cuban Missile Crisis*, Little, Brown, Boston.

Almond, G.A., and J.S. Coleman (eds) (1960), *The Politics of Developing Areas*, Princeton University Press, Princeton, N.J.

Almond, G.A., and G.B. Powell (1966), *Comparative Politics*, Little, Brown, Boston.

Alston, W.P. (1967), Motives and motivation, in P. Edwards (ed), *The Encyclopedia of Philosophy*, Vol. 5, Macmillan and Free Press, New York.

Andreski, I. (1965), *The Uses of Comparative Sociology*, University of California Press, Berkeley, Calif.

Arendt, H. (1959), *The Human Condition*, Doubleday, Garden City, N.Y.

Arrow, K. (1951), *Social Choice and Individual Values*, Yale University Press, New Haven, Conn.

Austin, J.L. (1961), *Philosophical Papers*, J.O. Urmson and G.J. Warnock (eds), Oxford University Press, London.

Austin, J.L. (1962), *How to Do Things with Words*, Harvard University Press, Cambridge, Mass.

Axelrod, R. (1970), *Conflict of Interest: A Theory of Divergent Goals with Applications to Politics*, Markham, Chicago.

Bachrach, P., and M.S. Baratz (1962), 'Two faces of power', *American Political Science Review*, 56, 947–52 (reprinted in Bell *et al.*, 1969, 94–9).

Bachrach, P., and M.S. Baratz (1963), 'Decisions and non-decisions: an analytical framework', *American Political Science Review*, 57, 632–42 (reprinted in Bell *et al.*, 1969, 100–9).

Bachrach, P., and M.S. Baratz (1970), *Power and Poverty: Theory and Practice*, Oxford University Press, New York.

Ball, T. (1975), 'Power, causation and explanation', *Polity* (forthcoming).

Banfield, E.C. (1961), *Political Influence*, Free Press, New York.

Banks, A., and R.B. Textor (1963), *A Cross-Polity Survey*, MIT Press, Cambridge, Mass.

Barber, B.R. (1974), *The Death of Communal Liberty: A History of Freedom in a Swiss Mountain Canton*, Princeton University Press, Princeton, N.J.

Barents, J. (1948), *De Wetenschap der Politiek: Een Terreinverkenning (Political Science: An Exploration)*, Stols, 's-Gravenhage.

Barry, B.M. (1965), *Political Argument*, Routledge and Kegan Paul, London.

Barry, B.M. (1970), *Sociologists, Economists and Democracy*, Collier-Macmillan, London.

Barry, B.M. (1973), *The Liberal Theory of Justice*, Clarendon Press, Oxford.

Bavelas, A. (1960), 'Communication patterns in task-oriented groups', in D. Cartwright and A. Zander (eds), Group Dynamics, Row and Peterson, Evanston, Ill., 669-82.

Bayles, M.D. (1972), 'A concept of coercion', in Pennock and Chapman (1972), 16-29.

Beer, S. (1966), *Decision and Control*, Wiley, New York.

Beer, S. (1972), *The Brain of the Firm*, Allen Lane, The Penguin Press, London.

Bell, R. (1969), 'The problem of measurement', in Bell *et al.* (1969), 13-27.

Bell, R., D.V. Edwards and R.H. Wagner (eds) (1969), *Political Power: A Reader in Theory and Research*, Free Press, New York.

Benjamin, A.C. (1942), 'Comparison', in D. Runes (ed), *The Dictionary of Philosophy*, Philosophical Library, New York.

Benn, S.I. (1967), 'Power', in P. Edwards (ed), *The Encyclopedia of Philosophy*, Vol. 6, Macmillan and Free Press, New York, 424-7.

Bentham, J. (1960), *An Introduction to the Principles of Morals and Legislation* and *A Fragment on Government*, W. Harrison (ed), Blackwell, Oxford.

Berger, P., and T. Luckman (1967), *The Social Construction of Reality*, Anchor Books, New York.

Berlin, I. (1957), *The Hedgehog and the Fox*, Simon & Schuster, New York.

Bierstedt, R. (1950), 'An analysis of social power', *American Sociological Review*, **15**, 730-8.

Bierstedt, R. (1957), *The Social Order*, McGraw-Hill, New York.

Bierstedt, R. (1959), 'Nominal and real definitions', in Gross (1959), 121-44.

Blain, R. (1971), 'On Homans' psychological reductionism', *Sociological Inquiry*, **41**, 3-25.

Blalock, H.M. (1964), *Causal Inferences in Non-experimental Research*, University of North Carolina Press, Chapel Hill, N.C.

Blau, P.M. (1964), *Exchange and Power in Social Life*, Wiley, New York.

Blau, P.M. (1974), *On the Nature of Organizations*, Wiley, New York.

Bloch, E. (1954), *Das Prinzip Hoffnung*, Aufbau Verlag, Berlin.

Bock, K.E. (1965), 'The comparative method of anthropology', *Comparative Studies in Society and History*, **8**, 269-80.

Bock, P.G. (1966), 'A study in international regulation: the case of whaling', Ph.D. dissertation, New York University.

Boudon, R. (1971a), *Les Mathématiques en sociologie*, Presses Universitaires de France, Paris.

Boudon, R. (1971b), *La Crise de la sociologie*, Droz, Geneva.

Boulding, K. (1973), *The Economy of Love and Fear*, Wadsworth, Belmont, Calif.

Bourdieu, P., and J.C. Passeron (1970), *La Reproduction*, Editions de Minuit, Paris.

Braam, G.P.A. (1973), *Invloed van bedrijven op de overheid* (Influence of enterprises on authorities), Meppel, Boom.

Brams, S.J. (1968), 'Measuring the concentration of power in political systems', *American Political Science Review*, **62**, 461–75 (reprinted in Bell *et al.*, 1969, 346–59).

Buchanan, J.M., and G. Tullock (1962), *The Calculus of Consent*, University of Michigan Press, Ann Arbor, Mich.

Buckley, W. (1967), *Sociology and Modern Systems Theory*, Prentice-Hall, Englewood Cliffs, N.J.

Burns, T. (1973), 'A structural theory of social exchange', *Acta Sociologica*, **16**, 188–208.

Campbell, A., P.E. Converse, W.E. Miller and D.E. Stokes (1960), *The American Voter*, Wiley, New York.

Carey, A. (1967), 'The Hawthorne studies: a radical criticism', *American Sociological Review*, **32**, 403–16.

Carnap, R. (1950), *Logical Foundations of Probability*, University of Chicago Press, Chicago.

Cartwright, D. (ed) (1959), *Studies in Social Power*, University of Michigan Press, Ann Arbor, Mich.

Chadwick, G. (1971), *A Systems View of Planning: Towards a Theory of the Urban Regional Planning Process*, Pergamon Press, Oxford.

Chazel, F. (1964), 'Réflexions sur la conception parsonienne du pouvoir et de l'influence', *Revue française de sociologie*, **5**, 387–401.

Chazel, F. (1974), *La Théorie analytique de la société dans l'oeuvre de Talcott Parsons*, Mouton, Paris.

Chomsky, N. (1964), 'Current issues in linguistic theory', in J. Fodor and J. Katz (eds), *The Structure of Language*, Prentice-Hall, Englewood Cliffs, N.J.

Churchman, C.W. (1968a), *The Systems Approach*, Dell, New York.

Churchman, C.W. (1968b), *Challenge to Reason*, McGraw-Hill, New York.

Churchman, C.W. (1971), *The Design of Inquiring Systems*, Basic Books, New York.

Clark, T. (1972), 'Structural functionalism, exchange theory and the new political economy: institutionalization as a theoretical linkage', *Sociological Inquiry*, **42**, 275–98.

Cochran, W.G., and G.M. Cox (1957), *Experimental Designs*, Wiley, New York.

Cohen, A. (1969), 'Political anthropology', *Man*, 4 n.s., 215–35.

Cohen, S. (1969), *Modern Capitalist Planning*, Harvard University Press, Cambridge, Mass.

Cole, G.D.H. (1955), *Studies in Class Structure*, Routledge and Kegan Paul, London.

Coleman, J. (1973), *The Mathematics of Collective Action*, Heinemann, London.

Collins, B.E., and B.H. Raven (1969), 'Group structure: attraction, coalitions, communication, and power', in Lindzey and Aronson (1968), Vol. 4, 166–80.

Conrad, A. (1967), 'Contribution to "Symposium on slavery as an obstacle to economic growth"', *Journal of Economic History*, **27**, 518–60.

Conrad, A., and J. Meyer (1958), 'The economics of slavery in the ante-bellum South', *Journal of Political Economy*, 66, 95–130.

Cornford, J.P. (1974), 'Review article: the illusion of decision', *British Journal of Political Science*, 4, 231–43.

Cox, D.R. (1958), *Planning of Experiments*, Wiley, New York.

Crenson, M.A. (1971), *The Un-politics of Air Pollution*, Johns Hopkins University Press, Baltimore, Md.

Dahl, R.A. (1956), *A Preface to Democratic Theory*, University of Chicago Press, Chicago.

Dahl, R.A. (1957), 'The concept of power', *Behavioral Science*, 2, 201–15 (reprinted in Bell *et al.*, 1969, 79–93).

Dahl, R.A. (1958), 'A critique of the ruling élite model', *American Political Science Review*, 52, 463–9 (reprinted in Bell *et al.*, 1969, 36–41).

Dahl, R. (1961), *Who Governs?: Democracy and Power in an American City*, Yale University Press, New Haven, Conn.

Dahl, R. (1963), *Modern Political Analysis*, Prentice-Hall, Englewood Cliffs, N.J.

Dahl, R. (ed) (1966), *Political Oppositions in Western Democracies*, Yale University Press, New Haven, Conn.

Dahl, R. (1968) 'Power', in Sills (1968), Vol. 12, 405–15.

Dahlström, E. (1966), 'Exchange, influence and power', *Acta Sociologica*, 9, 237–84.

Dahrendorf, R. (1959), *Class and Class Conflict in Industrial Society*, Routledge and Kegan Paul, London; Stanford University Press, Stanford, Calif.

Dalton, G. (1961), 'Economic theory and primitive society', *American Anthropologist*, 63, 1–25.

Danzger, H. (1964), 'Community power structure: problems and continuities', *American Sociological Review*, 29, 707–17.

Daudt, H. (1963), *Enige Recente Ontwikkelingen in de Wetenschap der Politiek (Some Recent Developments in Political Science)*, Stenfert Kroese, Leiden.

David, P., and P. Temin (1974), review of Fogel and Engerman, *Time on the Cross*, *Journal of Economic History*, 34, 739–83.

Davis, J.A. (1966), 'Structural balance, mechanical solidarity, and interpersonal relations', in J. Berger, M. Zelditch, Jr and B. Anderson (eds), *Sociological Theories in Progress*, Vol 1, Houghton Mifflin, Boston, 74–101.

Davis, K., and W. Moore (1945), 'Some principles of stratification', *American Sociological Review*, 10, 242–9.

Debreu, G. (1954), 'Representation of a preference ordering by a numerical function', in R. Thrall, C. Coombs and R. Davis (eds), *Decision Processes*, Wiley, New York.

Descartes, R. (1897ff.), 'Letter to the Princess Elisabeth', in *Oeuvres*, C. Adam and P. Tannéry (eds), Vol. 4, Vrin, Paris.

Deutsch, K.W. (1966), *The Nerves of Government: Models of Political Communication and Control*, Free Press, New York.

Devons, E. (1970), *Papers on Planning and Economic Development*, Manchester University Press, Manchester.

Domhoff, G.W. (1967), *Who Rules America?* Prentice-Hall, Englewood Cliffs, N.J.

Domhoff, G.W. (1971), *The Higher Circles: The Governing Class in America*, Vintage Books, New York.

Doorn, J.A.A. van (1957), 'Sociologische begrippen en problemen rond het verschijnsel macht' (for translation, see van Doorn, 1962/3), *Sociologisch Jaarboek*, 11, 73–135).

Doorn, J.A.A. van (1962/3), 'Sociology and the problem of power', *Sociologica Neerlandica*, 1, 3–51.

Doorn, J.A.A. van (1966), *Organisatie en Maatschappij (Organization and Society)*, Sternfert Kroese, Leiden.

Doorn, J.A.A. van, and C.J. Lammers (1959), *Moderne Sociologie (Modern Sociology)*, Het Spectrum, Utrecht.

Downs, A. (1957), *An Economic Theory of Democracy*, Harper, New York.

Droogleever Fortuijn, A.B. (1968), *Macht en Modernisering (Power and Modernization)*, Amsterdam, Sociografisch Instituut F.S.W., University of Amsterdam.

Duijker, H.C.J., and S. Rokkan (1954), 'Organizational aspects of cross-national social research', *Journal of Social Issues*, 10, 8–24.

Dummett, M. (1973), *Frege: Philosophy of Language*, Duckworth, London.

Durkheim, E. (1961), *Moral Education*, trans. by E. Wilson and H. Schnurer, Free Press, New York.

Durkheim, E. (1962), *The Rules of Sociological Method*, trans. by S. Solovay and J. Mueller, Free Press, New York.

Durkheim, E. (1964), *The Division of Labor in Society*, trans. by G. Simpson, Free Press, New York.

Durkheim, E., and P. Fauconnet (1903), 'Sociologie et sciences sociales', *Revue Philosophique*, 55, 465–97.

Easthope, G. (1974), *A History of Social Research Methods*, Longmans, London.

Easton, D. (1953), *The Political System*, Alfred A. Knopf, New York.

Easton, D. (1957), 'An approach to the analysis of political systems', *World Politics*, 9, 383–400.

Easton, D. (1959), 'Political anthropology', in B.J. Siegel (ed), *Biennial Review of Anthropology*, Stanford University Press, Stanford, Calif, 216–69.

Easton, D. (1965a), *A Framework for Political Analysis*, Prentice-Hall, Englewood Cliffs, N.J.

Easton, D. (1965b), *A Systems Analysis of Political Life*, Wiley, New York.

Easton, D., and J. Dennis (1969), *Children in the Political System*, McGraw-Hill, New York.

Eckstein, H. (1973), 'A structural basis for political inquiry', *American Political Science Review*, 67, 1142–61.

Eijk, C. Van der, and W.J.P. Kok (1974), 'Non-decisions reconsidered', a paper presented at Joint Sessions of Workshops, European Consortium for Political Research, Strasbourg, 28 March–2 April. Amsterdam: Institute for Political Science, University of Amsterdam.

Eisenstadt, S.N. (1966), 'Problems in the comparative analysis of total societies', in *Transactions of the Sixth World Congress of Sociology at Evian, 4–11 September*, Vol. 1, International Sociological Association, Geneva.

Eisenstadt, S.N. (1968), 'Social institutions, II: comparative study', in Sills (1968), Vol. 14, 421–9.

Eisenstadt, S.N. (1969), *The Political Systems of Empires*, Free Press, New York.

Eisler, R. (1930), 'Vergleichung', in R. Eisler (ed), Wörterbuch der philosophischen Begriffe, fourth Edition, Mittler, Berlin.

282

Ellemers, J.E. (1968), *Macht en Sociale Verandering (Power and Social Change)*, Boom, Meppel.

Elster, J. (1974), 'Is the concept of contradiction useful in the social sciences?' paper presented to the Fourth Bergen Seminar on Mathematical Sociology.

Emerson, R. (1962), 'Power-dependence relations', *American Sociological Review*, 27, 31–41.

Fararo, T.S. (1973), *Mathematical Sociology*, Wiley, New York.

Faris, R.E.L. (ed) (1964), *Handbook of Modern Sociology*, Rand McNally, Chicago.

Fester, M. (1971), 'Vorstudien zu einer Theorie kommunikativer Planung', *Architecture Plus*, 4, 42–72.

Festinger, L. (1954), 'A theory of social comparison processes', *Human Relations*, 7, 117–40.

Festinger, L. (1957), *A Theory of Cognitive Dissonance*, Stanford University Press, Stanford, Calif.

Festinger, L. (1964), *Conflict, Decision and Dissonance*, Stanford University Press, Stanford, Calif.

Festinger, L., S. Schachter and K. Back (1950), *Social Pressures in Informal Groups*, Stanford University Press, Stanford, Calif.

Festinger, L., H. Riecken and S. Schachter (1956), *When Prophecy Fails*, University of Minnesota Press, Minneapolis, Minn.

Finley, M.I. (1965), 'Technical innovation and economic progress in the ancient world', *Economic History Review*, 18, 29–45.

Finley, M.I. (1970), 'Aristotle and economic analysis', *Past and Present*, 47, 3–25.

Finley, M.I. (1973a), *The Ancient Economy*, Chatto and Windus, London.

Finley, M.I. (1973b), *Democracy: Ancient and Modern*, Rutgers University Press, New Brunswick, N.J.

Fisher, R.A. (1942), *The Design of Experiments*, Oliver and Boyd, Edinburgh.

Fogel, R. (1964), *Railroads and American Economic Growth*, Johns Hopkins University Press, Baltimore, Md.

Fogel, R., and S. Engerman (1971), 'The economics of slavery', in Fogel and Engerman (eds), *The Reinterpretation of American Economic History*, Harper and Row, New York.

Fogel, R., and S. Engerman (1974), *Time on the Cross*, Little, Brown, Boston.

Freeman, E.A. (1873), *Comparative Politics*, Macmillan, London.

Friedman, G. (1946), *Problèmes humains du machinisme industriel*, Gallimard, Paris.

Friedrich, C.J. (1950), *Constitutional Government and Democracy*, Revised Edition, Ginn and Company, Boston.

Friedrich, C.J. (1963), *Man and His Government*, McGraw-Hill, New York.

Gadourek, I. (1957), 'Macht en maatschappij' (Power and society), *Sociologisch Jaarboek*, 11, 136–61.

Galtung, J. (1967), 'Some aspects of comparative research', *Polls*, 2, 1–20.

Galtung, J. (1969), *Theory and Methods of Social Research*, Revised Edition, Universitetsforlaget, Oslo.

Gamson, W.A. (1966), 'Reputation and resources in community politics', *American Journal of Sociology*, 72, 121–31.

Genovese, E. (1965), *The Political Economy of Slavery*, Pantheon Books, New York.

George, A.L., D.K. Hall and W.E. Simons (1971), *The Limits of Coercive Diplomacy: Laos, Cuba, Vietnam*, Little, Brown, Boston.

Georgescu-Roegen, N. (1954), 'Choice, expectations and measurability', *Quarterly Journal of Economics*, **68**, 503–34.

Georgescu-Roegen, N. (1971), *The Entropy Law and the Economic Process*, Harvard University Press, Cambridge, Mass.

Gert, B. (1972), 'Coercion and Freedom', in Pennock and Chapman (1972), 30–48.

Gibson, Q. (1971), 'Power', *Philosophy of the Social Sciences*, **1**, 101–12.

Girard, A. (1964), *Le Choix du conjoint*, Presses Universitaires de France, Paris.

Glanzer, M., and R. Glaser (1959), 'Techniques for the study of group structure and behavior, I: analysis of structure', *Psychological Bulletin*, **56**, 317–32.

Glanzer, M., and R. Glaser (1961), 'Techniques for the study of group structure and behavior, II: empirical studies of the effects of structure in small groups', *Psychological Bulletin*, **58**, 1–27.

Goffman, E. (1959), *The Presentation of Self in Everyday Life*, Doubleday, New York.

Goffman, E. (1961), *Encounter*, Bobbs-Merrill, New York.

Goldman, A.I. (1970), *A Theory of Human Action*, Prentice-Hall, Englewood Cliffs, N.J.

Goldman, A.I. (1972), 'Towards a theory of social power', *Philosophical studies*, **23**, 221–68.

Goodman, R. (1972), *After the Planner*, Penguin, Harmondsworth.

Gould, J. (1964), 'Comparative method', in J. Gould and W. Kolb (eds), *A Dictionary of the Social Sciences*, Free Press, New York.

Gouldner, A. (1959), 'Reciprocity and autonomy in functional theory', in Gross (1959), 150–64.

Gregor, A. J. (1971), *An Introduction to Metapolitics: a Brief Inquiry into the Conceptual Language of Political Science*, Free Press, New York.

Gross, L. (ed) (1959), *Symposium on Sociological Theory*, Harper and Row, New York.

Gunsteren, H. R. van (1973a), 'Toward rational budgeting', *Proceedings of the Institute of Management Science*, **20**, 000–000.

Gunsteren, H. R. van (1973b), 'Filosofie en Politiek' (Philosophy and Politics), Leiden, *mimeo*.

Gunsteren, H. R. van (1974), 'Planning en politiek' (Planning and politics), *Bestuurswetenschappen*, **28**, 27–28.

Gunsteren, H.R. van (1975), 'Towards rational bugeting: the endless debate about PPBS' in E. Shlifer (ed), *Proceedings of the XX International Meeting of the Institute of Management Sciences*, Jerusalem. Academic Press, New York, 676–86.

Gunsteren, H. R. van (1976), *The Quest for Control*, Wiley; London.

Gurvitch, G. (1963), *La Vocation actuelle de la sociologie*, Presses Universitaires de France, Paris.

Guyau, M. (1904), *La Morale anglaise contemporaine*, F. Alcan, Paris.

Haavelmo, T. (1944), 'The probability approach to econometrics', *Econometrica*, **12** supp., 1–118.

Haavelmo, T. (1972), 'Variasjoner over et tema av Gossen' (Variations on a theme of Gossen's), memorandum from the Institute of Economics, University of Oslo.

Habermas, J. (1968), *Technik und Wissenschaft als Ideologie*, Suhrkamp Verlag, Frankfurt.

Habermas, J. (1971), *Theorie und Praxis*, Suhrkamp Verlag, Frankfurt.

284

Habermas, J. (1973), *Legitimationsprobleme im Spätkapitalismus*, Suhrkamp Verlag, Frankfurt.

Halévy, E. (1901), *La Formation du radicalisme philosophique*, F. Alcan, Paris.

Harsanyi, J. C. (1956), 'Approaches to the bargaining problem before and after the theory of games: a critical discussion of Zeuthen's, Hicks's and Nash's theories', *Econometrica*, 24, 144–57.

Harsanyi, J.C. (1962a), 'Bargaining in ignorance of the opposition's utility function', *Journal of Conflict Resolution*, 6, 29–38.

Harsanyi, J.C. (1962b), 'Measurement of social power, opportunity costs and the theory of two-person bargaining games', *Behavioral Science*, 7, 67–80 (reprinted in Bell *et al.*, 1969, 226–38).

Harsanyi, J.C. (1962c), 'Measurement of social power in *n*-person reciprocal power situations', *Behavioral Science*, 7, 81–92 (reprinted in Bell *et al.*, 1969, 239–48).

Heath, A. (1968), 'Economic theory and sociology', *Sociology*, 2, 273–92.

Heberle, R. (1966), 'The sociology of Georg Simmel: the forms of social interaction', in H. Barnes (ed), *An Introduction to the History of Sociology*, University of Chicago Press, Chicago, 249–73.

Heeger, R. (1972), 'Vad är en ideologie?' (What is an ideology?), *Statsvetenskaplig Tidskrift*, 75, 307–25.

Hegel, G.W.F. (1952), *Phänomenologie des Geistes*, ed. Hofmeister, Felix Meiner Verlag, Hamburg.

Held, V. (1972), 'Coercion and coercive offers', in Pennock and Chapman (1972), 49–62.

Helson, H. (1963), 'The theory of adaptation level', in D. Beardslee and M. Wertheimer (eds), *Readings in Perception*, Princeton University Press, Princeton, N.J.

Hempel, C.G. (1952), 'Fundamentals of concept formation in empirical science', in O. Neurath, R. Carnap and C. Morris (eds), *International Encyclopedia of Unified Science*, Vol. 2, University of Chicago Press, Chicago.

Hempel, C.G. (1966), *Philosophy of Natural Science*, Prentice-Hall, Englewood Cliffs, N.J.

Hempel, C.G. (1967), 'Scientific explanation', in S. Morgenbesser (ed), *Philosophy of Science Today*, Basic Books, New York, 79–88.

Hintikka, J. (1972), 'Leibniz on plenitude, relations and the "reign of law' ", in H. Frankfurt (ed), *Leibniz*, Anchor Books, New York.

Hirschman, A.O. (1970), *Exit, Voice, and Loyalty*, Harvard University Press, Cambridge, Mass.

Hobbes, T. (1960), *Leviathan*, M. Oakeshott (ed), Blackwell, Oxford.

Hoenigswald, H.M. (1963), 'On the history of the comparative method', *Anthropological Linguistics*, 5, 1–11.

Holt, R.T., and J.E. Turner (eds) (1970), *The Methodology of Comparative Research*, Free Press, New York.

Homans, G. (1950), *The Human Group*, Harcourt, Brace, New York.

Homans, G. (1961), *Social Behaviour: Its Elementary Forms*, Routledge and Kegan Paul, London.

Homans, G. (1964a), 'Bringing men back in', *American Sociological Review*, 29, 809–18.

Homans, G. (1964b), 'Commentary', *Sociological Inquiry*, 34, 221–31.

Homans, G. (1964c), 'Contemporary theory in sociology', in Faris (1964), 962–67.

Homans, G. (1968), 'A life of synthesis', *American Behavioral Scientist*, **12**, 2-8.

Homans, G., and D. Schneider (1955), *Marriage, Authority and Final Causes*, Free Press, Glencoe, Ill.

Hoogerwerf, A. (1972), *Politicologie, Begrippen en Problemen (Political Science, Concepts and Problems)*, Samsom, Alphen aan den Rijn.

Hopkins, T.K., and I. Wallerstein (1967), 'The comparative study of national societies', *Social Science Information*, **6**, 25-58.

Hughes, G. E., and M. J. Cresswell (1972), *An Introduction to Modal Logic*, Methuen, London.

Hunter, F. (1953), *Community Power Structure: A Study of Decision Makers*, University of North Carolina Press, Chapel Hill, N.C.

Hyman, H.H. (1953), 'The value system of different classes', in R. Bendix and S. Lipset (eds), *Class, Status and Power*, Free Press, Glencoe, Ill., 426-42.

Iklé, F.C. (1964), *How Nations Negotiate*, Harper and Row, New York.

Ishiguro, H.I. (1972), *Leibniz' Philosophy of Logic and Language*, Duckworth, London.

Jantsch, E. (1969), *Perspectives of Planning*, OECD, Paris.

Jantsch, E. (1972), *Technological Forecasting and Social Futures*, Halstead Press, London.

Jeidels, O. (1905), 'Das Verhältnis der deutschen Grossbanken zur Industrie mit besonderer Berücksichtigung der Eisenindustrie', in G. Schmoller and M. Sering (eds), *Staats—und socialwissenschaftliche Forschungen*, **24**, no. 12.

Jervis, R. (1970), *The Logic of Images in International Relations*, Princeton University Press, Princeton, N.J.

Kalleberg, A.L. (1966), 'The logic of comparison: a methodological note on the comparative study of political systems', *World Politics*, **19**, 69-82.

Karlsson, G. (1962), 'Some aspects of power in small groups', in J. Criswell, H. Solomon and P. Suppes (eds), *Mathematical Methods in Small Group Processes*, Stanford University Press, Stanford, Calif., 193-202.

Kaufman, H., and V. Jones (1954), 'The mystery of power', *Public Administration Review*, **14**, 205-12.

Kemeny, J.G., J.L. Snell and G.L. Thompson (1966), *An Introduction to Finite Mathematics*, Academic Press, New York.

Kerlinger, F.N. (1973), *Foundations of Behavioral Research: Educational and Psychological Inquiry*, Holt, Rinehart and Winston, New York.

Kornhauser, W. (1961), '"Power élite" or "veto groups"', in S. Lipset and L. Lowenthal (eds), *Culture and Social Character*, Free Press, New York, pp.252-67 (reprinted in Bell *et al.*, 1969, 42-52).

Kripke, S. (1972), 'Naming and necessity', in D. Davidson and G. Harman (eds), *Semantics of Natural Language*, Reidel, Dordrecht.

Kuypers, G. (1973), *Grondbegrippen van Politiek (Basic Concepts of Politics)*, Het Spectrum; Utrecht/Antwerpen.

Lasswell, H.D. (1958), *Politics: Who Gets What, When, How.* (With Postscript), Meridian Books, New York.

Lasswell, H.D. and A. Kaplan (1950), *Power and Society: A Framework for Political Inquiry*, Yale University Press, New Haven, Conn.

Lazarsfeld, P. F. (1970), *Philosophie des sciences sociales*, Gallimard; Paris.

Lazarsfeld, P. F., B. Berelson and H. Gaudet (1948), *The People's Choice*, Columbia University Press, New York.

Leach, E.R. (1968), 'Anthropology, VI: the comparative method in anthropology', in Sills (1968), Vol. 1, 339–45.

Leege, D.C., and W.L. Francis (1974), *Political Research: Design, Measurement, Analysis*, Basic Books, New York.

Lehner, F. (1973), *Politisches Verhalten als soziales Tausch*, Lang, Bern/Frankfurt.

Lehner, F. (1975), 'Cognitive structure, uncertainty, and the rationality of political action: a synthesis of economic and psychological perspectives', *European Journal of Political Research* (forthcoming).

Leibniz, G.G. (1947), *Textes inédits*, G. Grua (ed), Presses Universitaires de France, Paris.

Lenski, G. (1966), *Power and Privilege*, McGraw-Hill, New York.

Levins, R. (1968), *Evolution in Changing Environments*, Princeton University Press, Princeton, N. J.

Lévi-Strauss, C. (1969), *The Elementary Structures of Kinship*, Beacon Press, Boston.

Levy, M.J. (1952), *The Structure of Society*, Princeton University Press, Princeton, N.J.

Lewin, K., T. Dembo, L. Festinger and P. Sears (1944), 'Level of aspiration', in J. Hunt (ed), *Personality and the Behavior Disorders*, Ronald Press, New York.

Lewis, Sir G. C. (1898), *Remarks on the Use and Abuse of Some Political Terms*, Clarendon Press, Oxford.

Lewis, O. (1956), 'Comparisons in cultural anthropology', in W. Thomas Jr, (ed), *Current Anthropology: A Supplement to Anthropology Today*, University of Chicago Press, Chicago.

Lewis, C. I., and C. H. Langford (1932), *Symbolic Logic*, Dover Press, New York.

Lijphart, A. (1971), 'Comparative politics and the comparative method', *American Political Science Review*, 65, 682–93.

Lijphart, A. (1973), 'Comparative analysis: the search for comparable cases', paper presented at the International Seminar on Macro-contexts and Micro-variations in Cross-National Social Research, Helsinki, 17–21 September.

Lindzey, G., and E. Aronson (eds) (1968), *The Handbook of Social Psychology*, Second Edition, Addison-Wesley, Reading, Mass.

Loewenstein, K. (1944), 'Report of the research panel on comparative government', *American Political Science Review*, 38, 540–48.

Luce, R. D., and H. Raiffa (1958), *Games and Decisions: Introduction and Critical Survey*, Wiley, New York.

Luce, R. D., R. Bush and E. Galanter (1963), *Handbook of Mathematical Psychology*, Vols 1–3, Wiley, New York.

Luhmann, N. (1971), *Politische Planung*, Westdeutschen Verlag, Opladen.

Luhmann, N. (1973), *Zweckbegriff und Systemrationalität*, Suhrkamp Verlag, Frankfurt.

Lukács, G. (1923), *Geschichte und Klassenbewusstsein*, Malik, Berlin.

Lukes, S. (1973), *Individualism*, Harper and Row, New York.

Lynd, R. S., and H. M. Lynd (1929), *Middletown*, Harcourt, New York.

Lynd, R. S., and H. M. Lynd (1937), *Middletown in Transition*, Harcourt, New York.

McFarland, A.S. (1969), *Power and Leadership in Pluralist Systems*, Stanford University Press, Stanford, Calif.

McGlen, N. (1974), 'Strategy choices for political participation', PhD dissertation, University of Rochester.

McGuigan, F. J. (1960), *Experimental Psychology: A Methodological Approach*, Prentice-Hall, Englewood Cliffs, N. J.

McIntosh, D. (1972), 'Coercion and international politics', in Pennock and Chapman (1972), 243–71.

MacIntyre, A. (1967), review of *Exchange and Power in Social Life*, *Sociology*, 1, 199–201.

Mackenzie, W. J. M. (1967), *Politics and Social Science*, Penguin, Harmondsworth.

McLoughlin, J. B. (1970), 'Cybernetic and general-system approaches to urban and regional research: a review of the literature', *Environment and Planning*, 2, 369–408.

McLoughlin, J. B. (1973), *Control and Urban Planning*, Faber and Faber, London.

Macpherson, C. B. (1973), *Democratic Theory: Essays in Retrieval*, Clarendon Press, Oxford.

Mannheim, K. (1966), *Man and Society in an Age of Reconstruction*, Routledge and Kegan Paul, London.

Manning, D. J. (1968), *The Mind of Jeremy Bentham*, Longmans, London.

March, J. G. (1955), 'An introduction to the theory and measurement of influence', *American Political Science Review*, 49, 431–51 (reprinted in Bell *et al.*, 1969, 166–80).

March, J. G. (1957), 'Measurement concepts in the theory of influence', *Journal of Politics*, 19, 202–26 (reprinted in Bell *et al.*, 1969, 181–93).

March, J.G. (1966), 'The power of power', in D. Easton (ed), *Varieties of Political Theory*, Prentice-Hall, Englewood Cliffs, N.J. 39–70.

March, R. M. (1967), *Comparative Sociology: A Codification of Cross-Societal Analysis*, Harcourt, Brace and World, New York.

Markl, K. P. (1972), 'On the philosophical implications of systemic categories in integration research', a Research Paper at the Centre for Contemporary European Studies, University of Sussex.

Marmor, T. R., and D. Thomas (1972), 'Doctors, politics and pay disputes: *Pressure Group Politics* revisited', *British Journal of Political Science*, 2, 421–42.

Martin, R. (1971), 'The concept of power: a critical defence', *British Journal of Sociology*, 22, 240–56.

Martindale, D. (1959), 'Sociological theory and the ideal type', in Gross (1969), 57–91.

Marx, K. (1956a), *Die Klassenkämpfe in Frankreich*, in Marx and Engels (1956ff.), Vol. 7.

Marx, K. (1956b), *The Chartists*, in Marx and Engels (1956ff.), Vol. 8.

Marx, K. (1956c), *The Civil War in France*, in Marx and Engels (1956ff.), Vol. 17.

Marx, K. (1956d), *Das Kapital*, in Marx and Engels (1956ff.), Vol. 23.

Marx, K. (1956e), *Theorien über den Mehrwert*, in Marx and Engels (1956ff.), Vol 26.

Marx, K. (1967), *Capital*, trans. S. Moore and E. Aveling, ed. F. Engels, International Publishers, New York.

Marx, K., and F. Engels (1956ff.), *Werke*, 39 vols, Dietz Verlag, Berlin.

Mauss, M. (1954), *The Gift*, Cohen and West, London.

Mayo, E. (1960), *The Human Problems of an Industrial Civilization*, Viking Press, New York.

Merelman, R. M. (1968), 'On the neo-elitist critique of community power', *American Political Science Review*, 62, 451–60.

Merton, R. K. (1967), *Social Theory and Social Structure*, Free Press, New York.

Michels, R. (1925), *Zur Sociologie des Parteiwesens in den modernen Demokratie*, Kröner, Leipzig.

Midgaard, K. (1965), 'Co-ordination in 'tacit' games: some new concepts', *Cooperation and Conflict*, 2, 39–52.

Midgaard, K. (1973/4), 'Teori om internasjonale forhandlinger: forhandlingene 1958–59 om kvoteregulering av hvalfangsten i Antarktis' (A theory of international negotiations: the 1958–59 negotiations on quota regulations for whaling in the Antarctic), *Internasjonal Politikk*, 2, 453–73; 4, 923–46; 1, 77–100.

Mills, C.W. (1956), *The Power Elite*, Oxford University Press, New York.

Mills, C.W. (1963), 'The sociology of stratification', in I.L. Horowitz (ed), *Power Politics and People: The Collected Essays of C. Wright Mills*, Ballantine Books, New York.

Mokken, R. J., and F. N. Stokman (1974), 'Traces of power, II: interlocking directorates between large corporations, banks and other financial companies and institutions in the Netherlands in 1969', a paper presented at Joint Sessions, European Consortium for Political Research, Strasbourg, 28 March–April 2, Amsterdam: Institute for Political Science, University of Amsterdam.

Mommsen, W. (1965), 'Max Weber's political sociology and his philosophy of world history', *International Social Science Journal*, 17, 23–45.

Moreno, J. L. (1947), 'La Méthode sociometrique en sociologie', *Cahiers internationaux sociologie*, 2, 88–101.

Moreno, J. L. (1954), *Who Shall Survive?* Beacon House, Beacon, N.Y.

Mulkay, M. J. (1971), *Functionalism, Exchange and Theoretical Strategy*, Routledge and Kegan Paul, London.

Murdock, G. P. (1957), 'Anthropology as a comparative science', *Behavioral Science*, 2, 249–54.

Nadel, S. F. (1951), *The Foundations of Social Anthropology*, Cohen and West, London.

Naess, A. (1966), *Communication and Argument*, Universitetsforlaget, Oslo.

Needham, R. (1962), *Structure and Sentiments*, University of Chicago Press, Chicago.

Neumann, F. L. (1950), 'Approaches to the study of political power', *Political Science Quarterly*, 65, 161–80.

Nizard, L. (1973), 'Administration et société: planification et régulations bureaucratiques', *Revue française de science politique*, 23, 199–229.

North, D., and R. Thomas (1973), *The Rise of the Western World*, Cambridge University Press, London.

Offe, C. (1972), *Strukturprobleme des Kapitalistischen Staaten*, Suhrkamp Verlag, Frankfurt.

Olson, M., Jr. (1965), *The Logic of Collective Action: Public Goods and the Theory of Groups*, Harvard University Press, Cambridge, Mass.

Oppenheim, F. E. (1961), *Dimensions of Freedom*, St Martin's Press, New York.

Ossowski, S. (1963), *Class Structure in the Social Consciousness*, Routledge and Kegan Paul, London.

Parsons, T. (1951), *The Social System*, Harper and Row, New York.

Parsons, T. (1963a), 'On the concept of influence', *Public Opinion Quarterly*, 27, 37–62.

Parsons, T. (1963b), 'On the concept of political power', *Proceedings of the American Philosophical Society*, 107, 232–62 (reprinted in Bell *et al.*, 1969, 251–84).

Parsons, T. (1963c), 'Rejoinder to Bauer and Coleman', *Public Opinion Quarterly*, 27, 87–92.

Parsons, T. (1964), 'Some reflections on the place of force in the social process', in H. Eckstein (ed), *Internal War: Basic Problems and Approaches,* Free Press, New York, 33–70 (reprinted in Parsons, 1967, 264–96).

Parsons, T. (1966), *The Structure of Social Action,* Free Press, New York.

Parsons, T. (1967), *Sociological Theory and Modern Society,* Free Press, New York.

Parsons, T. (1968), 'Professions', in Sills (1968), Vol. 12, 536–47.

Parsons, T. (1969), *Politics and Social Structure,* Free Press, New York.

Parsons, T., and N.J. Smelser (1956), *Economy and Society,* Free Press, Glencoe, Ill.

Parsons, T., E.A. Shils and J. Olds (1965), 'Values, motives and systems of action', in T. Parsons and E.A. Shils (eds), *Toward a General Theory of Action,* Harper and Row, New York, 47–275.

Pateman, C. (1970), *Participation and Democratic Theory,* Cambridge University Press, London.

Pauly-Wissowa, (1958), 'Vicarius', in *Realencyclopädie der klassischen Altertumswissenschaften,* J.B. Metzlerscher Verlag, Stuttgart.

Payne, G. (1973), 'Comparative sociology: some problems of theory and method', *British Journal of Sociology,* 24, 13–29.

Pennock, J.R., and J.W. Chapman (eds) (1972), *Nomos XIV: Coercion,* Aldine Atherton, Chicago/New York.

Pitkin, H.F. (1972), *Wittgenstein and Justice,* University of California Press, Berkeley, Calif.

Plamenatz, J. (1973), *Democracy and Illusion,* Longmans, London.

Plato (1968), *Politeia,* trans. A. Bloom, Basic Books, New York.

Polanyi, K. (1957), 'The economy as instituted process', in K. Polanyi, C. Arensberg and H. Pearson (eds), *Trade and Market in Early Empires,* Free Press, Glencoe, Ill.

Pollak, R.A. (1968), 'Consistent planning', *Review of Economic Studies,* 35, 201–8.

Polsby, N.W. (1960), 'How to study community power: the pluralist alternative', *Journal of Politics,* 22, 474–84 (reprinted in Bell *et al.,* 1969, pp. 31–5).

Polsby, N.W. (1963), *Community Power and Political Theory,* Yale University Press, New Haven, Conn.

Popper, K.R. (1963), *Conjectures and Refutations,* Routledge and Kegan Paul, London.

Przeworski, A., and H. Teune (1970), *The Logic of Comparative Social Inquiry,* Wiley, New York.

Ramsey, F. (1928), 'A mathematical theory of saving', *Economic Journal,* 38, 543–59.

Rawls, J. (1962), 'Justice as fairness', in P. Laslett and W.G. Runciman (eds), *Philosophy, Politics and Society,* 2nd series, Oxford, Blackwell, 132–57.

Rawls, J. (1971), *A Theory of Justice.* Belknap Press (Harvard University Press), Cambridge, Mass.

Riesman, D. (1950), *The Lonely Crowd,* Yale University Press, New Haven, Conn.

Riker, W.H. (1962), *The Theory of Political Coalitions,* Yale University Press, New Haven, Conn.

Riker, W.H. (1964), 'Some ambiguities in the notion of power', *American Political Science Review,* 58, 341–9 (reprinted in Bell *et al.,* 1969, 110–19).

Riker, W.H., and P.C. Ordeshook (1973), *An Introduction to Positive Political Theory,* Prentice-Hall, Englewood Cliffs, N.J.

Robbins, L. (1932), *An Essay on the Nature and Significance of Economic Science,* Macmillan, London.

Rokkan, S. (1966a), 'Comparative cross-national research: the context of current efforts', in R. Merritt and S. Rokkan (eds), *Comparing Nations: The Use of Quantitative Data in Cross-National Research,* Yale University Press, New Haven, Conn.

Rokkan, S. (1966b), 'Norway: numerical democracy and corporate pluralism', in Dahl (1966), 70–115.

Rokkan, S. (1970), 'Cross-cultural, cross-societal and cross-national research', in *Main Trends of Research in the Social and Human Sciences, Part I: Social Sciences,* Mouton, Paris, 645–89.

Rokkan, S., S. Verba and E. Almasy (eds) (1969), *Comparative Survey Analysis,* Mouton, The Hague.

Rothschild, K.W. (ed) (1971), *Power in Economics,* Harmondsworth, Penguin.

Royal Ministry of Foreign Affairs (n.d.–c. 1971), *Glimpses of Norway,* Oslo.

Runciman, W.G. (1973), *A Critique of Max Weber's Philosophy of Social Science,* Cambridge University Press, London.

Russell, B. (1938), *Power: A New Social Analysis,* George Allen and Unwin, London.

Russett, B.M. (1968), 'Probabilism and the number of units affected: measuring influence concentration', *American Political Science Review,* **62**, 476–80.

Samuelson, P. (1969), 'The evaluation of real national income', in K. Arrow and T. Scitovsky (eds), *Readings in Welfare Economics,* Allen and Unwin, London, 402–33.

Santinello, G. (1957), 'Comparazione', in *Enciclopedia Filosofica,* Instituto per la Collaborazione Culturale, Venice.

Sartori, G. (1973), 'What is politics?' *Political Theory,* **1**, 5–26.

Sartre, J.-P. (1960), *Critique de la raison dialectique,* Gallimard, Paris.

Scarrow, H.A. (1969), *Comparative Political Analysis: An Introduction,* Harper and Row, New York.

Schäfers, B. (ed) (1973), *Gesellschaftliche Planung,* Ferdinand Enke Verlag, Stuttgart.

Schapera, I. (1963), *Government and Politics in Tribal Societies,* C. A. Watts, London.

Schattschneider, E.E. (1960), *The Semisovereign People: A Realist's View of Democracy in America,* Holt, Rinehart and Winston, New York.

Schelling, T.C. (1960), *The Strategy of Conflict,* Harvard University Press, Cambridge, Mass.

Scholten, G.H. (1972), *Politiek en Bestuur (Politics and Administration),* Samson, Alphen aan den Rijn.

Schroder, H.M., M.J. Driver and S. Streuffert (1967), *Human Information Processing,* Holt, Rinehart and Winston, New York.

Schütte, H.G. (1971a), *Der empirische Gehalt des Funktionalismus,* Hain, Meisenheim am Glan.

Schütte, H.G. (1971b), 'Über die Chancen einer Theorie sozialer Systeme', in H. Albert (ed), *Sozialtheorie und soziale Praxis,* Hain, Meisenheim am Glan.

Schütte, H.G. (1973), 'Markt und Konflikt', in G. Albrecht *et al.,* (eds), *Soziologie,* Westdeutscher Verlag, Opladen.

Schumpeter, J.A. (1961), *Capitalism, Socialism and Democracy,* Harper and Row, New York.

Selltiz, C., M. Jahoda, M. Deutsch and S.W. Cook (1959), *Research Methods in Social Relations,* Revised Edition, Holt, Rinehart and Winston, New York.

Sen, A. (1968), *The Choice of Techniques*, Blackwell, Oxford.

Sen, A. (1973), *On Economic Inequality*, Clarendon Press, Oxford.

Shakankiri, M. El (1970), *La Philosophie juridique de Jeremy Bentham*, LGDJ, Paris.

Shapley, L.S., and M. Shubik (1954), 'A method for evaluating the distribution of power in a committee system', *American Political Science Review*, **48**, 787–92.

Sills, D.L. (ed) (1968), *International Encyclopedia of the Social Sciences*, Macmillan and Free Press, New York.

Simmel, G. (1894), 'Le Problème de la sociologie', *Revue de métaphysique et de morale*, **2**, 497–504.

Simmel, G. (1950), *The Sociology of Georg Simmel*, K. Wolff (ed), Free Press, New York.

Simon, H.A. (1953), 'Notes on the observation and measurement of political power', *Journal of Politics*, **15**, 500–16 (reprinted in Bell *et al.*, 1969, 69–78).

Simon, H.A. (1954), 'Bandwagon and underdog effects of election predictions', *Public Opinion Quarterly*, **18**, 245–53 (reprinted in Simon, 1957).

Simon, H.A. (1955), 'A behavioral model of rational choice', *Quarterly Journal of Economics*, **69**, 99–118.

Simon, H.A. (1957), *Models of Man, Social and Rational: Mathematical Essays on Rational and Human Behavior in a Social Setting*, Wiley, New York.

Sjoberg, G. (1955), 'The comparative method in the social sciences', *Philosophy of Science*, **22**, 106–17.

Smelser, N.J. (1973), 'The methodology of comparative analysis', in D. Warwick and S. Osherson (eds), *Comparative Research Methods*, Prentice-Hall, Englewood Cliffs, N.J., 42–86.

Snyder, D.P. (1971), *Modal Logic and Its Applications*, Van Nostrand, New York.

Sorokin, P. (1956), *Fads and Foibles in Modern Sociology*, Henry Regnery, Chicago.

Sperlich, P.W. (1971), *Conflict and Harmony in Human Affairs: A Study of Cross-Pressure and Political Behavior*, Rand McNally, Chicago.

Spykman, N. (1966), *The Social Theory of Georg Simmel*, Atherton, New York.

Ståhl, I. (1972), *Bargaining Theory*, Economic Research Institute, Stockholm School of Economics, Stockholm.

Stout, G.F., and J.M. Baldwin (1928), 'Comparison', in J. Baldwin (ed), *Dictionary of Philosophy and Psychology*, Macmillan, New York.

Strotz, R. (1955–6), 'Myopia and inconsistency in dynamic utility maximization', *Review of Economic Studies*, **23**, 165–80.

Suret-Canale, J. (1967), 'Structuralisme et anthropologie economique', *La Pensée*, 135 n.s., 94–106.

Swanson, G.E. (1971), 'Frameworks for comparative research: structural anthropology and the theory of action', in I. Vallier (ed), *Comparative Research Methods in Sociology: Essays on Trends and Applications*, University of California Press, Berkeley, Calif., 141–202.

Tarski, A. (1944), 'The semantic conception of truth and the foundation of semantics', *Philosophy and Phenomenological Research*, **4**, 341–76.

Thibaut, J.W., and H.H. Kelley (1959), *The Social Psychology of Groups*, Wiley, New York.

Titmuss, R.M. (1970), *The Gift Relationship*, Allen and Unwin, London.

Tønnessen, J.N. (1970), *Den Moderne Hvalfangsts Historie (The History of Modern Whaling)*, vol. 4, Norges Hvalfangstforbund, Sandefjord.

Tranöy, K.E. (1970), *Vilkårslogikk* (*The Logic of Conditions*), Universitetsforlaget, Oslo.

Urmson, J.O. (1952), 'Motives and Causes', *Proceedings of the Aristotelian Society*, supp. 26, 179–94 (reprinted in A. White (ed) (1968), *The Philosophy of Action*, Oxford University Press, London, 153–65).

Valkenburgh, P. (1968), *Inleiding tot de Politicologie* (*Introduction to Political Science*), Agon-Elsevier, Amsterdam/Brussels.

Vree, J.K. De (1968/9a), 'De wetenschap der politiek: het vraagstuk van een definitie' (Political science: the problem of definition), *Acta Politica*, 4, 55–81.

Vree, J.K. De (1968/9b), 'Over theorievorming' (On the formation of theory), *Acta Politica*, 4, 275–98.

Vree, J.K. De (1972a), *Political Integration: The Formation of Theory and Its Problems*, Mouton, Den Haag.

Vree, J.K. De (1972b), 'Behaviour, Learning and Conversion: Elements of a General Theory of Politics', Amsterdam, mimeo.

Vree, J.K. De (forthcoming), *Foundations of Politics*.

Waldman, S.R. (1972), *Foundations of Political Action*, Little, Brown, Boston.

Walton, J. (1966a), 'Substance and artifact: the current status of research on community power structure', *American Journal of Sociology*, 71, 430–8.

Walton, J. (1966b), 'Discipline, method and community power', *American Sociological Review*, 31, 684–9.

Walton, R.E., and R.B. McKersie (1965), *A Behavioral Theory of Labor Negotiations: An Analysis of a Social Interaction System*, McGraw-Hill, New York.

Warner, W.L., and P.S. Lunt (1941), *The Social Life of a Modern Community*, Yale University Press, New Haven, Conn.

Warwick, D.P., and S. Osherson (eds) (1973), *Comparative Research Methods*, Prentice-Hall, Englewood Cliffs, N.J.

Weber, M. (1964a), *Wirtschaft und Gesellschaft*, Fifth Edition, Kiepenheuer und Witsch, Köln/Berlin.

Weber, M. (1964b), *The Theory of Social and Economic Organization*, trans. A.M. Henderson and T. Parsons, (ed) T. Parsons, Free Press, New York.

Weber, M. (1968), *Basic Concepts in Sociology*, trans. and ed. H.P. Secker, Peter Owen, London.

Webster, M. (1973), 'Psychological reductionism: methodological individualism and large scale problems', *American Sociological Review*, 38, 258–73.

Wertheimer, A.P. (1972), 'Political coercion and political obligation', in Pennock and Chapman (1972), 213–42.

Wildavsky, A. (1964a), *Leadership in a Small Town*, Bedminster Press, Totowa, N.J.

Wildavsky, A. (1964b), *The Politics of the Budgeting Process*, Little, Brown, Boston.

Wildavsky, A. (1973), 'If planning is everything, maybe it's nothing', *Policy Science*, 4, 127–53.

Williams, G.C. (1966), *Adaptation and Natural Selection*, Princeton University Press, Princeton, N.J.

Wilson, J.Q. (1961), 'The economy of patronage', *Journal of Political Economy*, 69, 369–80.

Wilson, J.Q. (1973), *Political Organizations*, Basic Books, New York.

Wittram, R. (1958), *Das Interesse an der Geschichte: Zwölf Vorlesungen über Fragen des zeitgenössischen Geschichtsverständnisses*, Vandenhoek und Ruprecht, Göttingen.

Wodehouse, P.G. (1973), *The World of Jeeves,* Manor Books, New York.

Wright, G.H. von (1951), *A Treatise on Induction and Probability,* Routledge and Kegan Paul, London.

Wright, G.H. von (1971), *Explanation and Understanding,* Cornell University Press, Ithaca, N.Y.

Wundt, W. (1921), *Logik: Eine Untersuchung der Principien der Erkenntnis und der Methoden wissenschaftlicher Forschung,* Vols. 1-3, Enke, Stuttgart.

Zetterberg, H.L. (1965), *On Theory and Verification in Sociology,* Bedminster Press, Totowa, N.J.

# Index